*The Settlement of Disputes in
Early Medieval Europe*

The Settlement of Disputes in Early Medieval Europe

edited by

WENDY DAVIES

Professor of History, University of London

and

PAUL FOURACRE

Lecturer in History, University of London Goldsmiths' College

CAMBRIDGE
UNIVERSITY PRESS

Published by the Press Syndicate of the University of Cambridge
The Pitt Building, Trumpington Street, Cambridge CB2 IRP
40 West 20th Street, New York, NY 10011–4211, USA
10 Stamford Road, Oakleigh, Victoria 3166, Australia

First published 1986
First paperback edition 1992

Printed in Great Britain at the University Press, Cambridge

British Library cataloguing in publication data

The Settlement of disputes in early medieval Europe.
1. Conflict management – Europe – History
2. Europe – Social conditions – To 1492
I. Davies, Wendy II. Fouracre, Paul
303.3'3 HN373

Library of Congress cataloguing in publication data

The Settlement of disputes in early medieval Europe.
Bibliography
Includes index.
1. Justice, Administration of – Europe – History.
2. Dispute resolution (Law) – Europe – History.
3. Law, Medieval. I. Davies, Wendy. II. Fouracre,
Paul.
KJ147.S48 1986 347.4'09 86–6783

ISBN 0 521 30788 0 hardback
ISBN 0 521 42895 5 paperback

WV

Contents

v

Figures

Preface

This book began with a belief, shared by all of us, that the charter collections of the early middle ages provide an exceptionally rich source of information for writing the social history of early medieval Europe – a source that has often been neglected. We also shared a belief that detailed study of particular localities is not well made in isolation – the East *can* illuminate the West, and even the North the South – and we thought it important to over-ride the sometimes excessively insular interests and approaches of English scholarship. The incomparable chance that charters give us to localize and particularize, and even to discuss the less than royal individual, could not be an excuse to ignore broad trends and common problems, for we shared an interest too in understanding the way that human communities organize themselves, as much now as in the distant past.

These shared beliefs have stood firm through some years of interaction, so much so that it seemed useful as well as manageable to produce a work concentrating on charters that record dispute settlements: these have allowed us to explore a class of the material with obvious potential for providing case material, a class whose subject matter is immediate to such central issues in the pattern of social, political and cultural change as definition of communal identity, the ebb and flow of state power, and the interaction between state and local community. We have worked on it in a genuinely collaborative way, meeting on many occasions during the last six years for long weekends of concentrated charter talk in rural isolation. We each did our primary research in the light of an agreed framework of questions; we endlessly chewed over each other's contributions; and we eventually arrived at a common view for Introduction and Conclusion – a process that was often difficult for the individual but undeniably stimulating for all of us. Although, then, the Introduction was written by Patrick Wormald and section 1 of the Conclusion by Roger Collins, section 2 by Paul Fouracre and section 3 by Chris Wickham, the pieces stand as an expression of the group approach.

This book is meant to be read as a book and not as a collection of separate essays. It was not conceived as a contribution to the technical study of diplomatic nor as a work of source criticism. We hope that it will be of interest to those who specialize in such fields, but our chief hope is that it will appeal to more than early medieval historians, or those interested in legal history, and reach anyone concerned with the way that societies regulate and institutionalize disagreement as well as those with more general interests in social change. We have therefore taken care to explain aspects and institutions with which the non-specialist may be unfamiliar, and hope that the specialist will tolerate some passages of basic orientation. Hence our Glossary: it is meant to be used as a simple guide (and does not pretend to be a definitive or exhaustive survey of semantic development). An * on the first occasion of use of a glossed term in each chapter will direct the reader to the appropriate Glossary entry.

We owe a great debt to each other and another to the various wives, husbands, lovers, children, who have suffered our absences and obsessions. We are also extremely grateful to the Syndics of the Cambridge University Press for being so ready to undertake publication, and to the following bodies for permission to reproduce parts of texts: the British Academy for Appendix XXV, XXVI, from *Charters of Rochester*, ed. A. Campbell; Istituto Storico Italiano for Appendix XX, for Appendix XIX, from *Cartulario de San Juan de la Peña*; Deutsches Historisches Institut in Rome for Appendix XXII, from *Quellen und Forschungen aus italienischen Archiven und Bibliotheken*, 41 (1961).

Bucknell
September 1985

Abbreviations

Aberdeen–Banff Illustrations	*Illustrations of the Topography and Antiquities of the Shires of Aberdeen and Banff*, ed. J. Robertson and G. Grub.
AHN	Archivo Histórico Nacional
App.	Appendix
Balfour's Practicks	*The Practicks of Sir James Balfour of Pittendreich*, ed. P. G. B. McNeill.
Barsocchini	*Memorie e documenti per servire all'istoria del ducato di Lucca*, ed. D. Barsocchini.
Basilika	*Basilicorum libri lx*, ed. C. E. Heimbach.
Becerro de Cardeña	*El Becerro gótico de San Pedro de Cardeña*, ed. L. Serrano.
Brühl	*Codice diplomatico longobardo*, vol. 3, pt 1, ed. C. R. Brühl.
Cartulario de Arlanza	*El Cartulario de San Pedro de Arlanza*, ed. L. Serrano.
ChLA	*Chartae Latinae Antiquiores*, ed. A. Bruckner and R. Marichal.
CIH	*Corpus Iuris Hibernici*, ed. D. A. Binchy.
CR	*Cartulaire de Redon*, ed. A. de Courson.
El.	*Liber Eliensis*, ed. E. O. Blake.
Grimoald	*Leges Grimvaldi* in *Leges Langobardorum*, ed. F. Beyerle.
Hib.	*Hibernensis. Die irische Kanonensammlung*, ed. F. W. H. Wasserschleben.
Liutprand	*Leges Liutprandi* in *Leges Langobardorum*, ed. F. Beyerle.
Manaresi	*I placiti del 'Regnum Italiae'*, ed. C. Manaresi.
MGH	*Monumenta Germaniae Historica.*
MGH AA	*MGH Auctores Antiquissimi.*
MGH Capit.	*Capitularia Regum Francorum*, ed. A. Boretius.

MGH LL	*MGH Leges* (folio series).
MGH LL in quarto	*MGH Leges* (quarto series).
MGH SRL	*MGH Scriptores Rerum Langobardicarum.*
MGH SRM	*MGH Scriptores Rerum Merovingicarum.*
MGH SS	*MGH Scriptores* (folio series).
n. s.	new series
Peira	*Practica ex actis Eustathii Romani* in *Jus graeco-romanum*, ed. J. and P. Zepos.
Pertz	*Diplomata regum Francorum e stirpe Merowingica* in *MGH Diplomata Imperii*, vol. 1, ed. K. Pertz.
Porro	*Codex diplomaticus langobardiae*, ed. G. Porro-Lambertenghi.
Prôtaton	*Actes du Prôtaton*, vol. 1, ed. D. Papachryssanthou.
Ram.	*Chronicon Abbatiae Rameseiensis*, ed. W. D. Macray.
Ratchis	*Legis Ratchisi* in *Leges Langobardorum*, ed. F. Beyerle.
RF	*Regesto di Farfa*, ed. I. Giorgi and U. Balzani.
Roch.	*Charters of Rochester*, ed. A. Campbell.
S	P. H. Sawyer, *Anglo-Saxon Charters: an annotated list and bibliography*.
Salvioli	G. Salvioli, *Storia della procedura civile e criminale*.
Schiaparelli	*Codice diplomatico longobardo*, vols. 1 and 2, ed. L. Schiaparelli.
SRO	Scottish Record Office.
Tessier, *Recueil*	*Recueil des Actes de Charles II le Chauve*, ed. G. Tessier.
Tírechán	Tírechán in *The Patrician Texts in the Book of Armagh*, ed. L. Bieler.
Volpini	R. Volpini, 'Placiti dell "Regnum Italiae"' in P. Zerbi (ed.), *Contributi dell' Istituto di storia medioevale*.
ZRG, Germ. Abt.	*Zeitschrift der Savigny-Stiftung für Rechtsgeschichte, Germanistiche Abteilung.*

Introduction

History is the debtor of many intellectual disciplines, but is often thereby enslaved. Archaeology, philology and sociology can be ruthless creditors. Many forms of a 'pure' historian's written evidence demand inside knowledge of their genre, from Egyptian papyri to Fleet Street tabloids. Understanding our means of perceiving the past risks becoming an end in itself. This is especially so in Europe's early middle ages: 'Dark Ages', not just because they were 'barbarous', nor even because shortage of documentary guides makes them relatively impenetrable, but because the waywardness of literacy in so much of the area for so much of the era raises particularly awkward questions about the motivation and audience of what texts we have, narrative or documentary. This book seeks to emancipate the historical perspective on two aspects of the evidence for the period where means have tended to be ends: the charter* and the law.

Early medieval historians lack the sort of bureaucratic records which are staple fare for students of politics, government and law in later ages. More or less formal documents were produced, sometimes in very large numbers. But no known text before Domesday Book (1086) survives today because it was kept by the secular government responsible for producing it. Until then – and in most of Europe for some time later – our archival repositories were churches. However apparently vulnerable themselves, only ecclesiastical corporations had a sufficiently continuous tradition to pass their records on to modern times. Churches exercised authority in their own right, but, except in the papacy's case, they much more often preserved what they received rather than what they issued, texts of which they were, or thought themselves, directly or indirectly, the beneficiaries. So we see the exercise of power in early medieval Europe from the outside looking in, and largely from the angle of a very specific, very powerful, interest. This raises suspicions that the records bestowing property or privilege which are generically known to English-speaking historians as charters have been doctored or fabricated to the advantage of those who preserved them; and scepticism is hard to dispel, not only because one cannot make checks in government archives but also because, at least in northern Europe, most charters survive not as

1

originally issued (with such authenticating features as seals or autograph signatures) but in later collections, or cartularies.

It was especially this last problem that gave rise to the historical science of diplomatic (diploma* being a term for the more formal type of charter), a technical and highly skilled discipline which has supplied excellent manuals of the subject (mostly in French or German), but which has been limited both by its own terms of reference and in its practical application[1]. First, an understandable pre-occupation with authenticity means that it is more concerned with what charters are than with what they say, or how they relate to wider issues of political, social and cultural history. Second, as so often in early medieval European history, the picture in these manuals is dominated by the Franks (in effect, France, Germany and Benelux). Byzantium has for these always been a place apart[2]. The rich Italian evidence has received limited attention, and the Anglo-Saxon material has been largely, the Spanish and Celtic traditions entirely, ignored. The group responsible for this book was formed in reaction to such tendencies. We felt that, by combining a common interest in charters with a range of specialist experience, we could widen perceptions of what, at most times and places, is the bulkiest category of early medieval historical evidence.

This book contains detailed studies of particular areas with special reference to select texts, followed by three essays of general conclusions, an Appendix of the texts highlighted, a Glossary of technical terms, and a full Bibliography[3]. It concentrates on one broad type of charter, the formal record of the settlement of disputes (often, then and since, called *placitum**). Dispute settlement is a subject of crucial importance to both sociologists and historians of other societies[4]. Of particular interest to us is the fact that the study of the settlement procedures which lay behind the records highlights the relationship between the charter's form (and the history of its form) and its social, political and cultural context. And without this understanding, legal history becomes another specialist taskmaster, written as it usually is, if not by lawyers, then with a legalist slant (the one obvious exception simply proves the rule: there has never been anyone else like Maitland).

The history of law in early medieval Europe – commonly and understandably, but not always helpfully, called Germanic law – has been dominated by the so-called *Rechtsschule**, the school of legal history created by nineteenth-century

---

[1] For a full bibliography of most western European diplomatic down to *c.* 750, see P. Wormald, *Bede . . . the charter evidence*, pp. 26–8.

[2] See Morris below, pp. 125–31.

[3] Appendix texts have been critically amended where necessary; here and henceforth, items in the Glossary are marked * when first introduced in an article; references in our notes throughout are partly abbreviated versions of what appears in full in the Bibliography.

[4] For example, S. Roberts, *Order and Dispute*; J. Bossy (ed.), *Disputes and Settlements*.

scholars, mostly German, who were inspired by the legal dimensions of the Romantic movement[5]. It remains a construct of immense intellectual power, but it too has drawbacks. First, like diplomatic, it focuses on the more 'purely' Germanic peoples, especially the Franks. Second, it is founded on faith in a fundamental Germanic law and its 'spirit (*geist*)', by which standard its selection of evidence is largely determined. Third, it prefers prescriptive to descriptive evidence, that of codes of law rather than records of their application[6]. Fourth, it considers that what it finds is 'irrational': pleading in fixed *formulae** so that a verbal stumble might lose a case, or the oath and the ordeal, whose only sanction was superstitious dread of divine judgement. Material evidence, even in writing, they maintained, only brought a party 'closer to the oath', that is gave him prior right to swear with his oath-helpers*, and by such support (rather than proof) win his case[7]. Finally, and perhaps paradoxically, the *Rechtsschule* view is essentially optimist: it acknowledges that corruption and tyranny distorted the law, but these were departures from a norm which it sees as equitable and fair, in recognizably modern terms.

By contrast, *we* begin with law in action, basing our argument on the *placita*, adducing narrative evidence where appropriate, and invoking that of edicts or formulaic norms only as a last resort. Our approach is inductive, and embraces areas with no pretence of being Germanic, in order to make contrasts and comparisons between the variety of early medieval western societies. We are also 'realists', in that we accept political pressure and social advantage as integral (and not always unfair) parts of legal procedure. We must not anticipate our conclusions here, but it needs emphasis that they emerged from collaborative study; each contribution was rigorously discussed by the group in a series of

---

[5] For a conspectus of the *Rechtsschule* and a critique of one of its basic tenets, see J. Goebel, *Felony and Misdemeanour*, pp. 1–122. The movement effectively began in 1828 with the publication of Jakob Grimm's *Deutsche Rechtsaltertümer*; Grimm was not only the famous folk-tale collector but also the close friend of Friedrich von Savigny, and his 'system' of Germanic law was a conscious reflection of that constructed by Savigny for Roman jurisprudence. The approach reached its apotheosis in H. Brunner's fine *Deutsche Rechtsgeschichte*. It is still influential but is now encountering criticism, even in Germany; for example, see H. Conrad, *Deutsche Rechtsgeschichte*, but contrast P. Classen (ed.), *Recht und Schrift im Mittelalter, Vorträge und Forschungen*, vol. 23 (1977).

[6] In the 1373 footnotes to his discussion of 'Der Rechtsgang' in *Deutsche Rechtsgeschichte*, 3rd edn, vol. 2, pp. 435–702, Brunner cites charters just over one hundred times, as against an extraordinary range of reference to normative, and indeed narrative, evidence; compare Wormald's analysis of the method used by F. Liebermann in *Die Gesetze der Angelsachsen*, below, p. 149. R. Hübner's still valuable list of 'Gerichtsurkunden der fränkischen Zeit', *ZRG, Germ. Abt.*, 12 (1891) and 14 (1893) was meant to be the foundation of an edition of *placita* in the *Monumenta Germaniae Historica* (whose editorial board overlapped with the *Rechtsschule*); perhaps significantly, the edition never appeared, though the *Monumenta* have supplied editions of all continental legislation in the early middle ages. For a survey of this legislation, and analysis of some problems, see P. Wormald, '*Lex Scripta* and *Verbum Regis*' in P. H. Sawyer and I. N. Wood (eds.), *Early Medieval Kingship*.

[7] For a succinct English statement of this approach, see D. Whitelock (ed.), *English Historical Documents*, vol. 1, pp. 366–9; and, for a French one, F. L. Ganshof, 'La preuve dans le droit franc' in *La Preuve*, vol. 2, *Recueil de la Société Jean Bodin*, vol. 17 (1965).

meetings; there are differences of view and emphasis throughout the book, because even our own disputes were not always resolved. Nevertheless, we think that our results are coherent overall, and they have surprised some of us as much as they may surprise the reader.

It should also be stressed that we are well aware of our exercise's limitations. The distribution of our evidence is to an extent arbitrary, allowing insight only into the perhaps rather special cases which somehow interested churchmen. Little is said of crime as such, though one of our messages is that in early medieval Europe, as in comparable societies, criminal proceedings are not easily distinguished from civil. Our selection of study areas may seem paradoxical to some: we begin in the fifth century where there is very little documentary material indeed, and end before the twelfth when it becomes plentiful; we almost ignore Scandinavian evidence, long supposed the most primitively Germanic available, and include not only Byzantium and Ireland but also early modern Scotland. Such idiosyncracies arise partly from the interests and expertise of the group's members, just as the nature of our chosen evidence concentrates attention on property disputes, whether in land or men. But there are also other reasons.

We focus on a world sandwiched between two others, the Roman Empire and the twelfth-century West, and we thereby isolate societies whose evidence was affected, quantitively and qualitatively, by the relative lack of bureaucratic government and of the academic study of law. Admittedly Irish law was as academically specialized as that of post-twelfth-century law schools and Byzantium inherited to a significant extent the bureaucratic procedures of the later Roman empire. But Irish government was anything but bureaucratic, and Byzantine legal procedure, at least outside the capital, owed less to legal theory than its machinery might lead one to expect. On the other hand, it is now known that the supposedly archaic Scandinavian evidence was significantly affected by the post-twelfth-century cultural climate[8]. Early modern Scotland was of course no less affected, notably in that its documentation was infinitely more prolific than that of early medieval Europe. But our concern is with social, not ethnic, patterns; and it seems reasonable to use a sixteenth-century Banffshire dispute as our post-script, because it reminds readers of what a few experts in the mighty edifice of English medieval justice, with its two or three million writs from just two hundred years, have begun to suspect even for their own world: that behind the sophisticated façade of later ages lie much the same procedural rhythms of dispute settlement as we have found in the rest of this volume[9].

[8] See P. H. Sawyer, *Kings and Vikings*, pp. 8–23; and *idem*, 'The Vikings and Ireland' in D. Whitelock *et al.* (eds.), *Ireland in early mediaeval Europe*.

[9] For the number of surviving judicial writs between the reigns of Richard I and II, see R. C. van Caenegem, *Royal Writs in England*, p. 3; for hesitation about the impression they give, see M. T. Clanchy, 'Law and Love' in Bossy (ed.), *Disputes and Settlements*, and *idem*, 'A medieval realist' in E. Attwool (ed.), *Perspectives in Jurisprudence*.

All contributors wish to thank our editors for the kindly firmness with which they have shepherded an awkward flock. Without them, an idea dreamed up at lunch in a London pub seven years ago would never have materialized.

1

Disputes in late fifth- and sixth-century Gaul: some problems

IAN WOOD

The procedures for settling disputes in the great law courts of the Roman empire are well known. For the fourth and fifth centuries the *Codex Theodosianus* provides an invaluable guide[1]. Similarly law books provide a key to the legal processes of the Germanic kingdoms, whilst specific cases are recorded in documents known to modern historians as *placita**, which survive, particularly in north Francia, from the seventh century onwards[2]. Despite the absence of such documents from earlier periods, it has been suggested with reason that the *placitum* developed out of the Roman charter*[3]. Nevertheless it is worth noting that the development of the *placitum*, like that of the charter itself, can only be inferred and not demonstrated directly. It may be significant that no genuine specimen is known from the Merovingian kingdom before 625 and that the surviving examples come from the relatively new monastic world of northern Francia, not from the well-established urban administrative centres of the south[4]. The towns of the north were undoubtedly less important than their southern counterparts and in all probability their rôle in local administration was correspondingly less significant. Moreover the monasteries of the region were young, powerful and rural, with no particular interest in upholding the remnants of the city-based administrative system of Roman Gaul. These factors may in part explain the emergence of the *placitum* in the early seventh century; if so, they provide a powerful illustration of the need to place the development of legal procedure in a general context.

The origins of the *placitum* in many ways provide a paradigm of the problems facing the would-be historian of sixth-century dispute settlement. The procedures involved are usually regarded as having developed from some earlier tradition, whether Roman or Germanic. More often than not, however, there is

---

[1] See H. F. Jolowicz, *Historical Introduction to the Study of Roman Law*, 2nd edn, pp. 457–70.
[2] See Fouracre below, pp. 23–5.
[3] P. Classen, 'Kaiserreskript und Königsurkunde', *Archiv für Diplomatik*, 2 (1956), 69; W. Bergmann, 'Untersuchungen zu den Gerichtsurkunden der Merowingerzeit', *Archiv für Dip.*, 22 (1976), 105–6.
[4] P. Classen, 'Fortleben und Wandel spätrömischen Urkundenwesens im frühen Mittelalter' in P. Classen (ed.), *Recht und Schrift im Mittelalter, Vorträge und Forschungen*, 23 (1977), pp. 48–9.

no clear evidence to prove the derivation of a particular legal process, and at times one may suspect that the grounds for identifying origins are little more than an assumption that Germanic law is more 'irrational' than its Roman counterpart. This is a particularly dangerous approach, given that very little is known about Roman procedure outside the great courts of the empire. The workings of Roman vulgar law* in minor provincial courts are completely obscure. Nevertheless it is possible to look at some of the procedures followed in sixth-century dispute settlement and to make suggestions about their origins; in particular, it is possible to examine methods of proof used in law-suits and to make deductions about the development of law in the sub-Roman period. Before doing so, however, it is useful to look briefly at the range of evidence relating to dispute settlement in the sixth century, in order to provide a background to a discussion of legal formalities.

Alongside the purely legal evidence there is information to be gleaned from the literary evidence, notably from the writings, both historical and hagiographical, of Gregory of Tours[5]. The majority of disputes which attract Gregory's attention, however, are of political significance and hence are unusual in form; ordinary cases are not his concern. Nevertheless he is at pains to emphasize the habitual rôle of the Church, especially the bishops, in arbitration and making peace. Moreover Gregory's anecdotes, albeit abnormal, bring out one other crucial point; that social, religious and political pressures which weighed in the settlement of disputes need to be taken into consideration, despite the fact that they are not apparent in the law codes or the *formulae**.

A similar point is to be found in other literary evidence of the late fifth and sixth centuries, in letter collections and in the related verses of Venantius Fortunatus. Although court-cases rarely figure in this material, there are numerous instances of individuals lobbying their friends for help in sorting out problems, both in order to produce settlement outside the court and also as preparation for trial. In the letters of Sidonius Apollinaris conflicts over land, slaves and rent are dealt with in gentlemanly fashion, without recourse to law, as are questions of violence and problems raised by illicit servile marriage and kidnapping. In the last case Sidonius explicitly attempted to find grounds for agreement before conflict escalated and reached the courts[6]. Likewise in a case of abduction Venantius Fortunatus resorted to addressing poems to four powerful men and relied on them rather than the law to secure the girl's release[7]. Rather less clear are two cases involving Avitus of Vienne, in which the bishop lobbied powerful laymen, not least because the defendants had impugned him[8]. This exertion of pressure

---

[5] E. James, '*Beati pacifici*: bishops and the law in sixth-century Gaul' in J. A. Bossy (ed.), *Disputes and Settlements*.

[6] Sidonius Apollinaris, *Lettres*, vols. 2 and 3, ed. A. Loyen, *epistolae* III. v, III. ix, VI. x, III. xii, VI. iv, V. xix.

[7] Venantius Fortunatus, *Opera Poetica*, ed. F. Leo, *MGH AA*, vol. 4, pt 1, X. xii. a–d.

[8] Avitus, *Opera*, ed. R. Peiper, *MGH AA*, vol. 6, pt 2, *epistolae*, nos. 44, 55.

on both friends and officials confirms the importance of the social context of any dispute and it shows that opposing parties could be brought to composition without invoking the law. Moreover agreements made out of court could be given formal sanction, since the Formularies* provide models for such settlements made through a third party of friends or clergy, as well as for rather more official compositions arranged by *boni homines**. Among the *formulae* there are records of final concord in cases of theft, seizure of land, violence, murder, illicit marriage and rape, despite the fact that Roman law disapproved of agreement over rape, while the *Pactus pro tenore pacis* of Childebert and Chlothar refused to countenance extra-judicial composition in the case of theft[9].

The *formulae* provide a useful bridge between the specific evidence of histories, hagiography and letters on the one hand and the more general statements of the law codes on the other. They therefore offer some compensation for the absence of authentic *placita* from sixth-century Gaul. More often than not the *formulae* appear to have been drawn from already existing documents, omitting merely the specifics of person and place. Unfortunately, however, the Formularies present problems of chronology. Although individual *formulae* from Angers and Clermont can be dated with some certainty to the early Merovingian period[10], the majority have no clear *terminus ante quem* other than the fact that they survive, often in connexion with the *Lex Romana Visigothorum*, in manuscripts of the ninth century and later. Even the Formulary which is apparently earliest in date, that from Angers, may reflect legal developments of the seventh century rather than the situation in the sixth, since a very high proportion of its *formulae* seem to be associated with a monastic or episcopal court and not with the municipal courts known to have been in existence in the post-Roman period. It may even be that the *Formulae Andecavenses* were drawn from the archives of one of the leading abbeys of Angers[11]. In short, only a handful of *formulae*, and those not the most important for the legal historian, can be used with any certainty as sixth-century evidence; the rest can only be cited in a supporting rôle.

9 *Formulae Andecavenses*, nos. 6, 26, 39, 43, 44, in *Formulae Merowingici et Karolini Aevi*, ed. K. Zeumer, *MGH LL in quarto*, sectio 5; *Marculfi Formularum Libri Duo*, ed. A. Uddholm, II. 18, 41; *Formulae Turonenses*, no. 32, in *MGH LL in quarto*, sectio 5. For the Roman condemnation of composition after rape, see *Codex Theodosianus*, ed. T. Mommsen and P. M. Meyer, IX. xxiv, 1–2 and *Lex Burgundionum*, ix. 2, in *Leges Burgundionum*, ed. L. R. de Salis, *MGH LL in quarto*, sectio 1, vol. 2, pt 1. For Frankish condemnation of composition after theft, see *Pactus pro tenore pacis domnorum Childeberti et Chlotharii regum*, iii, in *Capitularia Regum Francorum*, vol. 1, ed. A. Boretius, *MGH LL in quarto*, sectio 2; for the rôle of *boni homines*, see K. Nehlsen-von Stryk, *Die boni homines des frühen Mittelalters*, pp. 50–92.

10 *Formulae Andecavenses*, nos. 1, 34; *Formulae Arvernenses*, no. 1, in *Formulae, MGH LL in quarto*, sectio 5.

11 Thirty-three out of the sixty *Formulae Andecavenses* can be seen as ecclesiastical (these do not include the undoubtedly early *formulae* nos. 1 and 34). In his commentary in *Formulae, MGH LL in quarto*, sectio 5, p. 1, Zeumer radically underestimated the ecclesiastical nature of the collection. Recognition of the ecclesiastical *formulae* undermines his argument for an original compilation (nos. 1–36) made in 514–15, which was then expanded until it reached its present state *c*. 675–6.

By contrast, the major legal collections of the sixth century are well dated. In origin the *Pactus Legis Salicae* appears to be a product of the last years of Clovis's reign[12], while the crucial additions, most notably the *Edictus Chilperici*, are ascribed with certainty to individual rulers. The *Leges Burgundionum* present greater problems, not least because some of the manuscripts of the *Liber Constitutionum*, the official collection of Burgundian law, attribute the work to Gundobad, and some to his son Sigismund[13]. However, seeing that all manuscripts are agreed that the original collection was ratified in Lyons 'sub die IIII kalendas Aprilis' (29 March), in the second year of the king's reign, and seeing that we know from an edict appended to the collection that Sigismund was legislating in Lyons 'sub die IIII kalendas Aprilis . . . Agapito consule', that is 517, the second year of his reign[14], we can reasonably assume that the core of the compilation, as it now stands, was promulgated on that day. The *Lex Romana Burgundionum* is more difficult to date, and its status as law is not entirely clear; it need not be an officially recognized code. Nevertheless its close relationship with the *Liber Constitutionum* sugests that the two are almost, if not exactly, contemporary[15].

Over the procedure for making an accusation and bringing a case to court the *Lex Romana Burgundionum* openly excerpts the *Codex Theodosianus*. In criminal cases, doubtless involving accusations of homicide and certainly involving those of treason, 'obiectio criminum maiestatis', the accuser had to agree to face the same penalties as the accused[16]. In civil disputes (*lites*) the plaintiff had to make known the cause of his accusation in writing to the defendant before a judge within three days[17]. The *Liber Constitutionum* has little to say about bringing a case to the courts, although it is assumed that in the case of a slave being accused, his master will readily hand him over to justice[18]. The main procedural problems relate to the failure of a judge to give judgement within three months[19], and to the danger of barbarian *patrocinium* being sought in a case between Romans[20]. The contrast between this and the concerns about attendance at court in the *Pactus Legis Salicae* and more particularly the *Edictus Chilperici* is striking. The *Pactus* itself begins with a fine for non-attendance at the *mallus**[21], and subsequent

---

12 P. Wormald, '*Lex Scripta* and *Verbum Regis*' in P. H. Sawyer and I. N. Wood (eds.), *Early Medieval Kingship*, p. 108.

13 *Liber Constitutionum, prima constitutio*, in *Leges Burgundionum* ed. L. R. de Salis, p. 30.

14 *Liber Constitutionum, prima constitutio* and lii. On Sigismund's Easter court of 517, see further I. N. Wood, 'Avitus of Vienne: religion and culture in the Auvergne and the Rhône valley, 470–530' (Univ. Oxford D.Phil. thesis, 1980), pp. 221–2.

15 For a comparison of the two texts, see *Leges Burgundionum*, pp. 164–7.

16 *Lex Romana Burgundionum*, vii; compare *Codex Theodosianus*, IX. i. 14 and 19.

17 *Lex Romana Burgundionum*, xi. 1. On the judges in such cases, *Lex Romana Burgundionum*, xxxiii.

18 *Liber Constitutionum*, lxxvii. 1.

19 *Liber Constitutionum*, lxxxi. 1; compare *prima constitutio* xii.

20 *Liber Constitutionum*, xxii.

21 *Pactus Legis Salicae*, i, ed. K. A. Eckhardt, *MGH LL in quarto*, sectio 1, vol. 4, pt 1.

legislation deals at length with procedure for enforcing judgement on recalcitrant defendants, requiring witnesses to attest that the court had carried out all the appropriate formalities before calling for the intervention of the king[22]. In the case of one antrustion (military follower) accusing another the procedures are set out at greater length; the accuser must make his claim with witnesses before the judge for seven nights, thus giving the accused a chance to refute the charge. If the accused fails to turn up the procedure must be repeated for fourteen nights; if he then appears he must clear himself with an oath; if he still does not appear, or if he refuses to clear himself or to undergo ordeal, the case is then deferred for a further forty days. Non-attendance at this court leads to the case being transferred to the king fourteen days later[23]. This elaborate procedure, where the accused is given every chance of clearing himself and where there can be no opportunity for a case being overlooked accidentally is no more complex that that set out in the *Edictus Chilperici*, where a lord must bring an accused slave to judgement by divination (*sors*) within ten days; if not, the case is adjourned for forty-two days. If legitimate excuses for non-attendance are then forthcoming, the case is deferred for eighty-four days; if no apologies are offered, sentence is passed and must be carried out in fourteen days. In the event of the penalty not being exacted, complaint must be made within seven days, and at the next meeting of the *mallus* the *graphio** should be asked in the presence of the *rachymburgi** to take charge of the proceedings[24].

The complicated formalities of justice in the *Pactus* make most obvious sense in a small face-to-face community, whilst the concerns of the Burgundian *Liber Constitutionum* more obviously reflect the mixed society of the Rhône valley cities. Whether we can conclude that procedures specified in the *Pactus* are therefore entirely Germanic is a different matter. *Lex Salica* does not concern itself solely with Franks; it includes legislation on Romans, even in instances when they were not involved with their barbarian neighbours[25]. Similarly the *Edictus Chilperici* is addressed to all the king's subjects. Moreover, an underlying concern with non-attendance was not confined to Germanic legislation; it is to be found in Roman and Burgundian law and in the *formulae* and seventh-century *placita*[26]. In addition the details of procedure in the *Pactus* are themselves somewhat hybrid. A concern to reckon by nights is certainly Germanic and reckoning in units of ten may be[27], but an overlapping set of calculations in units of seven days must reflect the influence of the Judaeo-Christian week[28].

---

[22] *Pactus Legis Salicae*, lvi.　　　　　[23] *Pactus Legis Salicae*, lxxiii.
[24] *Pactus Legis Salicae*, cxiii. See Fouracre below, pp. 39–41.
[25] *Pactus Legis Salicae*, xvi. 5, xxxix. 5, xli. 8–10, xlii. 4, civ. 9, cxvii. 2.
[26] *Codex Theodosianus*, II. vi. 1, II. xviii. 2; *Liber Constitutionum*, viii. 4–5; *Formulae Andecavenses*, nos. 12–14. For the *placita*, see Fouracre below, p. 34.
[27] On nights, Tacitus, *Germania*, ed. J. G. C. Anderson, xi. 2; *Pactus Legis Salicae*, xl. 7–10, xlv. 2, xlvii. 1, lii. 1–2, lvi. 3–4, lxxiii. 1, 5–6, lxxxii. 1, lxxxviii. 1, cii. 1–2, cxiii. On multiples of ten, xlv. 2, xlvii. 1, lvi. 3, lxxiii. 6, lxxxii. 1, lxxxviii, cii. 3, cxiii.
[28] On multiples of seven, *Pactus Legis Salicae*, xl. 7, 9–10, lii. 2, lvi. 4, lxxiii. 1, 5, cii. 1, cxiii.

Turning from the processes of accusation and summons to those of proof, it is clear that in Burgundian law written documentation provided the best claim in cases of land dispute; the *Liber Constitutionum* reveals that royal grants were secured by charter and it lays emphasis on the need for signatures on deeds of gift and on wills because of conflict over title[29]. In addition the *Lex Romana Burgundionum* insists on the production of documents to claim precarial possession[30]. The *Pactus Legis Salicae*, by contrast, provides scarcely any indication of the use of written documentation[31]. It is nevertheless clear from Gregory of Tours not only that there were charters in use in the Frankish kingdom during the sixth century, but also that men were still able to detect forged charters on palaeographical grounds, as happened in the trial of Bishop Egidius of Rheims in 590[32]. The use of palaeography to check the authenticity of a document was known to Roman law and survived in the *Lex Romana Burgundionum*[33]. The absence of sixth-century charters does not, therefore, indicate that such documents were unimportant; their value is indeed apparent in numerous *formulae* concerned with replacing documents which had been destroyed, after a claim had been substantiated by witnesses[34]. Not only were documents replaced; a record of the claims was entered in the municipal archives, the *gesta municipalia*, where according to the *Lex Romana Burgundionum* all gifts were to be registered[35].

The entry of a claim in the *gesta* was an extremely formal and elaborate process which was indubitably Roman (though probably late Roman) in origin[36]. The full elaboration of the procedure, however, is only known from the *formulae*, of which perhaps the most illuminating is the first surviving document of the Clermont formulary[37]. This text (paraphrased below), albeit incomplete, has the additional merit of being relatively well dated, since it refers to Frankish hostilities, which are probably best equated with the raid led by Theuderic against the Auvergne in the mid 520s. This context also provides a vivid reminder of the endemic disorder and civil war in fifth- and sixth-century Gaul, factors which can only have complicated claims to land.

[29] *Liber Constitutionum*, i. 4, xliii. 1, *constitutiones extravagantes* xxi. 14.

[30] *Lex Romana Burgundionum*, xxxv. 2.

[31] But see *Pactus Legis Salicae*, xiv. 4.

[32] Gregory of Tours, *Libri Historiarum*, x. xix, ed. B. Krusch and W. Levison, *MGH SRM*, vol. 1, pt 1. For accusations of tampering with wills, IV. li, VI. xlvi.

[33] *Codex Theodosianus*, II. xxvii. 1, IX. xix. 2; *Lex Romana Burgundionum*, xlv. 1.

[34] *Formulae Andecavenses*, nos. 31–3; *Marculfi Form.* I. 33–4; *Formulae Turonenses*, nos. 27–8.

[35] *Lex Romana Burgundionum*, i. 1, xxii. 3. See also xi. 2 on registering concessions of the power of attorney in law cases; this is much in evidence in the *formulae*, for example *Formulae Arvernenses*, no. 2. For the entry of a will in the *gesta*, *Formulae Andecavenses*, no. 41.

[36] *Codex Theodosianus*, XIV. xv. 2; *Novella Valentiniani*, xv. 1 and 3, in *Codex Theodosianus*, ed. Mommsen.

[37] *Formulae Arvernenses*, no. 1; *Formulae Andecavenses*, no. 32; *Marculfi Form.* II. 37–8. See also *Lex Romana Burgundionum*, xliv. 3.

It is not unknown that as a result of the Frankish hostilities our documents were lost in our *mansus* [dwelling] at villa 'a' where we were living. Therefore I, 'b', and my wife ask and make known that our possession of all we are known to have held by those documents at that time should not be undermined on account of those events. Among the documents were certain letters relating to the *mansus* on villa 'a', by which we had complete possession, held according to a deed of purchase[?]. In addition there were all those things mentioned above, which we can scarcely remember, held by written judgements, briefs, notices, records of dowry, *conculcationes* [marriage documents?] and other deeds, both our own and ones which had been committed to us, all of which we lost in the aforesaid villa during those troubles; and we ask that we may be allowed to put together and affirm this appeal or plea through this document in our name, as we have done; and in accordance with the law issued during the consulship of the emperors Honorius and Theodosius we have posted and upheld these claims for three days at the gate of the church of saint 'c' in the fortress of Clermont, and in the public market, as directed by the council, the king or your agents or persons of this fortress, so that with this appeal or plea set out in your presence, according to the law, you may confirm it with your subscriptions and marks, authorizing restitution for our losses, as mentioned above, with just authority by your approval, so that with these documents we may regain control of our property by the authority of the law.

Therefore your worship (*vir laudabilis*) with *defensor** 'd' and you honourable men (*honorati*), who assiduously act in the common good, ought in this meeting of the council to approve on my behalf this appeal or plea, upheld for three days in the public places, with your signatures or marks affixed below, so that I may regain possession of my dwelling, as is necessary, either in the presence of the lords or of the judges of my opponents. For this we have taken care to set down this appeal or plea, so that when you wish or prefer or when it is necessary for me, you may enter it together with our petitions according to the custom in the municipal archives. For this may we offer you the greatest thanks. (App. I)

From this *formula* it is clear that in early sixth-century Clermont a vast range of legal documents were still in use, as were the municipal archives. It is also clear that in the case of documents being lost there were elaborate procedures for asserting one's claim to land, involving public advertisements maintained for three days. Similar claims are known to have been made elsewhere with the support of witnesses[38]. Unfortunately outside the *formulae* there is little to illuminate the significance of these procedures in sixth-century Gaul. Certainly the municipal archives are known to have continued into the seventh century in some centres, although these may have been exceptional[39]. In Le Mans, not an obvious centre of Merovingian literacy[40], Bishop Bertram had his will inserted into the municipal archives in 616[41]; the purpose of such registration, however, is not clear. Like the victims of Theuderic's Clermont raid, Bertram himself lost substantial lands in the civil wars between Chlothar and the grandsons of Brunhild, but he did not use the municipal archives to re-establish his claim over

[38] *Formulae Andecavenses*, nos. 31, 32; *Marculfi Form.* I. 33–4. Compare *Formulae Turonenses*, no. 28.
[39] Classen, 'Fortleben und Wandel', pp. 42–7. For a fuller bibliography on *gesta municipalia*, see Classen, 'Kaiserreskript und Königsurkunde', 30.
[40] Gregory of Tours, *Libri Historiarum*, VI. ix, p. 279.
[41] *Actus Pontificum Cennomanis in urbe degentium*, ed. G. Busson and A. Ledru, pp. 102–41.

land. Nor, apparently, did he regain his lost estates despite Chlothar's legislation that anything lost in the service of one's lord should be restored[42]. As for his will, it is not arranged in such a way as to help the reader, having no obvious organization and degenerating into a series of disconnected additions. In other words it is possible that in the sixth and seventh centuries registration in the *gesta municipalia* was a formality with no real function[43].

Against this there are sixth-century documents from Italy which not only illustrate the process of registration in the municipal archives[44], but also show that the *gesta* were used by interested parties[45]. Although the survival of Roman administration may have been greater in sixth-century Italy than in early Merovingian Gaul, the Italian papyri do show that land registration could be worthwhile in the post-Roman period. It thus becomes possible to take a much more favourable view of the evidence provided by the *formulae*. It may be that the comparative silence in the law codes and the literary sources over the use of documentary evidence in land disputes stems from the fact that where there was documentation few disputes ever reached the courts. If this is correct, then there is greater reason for linking the emergence of the *placitum* with the lack of municipal archives in northern Gaul, just as there is cause for relating the survival of individual charters from the seventh century onwards to the decline of public registration and the demise of the *gesta municipalia*[46].

The majority of the legal evidence for dispute in sixth-century Gaul centres not on land but on crimes such as theft, and the most revealing laws relate to accusations made 'per suspicionem', without clear evidence. Although these draw us away from the central area of land dispute, they provide an insight into questions of proof which are germane to a general understanding of post-Roman dispute settlement. For these the eighth chapter of the Burgundian *Liber Constitutionum* provides a useful starting point.

Concerning the rebuttal of accusations made against freemen.
(1) If any free man, whether barbarian or Roman, is accused of a crime out of suspicion, let him offer an oath, and let him swear, together with his wife, children [sons?] and twelve relatives; if indeed he has no wife or children but has a father and mother, let the father and mother fill up the required number. But if he has no father and mother, let him take the oath with twelve relatives.
(2) But if he who is to swear wishes to take the oath with his hand, those men who are ordered to witness the oath, three of whom we have ordered to be appointed by the judges always to witness the oath, may protest before they enter the church that they do not wish the oath to be taken, and after this announcement he who was to swear is

[42] *Edictum Chlotharii*, xvii, in *Capitularia*, vol. 1, ed. A. Boretius.
[43] For a parallel to the form of Bertram's will, with its unorganized additions, *Marculfi Form.* II. 17. Compare the difficulties of retrieving information from English medieval records discussed in M. T. Clanchy, *From Memory to Written Record*, p. 139.
[44] *Die nichtliterarischen Papyri Italiens aus der Zeit 445–700*, ed. J.-O. Tjäder, nos. 4–5, 7, 8, 10–11, 14–15, 18–19, 21, 29, 31, 32, 33.
[45] *Die nichtlit. Papyri Italiens*, nos. 10–11.   [46] Classen, 'Fortleben und Wandel', p. 49.

not allowed to take the oath, but those who are to be tried by the judgement of God should then be sent to us.

(3) If, however, he is allowed to swear and does so and is then convicted after the oath, let him know that he is to make ninefold compensation to those in whose presence the judge ordered the oath to be taken.

(4) If they fail to appear at the place on the appointed day, not as a result of sickness or official business, let them pay six *solidi** by way of fine. But if they have been detained by sickness or business, let them make this known to the judge or send appropriate people in their place, through whose faith they can discharge the oath there.

(5) If, however, he who is to be given the oath, does not come to the place let the other party wait until the sixth hour of the day, and if he does not come before the sixth hour, let the case be concluded without delay.

(6) But if the accuser does not come, let him who was to have offered the oath leave guiltless. (App. II)

The methods of proof envisaged here – primarily oath-taking, but also trial by ordeal – have little to do with those discussed in the *Codex Theodosianus*. The heavy reliance on oath-taking and the introduction of trial by ordeal have, as a result, been interpreted as an indication of Germanic legal tradition within the early barbarian law codes[47]. A simple primitive-Germanic interpretation of this material, however, does not find particularly strong support from what is known about barbarian law from the pre-migration period[48]. It is, therefore, necessary to look more closely at the oath and ordeal as methods of proof in order to form a clearer picture of the implications of this evidence for the history of sixth-century dispute settlement.

The crucial issue in *Liber Constitutionum* chapter 8 is that a man may clear himself by taking an oath in the company of twelve relatives; in normal circumstances proof depended entirely on the accused being permitted, being prepared and being able to swear with at least twelve other oath-takers. This pattern is similar to that in the *Pactus Legis Salicae*, although there are variations in the numbers of oath-takers (*iuratores**) required[49]. The *formulae* also illustrate the importance of oath-taking in rebutting charges of illegal action and evasion of obligation[50]. That the *formulae* reflect sixth-century practice here is confirmed by the evidence of Gregory of Tours, who records numerous cases of purgation by oath[51], alongside a host of moral anecdotes relating to the fate of perjurers[52]. He

---

[47] H. Brunner, *Deutsche Rechtsgeschichte*, 1st edn, vol. 2, pp. 377–91, 399–419.

[48] See especially the discussion of the origins of ordeal in Brunner, *Deutsche Rechtsgeschichte*, 1st edn, vol. 1, pp. 182–3. For a more cautious view of the origins of ordeal, see E. James, *The Origins of France*, pp. 88–90.

[49] *Pactus Legis Salicae*, xiv. 2, 3, xlii. 5, lxxiii; lxxix and cii (*Decretio Childeberti regis*); cxi (*Edictus Chilperici*); *Decretus Childeberti*, ii. 5, in *Pactus Legis Salicae*, ed. Eckhardt.

[50] *Formulae Andecavenses*, nos. 10, 28, 29, 50.

[51] Gregory of Tours, *Libri Historiarum*, v. v, xlix, pp. 201–2, 261; VII. xxiii, p. 343; IX. xxxii, p. 451; idem, *Liber in Gloria Martyrum*, ch. 33, in Gregory of Tours, *Miracula*, ed. W. Arndt and B. Krusch, *MGH SRM*, vol. 1, pt 2, p. 508.

[52] Gregory of Tours, *Libri Historiarum*, VIII. xvi, pp. 383–4; idem, *Liber in Gloria Martyrum*, cc. 38, 52, 57, 102; idem, *Liber de Virtutibus sancti Juliani*, ch. 19; idem, *Liber de Virtutibus sancti Martini*, I. xxxi;

also provides evidence for the use of oaths in land disputes[53]. It is clear from Gregory's writings that Romans and barbarians both accepted oath-taking as a normal method of proof[54].

The laws, however, may indicate that oath-taking was more common among Romans than barbarians in the early part of the sixth century. Chapter 8 of the *Liber Constitutionum*, as we have seen, envisages oath-taking by both Romans and Burgundians[55], while the closely-related chapter 45 provides the text of an edict issued by King Gundobad in 502 condemning a mercenary attitude towards perjury which had apparently become common 'in populo nostro' (amongst our people).

Concerning those who deny the charges made against them and offer to take an oath.
We know that many of our people have become depraved through the failure of litigation and through an instinct of cupidity, to the extent that they do not hesitate to offer oaths in uncertain matters and to perjure themselves over known facts. In order to undermine this criminal habit we decree by the present law that whenever a case arises among our people, and he who is accused denies on oath that the thing in question should be sought from him or that he is responsible for the crime, then a solution to the quarrel should be imposed in this manner; that is if the party to whom the oath has been offered does not wish to accept it, but says that the force of truth can only be brought to his adversary by dint of arms, and if the other party does not then withdraw the suit, licence to fight will not be denied. Then one of the witnesses who has come to give his oath shall undertake the challenge with God as judge; since it is right that if anyone says that he knows the truth of the matter without doubt and offers to take the oath, he should not refuse to fight. And if the witness of the party which offered the oath is defeated in battle, all the witnesses who promised to swear are condemned to pay three hundred *solidi* as a fine without any further delay. But if he who refused to accept the oath is killed, a ninefold payment of what he owed is due from his property to the victor's party, so that men may delight more in truth than perjury. Issued on 28 May at Lyons, in the consulship of Abienus, *vir clarissimus*. (App. III)

This edict, which doubtless lies at the heart of the later association of trial by ordeal with the Burgundian people, significantly called *Gundobadi*[56], is perhaps best seen as being directed towards Gundobad's Germanic followers. While oath-taking could be regarded as a primarily Roman institution, ordeal by battle might be interpreted as a specifically Germanic, even Burgundian, method of proof[57]. From this point of view the edict looks like an attempt to restore credibility to the process of dispute settlement by reviving ancestral procedures

---

idem, Liber Vitae Patrum, VIII. ix; *idem, Liber in Gloria Confessorum*, cc. 91, 92; all in Gregory of Tours, *Miracula*, pp. 512–13, 525, 527–8, 555, 572–3, 603, 699, 806–7.

[53] Gregory of Tours, *Liber in Gloria Confessorum*, ch. 70, in *idem, Miracula*, pp. 788–9.

[54] H. Jaeger has argued that *purgatio* in the works of Gregory the Great has no probative implications, 'La preuve judicaire d'après la tradition rabbinique et patristique' in *La Preuve*, vol. 1, *Recueil de la Société Jean Bodin*, vol. 16 (1964), pp. 529–50. The acceptance of oath-taking as a means of proof by the pope's ecclesiastical contemporaries, however, may weaken his case.

[55] *Liber Constitutionum*, viii. 1.

[56] Agobard, *Liber adversus legem Gundobadi*, ch. 10, ed. J.-P. Migne, *Patrologia Latina*, vol. 104.

[57] Brunner, *Deutsche Rechtsgeschichte*, 1st edn, vol. 2, pp. 415–18.

for the Burgundians who were insufficiently awestruck by the sacred nature of the oath.

A further indication of an indecently frivolous attitude towards oath-taking may be implied by a clause of the *Pactus Legis Salicae* in which men are apparently prevented from swearing in more than three cases[58]. It is possible that to the Franks, as to the Burgundians, oath-taking was a novel form of proof and that part of the irreverence shown towards it during the sixth century stemmed from this novelty. Such an interpretation may find additional support in the fact that in one clause of the *Pactus* relating to Romans alone there is an insistence on the assertion of innocence by oath[59]. Nor can this simply be an indication that the Romans in question are of lower status than their Frankish counterparts, since elsewhere there is provision for oath-taking in cases involving antrustions[60]. It is therefore possible that the system of proof by oath was drawn primarily from Roman vulgar law. One indication of such an origin for the procedure is the short clause in the *Lex Romana Burgundionum*, 'de sacramentis', which states that only the man from whom information is sought should swear in doubtful cases[61]. This law claims to follow *constitutiones Gregoriani et Ermogeniani* and it is certainly related to one of the sentences of the classical jurist Paul[62]. In fact Roman law did make considerable use of the oath and, although modern commentators have concentrated on the importance of sworn witness, it is clear that oath-taking could play a very substantial rôle in dispute settlement under the Empire[63]. Classical jurists welcomed the use of a system that did not differ greatly from that in the barbarian codes[64]. As Gaius commented 'judges often tend in uncertain cases to exact an oath and to judge in favour of the swearer'[65]. Essentially the judge asked the defendant to take an oath; if he refused, he had either to make restitution or to have the judgement go against him; if he agreed, the oath was then offered to the plaintiff, who also had to swear; if he did he won the case, if not he lost[66]. The major difference between this and oath-taking in the sub-Roman period is the apparent absence of oath-helpers, whose later rôle may derive from legal developments in late Roman provincial society rather than from Germanic law.

The oath as recorded by the classical jurists was not, of course, a Christian procedure. The conversion of the Empire and the association of the Church with law may, however, explain the increased reliance on the oath apparent in the sixth

---

[58] *Pactus Legis Salicae*, lxix; the manuscript variants for this law render its meaning open to question.
[59] *Pactus Legis Salicae*, xvi. 5, but compare xiv. 2–3.
[60] *Pactus Legis Salicae*, lxxiii; see also xiv. 3.
[61] *Lex Romana Burgundionum*, xxiii.
[62] Paul, *sententiae*, ii. 1, in *Lex Romana Visigothorum*, ed. G. F. Haenel.
[63] For a discussion of sworn witness, Jolowicz, *Historical Introduction to Roman Law*, p. 462.
[64] Justinian, *Digest*, XII. ii. 1, ed. T. Mommsen, *Corpus Iuris Civilis*, vol. 1.
[65] Justinian, *Digest*, XII. ii. 31.
[66] Justinian, *Digest*, XII. ii. 34 (9). See also XII. ii. 6.

century[67]. Although the very considerable jurisdiction granted by Constantine to the bishops was modified during the fourth century and, in secular affairs, was essentially transformed by Valentinian III into a process for arbitration[68], the *episcopalis audienta* (episcopal tribunal) survived and was a significant legal force at least among the clergy. Moreover, even outside the episcopal courts clerics presented problems for Roman law since priests could not be subjected to the indignity of torture[69]. At the same time the Church's own interest in perjury, apparent in the numerous instances of heavenly intervention against perjurors in sixth-century hagiography, is likely to be relevant to an understanding of the context in which legal oath-taking became the normal method of proof. Roman and ecclesiastical influences may therefore be the major factors in the development of the oath, although the legal procedures themselves were still developing in both Byzantium and the early barbarian kingdoms, as can be learnt from the fact that the Burgundian king ordered the judges to appoint three men to hear all oaths[70].

The same late Roman and ecclesiastical context may also be of relevance to the development of the ordeal. The *iudicium Dei* is mentioned in the earliest surviving legislation of both the Franks and the Burgundians, although from the start a variety of ordeals is envisaged[71]. The *Liber Constitutionum* refers vaguely to the *iudicium Dei* and specifically to trial by combat[72]. It appears that this second method of proof is Germanic in origin and that it was taken more seriously than the oath by the Burgundians, but it is not much in evidence in the sixth century, apart from one substantial and savage anecdote concerning royal forest rights in Gregory of Tours, where Guntram commanded that a forester, who had accused Chundo of killing a buffalo, should fight the latter's champion. Both forester and champion died, while Chundo was stoned to death[73]. The setting for the crime, the Vosges, and for the trial, Chalon-sur-Saône, are compatible with the assumption that the procedure was basically that laid down by Gundobad.

In the *Pactus Legis Salicae* two types of ordeal are apparent, ordeal by hot water (*inius*) and ordeal by lot (*sors*), which may have been thought particularly appropriate in the trial of men of low status[74]. It may also have been associated

---

[67] For sixth-century Byzantium, see Justinian, *Digest*, XII. ii, iii; *Codex Justinianus*, IV. i and especially II. lviii, ed. P. Krueger, *Corpus Iuris Civilis*, vol. 2.

[68] J. Gaudemet, *L'Église dans l'empire romain*, pp. 230–7.

[69] *Codex Theodosianus*, XI. xxxix. 10; Sirmondian constitution, iii, in *Codex Theodosianus*, ed. Mommsen.

[70] *Liber Constitutionum*, viii. 2. For Byzantium, see *Codex Justinianus*, II. lviii.

[71] For a survey of the various types of ordeal, see Brunner, *Deutsche Rechtsgeschichte*, 1st edn, vol. 2, pp. 399–419.

[72] *Liber Constitutionum*, viii. 2, xlv, lxxx. 2.

[73] Gregory of Tours, *Libri Historiarum*, X. x.

[74] *Inius: Pactus Legis Salicae*, xiv. 2, xvi. 5, liii, lvi, lxxiii. 5–6, lxxxi, cxii, cxxxii. *Sors: Pactus Legis Salicae*, lxxxii, lxxxiii. 2, lxxxvii, cxiii (*Edictus Chilperici*). *Sors* is apparently associated with the servile classes in lxxxvi. See Brunner, *Deutsche Rechtsgeschichte*, 1st edn, vol. 2, pp. 413–14.

with Germanic religion[75]. More important is the *inius*, whereby the accused plunged his hand into a cauldron of hot water in order to prove his innocence. Although on occasion this procedure applied specifically to members of the *leudes* and to antrustions[76], in two instances it is laid down as the practice in the trial of Romans but not Salians[77]. It is therefore at least likely that the origins of this form of *iudicium Dei*, like those of oath-taking, lie as much in Roman vulgar or ecclesiastical law as in Germanic tradition. Support for such a supposition is perhaps to be found in Gregory of Tours's reference to the use of the same procedure in theological debates[78]. Admittedly Gregory's account is later than the *Pactus* and may subsequently reflect the influence of Frankish tradition; nevertheless he ascribes the anecdotes to the fifth century. Once again an ecclesiastical background may be relevant to the development of a method of proof. It could be argued that the specific ecclesiastical background was Arian, since Gundobad subscribed to that heresy, while the theological debates recorded by Gregory involved Catholics and Arians. The fact that ordeal is mentioned in the *Pactus*, however, tends rather to favour the influence of the Catholic church of late and post-Roman Gaul.

The transmission of ecclesiastical ideas into early barbarian legislation is well known. The laws of Æthelberht have convincingly been associated with the influence of Augustine of Canterbury[79]. For sixth-century Gaul there is Sigismund's open acknowledgement of the inspiration of Gimellus of Vaison behind his edict on foundlings[80]. Clergy could thus affect legislation every bit as directly as the more famous lay experts like Asclepiodatus, who is known to have influenced Frankish law[81]. Such men could ensure the direct incorporation of Roman law into sixth-century codes, not that they always did so in an intelligent manner, as is apparent in various requirements for witnesses. Thus the *Liber Constitutionum*, like the *Lex Romana Burgundionum*, takes over the imperial ruling that wills required the signatures of five or seven witnesses[82], although it is doubtful whether they understand the point that five witnesses were required in civil and seven in praetorian law[83]. The appearance of the same numbers in Childebert II's Maastricht decree, where five or seven oath-takers are demanded in cases of theft or evil-doing, suggests that the borrowing had got out of hand[84].

[75] Tacitus, *Germania*, x. On the association between paganism and the *sortes* in the seventh and eighth centuries see I. N. Wood, 'Pagans and holy men 600–800' (forthcoming).
[76] *Pactus Legis Salicae*, liii, lxxiii. 5–6.   [77] *Pactus Legis Salicae*, xiv. 2 (compare xiv. 3), xvi. 5.
[78] Gregory of Tours, *Liber in Gloria Martyrum*, ch. 80, in *idem, Miracula*, pp. 542–3; compare *Liber in Gloria Confessorum*, ch. 14, in *idem, Miracula*, p. 756. See James, '*Beati pacifici*', p. 32.
[79] J. M. Wallace-Hadrill, *Early Germanic Kingship in England and on the Continent*, pp. 37–40.
[80] *Liber Constitutionum, constitutiones extravagantes*, xx.
[81] Wormald, '*Lex Scripta* and *Verbum Regis*', pp. 125–6.
[82] *Liber Constitutionum*, xliii. 1, xcix. 1; *Lex Romana Burgundionum*, xlv. 2. Compare *Codex Theodosianus*, IV. iv. 1, 3, 7.   [83] *Codex Theodosianus*, IV. iv. 3 *interpretatio*.
[84] *Decretus Childeberti*, ii. 5, in *Pactus Legis Salicae*.

Such specific borrowings, however, are less important than the general context in which the procedures of dispute settlement evolved. Indeed, as we have seen, there is no precisely identifiable antecedent for either oath-taking or ordeal, although a Roman and an ecclesiastical background seems probable. There is in any case a further complicating factor and that is the lack of a monolithic legal structure even in the Roman world. There are contradictions in plenty within the *Codex Theodosianus*, but within the amorphous legal traditions known as vulgar law there must have been even more variety. One indication of this can be found in a clause of the *Lex Romana Burgundionum* concerning gifts[85].

Official records should be made according to the custom of the places; nor does it matter before which *defensor* they have been declared, following the second Theodosian law entitled *De donationibus*.

In fact the relevant Theodosian law does not discuss custom at all and its *interpretatio*, which might have elucidated this matter, does not survive. Nevertheless it is clear from the *Lex Romana Burgundionum* that there was variety at least in the *gesta municipalia* of the early sixth century and that the variety was nothing new. A rather more forceful description of the state of affairs which prevailed at least by the seventh century can be found in the *cri de coeur* which opens one of the Angers *formulae*; 'What good luck! The law of happiness is in appropriate agreement, Roman law teaches, the custom of the *pagus* consents and the power of the ruler does not prohibit'[86].

One implication of this legal confusion is that historians have been rather too concerned to draw firm distinctions between legal systems. It is not in fact possible to distinguish at all clearly between vulgar law and the early barbarian codes, indeed in many respects the latter provide evidence for the former as important as that preserved in the Byzantine 'Farmer's Law' and the 'Excerpta de libris Romanorum et Francorum' from north-west France[87]. This blurring of differences between Roman and barbarian law also undermines the notion of the personality of the law, that is the right of each man to be judged by the law of his own nation, at least in a sixth-century context. That some peoples did deliberately retain their own legal traditions is suggested by Paul the Deacon in his account of those Saxons who left Italy because they did not wish to live under

[85] *Lex Romana Burgundionum*, xxii. 4; compare *Codex Theodosianus*, VIII. xii. 18.
[86] *Formulae Andecavenses*, no. 54; compare 'lex felicitatis', *ibid.*, no. 58.
[87] W. Ashburner, 'The Farmer's Law', *J. Hell. Stud.*, 30 (1910), 97–108 (text); 32 (1912), 87–95 (commentary and trans.). See the thought-provoking comments of R. Collins, *Early Medieval Spain*, p. 28. The observation that the Byzantine 'Farmer's Law' is to be seen as vulgar, not Germanic, law is convincing, and the legislation it shares with barbarian codes must therefore imply that these have a strong vulgar component. For the 'Excerpta de libris' see 'Canones Wallici' in *The Irish Penitentials*, ed. L. Bieler, pp. 136–9; see also D. N. Dumville, 'On the dating of the early Breton law codes', *Études Celtiques*, 21 (1984), 207–21; for the vulgar law component, W. Davies, 'Land and power in early medieval Wales', *Past and Present*, 81 (1978), 17.

the law of the Lombards[88]. Paul, however, was writing in the eighth century, and Gregory of Tours does not support his interpretation of the Saxon exodus[89]. It may be that the personality of the law became a more common idea in the Carolingian age; Agobard, for instance, was incensed by the notion[90]. In the sixth century it is scarcely credible that tribes which had emerged not many generations before should be totally wedded to a particular legal system which was only then in the process of formation[91]. Nor do the laws themselves support the notion that they were designed only for a single ethnic group. Indeed, given the recent formation of many of the tribes, ethnicity is scarcely a viable concept in this period.

The chief indications that a man's origins could affect the law to which he was subject in fact relates to the Romans, a heterogeneous group by any standards, and not the barbarians. In both Burgundian and Frankish legislation it is the Romans who are instructed to resort to their own law[92]. At the same time, however, they are not obviously exempted from the precepts and the edicts of their new rulers and they are explicitly dealt with in certain clauses of the *Liber Constitutionum* and the *Pactus Legis Salicae*[93]. How far the various communities in Francia actually followed Merovingian legislation is, of course, a moot point. In reality Romans and Germans must have stuck with the laws to which they were accustomed, but that is not to say there was a fully fledged notion of 'the personality of the law'.

Essentially all the sub-Roman kingdoms drew to some extent on a common fund of legal tradition whether imperial, vulgar Roman, or Germanic. As a result, for all the variety within the codes, the laws were mutually comprehensible. This is seen most clearly in a clause of the *Pactus Legis Salicae* concerned with raiders[94].

If any foreign slave has been seized and taken overseas, and if he is found there by his master and names in the *mallus publicus* the man by whom he was seized in his own country, he ought to gather three witnesses there. Again when the slave has been brought back from across the sea he ought to repeat his statement in another *mallus*, and again should gather three suitable witnesses. He ought to do the same at a third *mallus*, so that nine witnesses swear that they heard the slave make the same statement against his kidnapper in three *malli*, and afterwards he who seized him should be denounced in court (*mallobergo*) as a werewolf*, that is he should be judged as subject to paying his wergeld* as well as 1,400

[88] Paul, *Historia Langobardorum*, III. vi, ed. L. Bethmann and G. Waitz, *MGH SRL*.
[89] Gregory of Tours, *Libri Historiarum*, IV. xlii, pp. 175–6.
[90] Agobard, *Liber adversus legem Gundobadi*, ch. 4.
[91] R. Wenskus, *Stammesbildung und Verfassung*.
[92] *Liber Constitutionum, prima constitutio* viii, lv. 4, *constitutiones extravagantes* xx; *Lex Romana Burgundionum*, ii. 5; *Clotharii praeceptio*, iv, in *Capitularia*, vol. 1, ed. A. Boretius.
[93] *Pactus Legis Salicae*, xvi. 5, xxxix. 5, xli. 8–10, xlii. 4, civ. 9, cxvii. 2; *Liber Constitutionum, prima constitutio* xi, iv. 1, 3, 4, vi. 3, 9, vii, viii. 1, ix, x, xii. 5, xv. 1, xvii. 5, xxi. 1, xxii, xxvi. 1, 2, xxviii. 1, xxxi. 1, xxxviii. 5, 11, xliv. 1, l. 1, liv. 2, lv, lvii, lxvii, lxxxiv. 2, xcvi, c, *constitutiones extravagantes* xviii. 1, xx, xxi. 11, 12. Two manuscripts describe the *Liber Constitutionum* as 'Lex Gundobadi inter Burgundiones et Romanos', *Leges Burgundionum*, p. 109.
[94] *Pactus Legis Salicae*, xxxix. 2.

denarii, which makes 35 *solidi*. The slave's statement holds good up to three kidnappers, but on the grounds that he provides in each case the names of the men and of the villas. (App. IV)

This law should almost certainly be viewed in the context of Clovis's last years and of Frankish overlordship exercised over the south coast of England[95]. The crucial point, however, is that the legislator assumed that a single complex procedure could be carried out on two sides of the English Channel.

Clovis's legislation on captured slaves may have been somewhat ambitious, but there is no doubt that such ambition did affect the development of the law, not least in the commissioning of new codes. Royal law, however, was not the only factor in dispute settlement. There were the Gallo-Roman upper-classes lobbying each other to prevent quarrels getting to court, and there was also the kin group whose fear of bloodshed created 'peace in the feud'[96]. At the same time the emergence of new kingdoms with its attendant disruption, and, in Francia, the subsequent civil wars must have led to rival claims over property and certainly caused the destruction of documents which recorded ownership. Where the municipal archives still existed they may have prevented many property disputes, but elsewhere legal processes developed to make good the lack of a reliable land register. All these factors influenced the evolution of dispute settlement in the fifth and sixth centuries. So too did the Church, whether or not it directly influenced the development of oath-taking and of the ordeal; with its interest in perjury and divine vengeance it undoubtedly helped crystallize notions of proof. At the same time individual churchmen regularly acted as mediators, oiling the processes of settlement[97].

Some of these factors were new to post-Roman Gaul; some had evolved in the later Roman empire. The new influences themselves, however, can scarcely have reflected pure Germanic tradition; the Franks and the Burgundians had been on the frontiers of the empire for too long not to have been influenced by Roman law. It is not possible to decide when or where the various elements, Roman, Christian and Germanic, combined to create the procedures for disputes recorded in the *Pactus Legis Salicae* and the *Edictus Chilperici*; the process probably began before the sixth century. Nor was Roman law simply the law of the emperor; the vulgar law of the minor courts was probably not unlike that which was codified by barbarian kings. Looked at in this way the dichotomy between a supposed law of the Germanic forests and that of the Roman forum becomes a hindrance to the understanding of post-Roman dispute settlement.

---

[95] I. N. Wood, *The Merovingian North Sea*, pp. 12–17.
[96] M. Gluckman, *Custom and Conflict in Africa*, pp. 1–26; J. M. Wallace-Hadrill, 'The Bloodfeud of the Franks' in *idem, The Long-haired kings*.
[97] James, '*Beati pacifici*'.

2

'Placita' and the settlement of disputes in later Merovingian Francia

PAUL FOURACRE

Narrative sources for the study of later Merovingian history are sparse and notoriously difficult to use. The evidence provided by royal charters* is therefore invaluable, although traditionally they have been studied as much for their form as for their content[1]. Here, as always, the motive force behind the production, transmission and preservation of all kinds of charters was the conservation of property, and it is the establishment or description of the property ownership in the charter which illuminates the underlying human activity. When there is a formal dispute over property the recorded process of establishing ownership becomes far more complex and may reveal to us a vivid and detailed impression of contemporary activity. In the case of later Merovingian dispute settlement the very complexity of the records suggests that they may be most revealing. On the other hand, that complexity may lie in the form of the recording document rather than in the substance of the recorded dispute. This problem, the relationship of the formal record to the reality of dispute settlement, will be a continuing theme of the present paper.

Of the eighty-seven seventh- and early eighth-century Frankish documents printed in the *Monumenta* series, twenty-four are the formal records of disputes settled before the king. Such disputes, and hence the documents which record them, were known as *placita**, and a very high proportion of the *placita*, over two-thirds, have survived in their original form[2]. All of them are concerned with

[1] This area is particularly well served by a long tradition of diplomatic studies, partly because lasting Frankish hegemony in north-western Europe allows the study of unbroken charter development, and partly because it reflects the Francocentric nature of thinking amongst French, German and Belgian scholars. See: H. Bresslau, *Handbuch der Urkundenlehre*; P. Classen, 'Kaiserreskript und Königsurkunde', *Archiv für Dip.*, 2 (1956); G. Tessier, *Diplomatique Royale Française*.

[2] The *placita* are to be found in several printed editions of Merovingian charters: *Diplomata, chartae, epistolae, leges, aliaque instrumenta ad res Gallo-Francicas spectantia*, ed. J. Pardessus; *Archives de l'Empire – Inventaires et Documents. Monuments historiques*, ed. J. Tardif; *Diplomata regum Francorum e stirpe Merowingica*, ed. K. Pertz in *MGH Diplomata Imperii*, vol. 1; *Les diplômes originaux des Mérovingiens*, ed. P. Lauer, C. Samaran; *Chartae Latinae Antiquiores*, ed. A. Bruckner, R. Marichal, vols. 13, 14 (hereafter *ChLA*, cited by document number). In this paper, references to the original documents will be to the editions printed in *ChLA*; reference to non-original documents will be to the Pertz edition. The most recent, and thorough, study of the *placita* is by W. Bergmann,

property and in nearly all of the cases this means landed property. It is possible, as W. Bergmann has shown, to distinguish three basic types of *placita* according to the nature of the judgements contained within them: judgements are thus either simply definitive, or made on an interim basis delaying a definite judgement, or they confirm earlier judgements or transactions[3]. Such classification may, however, be misleading for our purpose. Abstracting from the documents those elements which can be compared or grouped serves to draw attention away from those elements which cannot, and it is in the latter that the narrative of each dispute unfolds[4].

Later Merovingian charters draw heavily on stock phrases (*formulae**) and they are also laid out according to a limited range of forms. *Placita* do not differ here: *formulae* are used to begin and end all the documents and the phrases used are also to be found in Book I of the Formulary* of Marculf which was compiled in the late seventh or early eighth century[5]. The general pattern of cases revealed in the *placita* is as follows: the plaintiff comes before a tribunal of magnates over which the king presides. The plaintiff first accuses the defendant before the tribunal. The defendant answers the case and an interchange between the two develops as points are raised and answered[6]. It is in this interchange that various kinds of evidence may be produced to support particular points. When, finally, one side is seen to lose the argument an official called the count of the palace sums up the case, indicating that the proper procedure has been followed. The final judgement and remedy are then given by the king and magnates together. The final document, the formal record of the case, seems to have been produced from the summary presented by the count of the palace, written out by notaries and then checked and finally sealed by the official called the *referendarius*[7]. Unlike

'Untersuchungen zu der Gerichtsurkunden der Merowingerzeit', *Archiv für Dip.*, 22 (1976). Bergmann's work is firmly in the traditions of diplomatic scholarship. He was thus concerned with the classification of the types of document and with relating dispute settlement to the documentary record, rather than vice versa. He was not concerned to place the documents in full historical context.

[3] See Bergmann, 'Gerichtsurkunden', 69–102, for a comparison of types, 70 for the full list of possible types.

[4] Bergman, 'Gerichtsurkunden', 68–9, noted this too before going on to make a comparative study of the documents according to their formulaic structure. He was looking, he stated, for their 'legal content'. It thus seems ironic that he chose to concentrate on their form rather than on their contents as actual court cases.

[5] *Marculfi Formularum Libri Duo*, ed. A. Uddholm, I. 25, 38 for the beginning of cases; I. 37 for the end. The formulaic element in *placita* is discussed in more detail below, pp. 29–30, and the evidence of the earlier Formularies is discussed by I. Wood, above, p. 9.

[6] The document presents the interchange as reported speech, but this must represent a précis of the argument of each party rather than the only words spoken.

[7] Bergmann is particularly useful when he describes how the document was drawn up, 'Gerichtsurkunden', 40–7. He assumes, however, the existence of a Merovingian chancery of which the *referendarius* was supposedly a member. It is an assumption for which corroborative evidence is lacking. What elements we can see of an operative chancery at this date would, from charter evidence, appear to have been under the control of St Denis. For further recent discussion

the other kinds of royal charter, the later Merovingian *placita* do not bear the king's signature. The basis for sealing the *placitum* document is that the *referendarius* has recognized (*recognovit*) that the due process has been followed. In other kinds of charter the seal signifies that a royal command has been given and the *referendarius* has offered up the document (*optulit*) to the king to sign. It was then sealed[8]. Although the *placita* follow a set pattern, the pattern differs from that seen in other types of document; it is structured, as we have seen, around the actual session of a judicial tribunal, whereas in other charters the formal structure includes reference to general considerations or statements of intention with which the particular matter of the document may not be direcly concerned[9]. *Placita* survive as originals in far greater numbers than any other kind of royal document; conversely they are rarely copied into later cartularies and none, as far as is known, has ever been used as the basis of a later forgery.

It may well be no accident that no *placita* survive from the period before the seventh century. P. Classen, though aware of the idiosyncracies of the *placita*, nevertheless did not exclude them in his scheme for the evolution of Merovingian document forms from the later Roman. Yet *placita* are, as he admitted, the documents least like any known form of late Roman document and it may be more sensible to see them as a form of document developed in the early seventh century to meet the needs of the newly emerging centres of royal justice in northern Francia in the context of a growing royal and ecclesiastical monopoly over receding bureaucratic skills[10]. If this is true, then the form of the document may have been specifically developed according to available skills to reflect with accuracy the settlement of disputes in the royal court. If we can read the documents thus, they may tell us a great deal – one case alone leaves a fuller record than, say, the chronicle account of King Dagobert I's reign in the *Liber Historiae Francorum*.

However trustworthy and informative this group of documents may be, we cannot simply assume that what they tell us is fairly representative of the way disputes were settled throughout society in this period. They do, nevertheless, contain hints that the processes they describe for the royal court were, in that context at least, in widespread use. Their production according to standardized form, and, in one instance, the issue of two documents on consecutive days, suggests that the process of dispute settlement was regular, not occasional, and

---

of this problem, see D. Ganz, 'Bureaucratic short-hand and Merovingian learning' in P. Wormald, D. Bullough, R. Collins (eds.), *Ideal and Reality in Frankish and Anglo-Saxon Society*, pp. 58–75.

[8] Bergmann, 'Gerichtsurkunden', 41.

[9] Namely in the *arenga* and *promulgatio* which include a strongly rhetorical element. See Classen, 'Kaiserreskript', 42–5.

[10] Classen, 'Kaiserreskript', 69–70. In later work dealing with document evolution in general, Classen did lay greater emphasis on the way in which documents could change in form to meet new needs, but he did not discuss the *placita* in this context: 'Fortleben und Wandel spätrömischen Urkundenwesens im frühen Mittelalter' in P. Classen (ed.) *Recht und Schrift im Mittelalter, Vorträge und Forschungen*, vol. 23 (1977).

that the royal court did possess a degree of bureaucratic competence[11]. The concern of some *placita* with disputes over property of a relatively minor order suggests that access to royal justice was, at least for certain magnates, fairly open and it may well be that one factor in choosing to have a case heard before the royal court was the desire to possess the resulting document[12]. We are dealing, if the references within the *placita* are to be believed, with a society used to, needing and demanding, documents. This belief is encouraged by the wide range of document models provided in the Formulary of Marculf. Perhaps most indicative of all of the widespread use of the royal court and of the desire for documents recording the tribunal's affirmation of property ownership is the existence of confirmatory *placita*, that is, of fictitious disputes held in order to reinforce ownership with documentation[13]. Such fake disputes are really a means of conveyancing and are usually, though not necessarily, associated with more bureaucratic ages[14].

Despite the indications that the *placita* do indeed reveal the regular use of the royal court for the settlement of disputes, we must also note that there is an uneven distribution in the sample of surviving documents in terms of time and in terms of preservation. Most documents are from the period *c.* 670–716 and nearly all our documents, including all the originals, survived because they were preserved in the archives of the monastery of St Denis. The *placita* are overwhelmingly concerned with civil disputes involving churchmen and are usually representative of monastic interests, in particular those of St Denis. The vast majority of cases involve property in the Seine–Oise area, and all those

[11] Or, at least, the royal court had access to bureaucratic skills which may, by this date, have lain in ecclesiastical hands. So Ganz, 'Bureaucratic short-hand and Merovingian learning', 69–75.

[12] The royal court may here be filling the gap left by the eclipse of the *gesta municipalia*, as Ian Wood suggests, above, p. 14. Classen too noted the similarity between the rôle of the *gesta municipalia* and that of the confirmatory *placita* in strengthening legal title to property, 'Kaiserreskript', 70.

[13] Bergmann, 'Gerichtsurkunden', 153–80, identifies eight such fictitious disputes (*Scheinprozesse*), thus *ChLA*, vol. 14, 575, 578, 584, 585, 586, 587 and Pertz nos. 79, 94. I would question this identification for *ChLA* 586 and 587 as they are concerned with genuine disputes, although the disputes have apparently been settled before the sitting of the royal court of which the documents are a record. In other *Scheinprozesse* there is no dispute at all.

[14] They are usually associated with more bureaucratic ages when the familiarity with and facilities for documentation are said to engender the desire and opportunity to use the formal process thus. This, for example, is seen as a development in twelfth-century England resulting from Henry II's 'legal reforms' and subsequent increase in the use of the royal courts. For the use of the final concord as a means of conveyancing in this context, see W. L. Warren, *Henry II*, pp. 348–9. But, as Pollock and Maitland observed much earlier, 'in Frankland the use of litigious forms for the purpose of conveyancing can be traced back to a very distant date', F. Pollock and F. W. Maitland, *The History of English Law*, vol. 2, p. 95. It might be more helpful to see this form of conveyancing as a normal aspect of influence on the formal legal process exercised by those wielding power based on property ownership in a whole range of societies. If it is more apparent in more bureaucratic societies, it may be because this is where it is better recorded. For fictitious disputes in Italy, see Wickham below, pp. 115–16, 117.

involved in cases are drawn from within a small circle of the political élite, seen in
a court which is unique because it is royal. The *placita* cannot tell us how disputes
were settled in other courts, involving persons of lower status, or what happened
in cases of a criminal nature. Further, we must seek to reconcile the orderly
settlement of disputes seen in the *placita* with the violent remedies seen in other
sources[15]. To tackle this we must seek a context for the *placita* by examining other
sources which deal with disputes. First I will discuss two *placita* in detail and then,
in order to bring non-magnate, non-civil dispute settlement into the picture, turn
to materials other than the records of actual disputes brought before the royal
courts in the late seventh and early eighth centuries. I have chosen these two
cases because they show more of the settlement procedure than most and were
not simply disputes between churchmen over landed property. For the sake of
clarity I give full summaries of the cases rather than literal translations of the
original texts. In subsequent discussion the cases will be cited by reference to the
respective defendants, Ermenoald and Amalbert.

King Clovis III makes a judgement in favour of Chaino abbot of St Denis
against Abbot Ermenoald (held 5 May, 691 or 692).

The *agentes** of the monastery of St Denis, where Chaino is abbot, have come to the royal
palace at Nogent-sur-Marne to bring suit against Abbot Ermenoald [see fig. 1]. The
latter, they say, before this year [last year?] pledged to Chaino 1,500 pounds of oil and 100
barrels of good wine on behalf of Bishop Ansbert[16]. Ermenoald promised he would make
good this pledge, but did not do so. Thereupon both parties received identical warrants of
suit and had hearings before Bishop Sigofred, the outcome being that the day after mid
April Ermenoald with three men, himself making the fourth, should swear before Sigofred
that he had never contracted the pledge nor promised to pay it. If he failed to do this he
would have to pay ten pounds of silver on the aforesaid day. If he did not do this, then on
the second day of May he should come before the royal court to make his oath before the
king and when the warrants of suit had been inspected, the case would be heard. So, the
warrants were seen and the hearing begun. Chaino's *agentes* came to this hearing at
Nogent and defended their suit for over three days, as is the law, and charged Ermenoald
with the fault of not attending to produce any evidence against them: Ermenoald did not
turn up, did not send anyone in his place, nor did he provide any valid excuse for not
complying with the summons.

The king and magnates then judged that they had seen the warrants of suit and that
there was thus a case to be heard. Warno, the count of the palace, then formally stated that
Chaino's *agentes* had defended their suit according to law and that Ermenoald had failed to
defend his suit. The king and magnates then made the judgement that, according to
whatever the law of the locality said on the matter, Ermenoald should make satisfactory
payment to Chaino's *agentes* and be subject to their distraint*. (App. V)

---

[15] For example, the lengthy feud (not, in the chronicle's account, about land) between Flaochad and
Willebad reported by the Chronicle of Fredegar, a feud which ended in a pitched battle: *The Fourth
Book of the Chronicle of Fredegar*, ed. and trans. J. Wallace-Hadrill, ch. 90.

[16] The precise rôle of the pledge (*wadium*) in this case is unclear. The general context of the dispute
makes it likely that the oil and wine was pledged as security for a loan.

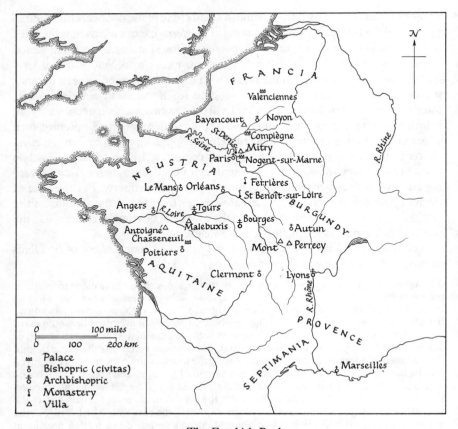

1 The Frankish Realm

King Clovis III makes a judgement in favour of the deacon Chrotcharius, representing the orphan Ingramnus, against Amalbert (held 28 February, 692 or 693).

The hearing takes place at Valenciennes in the presence of king and magnates. The latter are made up of twelve bishops, twelve leading men, seventeen counts, four officers of the king's court, four referendaries, two seneschals and Audramnus, count of the palace, as well as other unnamed followers. The plaintiff is Chrotcharius the deacon, appearing on behalf of Ingramnus an orphan and son of one Chaldedramn. The hearing is held at the behest of Nordbert and Chrotcharius has taken Ingramnus's brief at royal command. Chrotcharius's case is that one Amalbert is in illegal possession of a small property called Bayencourt (on the River Matz) which had once belonged to Chaldedramn. Because of this, Chrotcharius and Amalbert had already attended many court hearings begun by royal warrant. And now, on the fifth day before the Kalends of March, there is another hearing begun by yet another royal warrant.

Chrotcharius came to the hearing at Valenciennes and guarded his suit according to law and accused Amalbert of default. But Amalbert's son Amalric appeared on his father's behalf instead and denied the accusation of default. Amalric was then asked by the court whether his father had received warrants to begin a hearing with Chrotcharius and by what right he [Amalric] had come to the hearing in his father's place. Amalric could show no record of being ordered to appear, and it was found that his denial of Amalbert's default and his own appearance in the case were in contempt of court proceedings. It was thus judged that he be fined fifteen *solidi**. Then, with Amalric grasping the *festuca**, this act was symbolically concluded. Thereafter Chrotcharius guarded his suit for over three days according to law and accused Amalbert of default. Amalbert did not turn up, nor did he order to appear his pledge-guarantor*, one Ermecharius who could, according to the warrants, have appeared for him. Amalbert thus defaulted without legitimate excuse.

The king and magnates then moved to judgement, the count of the palace first testifying that the hearing was complete. Amalbert had to return to Chrotcharius, on Ingramnus's behalf, the Bayencourt property just as it had been when Chaldedram had possessed it. Chrotcharius, on behalf of Ingramnus, should hold the property for all time by unchallengeable right. Further, Amalbert had to compensate Chrotcharius for anything he or his serfs had taken from Bayencourt. This was to be the end of the matter and, finally, the ten *solidi* promised to Chrotcharius on account of Amalric's contempt had to be paid. (App. VI)

These two documents are similar in form, and where they coincide – on default, on warrants and on the count of the palace's *testimonium* – similar phrases dealing with the same subjects are to be found in the Formulary of Marculf[17]; and the opening sentences of the Amalbert case are to be found word for word in Marculf[18]. A closer examination of the formulaic element in the two cases is necessary. It is noticeable that in both cases where *formulae* were used they had been carefully adapted to suit the facts of each case. The *formulae* for stating that the defendant did not turn up to the hearing had to be adapted in the Ermenoald case to take account of the fact that it was Chaino's *agentes* who defended the suit – a *formula* found in the singular in Marculf and in the singular in the Amalbert case is thus seen in the plural in the Ermenoald case. In the Amalbert case the *formula* broke down on Amalbert's first default because Amalric turned up, and on his second default it was adapted to take account of the fact that he had a pledge-guarantor whom he failed to have appear on his behalf.

There is good reason to believe that the source for these *formulae* was indeed the Formulary of Marculf, or some closely related document. The Ermenoald case ended with the instruction (to Chaino's party) that Ermenoald should be made to make satisfactory payment according to 'what the law of your locality says on the matter'. This phrase makes little sense in the context of the case. St Denis is less than sixteen kilometres from Nogent-sur-Marne where the hearing took place, hardly a separate locality (see fig. 1). Such an address in the second person is unknown in any other document. The phrase does occur, however, in the

---

[17] *Marculfi Form.* I. 37 on default; I. 38 on warrants; I. 37 on *testimonium*.
[18] *Marculfi Form.* I. 25.

Formulary of Marculf, Book 1, chapter 37, which deals with default and distraint, but in another context.

There is, I think, more to be read into this than simple scribal incompetence. It relates, rather, to the general difficulty of applying *formulae* to the records of court cases, a difficulty visible in the Marculf collection itself. Where the collection is concerned with matters of judicial procedure it sets the *formulae* in hypothetical court cases, and in order to illustrate the form of judgement, contextual detail is included to show how the judgement was arrived at. When the collection deals with grants, privileges and immunities, however, the appropriate administrative procedure is expressed by *formulae* alone. So, whereas in most dispositive documents the Formulary models could be incorporated without modification, in *placita* the models had to be substantially modified to suit the circumstances of the specific case[19]. In the Marculf collection, Book 1, chapter 37 presents perhaps the clearest example of the use of contextual detail to illustrate the form of a judgement[20]. The draughtsman of the Ermenoald judgement appears to have borrowed heavily from the model presented in chapter 37, but failed to modify it to suit the circumstances of his own case[21]. Though this should warn us to be wary of the formulaic element in the *placita*, we should also note that the way in which contemporaries experienced difficulty in selecting appropriate *formulae*, and did usually take care to adapt them when necessary, suggests that in the main the use of *formulae* did not detract from the accurate reporting of cases. There would seem to be a significant difference here between the formulaic element in the later Merovingian *placita* and its free employment, to the point of dominating content, in the Italian records from the late ninth century onwards[22].

To both our cases there was probably a political dimension. In the Ermenoald case the pledge had originally been made on behalf of Bishop Ansbert. Of Ermenoald nothing more is known. Ansbert has traditionally been identified, following L. Duchesne, as Ansbert bishop of Autun, but given the situation in this case it would be reasonable to think that Ansbert bishop of Rouen was

[19] *Marculfi Form.* I. 15. This model, for *Cessio ad loco sancto* (grant to an ecclesiastical institution), can be used with only minor adaptations. Gaps are left in the model for the insertion of the particular details of the grant. For how it was applied in practice, see *ChLA*, vol. 14, 566. I. 25, which does apply to court-cases, which can be used without alteration as it presents the model for the introduction to a *placitum* but ends at the point at which the plaintiff begins to speak.

[20] *Marculfi Form.* I. 27 and 38 provide further examples.

[21] Thus in the Ermenoald case: '(ut) inluster uir Warno, comis palacii nostri, testimuniauit quod memorati agentis iam dicto Chainone abbati placitum eorum ligebus custudierunt, et suprascriptus Ermenoaldus abba placitum suum custudire neclixsit, iobemmus ut quicquid lex loci uestri de tale causa edocit, memoratus Ermenoaldus abba partibus ipsius agentibus ad parte suprascripti Chainone abbati uel basilice sui domni Dionisii, omnemodis uobis distringentebus, conponire et satisfacire non recusit'; and in *Marculfi Form.* I. 37: 'dum et inluster vir ille comis palatii nostri testimoniavit quod antedictus ille placitum suum legibus custodivit et eum abiectivit vel solsativit et ipse ille placitum suum custodire necglexit, jobemus ut quicquid lex loci vestri de tale causa edocet, vobis distringentibus, antedictus ille partibus illius conponare et satisfacire non recusit'. [22] See Wickham below, pp. 107, 112, 117–18.

involved[23]. Ansbert of Rouen was ousted from his see in *c.* 690 at the urging of his political opponent Pippin of Heristal, was imprisoned by the latter in the monastery of Hautmont and died there sometime in 692 or 693[24]. It could be that Ermenoald pledged the oil and wine to St Denis to raise cash for a fine to be paid on Ansbert's behalf in connexion with his deposition, or to pay some kind of bail to Pippin in the negotiations for the bishop's release which the *Vita Ansberti* tells us followed his imprisonment[25]. According to the *Vita*, Pippin at first agreed to release Ansbert but then did not do so. In his last request to Pippin Ansbert begged that his bones be allowed to leave Hautmont to rest at St Wandrille[26]. Perhaps the dispute in the Ermenoald case went back to the breaking of some kind of agreement with a third party here. Ermenoald is not said to have denied that he made the pledge and promise to pay but he was plainly contesting the payment. To see the case involving Ansbert of Rouen, rather than Ansbert of Autun, also helps to explain the otherwise odd position of Ermenoald as a liable intermediary. Ansbert of Autun appeared, in fact, in the Amalbert case as a member of the tribunal. He was not, it seems, estranged from the judicial and political establishment. Another point in favour of thinking that Ansbert's pledge to St Denis might have been made to raise cash to pay a fine is that there is further evidence to show St Denis lending money on pledge for this purpose: a confirmatory *placitum* from 694 or 695 refers to a case of 676 when St Denis put up 600 *solidi* for one Ibbo to pay a fine and was pledged land in return[27].

For the person of Amalbert there are likewise two candidates, unless they are one and the same person[28]. Of his son Amalric nothing more is known. An Amalbert is named in conjunction with one Ingobert as the murderer of the Austrasian king Childeric II in 675[29]. Ingobert was apparently rewarded by the Neustrian régime under Ebroin which reasserted itself after the murder. It is thus

---

[23] L. Duchesne, *Fastes épiscopaux de l'ancienne Gaule*, vol. 2, p. 181. Dating the Ermenoald case to 693, Duchesne must have omitted Ansbert of Rouen from consideration as the latter was by that date dead. Dating the case to 691 or 692, Bergmann, 'Gerichtsurkunden', 166, noted that Ansbert of Rouen had to be considered, but he did not explore the contextual grounds for shifting the identification.

[24] *Vita Ansberti*, ch. 21, ed. W. Levison, *MGH SRM*, vol. 5, for his imprisonment; ch. 24 for his death.

[25] A royal *praecepcio* of 677, authorizing the deposed bishop Chramlinus to retain his property despite exile, suggests that deposition and exile could be accompanied by confiscation, *ChLA*, vol. 14, 565.

[26] *Vita Ansberti*, cc. 22, 24.   [27] *ChLA*, vol. 14, 578.

[28] H. Ebling identified three people bearing the name of Amalbert and seems, rather arbitrarily, to have fixed on one, the brother of Flaochad, as one of the murderers of Childeric II, who is thus a likely candidate for this case. The brother of Flaochad is, I would argue, the least likely candidate as he was of the generation at the height of its activity in the 640s, which would make it very unlikely that he survived into the 690s, as may have Ingobert, another named murderer. There is no way one can actually show that the other Amalberts are two people. The orthographic grounds on which Ebling apparently distinguished between the two are spurious. There is nothing in the little we know of the two which would be contradictory in the career of one person. See H. Ebling, *Prosopographie der Amtsträger des Merowingerreiches*, pp. 46–8.

[29] *Liber Historiae Francorum*, ch. 45, ed. B. Krusch, *MGH SRM*, vol. 2.

tempting to see Amalbert as similarly benefiting and then suffering under Pippin of Heristal. We know, from the *Vita Eligii*, of an Amalbert who was count of Noyon not long after 660, and the land in question in this case is within fourteen kilometres of Noyon[30]. That Pippin's right-hand man Nordbert ordered the case to come before the court and that the case was heard before the annual spring gathering of magnates (hence the spectacular list of those present, including men from as far away as Lyons) suggests that the case was indeed of a political nature. In both cases, then, it seems highly likely that the final judgement was politically influenced.

The two plaintiffs, Chaino and Chrotcharius, appeared several times in royal court cases. Chaino, as abbot of St Denis from 678 to 706, represented the institution which was the focus of so many of the *placita*[31]. Chrotcharius appeared in a dispute over land in 690 and is seen in a document of 696 as an abbot[32]. He may have been something of a specialist in legal matters and seems to have represented Ingramnus on more than one occasion. Of the orphan Ingramnus and his father Chaldedram, nothing more is known.

The prominence of churchmen in these cases may reflect more than just the ecclesiastical bias in the sample of surviving documents. Here, for instance, Chrotcharius, a deacon, represented a lay person in dispute with another lay person. That the involvement of churchmen in the legal affairs of lay persons may have been common is suggested in a canon of the Council of Bordeaux, held *c*. 674, which warned churchmen to seek the permission of their bishop before taking on the *mundeburdium** of laymen. The introduction to the same council complained bitterly that the clergy was involved in disputes more frequently than lay persons[33]. Such involvement in the courts does not seem surprising, for gift of land by an individual to the church meant alienating land from a kindred group, other members of which might dispute the church's right to have the land. Whereas disputes within a kindred might be settled within the group, dispute with the church was likely to mean a formal contest[34]. The church had thus pioneered the right to and the defence of property through the formal procedure of the law courts, and acquiring a vested interest in the development of legal expertise, became a leading force in the documentation, prosecution and defence of property rights[35].

In these *placita*, as always, a *formula* was used to show that the king and

---

[30] *Vita Eligii*, II. lxvi, ed. B. Krusch, *MGH SRM*, vol. 4.

[31] Chaino appears in *ChLA*, vol. 14, 565, 575, 578.

[32] Chrotcharius appears in *ChLA*, vol. 14, 566, 576, 580.

[33] 'Concilium Burdegalense', Intro. and ch. 2, in C. de Clercq (ed.), *Conciliae Galliae 511–695*, pp. 311–13.

[34] The Cartulary of Redon, by contrast, contains many cases of inter-family disputes in ninth-century eastern Brittany. It may be significant that the material here relates to disputes at village level, a level invisible in the Frankish material. See Davies below, p. 70.

[35] J. Goody, *The development of family and marriage in Europe*, pp. 46, 111–13.

magnates together made the final judgement: *nus una cum nostris procerebus constetit decriuisse*. This arrangement of co-judgement relates to the procedure of the courts in which the count presided over a tribunal of *rachymburgi*[36]. Though judgement was made collectively, it was the king or count president who enforced it and the collective and public nature of the judgement may relate to the consensus and support the president needed for effective enforcement. In our cases consensus and support for the judgement of the court may have been particularly relevant because the king, Clovis III, was still very young in 692.

Attention has already been drawn to the spectacular gathering of fifty-two magnates which made up the tribunal for the Amalbert case. On two other occasions we are given a list of names. Twelve are named in a document of November 691, twenty-one in one of March 697 and the two longer lists end with a statement that other *fideles* were present too[37]. The other *placita* speak of magnates in the plural but do not give names. If such magnates were acting as *rachymburgi* then, according to Frankish custom, they would be required to 'know the law'[38]. There are references to *lex* – law – in both our cases but it is hard to know what is meant by the term. In the Ermenoald case, as we have seen, the phrase 'the law of your locality' would seem to relate more to the ham-fisted use of *formulae* than to the actual proceedings. Other references to *lex* in both cases also occur as part of the *formulae*, those used to describe default, although here it is highly likely that the *formulae* do reflect the proceedings. We thus have 'to defend suit for three days *ut lex habuit*' and 'defending suit *ligebus*'. Elsewhere judgement refers to *lex* only in a general sense, for instance in a *placitum* of *c.* 690 'quod lex de tale causa edocit, exinde susteniat'[39]. Such vagueness, the seeming interchangeability of *lex* and *leges* and the participation in judgements by large numbers of apparent non-specialists, suggest that for the term *lex* we should generally understand a body of accepted custom rather than specific legal doctrine[40]. It is in relation to a visible adherence to custom that we may seek an explanation of the very strong emphasis on the observation of correct procedure which is a basic feature of the *placita*.

---

[36] On the *rachymburgi* and their relationship to the courts, see A. Schmitt-Weigand, *Rechtspflegedelikte in der Fränkischen Zeit*, pp. 8–20.   [37] *ChLA*, vol. 14, 575 and 581 respectively.

[38] *Pactus Legis Salicae*, lvii (*De rachineburgiis*), ed. K. Eckhardt, *MGH LL in quarto*, sectio 1, vol. 4, pt 1.   [39] *ChLA*, vol. 14, 572.

[40] This is not to say that *lex* could never mean an authoritative written text, as plainly on occasion it could – with Canon Law, for instance. The point is that the use of certain written texts was integral to accepted custom, and elements of authority could have determinant influence on what was accepted as custom. In the *placita* generally *lex* refers to custom. In historiographical terms, confidence in the supremacy of *lex scripta* has been replaced by a new orthodoxy which views custom in functionalist terms as the base for the entire legal structure in this period. So, for instance, H. Vollrath, 'Herrschaft und Genossenschaft im Kontext frühmittelalterliche Rechtsbeziehungen', *Historisches Jahrbuch*, 102 (1982), 47. This view is unhelpful if the effect of authority on custom is ignored. Custom is then invoked, perhaps romantically, as a bulwark against loss of rights. But it would seem more likely that a manipulation of custom, which was always liable to change, actually facilitated expropriation here.

The observation of correct procedure is prominent in both the Ermenoald and the Amalbert cases. Amalric, remember, was fined fifteen *solidi* in contempt of procedure. Ten of the *solidi* were given to Chrotcharius in *exfaida**, literally, to avoid a feud because his word had been wrongly challenged. The other five were paid to the king *in fredo**, his normal cut in any fine. Throughout, the terminology of procedure stands out: *sulsadire**, to establish the fault of the opposing party; *adchramire**, to bind to a court decision; *sunia**, a legitimate excuse for non-appearance in court; *festuca*, the symbolic rod or speaking baton. These are technical terms used, as they were used in *Lex Salica* too, to indicate particular aspects of procedural significance[41]. There is in such procedure a marked physical, even dramatic, element. Default is established by the plaintiff Chrotcharius, for instance, actually waiting three days 'and a bit more' at the appointed place. Acceptance of a court decision is shown by a grasping of the *festuca* – Amalric, for example, showed acceptance of the fifteen *solidi* fine *per festucam* and, importantly, this was formally witnessed by all those present (*visus est ficisse*). It would seem that we are seeing here procedure of a ritualistic nature and that ritual is one element in custom and, in turn, one element contained in the term *lex*.

The procedural framework of Frankish dispute settlement can be overemphasized to the point where the process of settlement is seen as a test of skills in the observation of correct procedure, a kind of ordeal by rule book[42]. It is more likely that the sense of being seen to do things properly was related to the public demonstration of the judges' decision which was a prerequisite for its enforcement. One can, further, contrast the elements of ritual procedure in the *placita* with the more bureaucratic elements in the process of settlement. We know of these procedural details precisely because they were encapsulated in the recording documents and we know, from the practice of holding fictitious disputes in order to acquire such documents, that they were valued as indicating in writing a public recognition of rights at that time. Emphasis on this aspect of the demonstration of judgement would lead us, in any search for the roots of the *placita*, in the direction of the Theodosian Code rather than towards a largely undefinable mass of 'Germanic Custom'[43]. In the final hearing the judges' decision was meant to be final and the recording document proof that there could be no grounds for further dispute[44]. There is here no sense of *amica pactuatio**, no procedure for bringing the disputing parties to agreement.

[41] *Pactus Legis Salicae*, xlvi. 1 (*De acfatmire*), for example.

[42] For this view, its origins and its development, see Schmitt-Weigand, *Rechtspflegedelikte*, pp. 102–4.

[43] Note, for instance, the stress in the Code on the public nature of judgement, *The Theodosian Code*, I. xvi, trans. C. Pharr; IV. xvii, 1 for the stricture that judgements must be written down. For a treatment of post-Roman proprietary remedies as 'neither non-Roman nor specifically German development' see E. Levy, *West Roman vulgar law*, pp. 240–2.

[44] This is strongly stated in the documents, as, for instance, in the Amalbert case. Chrotcharius, on behalf of Ingramnus, is to hold Bayencourt: 'Omni tempore habiat evindecatum adque elidiatum . . . et sit inter ipsis ex ac re in postmodo subita causacio'.

In both cases the use of warrants again shows the use of documents as an integral part of customary procedure. These warrants were written instructions supplying permission to take a dispute before a court and in each case both plaintiff and defendant appear to have received identical warrants, *notitiae paricolae* in the Ermenoald case, *equales praecepciones* in the Amalbert case. The dispute hearing did not begin until the warrants had been seen. In the Ermenoald case they were *inspecta*, in the Amalbert case, Amalric was asked why he had appeared when the warrant was for his father. In the former case the warrants were mentioned yet again before judgement was delivered and here they had the effect of holding off judgement until the *placitum* had been held[45]. This might also mean that once warrants had been issued a *placitum* had to be held, thus preventing an out of court settlement. Overall, the presentation of warrants in these cases was an important part of the procedure. They would seem to have had some of the qualities of the later judicial writ and it should be noted that they were valid in a series of courts. In the Ermenoald case the warrants had been used in the court of Sigofred bishop of Paris before being taken into the royal court[46]. In the Amalbert case, one set of warrants had taken the parties through 'several hearings' but a fresh set seems to have been issued for the final hearing. Both disputes had obviously been going on for some time before the final hearings. A defendant such as Ermenoald who, basically, did not contest the case after the first hearing was still presented with two other opportunities to defend himself before judgement was delivered in the final court session. The holding of multiple hearings should thus be seen as part of the dispute settlement procedure – another element, I would suggest, in the demonstration that there could be no possible grounds for dissent from the final verdict.

Our cases, and the other *placita*, show the use of a variety of forms of proof. Documentary forms of proof have already been alluded to. The warrants served as written evidence of the right to be at a hearing – Amalric could produce *nulla evidens* of his right to be there. Other sorts of written evidence in the form of charters are mentioned in eighteen of the twenty surviving original *placita* documents, though six of these *placita* are of confirmatory type and were held, therefore, to confirm the validity of the documents in question. So, in just over half of the genuine disputes in this sample, the use of documentary evidence was part of the procedure. Included here are deeds of sale, of inheritance, exchanges, grants and leases, as well as warrants. It is a picture which accords well with the impression, derived from Marculf, that this society documented a wide range of activities.

As we have seen, the use of documents was perfectly consistent with a stress on

---

[45] Thus too in *Marculfi Form.* I. 38, *De carta paricla*: 'Interim vero usque ipso placita necutra pars ex ipsis iectita non appareat'.

[46] Note also that there is no obvious distinction here between the jurisdiction of secular and ecclesiastical courts.

customary procedure. Observation of correct procedure itself served as a kind of proof when, as in both our cases, contempt of procedure was stated in the count of the palace's *testimonium* as a fact on which judgement rested. Oath-swearing and oath-helping* furnished another kind of proof. Ermenoald was asked to swear along with three others that he had never undertaken the pledge. In four other case oaths decided the issue and an especially strong oath was one taken over the cloak of St Martin, by 679 possessed by the palace and to be regarded as an important adjunct to the machinery of the royal court[47]. Finally, we see in one case of 710 the questioning of 'several persons' in conjunction with the examination of royal *praecepciones* in order to establish the legality of what Pippin of Heristal's son Grimoald claimed was an old custom allowing him to levy tolls at the St Denis fair[48].

Given the small numbers of extant *placita* records, any listing of all the kinds of proof admissible in court cases is likely to be incomplete[49]. For instance, the last quoted example, the case of 710, hints at some kind of sworn inquisition (*inquisitum est per plures personas*) but the expression is unique to this document, so we cannot read regularity into its use. We can, however, argue that contemporaries recognized that it was possible to prove things in different ways and that this could mean drawing on different concepts of proof, sometimes in one and the same case[50]. There was here, as in Lombard–Carolingian Italy, something of a pragmatic approach to questions of evidence[51]. Documents were called for when they were available and appropriate to the case and then they were valued for the legal title that they conveyed. They might, on the other hand, not have existed or have been inappropriate. One case, to be sure, was decided against a defendant because he had no document, when the logic of his argument demanded that he did have written evidence to support his claim[52]. The evidence of legal title held in writing is most clearly associated with, and appropriate to, cases involving the church in disputes about land ownership. In contrast, in one dispute about land ownership between lay persons no written evidence was mentioned and the case was decided by an oath taken on the cloak of St Martin[53].

---

[47] That it was in regular use in the royal court is suggested by its appearance in *Marculfi Form.* I. 38. Its first appearance in a *placitum* of 679 (*ChLA*, vol. 14, 567) is, in fact, an important *terminus* in the dating of the Marculf collection itself. On the palace's acquisition of the *cappa* and other relics, see J. Nelson, 'Queens as Jezabels: the careers of Brunhild and Balthild in Merovingian history' in D. Baker (ed.), *Studies in Church History, Subsidia*, vol. 1, pp. 67–72.

[48] *ChLA*, vol. 14, 586.

[49] This is true also of the Carolingian period. In his famous article on proof in this period, F. Ganshof drew on only four documents 'La preuve dans le droit franc' in *La Preuve*, vol. 2, *Recueil de la Société Jean Bodin*, vol. 17 (1965).

[50] In *ChLA*, vol. 14, 586, for instance.   [51] See Wickham below, p. 114.

[52] *ChLA*, vol. 14, 581. Pippin's son Drogo claimed that an exchange of land had actually taken place, whereas his opponent, Abbot Magnoald, claimed that the exchange had only been discussed. Drogo, asked how he knew that it had taken place, stated that there was a letter of exchange to prove it. But asked to produce this written evidence, he failed to do so and thus lost the case.

[53] *ChLA*, vol. 14, 566.

Both the Ermenoald and the Amalbert cases, warrants apart, were decided on grounds other than proof by written evidence. The latter may have existed but given the default of the defendants it was not necessary to produce it. We cannot say in this context that written evidence had any kind of primacy, nor can we believe that there was any sense of contradiction in the use of different kinds of evidence[54]. Acceptance as custom was a denominator common to the different modes of proof and custom reflected a world in which it remained possible to maintain power and property without recourse to writing.

We have seen thus far that the settlement of disputes in the royal court was based on an elaborate customary procedure and that even in cases of a political nature with a probably predetermined outcome the losing parties were given several opportunities to defend themselves before the final judgement. In the absence of actual case records, it is impossible to build up such a detailed picture for the workings of other courts. Of the episcopal courts we know almost nothing. However, of the count's court, the *mallus publicus**, the apparent mainstay of the Frankish judicial system, there is evidence from the Formularies to tell us more[55]; and of counts themselves we know quite a lot[56]. Hagiographic material is instructive here. It shows counts on several occasions acting in the context of what we would term criminal justice. The late seventh-century *Vita Amandi*, for example, gives what purports to be an eye-witness account of a count in action: a count called Dotto gathered together a 'fair number' of Franks 'as he was supposed to do in order to sit in judgement over law cases'. A defendant was thrust before the count and the crowd shouted for his death. He was then tortured and when he was but *semivivus*, Dotto had him hanged[57]. There is some contrast here with the intricate procedures revealed in the *placita*.

Dotto is described in this story as, 'savage and more cruel than any wild beast'. The presentation of counts as unfeeling and cruel in the Saints' Lives is common and is strongly influenced by literary convention[58]. The *Vita Eligii* even has a miracle story in which by prayer the saint freed men convicted of killing a count[59]. Such an unfavourable attitude towards counts may well have its roots in the treatment of the unfree at law. A famous clause of *Lex Salica* states that the unfree are to suffer the death penalty for all those crimes for which a free man would be

---

[54] That written evidence did have primacy is a strong assumption in Vollrath's work. She sees the growing predominance of the written record as an agent of determinant change in society, eating away at the custom which protected a *status quo* relatively beneficial to the mass of freemen, 'Herrschaft und Genossenschaft', 41–59.

[55] On the *mallus*, with useful references, see Schmitt-Weigand, *Rechtspflegedelikte*, pp. 16–20.

[56] On the counts, D. Claude, 'Untersuchungen zum frühfränkischen Comitat', *ZRG, Germ. Abt.*, 42 (1964).

[57] *Vita Amandi*, ch. 14, ed. B. Krusch, *MGH SRM*, vol. 5.

[58] For the development of this motif and for the relationship of the Saint to the representatives of the State in the *Vitae*, see F. Graus, *Volk, Herrscher und Heiliger im Reich der Merowinger*, pp. 334–90. Graus concentrates on the relationship between the Saint and the dynasty and thus does not discuss potential conflict at a more local level.   [59] *Vita Eligii*, ch. 15.

punished by a fine of 45 *solidi* or more[60]. Lots of crimes carry fines above this mark – bee-stealing, for instance. Counts were indeed frequently involved in executions and those suffering the penalty were, most often, the powerless.

The narrative sources for this period mention the settlement of disputes through the courts only very rarely but they do give prominence to the way in which people resorted to violence when they fell out with each other. The main reason for this, I would suggest, is that such sources are particularly concerned with episodes which led to violence, rather than that the settlement of differences through violence generally predominated. The two chronicles of the period give us but a thin record of the doings of the élite[61]. They are concerned with power and the struggle for power and this is presented as power based on military might. Hence the catalogue of violence which is at times portrayed in graphic and sensational detail[62]. Violence is also prominent in hagiographic sources, largely because those church leaders who died violently came to be regarded as martyrs. This explains the concern to write their Lives, which dwell on the detail of their heroes' suffering. The explanation of this violence towards church leaders must be sought in each particular instance, but in several cases, those of Aunemundus, Praejectus and Leudegarius, for example, death occurred in the context of the kind of struggle for political power on which the chronicles concentrate. A struggle over power cannot be reduced to the sort of dispute over a limited issue that we find recorded in the *placita*, and the enforcement of a judicial decision against a group of dissenting powerful could, anyway, have led to armed conflict.

The demise of Praejectus, bishop of Clermont, illustrates well how the settlement of a dispute through the courts could be overshadowed and then overwhelmed by political conflict[63]. Clermont claimed land taken by Hector ruler of Marseilles. Praejectus thus attended the royal court at Autun at Easter 675 to press suit against Hector. Midway through the proceedings the political tensions brought about by an assembly of divided magnates burst into open conflict which ended in Hector's death. It is as if the fifty-two magnates attending Amalbert's case had suddenly turned on each other halfway through the hearing. Praejectus thus by default emerged as victor in his case, but, on returning to his see, found himself at the mercy of Hector's followers, and mercy they did not show. This case illustrates a limit to the effectiveness of the royal court in settling disputes: effective settlement required consensus amongst the members of the tribunal which in times of political crisis might not be forthcoming and, at all times, in areas where particular kings lacked supporters the decisions of the royal court may not have been upheld. The *regale edictum* which Praejectus proudly carried back to the Auvergne was, in the event, useless to him.

[60] *Pactus Legis Salicae*, xl. 5.
[61] *The Fourth Book of the Chronicle of Fredegar* and the *Liber Historiae Francorum*.
[62] See, for instance, the description of Brunhild's death: *The Fourth Book of the Chronicle of Fredegar*, ch. 42, and *Liber Historiae Francorum*, ch. 40.
[63] *Passio Praejecti*, cc. 23–30, ed. B. Krusch, *MGH SRM*, vol. 5, pp. 239–43.

In two other cases we see a challenge to the growing establishment of the church result in violence. These events, the murder of Germanus, abbot of Grandivalle and the sacking of his monastery, some time in the 670s, and the slaughter of Landibert bishop of Tongres and his clerical entourage *c.* 703, occurred in outlying areas where church persons and property were vulnerable whenever there was a clash with other powerful interests[64]. Though it is in the main correct to highlight the emerging legal expertise of the church and its pioneer work in the defence of property through the courts, we must also remember that success here was conditional upon the will and the ability of the powerful to oversee the workings and guarantee the results of the legal process. It was possible, *in extremis*, for powerful magnates to ignore the courts and look to their own armed strength. Conflict between groups of such people could become civil war. It remains likely, however, that armed clashes between groups of the powerful and violent attacks on church leaders are heavily over-represented in the narrative sources, events famous because they were unusual. Far more normal was a balance of interests which allowed the church protection through the courts and maintained customary legal procedure as a primary instrument of social regulation. Though we see various groups in society coming into contact with the courts, there is an obvious contrast between the powerful and the powerless in their relationship to the legal process. My third text is one which to some extent helps to explain that contrast. It is not the record of a late seventh-century court case but an extract from an earlier normative text, the Edict of Chilperic which was issued *c.* 575. Again I present a full summary rather than a literal translation.

This is a royal Edict dealing here with theft by slaves and by free people who have little or no property: if a slave is accused of theft, his master must present him at court within ten nights, or forty-two nights at most. The victim of the slave and six others will then sit in judgement on him. If the slave does not appear at court and has no legitimate excuse, his master can either yield him up for punishment or redeem him by paying compensation to the court and to the victim of his crime. If, however, a legitimate excuse is given within forty-two nights, the latter period will be extended to eighty-four nights and a future court appearance arranged. Non-appearance will have the same result as before. If a legitimate excuse is not given within forty-two nights, then a 15 *solidi* fine is payable – and a promise to pay this within fourteen nights must be made (though the latter period can be extended to twenty-one nights if necessary). If promise or payment is not forthcoming, then the case must go before the next *mallus*. Here it will be heard by the *rachymburgi* and the count. The count will then take up the *festuca* and go to the property of the accused and take from it an amount decided upon by the *rachymburgi* – seven *rachymburgi* of good character, or who know the procedure, will go with him to take the correct amount. The count may not move until the *rachymburgi* ask him to do so. If he does, or if he takes an illegal amount, he will be liable to punishment by death.

The legislation now outlines the procedure to be followed if there is a complaint that the

---

[64] *Vita Germani Grandivallensis*, ch. 12, ed. B. Krusch, *MGH SRM*, vol. 5, and *Vita Landiberti Vetustissima*, cc. 14–17, ed. B. Krusch, *MGH SRM*, vol. 6, pp. 367–70.

count has confiscated property illegally: the count and whoever asked for the confiscation must answer the charge within forty-two nights. If the one who asked for the confiscation does not deny the charge, then the seven *rachymburgi* who first heard the case must be called in as witnesses and the case heard before the royal court. If the seven cannot come and have legal excuse, then three will do. If none can come, then the count and whoever asked for the confiscation must return the property plus compensation.

The legislation now deals with criminals who are free but have little or no property: if someone commits a crime but does not have enough property to make compensation to the victim, he will nevertheless come before the *mallus* at three sessions so that his relatives can redeem him by payment. If they refuse to do this, the criminal, after a fourth session of the *mallus*, shall appear before the royal court and there it will be decreed that he should be handed over to the victim of his crime who may do what he likes with him. (App. VII)

Despite the fact that this Edict was issued over a hundred years before the other cases we have looked at took place, most of its provisions accord well with what we know of the legal process of the later period. It reflects the contrast between the operation of the courts seen in the *placita* and in the hagiographic material by showing both stress on the observation of correct procedure and the ultimate vulnerability of the unfree and poor. It also shows how property ownership provided the free man with some safeguard against arbitrary treatment by the count and the *rachymburgi*.

The Edict's provisions appear complex. The final judicial remedies are simple enough: the guilty slave is either given to his victim or redeemed by his master's money payment; the master, a propertied free man, has property taken away from him if he fails to compensate his slave's victim, and the free but poor man loses his liberty if he cannot compensate his victim. The complexity lies in what seems to be a process of associative reasoning which attempts to build up a water-tight procedure to produce a definitive judgement.

The strictures on following the correct procedures are remarkably strong where the count is concerned. If he acts wrongly in confiscating property or does not act when called in he is liable to suffer the death penalty. This provision is there too in *Lex Salica*, though with a wergeld* fine as an alternative to the death penalty[65]. It may, as has been suggested, have its origins in some royal command which counts subsequently disobey at their peril, but there is surely rather more involved than royal anger at direct disobedience[66]. The count is here the key man in the court process. If he does not follow the correct procedure, the whole process becomes invalid. The confiscation of property must be seen to be indisputably correct, for this is where visible injustice could occur and those monitoring the count, the *rachymburgi*, were themselves property owners, thus likely to have a strong interest in the protection of property through due legal procedure. As with the *placita* we see a consensus of interests underlying the legal process. The count, as president of the tribunal and chief enforcer of its

---

[65] *Pactus Legis Salicae*, l. 4.
[66] Schmitt-Weigand, *Rechtspflegedelikte*, pp. 15–16.

decisions, was in a position to ruin that consensus. How far in practice he was restricted by these dire threats we can only speculate.

That Chilperic's Edict and the *placita* have elements of procedure common to both strengthens the impression that the procedures of the latter draw heavily on the custom of the *mallus*. Both, for instance, have a fifteen *solidi* fine for non-appearance without *sunia* and both indicate that there could be a series of court hearings culminating with a final hearing before the king[67]. It may seem at first sight striking that the process of criminal trial before the *mallus* has much in common with the process of dispute settlement in the royal court, but at the heart of both lay claims to property. Both the slave (and, in effect, his master if he refuses to yield him up) and the insolvent free man have taken property which others are trying through the court to regain along with an extra amount due as compensation. The unredeemed slave and the poor free man are given to the victim of their crime when they cannot meet the latter's claim. The propertied master is in a much more favourable position. He can meet the claim without loss of liberty and has the right to challenge if property is unjustly taken from him. The emphasis on property transfer to the victim in criminal cases narrows any distinction to be made between criminal and civil justice[68]. What distinction there is lies in the element of compensation in criminal cases. Such compensation in effect punishes and the state, in the person of king or count, guarantees the enforcement, enforcing it directly in the case of capital punishment, the ultimate form of compensation. A precise penalty is lacking in *placita*. When Amalric was fined, it was because he had wronged Chrotcharius and was not connected directly with the occupation of Bayencourt. In *placita*, compensaton is sometimes mentioned, but only to cover damage and loss of income from land. Ermenoald faced distraint, but only for what he owed St Denis. Chilperic's Edict, in the use of a tribunal and a president, the strict adherence to elaborate procedure, the holding of multiple hearings and the production, ultimately, of a definitive judgement, shows that, in theory at least, the late sixth-century *mallus* worked very much like the courts in which disputes were settled before the king in the later Merovingian period.

I began by asking how far the formal record of the *placitum* reflected the reality of the settlement of disputes both in and beyond the royal court. Despite the fact that we have as evidence only a tiny sample of documents which are over-whelmingly representative of monastic interests, I would, in conclusion, argue that they do indeed convey an accurate picture of the process of settlement. They

---

[67] An important difference between the two is that there is nothing in the Edict on proof. It is assumed that the defendant is guilty. In *Pactus Legis Salicae*, xl. 2, the implication is that when a *servus* is accused, guilt will be established by torture.

[68] One can, in this context, view the penalties of *Pactus Legis Salicae* as a list or tarif for compensation. For the tarif element in early medieval law in general, Vollrath, 'Herrschaft und Genossenschaft', 61–2.

allow us to see Frankish legal procedure of this period in motion and where we can glimpse that procedure beyond the royal tribunal, other courts seem to move in the same ways.

Common to the conduct of all courts was a visible adherence to accepted custom, manifested most strongly in elaborate customary procedure. But custom could change, and although it is true that consensus was a prerequisite for change, we must also note that an operative consensus meant the acceptance of change by those with the power to enforce it[69]. Chilperic was redefining custom in his Edict in favour of the smaller landholders who were given greater opportunity to redeem errant slaves[70]. It was change which would thus have been supported by the very people who sat on the tribunals of the local courts. Change in this view was aligned towards a reinforcement of dominant power and property relationships. The *placita* provide some measure of this. They show how to the traditional, and oral, judicial process there was added the use of written evidence, warrants and, indeed, the employment of customary procedures to affirm ownership publicly and in writing. The *placita* thus reveal the royal court in the seventh century doing much of the work that the *gesta municipalia* had done in the sixth century.

These changes mark the growing influence of the church on property relationships and upon political society as a whole, an impression which rests on more than one batch of documents produced in favour of and conserved by the church. Yet just as we can infer change from the *placita* form of the seventh century, we should also note that form is thereafter remarkably stable. There is very little difference between a royal *placitum* of the seventh century and one of the ninth[71]. This may suggest that not only was the later Merovingian blend of customary procedure and bureaucratic refinement efficacious in the settlement of disputes, but also that there was continuity in the underlying social and political structures from the seventh to ninth centuries. We may see there a balance of interests within which the process of the royal court provided, at least for the magnate community, a convenient and acceptable way of settling disputes over property of a relatively minor order. It seems likely that the *mallus* similarly operated within a balance of local interests – a balance which operated against those without property. The possible fate of the latter before the courts points up

---

[69] This is an important *caveat* to the notion of the impact of authority on custom. In this society the power to enforce change was diffused horizontally in the partnership between king and magnates, and vertically in the relationship between the magnates and their followers in a local context. No group could act independently of the other, hence the consensus necessary for change. A *decretio* issued by King Childebert II *c.* 596 seems to alter custom almost at will, for instance suspending wergeld for those who have killed on the basis that 'qui novit occidere, discat morire', *Childeberti Decretio*, ch. 5, ed. G. Pertz, *MGH LL*, vol. 1, pp. 10–12. This kind of drastic change, which expresses what is by now an anachronistic notion of Roman authority, seems to have been ignored by the magnates and their followers.

[70] F. Beyerle, 'Das legislativ Werk Chilperichs I', *ZRG, Germ. Abt.*, 78 (1961).

[71] See Nelson below, p. 49.

a repressive element in the Frankish judicial structure. It is noteworthy that even where the powerful were concerned, the tribunal's final verdict was meant to be decisive – there were, it was stated, no possible grounds for dissent. But in practice, as we have seen, where the stakes were too high, the king too remote, or the magnates too divided to form a tribunal, the entire court process could be bypassed.

The latter alternative to the formal process, the stuff of the chronicles, should, however, be seen as an option chosen but rarely. All too often, though, it has been taken as a model for Frankish life in general in this period. Ganshof, for example, saw a later Merovingian anarchy as the seed-bed of 'feudalism', claiming that 'Even apart from the struggle for power, the state was quite unable to maintain the public peace or secure the safety of its inhabitants'[72]. The *placita*, Marculf, hagiography and Chilperic's Edict tell a rather different story. Apart from occasional struggles for political power, the powerful in society, who were the basis of the state, had a great interest in maintaining the public peace through customary legal procedures. Because their interests were reinforced by the maintenance of peace, those procedures evolved in line with those interests. In this period facilities for formal litigation existed at all levels of Frankish society, guaranteed, ultimately, by the king drawing on the collective power of the magnates. The strength of customary procedure meant that disputes could be settled effectively in the royal court even when the king was an infant. In this context the *placita* give us another view of the famous later Merovingian royal *fainéance*. They show how custom and consensus gave a momentum to the practice of kingship which allowed it to continue even when the kings themselves were too young to do anything[73].

[72] F. Ganshof, *Feudalism*, p. 3.
[73] I am grateful to David Killingray for reading a draft of this paper, and for his helpful and encouraging comments.

3

Dispute settlement in Carolingian West Francia

JANET L. NELSON

About the year 830, the monastery of St Benedict at Fleury was in dispute with another monastery over possession of some serfs. The abbot of Fleury, learning where and when the case was to be heard before the local *vicarius**, and 'not wishing to be thought careless', sent two monks to the *vicarius* with a gift of two silver bowls and a message begging him 'to favour justice and righteousness'. Unfortunately for the abbot, the *vicarius* had already received presents from the other monastery, and thus 'corrupted' and 'diverted from the righteousness of equity', he spurned Fleury's offerings, 'Go away, you monks, and take your bowls with you'. But St Benedict was watching over his community, and saw to it that the *vicarius*, in his pride, was thrown from his horse and killed. Thus Fleury's *advocatus** could have his case heard by different judges and settled by a 'lawful judgement' in Fleury's favour[1].

This case is typical in several ways of dispute settlement in Francia in the Carolingian period. It arose from the pursuit by a powerful lord of a property claim – the parties involved being saints, represented by monastic communities; the property, manpower; and the claim pursued through courts and judgements supported by the Carolingian régime[2]. But the case is untypical in that it is recorded in a collection of miracle stories and reveals something of the social mechanisms as well as the legal procedures by which disputes were settled[3]. Usually the evidence for dispute settlement survives in sources that are either prescriptive and normative (laws, *formulae**) or formal records of particular cases (charters*, *notitiae**). Sources of both kinds are far more plentiful for the Carolingian than for the preceding Merovingian period[4]. Moreover, most of the

---

[1] Adrevald of Fleury, *Ex Miraculis S. Benedicti*, ch. 24, ed. O. Holder-Egger, *MGH SS*, vol. 15, pt 1.

[2] The régime's institutions are well described by F. L. Ganshof, *Frankish Institutions under Charlemagne*; K.-F. Werner, 'Missus – marchio – comes' in W. Paravicini and K.-F. Werner (eds.), *Histoire comparée de l'administration (IVe–XVIIIe siècles)*; R. McKitterick, *The Frankish Kingdoms under the Carolingians*, p. 77–105.

[3] Adrevald's collection is unusually rich in this kind of information. See G. Lysaght, 'Fleury and S. Benedict', Univ. Oxford D.Phil. thesis, 1985. See also M. Heinzelmann, 'Une source de base de la littérature hagiographique latine' in *Hagiographie, cultures et sociétés*, pp. 235–57.

[4] For these Merovingian sources, see Wood and Fouracre above, pp. 7–11, 23–4.

evidence usually labelled 'Merovingian' is contained in the undated *formulae* of formularies* that were written out in the Carolingian period, mainly in the ninth century[5]. In fact, there may well have been continuities in Frankish legal practice through the early middle ages, notably in those parts of the Carolingian empire which had constituted the Merovingian realm and from which most of the formularies come.

An invaluable guide to the Carolingian evidence was long since provided by Hübner's inventory of records of judgements: for the regions north of the Alps, Hübner listed some 600, dating from between the mid seventh century and *c.* 1000[6]. Of these, 257 are records of actual cases from the ninth century. Roughly half of them relate to the western part of the Carolingian empire, the regions which constituted the West Frankish kingdom of Charles the Bald (840–77)[7]. Within this area, however, the regional distribution is uneven. Thanks to the survival of rich monastic or cathedral archives, Brittany, Burgundy, the Rhône valley and Septimania are relatively well represented; Neustria, western Francia and Aquitaine much less so. But though there are some regional peculiarities of documentary style, *placita**, the records of cases, show basic similarities across the whole West Frankish kingdom. This mass of ninth-century case material has two advantages compared with the smaller Merovingian dossier; firstly, while there are a few royal judgements (and these show a remarkable resemblance to their Merovingian forebears) the great majority of ninth-century *placita* come not from the palace but from county courts. Secondly, whereas in the Merovingian period the prescriptive evidence comes from the century and a half before *c.* 650 from which no case material survives, while the *placita* come from the century after *c.* 650 from which we have no legislation, the central Carolingian period offers a happy conjunction of case material with legislation about dispute settlement.

Into what framework can this ninth-century case material be set? The historiography presents two rather different perspectives on Carolingian justice. On the one hand, there is the view from the twelfth century, the view of R. van Caenegem and M. Boulet-Sautel, in which Carolingian practice is seen as a compound of custom-bound, ritualistic, formal procedures and appeals to the judgement of God, and is contrasted with the 'new' rationality allegedly characteristic of the twelfth century[8]. On the other hand, there is the view from the capitularies, the view of F. L. Ganshof, of a system of local courts regularly

---

[5] See the information on manuscripts in K. Zeumer (ed.), *Formulae Merowingici et Karolini Aevi*, *MGH LL in quarto*, sectio 5; also H. Brunner, *Deutsche Rechtsgeschichte*, 2nd edn, vol. 1, pp. 575–88; R. Buchner, *Die Rechtsquellen*, pp. 49–55. The Formulary of Angers, preserved in an early eighth-century manuscript, contains some seventh-century *formulae*: Brunner, *Rechtsgeschichte*, vol. 1, pp. 577–8, and see Wood above, p. 9.

[6] R. Hübner, 'Gerichtsurkunden der fränkischen Zeit. Erste Abteilung', *ZRG, Germ. Abt.*, 12 (1891).

[7] See above, p. 28, fig. 1.

[8] R. C. van Caenegem, 'La preuve dans le Droit du moyen âge occidental' in *La Preuve*, vol. 2, *Recueil de la Société Jean Bodin*, vol. 17 (1965); M. Boulet-Sautel, 'Aperçus sur le système des preuves dans

inspected by impartial *missi** sent out from the palace, with officers (counts and their subordinates) helped by permanent panels of expert judgement-finders, the *scabini**, who replaced the old Merovingian *ad hoc* tribunals of amateur local free men, the *rachymburgi**. Ganshof acknowledged that much Carolingian procedure remained traditional. But he also stressed Carolingian improvements: the use of sworn witnesses as distinct from oath-helpers*, and of documentary proofs. The new efficiency injected into the system by the *scabini* was, Ganshof believed, strengthened by two further innovations: one, the adversarial pattern of witnessing whereby witnesses were produced by both sides, not just by the accused; the other, the inquest* whereby the president of the court was empowered by the king to empanel local free men to give sworn, impartial evidence to the facts (rather than partial witness to good character) in a given case[9].

Levillain too believed that justice was done in Carolingian courts, thanks to the collective judgement of *scabini* and other *boni homines**. Confronted by a case heard before the *missus* Hildebrand in which that same Hildebrand was a party, he assured himself that 'A case in which a count could appear as both judge and party must have been quite normal and had nothing even that could appear shocking . . . It mattered little that the judge was a party to the case, for in reality the judges did not have to offer a personal opinion on the substance of the case: guardians of Right, they ensured that the formalities were observed'[10].

Both the views sketched above offer useful perspectives on Carolingian dispute settlement. But both are too narrow, and both involve some questionable assumptions. The inappropriateness of applying modern categories of 'rational' and 'irrational' to Carolingian procedures, for instance, emerges from the prescriptions for the use of witnesses in a Capitulary of 816:

If a party suspects the witnesses brought against him, he can put forward other, better, witnesses against them. But if the two groups of witnesses cannot agree, let one man be chosen from each group to fight it out with shields and spears. Whoever loses is a perjuror, and must lose his right hand; but the other witnesses in the same group can redeem [i.e. pay compensation for] their right hands . . . Witnesses must be assembled from the county in which the disputed property lies, for it is not credible that . . . the truth of such a case can be better known through persons other than neighbours[11].

The drafter of this capitulary seems not to have seen his mutilated combatant and knowledgeable neighbour as strange bedfellows. It is instructive to share a Carolingian legislator's notion of improvement.

la France coutumière au moyen âge', *ibid.*, p. 277. Compare also J. Gaudemet, 'Les ordalies au moyen âge', *ibid.*, pp. 99–102. Cf. P. Brown, 'Society and the Supernatural', *Daedalus*, 104 (1975), and R. V. Colman, 'Reason and unreason in early medieval law', *Journal of Interdisciplinary History*, 4 (1974).

[9] F. Ganshof, 'La preuve dans le Droit franc' in *La Preuve*, vol. 2, *Recueil de la Société Jean Bodin*, vol. 17 (1965).

[10] L. Levillain, 'Les Nibelungen historiques', *Annales du Midi*, 49 (1937), 350–1, n. 3.

[11] *Capitularia Regum Francorum*, ed. A. Boretius, *MGH LL in quarto*, sectio 2 (hereafter *MGH Capit.*), vol. 1, no. 134 (816), cap. 1, p. 268.

Capitularies are an essential part of the context of dispute settlement. But the context's wider political and social dimensions also have to be considered. The law that can be seen as an instrument of the Carolingian state was also the instrument of an aristocracy whose incorporation into the state was partial and qualified. The further we move away from the palace and the more closely we inspect the workings of justice in the county courts, the keener our sense of the entrenched power of local *potentes* (powerful men). At that level, the interests of churches and of lay aristocrats often conflicted; and for all its royal backing, the church did not always triumph. Lords, ecclesiastical and secular, had a common interest in maximizing the profits of lordship. The law underwrote that exploitation in the case of the unfree. But for the free, however politically and economically weak, the law offered some protection. There was a possibility of short-circuiting local power by direct appeal to royal justice. Carolingian kings who sometimes needed the military and fiscal services of such *pauperes liberi homines* (lesser free men) could protest against their oppression by the powerful, denouncing, for instance, the abuse whereby counts and their subordinates held excessive numbers of local assemblies requiring the presence of lesser free men and then used these occasions to impose exactions[12]. Royal authority could also overturn the false judgements of corrupt local judges. But such reversals seem to have been rare. Few royal *missi* descended on the provinces like avenging angels from on high. Levillain's Hildebrand case illustrates a widespread phenomenon: the *missus* was a magnate (whether count or bishop) of the area he served in[13]. Thus the jurisdiction of count or *missus*, in principle delegated from the king, in practice became the acceptable face of existing local power. The king could find himself in the contradictory business of arming the hunters while attempting to protect the prey. Given a localized, hierarchical society and office-holding that was very often hereditary, the check of central control over arbitrary local power was at best intermittent. Levillain believed that custom and a sense of right, voiced by representatives of the local community, exercised a more permanent and effective restraint than could any central authority.

The first case I shall consider comes from Aquitaine. It is dated 828 and is a royal judgement given by Pippin I who ruled the Aquitanian kingdom from 817 to 838 under his father, the emperor Louis the Pious[14].

---

[12] *MGH Capit.*, vol. 1, no. 44 (805), cap. 16, p. 125; no. 159 (?823), cap. 2, p. 320; *Capit.*, vol. 2, no. 193 (829), cap. 5, p. 19: similar complaints against *vicarii* and *centenarii**. Thirteenth-century English sheriffs practised similar tricks: J. R. Maddicott, 'Magna Carta and the local community', *Past and Present*, 102 (1984), 31–6.

[13] Above, p. 47, n. 10.

[14] For the political history of Aquitaine in the ninth century, see Levillain's introduction to *Recueil des Actes de Pépin I et de Pépin II, rois d'Aquitaine*, pp. clxviii–cxc; J. Martindale, 'Charles the Bald and the Government of Aquitaine' in M. Gibson, J. Nelson, D. Ganz (eds.), *Charles the Bald: Court and Kingdom*; *idem*, 'The kingdom of Aquitaine', *Francia*, 13 (1985). Chasseneuil (dép. Vienne), just north of Poitiers, was one of the main palaces of this kingdom.

Pippin, by the grace of God king of Aquitaine. When we in God's name, on a Tuesday in our palace at the villa* of Chasseneuil in the county of Poitou near the River Clain, were sitting to hear the cases of many persons and to determine just judgements, there came certain men, named Aganbert, Aganfred, Frotfar and Martin, they as well as their fellows (*pares*) being *coloni** of St Paul from the villa of Antoigné belonging to the monastery of Cormery and its abbot Jacob. There they brought a complaint against that abbot and his advocate, named Agenus, on the grounds that the abbot and his officers had demanded and exacted from them more in rent and renders than they ought to pay and hand over, and more than their predecessors for a long time before then had paid and handed over, and that they [the abbot and his officers] were not keeping for them such law as their predecessors had had.

Agenus the advocate and Magenar the provost of monastery were there present, and made a statement rebutting that claim, as follows: neither the abbot nor they themselves had exacted, or ordered to be exacted, any dues or renders other than their predecessors had paid to the monastery's representatives for thirty years. They forthwith presented an estate survey (*descriptio*) to be read out, wherein was detailed how, in the time of Alcuin's abbacy, the *coloni* of that villa who were there present, and also their fellows, had declared on oath what they owed in renders, and what was still to pay, for each manse on that estate. The survey was dated to the thirty-fourth year of King Charles's reign.

The *coloni* there present were then asked if they had declared [the statements in] that survey and actually paid the renders stated in the survey for a period of years, and if that survey had been true and good, or did they wish to say anything against it or object to it, or not? They said and acknowledged that the survey was true and good, and they were quite unable to deny that they had paid that render for a period of years, or that they themselves, or their predecessors, had declared [the statements in] that survey.

Therefore we, together with our faithful men, namely Count Haimo [and twenty-three named men ending with John, count of the palace] and many others, have seen fit to judge that, since those *coloni* themselves gave the acknowledgement as stated above that the survey was as they had declared it, and as it was written down in the document there before them, and that they had paid the said renders for a period of years, so also must they pay and hand over the same each and every year to the representatives of that house of God.

Therefore we order that, since we have seen the case thus heard and concluded, the above Agenus the advocate and Maginar [*sic*] the provost should on behalf of that house of God receive a record of it, showing that it has been done in this way and at this time.

I Deotimus, deputizing for John count of the palace, have recognized and subscribed.

Given on 9 June in the fifteenth year of the reign of our lord Louis the serene emperor. Nectarius wrote out and subscribed it. (App. VIII)

This royal judgement is in the thoroughly traditional form of Merovingian *placita*, produced in the office of the count of the palace whose job it was to organize the royal tribunal. The scribe's 'barbarous Latin' contrasts with the expertise of notaries in the king's writing office where royal diplomas* were drawn up[15]. This text, an original, was kept in the archive of the monastery of St Paul at Cormery, a daughter house of St Martin, Tours[16].

The procedure follows standard form: a complaint is laid before the court, the

[15] As pointed out by Levillain, *Actes de Pépin*, p. 45. *Recueil des Actes de Charles le Chauve*, ed. G. Tessier (hereafter Tessier, *Recueil*), vol. 3, p. 195.

[16] Levillain, *Actes de Pépin*, p. 45. Cormery (dép. Indre-et-Loire) is about 15 km south east of Tours.

defendant rebuts the charge, and judgement is given by the king with twenty-four named faithful men 'and others' in favour of the defendant. The social context of the case is a conflict between a lord, the abbey of Cormery, and some tenants at Antoigné, one of the lord's estates (see fig. 1)[17]. Aganbert, Aganfred, Frotfar and Martin are *coloni*, who acknowledge only fixed customary obligations to their lord. They appear in court not only in their own behalf but as representatives of their fellow-*coloni* at Antoigné. The conflict had arisen over payments, presumably in cash, and renders, not over labour services. The case of Aganbert's side rests on their 'law', that is, the custom that operated for their predecessors as holders of particular tenements (manses) on the estate[18].

Aganbert and his fellows assume that the king will assure their 'law'. This fundamental royal obligation was acknowledged in exactly these terms by a succession of Carolingian rulers in their capitularies[19]. Aristocrats regularly appealed to kings on these grounds. Faithful men clearly felt justified in opposing a king who breached an individual's 'law', the status and treatment to which he, and his fellows, thought him entitled[20]. How often free peasants made similar appeals to kings, we can only guess from the very small number of surviving cases[21]. It may be that appeal was only possible from peasants whose lord was a church under special royal protection: there are no recorded cases of such appeals from peasants on the lands of secular lords. But secular cases are extremely unlikely to have been preserved. Further, Aganbert's 'law' is grounded in 'right' (*drictum*), a broader term denoting the whole framework of shared norms and values, embracing all individual statuses and claims, including those of kingship. Such rare and indirect bits of evidence for peasant perceptions suggest that the same basic assumptions were shared by men at all levels of Carolingian society.

Naturally, Cormery's representatives lodge their counterclaim too in right. But they also adduce proofs of three kinds: the thirty-year rule*, the survey document, and the sworn declarations that had accompanied the survey's compilation. Thirty-year prescription was often offered as proof in Carolingian land disputes; legislation in 829 made it the standard basis for ecclesiastical

---

[17] Antoigné (dép. Maine-et-Loire) seems the likeliest identification of 'Antoniacus': Levillain, *Actes de Pépin*, pp. 44–5, who also pointed out that while this villa was within Pippin's kingdom of Aquitaine, Cormery lay outside it. If this identification is right, the plaintiffs came some 70 km to seek the royal judgement.

[18] The existence of manses, and Alcuin's survey, suggest that Antoigné was organized as a demesne with dependent tenures: see A. Verhulst, 'La genèse du régime domanial classique' in *Agricoltura e mondo rurale, Settimane di Studio*, vol. 13 (1966).

[19] E.g. Charlemagne in *MGH Capit.*, vol. 1, no. 25 (787/93), p. 67; Charles the Bald in *Capit.*, vol. 2, no. 254 (843), cap. 3, p. 255; Lothar, Louis the German and Charles the Bald, *ibid.*, no. 204 (847), cap. 5, p. 69. See J. L. Nelson, 'Kingship, law and liturgy', *Eng. Hist. Rev.*, 92 (1977), 255.

[20] J. L. Nelson, 'Kingship and Empire' in J. H. Burns (ed.), *The Cambridge History of Medieval Political Thought* (forthcoming).

[21] For one other case north of the Alps, see below, pp. 51–3. For a few similar Italian cases, see C. Wickham, *Early Medieval Italy*, pp. 109–11.

claims[22]. It could also be used, as here, in a case involving personal obligations[23]. This proof is quite distinct from that of the survey document, dated 801 and hence only twenty-seven years before this judgement.

If the information supplied by Cormery is taken at face-value, the *coloni* seem to have had no case. Aganbert and his three colleagues (Aganfred was perhaps a brother) were presumably middle-aged men who represented their fellows because of their seniority and their long memories. Could they have forgotten their own sworn declarations of twenty-seven years before? Or had Cormery falsified the record, confident that its superior power could overcome the 'law' of the *coloni*? Another, perhaps likelier, possibility is that the survey was accurate, as was the thirty-year prescription claim, but that these both reflected fairly recent impositions introduced during the abbacy of Alcuin (who died in 804). If the alleged exactions were only a generation old, the *coloni* of Antoigné were perhaps trying to recover the situation on the horizon of living memory, before Alcuin's abbacy, asserting too late, hence unsuccessfully, the changelessness of custom. As for the timing of their plea, they may have hoped to forestall the abbey's becoming able, as it would in 831, to present documentary proof for its thirty-year claim.

Further possibilities in interpreting this case arise from comparison with another dispute which involved peasants seeking a royal judgement against their lord. On 1 July 861, twenty-three named men (*homines*) of St Denis, from the villa of Mitry, including 'Grimbald, notary', came before the tribunal of Charles the Bald at the palace of Compiègne (see fig. 1). With them came eighteen women, of whom ten brought their children – making a total of at least sixty-one persons[24]. The text details their claim:

that they ought to be [treated as] free *coloni* by birth, like the other *coloni* of St Denis, and that Deodadus the monk [responsible for running the Mitry estate] wanted unjustly to bend them down into an inferior service by force, and to afflict them[25].

In reply, Deodadus and the *maior** of Mitry stated that they had with them as 'suitable witnesses' *coloni* from Mitry through whom they would prove that

in the time of Louis [the Pious] those men listed above and their antecedents had always been serfs (*servi*) of that villa, bound to inferior service, and in right and in law had done more than *coloni* do, as is obvious[26].

Where the issue in the Antoigné case turned on customary rents and renders, the Mitry case was about the status of a group of peasants: were they free or unfree?

---

[22] *MGH Capit.*, vol. 2, no. 191 (829), cap. 8, p. 13.

[23] *Formulae Andecavenses*, no. 10, in *Formulae*, ed. K. Zeumer, p. 8.

[24] Tessier, *Recueil*, vol. 2, no. 228, pp. 7–9. This text is reprinted, and discussed from a rather different standpoint, in Ganshof, 'La preuve dans le Droit franc', pp. 81–7. Mitry (dép. Seine-et-Marne) is roughly 60 km south west of Compiègne.

[25] Tessier, *Recueil*, vol. 2, p. 8.   [26] *Ibid.*, p. 9.

There are a number of similar judgements from various parts of the Carolingian empire in the eighth and ninth centuries[27]. Lords were clearly short of manpower, and used the courts to impose their demands on refractory peasants, sometimes putting the machinery in motion to secure a judgement on the servile status of a single man or woman. A capitulary almost exactly contemporary with this case suggests that lords in the Seine valley were increasing their demands for labour services, perhaps to increase returns rather than to compensate for labour shortage[28]. This operation through legal procedures is as remarkable as the lordly determination to exploit where they could. Because unfreedom was transmitted through the mother to her children, the peasant plaintiffs of Mitry had to bring women and children to the tribunal, though the women were evidently not held legally capable to testify (hence St Denis's representatives only needed to produce twenty-three witnesses against the twenty-three male plaintiffs). Inferior service meant service at the lord's discretion[29]. Against the plaintiffs' assertion that such service had been extracted by force, and therefore unjustly, the abbey's officers produced twenty-three indisputable *coloni* as 'suitable witnesses' to the fact of the plaintiffs' servile status – *per legem*; and hence of their obligation in principle – *per dictum* – to perform the 'inferior service' the abbey wished to impose. There is no mention in the record of documentary proof in addition to the testimony of sworn witnesses, but it is interesting to note that the plaintiffs included a notary, perhaps a local priest of servile origin, who could have recorded his side's victory[30]. But the court found in favour of St Denis: hence the record's survival in St Denis's archives. The plaintiffs were ordered to acknowledge their defeat publicly by offering compensation and a pledge[31].

One further comment is needed on the way in which the law worked. The documentary record, freezing an ongoing conflict into a single scene, also elides procedural stages. Presumably there was a preliminary hearing (evidence of this survives in two other ninth-century cases) in which the plaintiffs lodged their plea and the court decided what proof the defendant must furnish and specified the date and place of judgement[32]. Summonses would then have been issued,

---

27 Hübner, 'Gerichtsurkunden', nos. 72, 86, 99, 144, 154, 155, 251, 254, 300–5 are from formularies; nos. 162, 171, 215, 217, 220, 226, 234, 323, and 372 are case records.

28 An example is the case considered by Levillain, cited above p. 47. Hübner, 'Gerichtsurkunden', does not list this, but all his case records listed above in n. 27, except no. 323, also involve only one person. Edict of Pîtres, *MGH Capit.*, vol. 2, no. 273 (864), cap. 29, p. 323.

29 Hence the distinction between *coloni*, owing fixed renders, and *servi*, unprotected by customary limits. For an exception that proves the rule, see *Cartulaire de Cormery*, ed. J.-J. Bourassé, no. 19 (851), p. 40: 'Hos servos vel ancillas . . . sub conditione colonorum constitutos, tributum amplius ut non requiratur quam unicuique mansum tenenti biduam in hebdomada 2' and so on.

30 W. Davies, 'Priests and rural communities in East Brittany', *Études Celtiques*, 20 (1983), 185, cites evidence for priests acting as scribes for 'members of the local community'; see also below, pp. 68–9. Carolingian councils had to repeat the canonical prohibition of the ordination of *servi*: *MGH Capit.*, vol. 1, no. 138 (818/9), cap. 6, p. 276; *Capit.*, vol. 2, no. 252 (895), cap. 29, p. 230.

31 Tessier, *Recueil*, vol. 2, p. 9.

32 Two examples of successive hearings are preserved in *Recueil des chartes de l'abbaye de*

bringing eighty or more people from Mitry to Compiègne, some 60 km away, for 1 July (see fig. 1).

The next case, a few years later than the Mitry hearing, takes us to Burgundy and a county court. The dispute this time is over property:

Bishop Leudo and Count Adalard, *missi dominici* in the county of Autun, came to the villa called Mont, and they caused to come there by the command of the lord king the more noble men of the county and many other men of the said county. And they held an inquiry between Bishop Wulfad [of Bourges] and Count Eccard [of Mâcon] by means of those whom Wulfad there named, and others, through the oath which they had sworn to the lord king Charles, and through the profession which they had sworn in baptism. They promised that they would speak the truth about the villa of Perrecy, which Wulfad said ought to belong to his church.

Wulfad therefore showed charters there, and had them read out, from the times of Kings Childebert and Chilperic, and one from the times of King Pippin in the name of Nibelung, which recorded a *precaria**, to the effect that, by means of the consent of good men (*boni homines*) and by the wish of the bishop of Bourges the said Nibelung had held [Perrecy] as a *precaria* and paid three pounds on the Feast of St Mary [each year].

Eccard there presented a charter of the lord emperor Louis to be read out, and also his own record of a judgement by which, in a general assembly of our lord Charles [the Bald], against the claims of John, he had recovered property, part of that granted in the [precarial] document, which had been taken away from him.

Then through these men, inquiry was made of Leutbald, Ildric, Suavo, Girbald, John, Ildebod, Eriulf, Wulfad, another Leutbald, Honesteus and others, on their oath to tell the truth, whatever truth they knew concerning this case.

Then [Eccard's witnesses] unanimously declared, 'We have never heard our antecedents say, nor have we ourselves ever heard or seen it told as truth, that that villa had been otherwise than belonging to the fisc of the lord Pippin and the lord Charles [the Great] and the lord Louis the emperor, without any dues or any render or any mark of lordship, until the lord emperor gave it by his charter to Eccard'.

Then inquiry was made of Leutbald and Jacob, at whose instance Wulfad had come to that assembly, as to what they knew about the case. They stated that (*sic*), 'We have seen that Eccard had that villa, and we have heard it said that it ought to belong to the church of Wulfad', and that 'many have been hearing this just now since this case was raised, but [they have] not [been hearing] about what truth there ever was in this [claim]'.

Then inquiry was made of Guntfrid, and he said that, 'I have seen [that] Hildebrand [Eccard's father] had it from the royal fisc and then Eccard [had it] as an allod'. And he had 'heard it said that it belonged to Wulfad's church'.

Then inquiry was made of Mauronus and he said that Suavus (*sic*) came to him saying that he had spoken with Odalric his lord and [suggested that] he [Odalric] should acquire that villa and give it to him [Suavus], but in [Odalric's] view there was no case for doing that and he dismissed the idea. Then he spoke with Winfred, another of his lords, and he took the view that there was no case for doing that and likewise dismissed the idea. And then he [Mauronus] heard that Suavus came to Count Odo on that same business, but he did not know what he [Odo] said about it, and he knew nothing further. (App. IX)

The record of this case, incomplete as it clearly is, survived in the now lost

St-Benoît-sur-Loire, ed. M. Prou and A. Vidier, nos. X and XI, pp. 24–7, and nos. XII and XVI, pp. 28–9 and 36–7.

cartulary of the priory of Perrecy, a dependent house of Fleury (see fig. 1)[33]. The bequest of Perrecy to Fleury by Count Eccard in his will in January 876 both reveals the outcome of the case and helps to date it[34]. The appearance in the Perrecy cartulary of eleven documents from the years before 876, relating to this and other estates, implies the existence of a family archive transferred to Fleury on Eccard's death[35]. Perrecy was an important estate and the disputants in this case were magnates[36]. The date must be later than Wulfad's appointment to the archbishopric of Bourges in 866[37].

Wulfad brought the case, and supplied documentary proofs: two Merovingian diplomas* and the record of a precarial grant over a century old[38]. Against these, Eccard offered documents of his own: a diploma of Louis the Pious dated 29 December 839 which confirmed a grant by Pippin I of Aquitaine, and a more recent *notitia*[39]. Oral testimonial proofs were also sought: they were the more needful when the documentary proofs conflicted. Both Wulfad and Eccard presented witnesses to the court: the ten named in the record seem to include those of both parties. The testimony of the defendant's witnesses is given first, followed by that of Wulfad's witnesses. Leutbald, Jacob and Guntfrid supported Bourges's claim straightforwardly, if rather weakly, on hearsay evidence. Mauronus's testimony is more puzzling but may be interpreted as implying that the two named magnates, Odalric and Winfred, and perhaps Count Odo too, in dismissing the idea of acquiring Perrecy, doubted the validity of Eccard's right[40]. Though the record omits the final judgement, we know from Eccard's will, and its fulfilment, that Wulfad's attempt to recover Perrecy for Bourges was unsuccessful.

The timing of Wulfad's bid, and the dating of this text, may be fixed more precisely. Thanks to Levillain's researches, Eccard's family, under the evocative name of 'les Nibelungen historiques', has acquired the status of a paradigm in the historiography of the Frankish aristocracy[41]. Eccard was a major landholder in the Autunois, *c.* 870, whose father had been the local count and sometimes *missus*. If – as seems probable – Wulfad was a close kinsman of the presiding

---

33 *Recueil des chartes de St-Benoît*, pp. lviii–lxvii.
34 'Elemosina Heccardi comitis', *ibid.*, no. XXV, pp. 59–67.
35 *Ibid.*, nos. IX–XIV, XVI, XVII, XX, XXI–XXIV.
36 Perrecy's bounds as given, *ibid.*, no. XXVI, p. 69, can be traced on a modern map. Its extent was roughly 700 km².
37 *Annales de St Bertin*, ed. F. Grat *et al.*, s.a. 866, p. 129.
38 Levillain, 'Nibelungen Historiques', 354, identifies the Merovingian grantors as Childebert III (695–711) and Chilperic II (715–21). The precarial grant was made to Eccard's grandfather, Nibelung, by Pippin, the first Carolingian king of Francia (751–68).
39 The two royal grants are preserved in the dossier: *Recueil des chartes de St-Benoît*, nos. XX and XXI. The *notitia* is not preserved.
40 For the Odalric–Winfred (Humfrid) familial group, see R. Hennebicque, 'Structures familiales et politiques', *Revue Historique*, 265 (1981), 294–301.
41 For further references, see J. L. Nelson, 'Public *Histories* and private history in the work of Nithard', *Speculum*, 60 (1985), 286–9.

missus here, Adalhard, a date towards 875 is likely for his attempt to regain Perrecy[42]. His kinsman had recently won influence with King Charles and his securing of the post of *missus* for the Autunois would have encouraged Wulfad's optimism. In the event, however, Eccard's support held firm, suggesting a residual strength in the 'Nibelungen' network that had much to do with the interest of close kinsmen in the family holdings[43].

The Perrecy hearing is by far the most typical ninth-century case we have so far considered. Records of judgements reached in the *mallus** are the commonest type of evidence of Carolingian dispute settlement. Such records survive in the archives of the churches in whose favour the judgements were given, or, as in the Perrecy case, to whom the once-disputed property was subsequently given by the lay holder. Hübner lists 141 such judgements for ninth-century Francia, seventy-nine of them relating to the West Frankish kingdom. Property disputes, often between lay and ecclesiastical claimants, were the likeliest type of case to be dealt with in the county court. Perhaps because this was the kind of case it handled, the *mallus* was the scene of such eminently 'rational' procedures as adversarial witnessing. Disputes between close kinsmen over shares in a patrimony, or disputes over women involving the honour of individuals and families, were probably more often dealt with out of court, by feud or by arbitration[44]. Property disputes between lesser land-holders may have been heard and settled in the lower courts of the *centenarii**, but no records of their judgements have survived[45]. The county court settlements show the Carolingian system working according to the rules: public officers hearing cases, whether in the county town (*civitas*) or at some other meeting place within the county (as in the Perrecy case), and settling them with the help of the men of the county[46]. Public jurisdiction was assiduously maintained by Carolingian rulers until late in the ninth century, and in some areas well beyond that. The abundant records suggest that the courts were much used, though it is not easy to determine how many 'less powerful free men' availed themselves of the justice to which they were entitled in theory. What the Perrecy case also shows is that the system could readily lend itself to exploitation by the powerful.

---

[42] K.-F. Werner, 'Die Nachkommen Karls des Grossen' in W. Braunfels and H. Beumann (eds.), *Karl der Grosse*, vol. 4, pp. 431–6.

[43] Eccard's family in fact tried to retain the estate after it had been assigned to the monastery of Fleury in his will, treating it 'quasi hereditarias': *Recueil des chartes de St-Benoît*, no. XXX, pp. 83–5.

[44] See Conclusion 'Dispute processes and social structures', below, pp. 232–5.

[45] Carolingian legislation forebade *vicarii* and *centenarii* to hear cases involving property or personal status: *MGH Capit.*, vol. 1, no. 64 (810), cap. 3, p. 153. But for a *vicarius* hearing a property dispute, see above, p. 45. Capitularies refer to centenarial courts and judgements: *Capit.*, vol. 1, nos. 80 (811/813), cap. 4, p. 176; 104 (?803), cap. 4, p. 214; 156 (814–840), cap. 3, p. 315; *Capit.*, vol. 2, no. 193 (829), p. 19. The *centenarius*'s oath, *Capit.*, vol. 2, no. 260 (853), p. 274, shows his rôle in dealing with local crime.

[46] Mont has been identified with a village some 60 km south west of Autun. But the name is common in the Autunois: *Recueil des chartes de St-Benoît*, p. 57, n. 1.

The last case to be considered here takes us to the Loire valley, and to an area quite distinct from the county in governmental terms: the lordship of an ecclesiastical immunity*, that of St Martin, Tours. Here again the evidence consists of a *notitia*, this time clearly dated:

This notice has been lawfully validated, telling how and in whose presence in AD 857 ... while through the whole area of jurisdiction (*dictio*) of the most distinguished abbot Hilduin [of St Martin] and at his order and command his *missi* were striving to do justice, a certain priest of the church of St Hispanus in that area of jurisdiction, a man called Nortbert, came into the presence of Saramian, provost of the community of St Martin, and of other noble men of that same lordship (*potestas*) on 10 June and made complaint as follows: a property of the church of St Hispanus, which was listed along with other estates in the document of that church, and which had been under his control (*potestas*) since the death of his uncle Isaiah who had bought that property, and which he had for a long time possessed lawfully on behalf of that church on the villa of Malebuxis, had been unjustly taken away from St Hispanus's control through the action of Autbert and his sister Agintrude and her husband Amalgar.

Then Saraman (*sic*) the provost ordered that those persons who were in possession of that property should show their title deeds (*auctoritates*) at the appointed assembly in his presence. These title deeds they then brought before his sight and that of other noble men at Tours. But they could not settle the issue because of the absence of the neighbours to whom the case was known. It was therefore decided there that the case should be settled by judgement of the neighbours and of other *boni homines* at that villa to which the disputed property belonged.

A little while later, on 30 July, Saraman the provost above-named, with other clergy of the flock of St Martin, and other good men, came to the villa of Briusgalus to which the above-mentioned property belonged. There, on the orders of his lord, he was to settle and deal with various cases. And they sat in the forecourt of the church for the convenience of the assembly of important persons. The time came for discussing this dispute. Then it was adjudged there by many noble men and by the *coloni* whose names are put in below, that Nortbert the priest should appoint his advocate, and the above-named persons [in possession of the property] should present their title deeds.

Soon one of them, Autbert, by God's inspiration it seemed, openly confessed that their title deeds were false. And to avoid having to go to Hell because of this, he refused to persist in his obstinacy, and he threw the title deeds down on the altar of St Hispanus. Then the above-named Amalgar, acting on behalf of his wife Agintrude, accused Autbert of unjustly disputing [the validity of] his wife's title deeds.

All those who were there sitting, or standing by (*adstantes**), were amazed at this. They discussed the matter for a long time. [They decided that] Autbert should show his documents publicly. This he did. But he was the first to testify that [both of them], that is, the one which he presented as being in the name of Isaiah, and the one which had been drawn up deceitfully at Tours, were found publicly, when read out, to be false. The reason was that those whose names were attached [to the first document], that is Notfred and Geroin, gave witness on oath that they had in no way confirmed it at any time, nor had it ever been corroborated. Moreover, the scribe of that document was also present, and he there admitted openly that he had written that document but had not corroborated it. So too nearly all the *coloni* gave witness that they had not seen it being corroborated, nor were the names written down there those of *coloni* of that villa of which the disputed property formed part, but they were from another villa which was not that of the *coloni* whose names were recorded.

Thereupon, by the judgement of all present, Amalgar held the charters in his hand and was asked formally by those there sitting whether he could produce witnesses from that lordship who would declare on oath that those documents were true. He straightaway admitted openly that he could not.

Then the woman Agintrude protested: [she said] that it was through fear of the priest [Nortbert] that they were unable to find witnesses for this matter, and she named certain *coloni* who, she said, were knowledgeable about this case.

Then the provost ordered relics to be brought forward, and he named the following *coloni* [nine names follow] and he caused many others to swear, by God and by their christianity and their good faith and the relics of the saints there present, [to say] whether that document, namely the title of sale in favour of Agintrude's side, had been lawfully and rightly corroborated; whether she had lawful tenure; and whether that property ought to belong by right to the priest Nortbert, representing St Hispanus, rather than to Agintrude. To these questions, each and every one called to witness straightaway testified on oath in the same way: that that title of sale had not been corroborated rightly, but fraudulently, and so could not confer rightful tenure; likewise that that document which they had obtained under false pretences at Tours was useless and of no effect; and that that property rightfully belonged to St Hispanus's side rather than to Agintrude's side.

Then Amalgar admitted openly that he had been unable to supply witnesses there [at Tours] or thereafter, and that therefore those documents which he held were of no effect.

Then, by judgement of all there present, the provost Saraman asked Otbert, the advocate of Nortbert the priest, if he could prove false the documents which Amalgar still held in his hand. He replied immediately that he could prove them utterly false. Then, by the right above established and with the witnesses above noted, he made [the documents] utterly false by piercing them there in Amalgar's hands and thus tearing them through, as it had been adjudged and decided in his favour by all.

That property is at the villa called Malebuxis. The late Isaiah the priest bought it from Amalbert after paying his price, and it is described with its boundaries in the title of sale.

Thus, now that that property had rightly been returned to St Hispanus's side by the judgement of all there sitting or standing by, and vindicated by their counsel, Nortbert the priest thought that he should receive this *notitia* of the outcome, so that . . . it should be clear in future how rightly and reasonably the case had been tried and settled by many noble men, some of whom are noted here.

I Saraman the provost have subscribed. I Autbert the priest have subscribed. I Azaneus the deacon have subscribed. I Gislemar the acolyte have subscribed. I Gislar the subdeacon have subscribed. Sign ✠ of Nautfred the judge. Sign ✠ of Gervin. S. [three names]. S. ✠ Restodonus. S. [two names]. (App. X)

This text, whose style links it with Neustrian formularies, contains one of the most detailed extant accounts of a ninth-century dispute settlement[47]. Its date fits the abbacy of Hilduin at St Martin, Tours, and shows, interestingly, an energetic local potentate seeing to the smooth running of the machinery of justice in this lordship in the very year when, according to the Annals of St Bertin, our main narrative source for the West Frankish kingdom, Vikings ravaged widely in the Touraine and aristocratic rebels in Neustria and Aquitaine 'committed many acts of violence'[48]. Our case had arisen from the claim of a priest, Nortbert, to have

---

[47] See above, n. 5 and also K. Nehlsen-von Stryk, *Die boni homines des frühen Mittelalters*, pp. 143–5.
[48] For Hilduin's career, see J. Fleckenstein, *Die Hofkapelle*, pp. 144–5. For the disturbances of 857, see *Annales de St Bertin*, s.a. 857, p. 75.

inherited some property from his uncle, the priest Isaiah. Nortbert's opponents claimed that Isaiah had sold the property to Agintrude, sister of Autbert. The text is ambiguous, or inconsistent, on the woman's legal standing: at first, her brother and husband took all the action, and only halfway through the account does it emerge that the disputed property was in fact held by Agintrude. Women were held unfit to act as witnesses in Frankish law, and were usually legally represented by male kin or advocates, though some ninth-century women shocked male contemporaries by fighting their own legal battles in court[49].

The case fell into three stages. The first turned on documentary proof. Nortbert came before the court during its judicial tour, at an unnamed place, and claimed that the property figured on a list of his church's estates. The president of the court required the defendants to present title deeds at a subsequent hearing at Tours. At this second stage, it transpired that documentary proof was insufficient without further oral testimony, so the case was again adjourned, to a third hearing to be held this time on the villa where the disputed property lay[50]. At this third stage, it emerged that the documentary proofs themselves were of questionable validity, and this issue could be settled only by the testimony of local free men (*coloni*) whose holdings were presumably on the disputed property. It was their (unsworn) statements, and the admission of the scribe of the earlier of the two documents presented by the defendants, together with the testimony of two named witnesses, which established the legal defect in both documents. The defendants failed to produce contrary proof, but one of them, Agintrude, assailed the witnesses' reliability. At this point, the president of the court demanded sworn testimony from all the *coloni* witnesses 'and many others'. Once the defendants' documentary proof had fallen as a result of this further testimony, the judgement followed: the plaintiff had to perform a ritual cancellation of the false documents by a *transpunctio* – a piercing through of the parchment before the court[51].

Collective judgement is a striking feature of this case. As in the seventh- and eighth-century Neustrian formularies, the *boni homines* of the neighbourhood (who included clergy as well as laymen of standing) participated in settling the issues of proof and in the final decision of the court. But these men, whom the author of our text seems at one point to identify as *nobiles viri* ('noble men'), were not the only ones to share in judging: so too did the 'neighbours', the *coloni* whose testimony was acknowledged by both sides as definitive, for it was they who, in Agintrude's words, were 'knowledgeable (*periti*) in this case'. They did not attest

---

49 Council of Nantes (895), cap. 19, *Sacrorum Conciliorum collectio*, ed. J. D. Mansi, vol. 18, cols. 171–2: 'shameless women', later specified as 'nuns and widows', were attending assemblies and discussing men's disputes.

50 The villa 'Briusgalus' can perhaps be identified with 'Burgogalus' where a chapel of St Hispanus belonged to St Martin, Tours, in 861: Tessier, *Recueil*, vol. 2, no. 239, p. 37. Tessier, *Recueil*, vol. 3, pp. 282, n. 1, and 384, appears to identify the place as Saint-Épain (dép. Indre-et-Loire).

51 Brunner, *Rechtsgeschichte*, 2nd edn, vol. 2, pp. 562–3.

the notice of the judgement, however; that was the privilege of the 'noble men', first the provost and five others in clerical orders, all able to subscribe the document, then a 'judge' (*iudex**) and seven other laymen who simply put their hands to the text, with or without the sign of the cross. These laymen are given no title, but they look like *scabini*.

Agintrude lost on a technicality: her title of purchase had been incorrectly corroborated, that is, it lacked the attestations of specified witnesses. Hence the second document involved, apparently a confirmation of the first, was also invalidated. The nature of the second document is never made explicit in our text. But it was evidently significant that it was 'made' and 'obtained' at Tours, the centre of the 'area of jurisdiction' mentioned at the beginning of the text. So it looks like a confirmatory grant by the holder of the lordship, St Martin's deputy. The impression given is that such confirmations of private transactions were routine, and this impression is reinforced by the familiarity of *coloni* with the technicalities of legal documents. Their *peritia* included a capacity to spot false attestations.

In these procedures there was much formality and some ritual. But those characteristics did not preclude what modern historians are prone to label 'rational proofs', and a shift of locale dictated by the need for informed witnesses. The author of the *notitia*, who knew his legal forms, was a cleric in the provost's entourage and an experienced recorder of the judgements wrought at Abbot Hilduin's behest[52]. The document conveys the impact of Hilduin's justice, but at the same time stresses the participation in its exercise of all the free men in the lordship. This idealized picture of local consensus and smooth-running procedure is belied by a single piece of information: Agintrude's allegation that the witnesses had been intimidated by her priest-opponent. Only at this point does our author identify Agintrude as 'the woman': the redundant label (she bore an unequivocally female name and had already been identified as Amalgar's wife and Autbert's sister) perhaps reveals the prejudice of a male, and clerical, opponent for whom 'justice' self-evidently coincided with ecclesiastical interests. We may recall that the priest hosted the court, for its 'convenience', in the forecourt of his church.

The cases considered above help us to reassess the stereotypes with which I began. The view from the twelfth century clearly will not do: our cases suggest that witnesses to fact were routinely required and that documentary proofs were commonly used. These impressions are confirmed by a wider survey of Hübner's 257 ninth-century judgements: and these also show oath-helping* used very seldom, and the ordeal not once. Our cases indicate, further, that the procedure was flexible within the framework of acceptable proofs: additional hearings could

[52] P. Gasnault, 'Les actes privés', *Bibliothèque de l'École des Chartes*, 112 (1954), 37.

be arranged, sometimes with a shift of locale, to enable more testimonies to be collected from knowledgeable neighbours. While the number of participants in hearings could vary greatly, collective judgement was the rule. Ritual elements were not substitutes for, but reinforced, decision-making based on testimonial and documentary proofs. Oaths operated no more, and no less, as a kind of judgement of God in the ninth than in the twentieth century: they solemnized proceedings and reduced the risk of perjury[53].

The view from the capitularies also needs modifying. Some ninth-century counts may have had copies of law codes or capitularies, and been able to read them, but there is a striking absence of reference to the use of written law in the records of actual cases from the Carolingian empire north of the Alps[54]. Admittedly in a very small number of cases, all of them from regions outside Francia proper, an individual identifies himself as a user of Frankish or Salic Law: but this may be understood as little more than a symbolic statement of personal status in provinces where the memory of Frankish conquest or domination was still so vivid in the ninth century that to assert one's Frankishness was to claim membership of the élite, the ruling *gens* (people)[55]. The case material shows that the customary norms and procedures actually applied did not differ perceptibly in the Rhône valley or the Midi from those in Neustria or Francia. The resemblances seem to have resulted not from a standardization of legal practice imposed by rulers, but from underlying similarities of social structure, and inherited traditions and values, Roman and Christian, common to all areas. Recourse to the collective judgement of 'the more noble and the more truthful' was prescribed and legitimated by custom and prudential considerations alike[56]. There was never any formal abrogation of the principle of the personality of law; it withered away. Strengthened by the superstructure of Carolingian government, the law of the locality, the *lex terrae*, gained a new currency[57].

Ganshof assigned a central place to the Carolingian inquest in terms of both greater rationalization and more state control of justice. Certainly, one side of the inquest's ancestry could be traced, respectably, to the right of the Roman imperial fisc to pursue claims against local misappropriations of public lands or funds[58]. Charlemagne's *missi* too used the inquest so vigorously for this purpose that the jurors empanelled to testify to Crown rights had to be offered protection

---

[53] Cf. S. Reynolds, *Kingdoms and Communities in Western Europe, 900–1300*, pp. 25–6.

[54] R. McKitterick, 'Some Carolingian law-books' in B. Tierney and P. Linehan (eds.), *Authority and Power: Studies on Medieval Law and Government*, pp. 13–28; Nelson, 'Public *Histories*', 256–60, 282–5. Compare P. Wormald, '*Lex Scripta and Verbum Regis*: Legislation and Germanic Kingship' in P. Sawyer and I. N. Wood (eds.), *Early Medieval Kingship*, pp. 119–23.

[55] For instance, in *Recueil des Chartes de Cluny*, ed. A. Bruel, vol. 1, no. 15, p. 18. See also A. Lewis, *The Development of Southern French and Catalan Society*, pp. 59–60, 126, 157.

[56] Tessier, *Recueil*, vol. 2, no. 401, p. 395. Cf. Reynolds, *Kingdoms and Communities*, pp. 23–38.

[57] *MGH Capit.*, vol. 1, no. 18 (768), p. 43; *Capit*, vol. 2, no. 273 (864), cap. 20, pp. 318–19.

[58] Brunner, *Rechtsgeschichte*, 2nd edn, vol. 2, pp. 690–1.

against the reprisals of resentful neighbours whose claims had been denied[59]. But on the other side, the inquest's antecedents were distinctly shadier from Ganshof's point of view: they lay, according to Van Caenegem, 'in some ancient form of consultation of the notables of the neighbourhood', particularly relevant in the case of criminal justice[60]. If Van Caenegem is right, then there would be no reason to believe that Charlemagne brought the inquest back from Italy after his conquest of the Lombard kingdom in 773[61]. But perhaps the question of origins need not be posed in terms of stark alternatives: of Roman *fora* or Germanic forests. It must have been obvious to powerful Frankish kings that the only way they could impinge on dispute settlement at local level was to mobilize local opinion and local sanctions, which meant, in practice, co-operating with, as well as containing, local power.

Such co-operation is clearest in the Carolingians' offering of the inquest as a privilege to favoured recipients. Louis the Pious granted all churches the right to use the inquest process when claiming property under the thirty-year rule[62]. This was a valuable concession because the main threat to a church's lands in the ninth century came from precisely those lay neighbours who might well be able to 'fix' a hearing's outcome through sheer weight of partial witnesses in the *mallus*. Our Perrecy case seems to offer an example. But as long as *missi* were appointed by the king, sometimes with instructions to offer aid and solace to a particular church's advocate, as long as the royal tribunal functioned as a court of appeal, and as long as royal protection could be extended to impartial witnesses, a church stood a chance of success[63]. Most of the nineteen inquest cases listed by Ganshof record the victories of ecclesiastical institutions in property disputes[64].

Perhaps, in any case, too sharp a line ought not to be drawn between the inquest and adversarial witnessing. Were the *coloni* empanelled to testify in our Tours case those named by Agintrude, or were they chosen by the president of the court? And in how many cases – that of the Mitry peasants, for instance – would that have made any difference to the outcome? Similarly, it is difficult to detect from the case material that *scabini* were any more 'expert' than *rachymburgi*: *notitiae* do not always distinguish between the two terms[65].

The 'disintegration' of the *pagus* (county) has been identified as a post-Carolingian phenomenon, symptom of the 'feudal mutation' of the tenth

---

[59] *MGH Capit.*, vol. 1, nos. 33 (802), cap. 31, p. 97; 34 (802), cap. 16, p. 101.

[60] Van Caenegem, 'La Preuve dans le Droit du moyen âge occidental', pp. 707–8.

[61] But see D. Bullough, '*Europae Pater*: Charlemagne and his achievement in the light of recent scholarship', *Eng. Hist. Rev.*, 85 (1970), 92–6.

[62] *MGH Capit.*, vol. 2, no. 191 (829), cap. 8, p. 13.

[63] E.g. Tessier, *Recueil*, vol. 2, no. 375, p. 336.

[64] Ganshof, 'La Preuve dans le Droit franc', p. 96, n. 54. Most of the other cases involve claims of the fisc.

[65] F. Estey, 'The *Scabini* and the Local Courts', *Speculum*, 26 (1951). *MGH Capit.*, vol. 2, no. 192 (829), cap. 2, p. 15, orders *missi* to throw out bad *scabini* and choose good ones 'totius populi consensu'.

century, symbolic of a collapse of public authority and justice[66]. The implied contrast is with the 'integration' of the Carolingian *pagus*, as exemplified, presumably, in the settlement of disputes like that between Wulfad and Eccard, with massed *pagenses** attending a county court at a villa in the countryside of the Autunois. Yet, for all the apparatus of public justice and a *missus* dispatched from the palace, the outcome in that case was swayed by one party's predominant local influence. It is hard to believe that such influence was less pervasive in centenarial courts. A castle is more glamorous than a stockade; but the function of a ninth-century count's fortified house on a villa may have differed little from that of a tenth-century count's keep, so often taken to epitomize private or seigneurial justice[67]. Of course there is a difference between, on the one hand, a Carolingian count who attends the king's court, who may even be a royal appointee and must sometimes yield his presidential seat in the county court to a royal *missus*, and on the other hand, the tenth-century ('feudal') count who stays in the county he inherited, has little if any contact with the king and is himself the only local wielder of even nominally delegated royal authority. But the difference here is one of political relations, and communications, at the highest level: between king and aristocracy. In the county itself, or out in the villas of the countryside, local power in the ninth century operated with little demonstrable intrusion from outside and above.

The picture of 'integrated' Carolingian county dissolves a little further if we add to it records like that of the Tours case. Here justice was in the hands of the holder of an immunity: the great monastery and landlord of St Martin, Tours. We can only guess at how many immunities blotted our imaginary tidy map of comital jurisdictions. Though virtually all the evidence relates to ecclesiastical immunities, lay *potentes* could hold them too[68]. In either case, what was involved was local lordship recognized and legitimized by royal concession. The Tours case shows that here public jurisdiction *was* local lordship. The coexistence of regalian and seigneurial rights was already characteristic of the Carolingian period: the view from the capitularies has to accommodate both.

It will also have to accommodate a large participatory element in ninth-century legal practice. Such participation cannot be assumed to have operated as a collective restraint on local power or a collective resistance to central authority. As our Mitry case shows, participation by interest groups is not the same thing as the collective action of whole village communities, while the Tours case suggests that an aura of collective judgement may be the instrument of a powerful interested party. Local opinion, though poorly registered in the record, may have had more genuine impact on the outcome of the Perrecy case than on any of the

---

[66] J.-F. Lemarignier, 'La Dislocation du *pagus*' in *Mélanges dédiés à L. Halphen*, pp. 401–10; J.-P. Poly and E. Bournazel, *La Mutation féodale*, pp. 59–103.
[67] For a *casa firmissima*, see *Annales de St Bertin*, s.a. 868, p. 141.
[68] For example, *MGH Capit.*, vol. 2, no. 273 (864), cap. 18, p. 317.

others dealt with in this paper. In all our cases, however, political influences were at work. It was in a broader administrative context that Hincmar of Rheims observed of judges, that is, counts and their deputies, 'when they hope for profit of some kind, they invoke [customary] law, but when they reckon there's no advantage to be had there, they seek refuge in capitularies: thus it comes about that neither capitularies nor law are properly observed'[69]. Hincmar knew that those who were in theory presidents of courts and guardians of 'Right' could, even with law-book in hand, sway judgements to suit their *own* book.

The Fleury monks we began with seem to have agreed with Hincmar here. A second Fleury case makes the point explicitly. Again involved in a dispute over serfs, this time with St Denis, Fleury and its opponent each assembled a battery of 'masters of the law, and judges' to witness for them[70]. Predictably, the experts of the two sides disagreed. It was finally decided, following the procedure in a capitulary cited earlier in this paper, to choose one witness from each side to fight it out 'and so put an end to the dispute'[71]. But just when everyone had agreed, reports our Fleury source with evident regret, 'a legal expert from the Gâtinais, with an appropriately beast-like name, who was on St Denis's side and had been corrupted by a gift, argued that combat was not right for ecclesiastical witnesses, and that representatives of the two sides should instead negotiate an agreement to divide the serfs between them[72]. The deputy count favoured this advice . . . and bent the whole court to that view.' So a settlement was what Fleury had to swallow – its patron St Benedict contenting himself this time, by way of revenge, with striking dumb the beast-like expert (we can surely recognize Lupus of Ferrières!) 'for almost a month'[73].

This story of legal compromise comes from a book of miracles. The judicial records, by their very nature, stress adversarial procedure: winners and losers. Agreements, mediations and arbitrations must have resolved very many ninth-century disputes, but either they were unrecorded, or the records have been lost, partly because churches, as disputants, were more interested in victory than in compromise. Churchmen are far more often to be found, in literally hundreds of early medieval cases, asserting rights to dues, as Cormery did with the men of Antoigné, or worrying away at old property claims, as Bourges did with Perrecy, than as the peace-makers of clerical ideology[74]. It must sometimes have happened in the ninth century, as later, that 'agreement prevailed over law, love

---

[69] *Ad Episcopos Regni*, ch. 15, *Patrologia Latina*, ed. J. P. Migne, vol. 125, col. 1,016.
[70] Adrevald of Fleury, *Ex Miraculis S. Benedicti*, ch. 25.
[71] Above p. 47 and n. 15.
[72] The expert was correct: the abolition of the cross ordeal shortly afterwards had brought precisely this modification: *MGH Capit.*, vol. 1, no. 139 (818/819), cap. 10, pp. 282–3.
[73] See further V. H. Galbraith, 'The Death of a Champion' in R. W. Hunt, W. A. Pantin and R. W. Southern (eds.), *Studies in Medieval History*, pp. 288–9. Ferrières was in the Gâtinais (dép. Loiret, Seine-et-Marne).
[74] Cf. E. James, '*Beati pacifici*: bishops and the law' in J. Bossy (ed.), *Disputes and Settlements*.

over judgement'[75]. Yet the spirit of the Carolingian records is better (if uniquely) captured in Agintrude's perception that the witnesses who in the end betrayed her were driven, not by love, but by 'fear of the priest'.

[75] Cf. M. Clanchy, 'Law and love in the middle ages' in J. Bossy (ed.), *Disputes and Settlements*.

4

People and places in dispute in ninth-century Brittany

WENDY DAVIES

The records of dispute and dispute settlement from northern Europe, although few by comparison with those of the South, include an unusually large set of useful material in the collection of charters relating to the monastery of Redon in eastern Brittany. Redon, on the River Vilaine, 65 km south-west of Rennes, was founded in 832 and soon gained the patronage of the Carolingian emperor Louis and of his representative in Brittany, Nominoe. It received many small grants of property in its neighbourhood in the decades following the foundation, and records of the grants, along with other documents, were copied in the eleventh century into the *Cartulaire de Redon*[1].

This cartulary contains 283 charters* of the ninth and early tenth centuries; and a further sixty-two charters, which may not have been included in the medieval cartulary, are known from early modern transcripts[2]. Three-quarters of these charters relate to the forty years following the monastery's foundation and constitute – for the ninth century – an unusually large number of documents to deal with a small region[3]. The lands with which the charters are concerned lie between Rennes, Nantes and Vannes, but most of the properties fall within 40 km of Redon itself (fig. 2). Many of the grants were of small areas (in the order of

---

[1] I have discussed several aspects of the dispute material in 'Disputes, their conduct and their settlement', *Hist. and Anth.*, 1, pt 2 (1985) and 'Suretyship in the *Cartulaire de Redon*' in T. Charles-Edwards, M. E. Owen, D. Walters (eds.), *Lawyers and Laymen*. In this present paper I summarize those discussions and only deal in detail with other aspects. The material in the latter part of the paper depends on analysis of the results of programs run on my Redon database, filed on the mainframe computers at University College London. I am indebted to the British Academy for financial support in setting up the database and to the staff of UCL Computer Centre, and in particular to Chris Horsburgh, for considerable assistance in creating the database and for writing the appropriate programs. I am also grateful to Rosamond McKitterick for her comments on a draft of this paper.

[2] *Cartulaire de Redon*, ed. A. de Courson (hereafter *CR*, with charters cited by number); most of the additional charters are printed by de Courson in an Appendix to *CR* and the rest can be found in H. Morice, *Mémoires pour servir de preuves*, vol. 1, cols. 265, 271f, 272, 295, 297, 308; the transcripts from which they were printed can sometimes be identified but many are difficult to locate.

[3] The density of coverage only seems to be paralleled by east Frankish collections such as those of St Gallen; *Urkundenbuch der Abtei Sanct Gallen*, ed. H. Wartmann, vols. 1 and 2. See further Nelson above, pp. 45–6, for comment on other Frankish material of the same period.

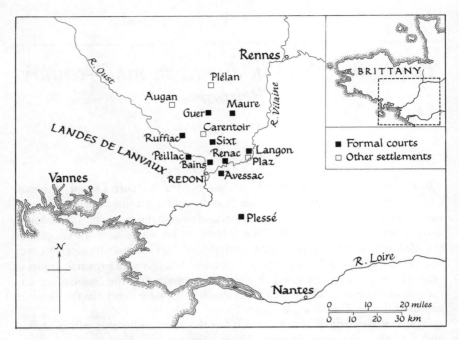

2 Formal and informal courts in the *pays de Redon*

10–25 hectares), and the donors, vendors and plaintiffs of the records were
peasant farmers: most of the individuals mentioned worked the land themselves
and confined their business to their own village communities[4]. The collection,
then, is largely a collection of private, rather than government, acts and is
particularly valuable in allowing insight into the workings and relationships of
peasant communities[5]. It is also valuable in the range of its material: since many
properties passed to Redon together with extant documentation about them, the
collection includes records from at least one generation previous to 832 and
records of transactions to which Redon was not party, both before 832 and after[6].
It therefore preserves far more than a dossier of grants to the monastery.

The area which is most frequently the subject of the charters was well worked
in the early middle ages, largely for arable production, and had many settlements.
Agrarian society was organized in village-based units, known as *plebes* in Latin

---

[4] For detailed discussion see my forthcoming book, *Villages, Villagers*.

[5] See below, pp. 78–82, for discussion of the means and social status of the men of these records.

[6] This is not unknown in other charter collections of the same period, although the proportion in *CR*
is notable; cf. *Cartulaire de Beaulieu*, ed. M. Deloche, which includes six charters previous to
Beaulieu's foundation date of 855; the material in the several Cluny collections includes several
score of records from the generation before the foundation, that is, from the 870s onwards, *Recueil
des chartes de l'abbaye de Cluny*, ed. A. Bruel, vol. 1. See also above, p. 54.

and as some similar-sounding term in the vernacular (hence Medieval Breton *plou*, a loanword from Latin *plebem*). Men referred to themselves as members of this or that *plebs* and transactions might be formally notified to the men of the *plebs*, although by the ninth century the term was used to refer to the land inhabited by the group as well as to the group itself. The territories of the *plebes* were quite small, ranging from 3 to 10 km across (but were often about 5 km): on the accompanying figure, Ruffiac and Carentoir are neighbouring *plebes*, as are Langon and Renac, Augan and Guer (fig. 2)[7]. Each *plebs* appears to have had its own officer for public business, called a machtiern*. This man presided over transactions involving the transfer of property rights, which were performed in public; he might also be approached to find a solution for village problems, and accordingly might order an investigation or preside over any consequent hearing[8]. He was usually the most powerful character in the locality and in practice might serve several *plebes* and have relations who served neighbouring communities. Characteristically he lived at a distinctive type of settlement, away from the nucleated focus of the *plebs*, known as the *lis*.

Although the material in the Redon cartulary is exceptionally useful as evidence of social process at village level, it also allows some glimpses into a wider world. There was an aristocracy, of counts and major landowners, although there were few large-scale property interests in these particular *plebes* until the extension of those of Redon itself. There was also a Breton ruler (the *princeps*), at least from *c.* 830, when the emperor Louis appointed the Breton Nominoe as his representative for government, following a series of Carolingian expeditions across the country. Thereafter, the whole of modern Brittany, and sometimes some of the lands to the east of it, seems to have been ruled as a single polity, although rule was sometimes shared by two leaders. The relationship of these rulers with the Carolingians was unstable, for Nominoe rebelled in the early 840s; afterwards some of the rulers – notably Salomon (*princeps* 857–73) in the 860s and early 870s – were effectively independent[9]. Since the *principes* favoured Redon with their patronage and especial protection, their presence was sometimes felt in the village communities considered here.

There are forty-nine ninth-century texts in the Redon collection which record dispute settlement processes, although six make only indirect reference to

---

[7] For further discussion of the *plebs* see my 'Priests and rural communities', *Études Celtiques*, 20 (1983), 177–80.

[8] See further below, pp. 72–3; for machtierns see also my 'On the distribution of political power' in M. Gibson, J. Nelson, D. Ganz (eds.), *Charles the Bald*, and M. Planiol, *Histoire des Institutions*, vol. 2, pp. 63–96.

[9] The relevant sources for the political history of this period are cited by A. Le Moyne de La Borderie, *Histoire de Bretagne*, vol. 2, pp. 3–122; interpretations differ nowadays. For more recent consideration see A. Chédeville and H. Guillotel, *La Bretagne des saints et des rois, V^e–Xe siècle*, pp. 201–332.

them[10]. These average five per decade between 832 and *c.* 880 but there are at least eleven from the 860s and a further eight, which cannot be dated more precisely than to the abbacy of Conuuoion (832–68), are probably also from the 860s. There are also four from the generation before the foundation of Redon and four that occurred after *c.* 880. The records do not conform to a standard pattern: some briefly indicate the essential details of a judgement; others have a narrative of the events leading up to a case, or of a settlement, or of proceedings in court, the latter sometimes including what look like verbatim reports; others are too cryptic to make much sense. Despite the variety of recording practice, it seems to have been usual to record court proceedings. Although there is only occasional mention of a notary, many of the Ruffiac and Carentoir records – of transactions as well as of disputes – conclude with a statement of the writer's identity and make it clear that the task of making a written record *was* someone's responsibility. Haeldetuuid, for example, cleric then abbot, recorded at least eighteen transactions of sale and pledge in Ruffiac and Carentoir (and also one in Pleucadeuc) between 821 and *c.* 850, and he was preceded as recorder by the cleric Latmoet[11].

Twenty-three individuals are named as scribes in the complete corpus of ninth-century records and this has some bearing on the recording of disputes[12]. Of the twenty-three scribes, three seem to have been working for Redon, since they either were termed monks or produced records for a wide range of locations in which Redon had interests[13]. The rest of the scribes are notable for their limited range: there were some at major centres like Angers and Nantes but the others only appeared in one of the *plebes* of, for example, Laillé, Grandchamp or Derval in the more Frankish East or at Médréac, Augan or Peillac in the more Breton West (see fig. 3). Records were made at seven of these places, and at another unidentified place, *before* 832 (by nine of the scribes) and therefore *cannot*

---

[10] Princely courts: *CR* 21, 29, 105, 107, 108, 215, 216, 242, 247, possibly 258, 274, A40, A53. Formal, local courts: 46, 47, 61, 96, 106, 124, 129, 139, 147, 162, 180, 191, 192, 271, A3, A20. Informal, local meetings: 32, 56, 88, 103, 118, 127, 144, 163, 184, 185, 190, 195, 202, 205, possibly 236, 237, 246, 261, possibly 265, 267. R. Hübner, 'Gerichtsurkunden', *ZRG, Germ. Abt.*, 12 (1891), omitted the twenty records of settlement in which no judgement was given.

[11] Haeldetuuid is named as scribe in *CR* 34, 53, 58, 64, 111, 112, 121, 131, 133, 143, 146, 148, 152, 153, 155, 160, 171, 193, 196, 198, 220, 255, 264, A11. Transactions of pledge were those in which a loan of cash was raised using landed property as security; see my 'Suretyship'.

[12] The scribes are Agnus, Benignus, Bernarius, Condeloc, Conuuoion, Cumdelu, Daramnus, Frodebert, Fulcric, Gallianus, Gundobald, Hilric, Landebert, Lathoiarn, Letaldus, Liberius, Mailon, Otbert, Ratuuethen, Siguinus, Tethion, Tuthouuen. The usual way of referring to a scribe is 'N scripsit'. Notaries are named in *CR* A6, A28, apparently attached to the Carolingian court.

[13] Fulcric (*CR* 69, 234); Liberius (213, 260); Conuuoion (128, 177, 179, A1, A4). In the case of Haeldetuuid it might be argued that he ended his life working for Redon: although his association with Ruffiac and Carentoir was consistent for about twenty-five years, from the middle of the 840s he also made records for the Bains and Renac area; *CR* 53, 121, A11 (although 58, dated to 838, seems to refer to Brain; if so, it is anomalous). We do know of several local priests who retired to Redon in old age, so the pattern is quite credible.

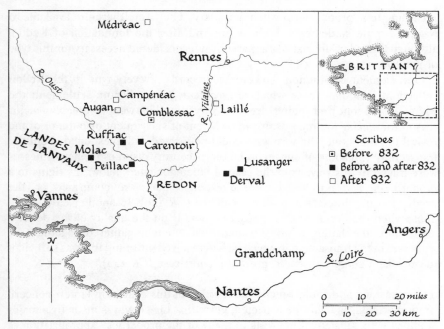

3 Scribes in the *pays de Redon*

have been made using services provided by Redon. Hence, scribal facilities were available at an early date in at least Molac, Ruffiac and Carentoir (both served by one scribe), Comblessac, Peillac, Derval and Lusanger. Not surprisingly, at least four of the early scribes – like Haeldetuuid and Latmoet – were in orders, termed priest or cleric: acting as scribe for local business may have been a normal part of the priests' duties in the *plebs*, although the records were sometimes made at the machtiern's residence, the *lis*, which occasionally seems to have functioned as an office for the performance of local business[14]. Now, more than half of the records that name scribes deal with sales, and these records have a consistency in form and *formulae** which is notably absent from the dispute records. In effect there seems to have been provision of secretarial services for the transfer of property rights in these villages, perhaps the consequence of a need to record sales correctly[15]. So, there were skilled people in the villages, who could write

---

[14] *CR* 34, 112, 152, 255; cf. R. McKitterick, *The Carolingians and the written word*, ch. 4.

[15] A concern that the correct legal procedure should be followed in cases of sale is indicated at least by the unprovenanced 'Excerpta de libris Romanorum et Francorum', cl. A18–20, in *The Irish Penitentials*, ed. L. Bieler, p. 140; see further my 'Suretyship', pp. 85–6. (This text may be Breton but if not it is likely to derive from Anjou or Maine; it may be of sixth-, seventh- or eighth-century date.) See L. Fleuriot, 'Un fragment en Latin de très anciennes lois bretonnes', *Ann. de Bret.*, 78 (1971) and D. Dumville, 'On the dating of the early Breton lawcodes', *Ét. Celt.*, 21 (1984).

according to a 'proper' form when necessary. They were therefore available to record dispute settlements, both before and after the foundation of Redon, although a standard format was apparently not considered necessary for this type of record.

One element is common, however, to records of every type in the Redon collection, including those which are explicitly about dispute settlement: the witnesses of public proceedings are listed very fully. This was presumably a major reason for *making* the records, for in the event of subsequent dispute, or of the revival of an old one, the witnesses could be located and questioned about the transaction[16]. In some of our recorded ninth-century disputes former witnesses were traced in this way, as in the case of Uuetenoc cited below: his rights to a property he had purchased were questioned but were confirmed on the production of witnesses and other evidence (*CR* 139). In another case of the 860s, when the donor of a property cast doubts on the quality of the donee's ownership, the latter, a priest called Maenuueten, gathered together the witnesses of the transaction in which he had received the grant; this was sufficient to provoke a compromise and prevent a court case (*CR* 144).

The occasions of dispute which are recorded in this collection largely concern property rights, as might be expected, given that the copy was made by a major landlord with substantial interests in many of the properties. Appropriation of land or income from the monastery of Redon is the commonest cause of dispute. Accusations were made by the abbot (or occasionally by his deputies) against men who continued to work and profit from properties given to Redon by their kinsmen; against others who encroached on the monastery's land, often when it was sharing a boundary with their own; against tenants who had defaulted on the payment of rent; and occasionally against men who went to monastic property, stole stock and attacked the farmers who lived there. These account for about half of the cases. Nearly as common, however, are records of disputes within lay families, especially disputes about the allocation of property rights between members of the family and about powers to alienate individual shares. Hence, brothers quarrelled with brothers, and cousins with cousins. In addition to these types of case there are records of lay quarrels in which there seems to have been neither strong family nor monastic interest; and, rarely, there are accounts of the procedures that followed assault and killing[17].

The means of arriving at a settlement in these disputes varied in accordance

---

16 See my 'Latin charter tradition' in D. Whitelock, R. McKitterick, D. Dumville (eds.), *Ireland in Early Mediaeval Europe*, pp. 275f, for the importance of witnesses to registration of property transfer in late Roman Europe.

17 See my 'Disputes' for full discussion of the subject of this paragraph and for what follows in the succeeding few pages. Cf. 'Gesta Sanctorum Rotonensium', I. viii, in L. d'Achéry, *Acta Sanctorum ord. s. Benedicti*, ed. J. Mabillon, for a comparable ninth-century Redon case recorded in a Saints' Life: Abbot Conuuoion offered Risuueten 20 *solidi** to withdraw a claim on hereditary lands.

with the status of the parties. In normal circumstances, when a dispute arose, requests to solve the problem might be made to political leaders – notably to the *princeps* but also to machtierns, counts and, very occasionally, village elders. But there were also other methods of initiating settlement proceedings: sometimes a grievance appears to have had its first airing in court, recorded in such terms as 'N came to court and there accused NN'; at other times demands were made privately of the offender by the injured party, with the knowledge of friends and neighbours. In fact, it seems highly likely that the latter procedure was normal: presumably most cases first recorded in court had already been through some such process.

In practice, many disputes seem to have been settled before they reached litigation, and settled locally, without recourse to political leaders. For example, the following case, which took place on 29 January 852, in Augan, was not taken to court since the abbot of Redon, who was here the subject of an accusation by a layman, sent some monks to test local feeling on the matter as a preliminary to reaching an agreement.

Notice of the way that Fomus came to accuse the monks of the Holy Saviour of Redon about the Arbiuan Inheritance (*hereditas*[18]), for he said that it was his. Abbot Conuuoion consulted with the brothers about this and they advised him to send three of the most learned brothers to the land to meet the respected men who lived in the *plebs* and ask them whether the complaint were true or not. Leumelus, priest and monk, Uuinkalunus, priest and monk, and Rituuere, monk, went off to the land, on Wednesday the feast of St John. The gave him (Fomus) a third of the Dignum Inheritance; and he gave them sureties* (*fideiussores* and *dilisidos*), Iarnhobrit and Dumuuoret, so that he would not complain further over the Dignum Inheritance nor the Arbiuan Inheritance, nor [would] his son, nor his son's son, for ever as long as the world lasted. He promised to give them, from the third part [i.e. from Dignum], a half measure of wheat and 18 pence every year. This was done in the *plebs* of Augan, at Coluuoretan, before many respected men. Their names are Reinbert (priest), Haelhoiarn (priest), Catuueten, Cenetlor (priest), Arthanael, Uuoletec, Rethuualt, Alunoc (cleric), Iarnican, Uuorbili, Maenuuallon, Pascuuoret, Seferia. It was done . . . in the twelfth year of the reign of King Charles, with Erispoe [*princeps*] governing Brittany (*CR* 127). (App. XI)

Since Fomus was given tenancy of a third of a property which was not the subject of recorded dispute, and since he appears to have remained in control of the disputed property, although as tenant, it looks as if the abbot and his advisers did a deal; by this Fomus kept the use, but not the ownership, of the Arbiuan Inheritance but his acquiescence and silence were bought by allowing him use of a further property, a third of the Dignum Inheritance. Full reconstruction of the episode is impossible, since there is no further documentation. Even in this out-of-court settlement witnesses were noted – local Augan priests and peasants – implying some local informal meeting. Fomus himself was clearly a well-off

---

[18] *Hereditas* refers to land, and to family rather than acquired land; in practice I think the *hereditas* was often managed as a unit.

peasant and appeared in Augan as ordinary witness; in 867 he pledged another property in Augan for 24 *solidi** (*CR* 68).

The drive to settle amicably was a forceful one and even in formal court proceedings a compromise solution was often reached[19]. It was in most people's interest to establish and preserve harmony, especially in relationships within the *plebs*. It is only at a higher – supra-*plebs* – social level that there are suggestions of resistance to compromise: the abbot was often persistent in his attempts to preserve and extend Redon's rights, especially against local machtierns, and could make repeated visits to the *princeps* to do so; at the other end of the social scale, peasant farmers sometimes refused to accept the extension into their communities of seigneurial interests from outside.

What happened when there was no immediate settlement? When a request for intervention was made to the *princeps*, he referred the case to a local court, or he sent representatives to the locality to gather information, or he commanded the accused to appear at his own court and answer the accusation. It was usually peasant problems that were referred back to their local community machinery (*CR* 106, 261), while the *princeps* showed an interest himself in cases involving machtierns and major landlords. Aristocrats might well be given time to gather evidence, as in the case quoted below, and local knowledge might be used to arrive at a solution. In the end, however, it was the *princeps* himself who made the judgement and ordered what consequences should ensue. This was very different from the procedure followed in local courts[20].

The following record is representative of the aristocratic process. In it the abbot of Redon complained to Salomon about a machtiern called Ratfred and his attacks on monastic property in Bains and Sixt. It was heard soon after 857.

Notice that Salomon, *princeps* of Brittany, asked Ratfred why he had broken his protection of Abbot Conuuoion and the monks of the Holy Saviour during the disturbances that followed the death of Erispoe. Ratfred and his brothers had gone to the monastery of Redon, saying that they were heirs of Bains and that, unless the abbot and his monks returned their inheritance, they would burn the entire abbey and loot it. Then the abbot and monks, unwilling but driven by necessity, gave them what they sought, that is, eight parcels of land (*partes*) in Bains and four and a half in Sixt. Even this was not enough for they required the monks to give them four sureties for the gift; forced by this, the monks did so, lest the whole *plebs* be burned. Afterwards Salomon acquired control of the whole of Brittany and heard about it, and he was very annoyed. He ordered Ratfred to come to him and asked him why he held monastic property by force and tyranny. He replied that he did not hold anything by force, for Abbot Conuuoion and his monks had given the

---

[19] *CR* 47, 96, for example. Compare the comments of S. Weinberger, 'Cours judiciaires, justice et résponsabilité sociale', *Rev. Hist.*, 267 (1982), 282–6, on compromise in Provençal courts of the tenth and eleventh centuries (although he is somewhat quick to link this with a decline in 'state' power).

[20] Most of the aristocratic cases involve machtierns, although the case of Pricient appears to have been about a wealthy man, with large and wide-spread property interests, who held no office (*CR* 242).

property freely, willingly and peacefully. Salomon, angered, then asked Conuuoion and the monks why they had given the religious property (*monachia sempiterna*[21]) of the Holy Saviour to tyrants (*tirannis*[22]) . . . [The abbot objected but] Salomon took over the disputed property and said to Ratfred, 'Now I have in my hands what you held of the property of Redon. Now lay your charge and show that it is your inheritance, according to law, truth and right, and I will show that "proof" to the monks and return it to you.' Ratfred replied that he could not produce proof because he did not have any law-worthy local men (*pagenses**) there. So Salomon said, 'I give you ten days to gather your proof and your witnesses in the court of Penard.' Then Ratfred confessed that he had neither witnesses nor proof to show that he had an inheritance in Bains. Then Salomon said, 'If you cannot prove that it is your inheritance, promise and give security, for yourself and all your family, that neither you nor your family will seek an inheritance in Bains.' [He did so.] Then Salomon returned the property to Abbot Conuuoion and the Holy Saviour in eternal alms, for his own soul and that of Nominoe his fosterfather. It was done in the court of Colroit, before many noble men, whose names are Salomon, Bran, Boduan [and thirteen further names] (*CR* 105). (App. XII)

This was a very explicitly aristocratic occasion, the witnesses at Salomon's court including several counts, with Salomon using his power as ruler to control the machtiern and allocate (perhaps re-allocate) the property. Ratfred was presumably the man called Ratfred who was machtiern of Sixt, who appeared often in the *plebes* near Redon as ordinary witness and who acted as surety in the very special case of the arrangement following an assault made by one Anau. He was frequently at Salomon's court in the 860s and 870s. He is probably to be identified with Ratfred brother of Ratuili (*CR* 221) and this would make him the brother of the machtiern of Bains. His interest in these properties is therefore understandable and he might have regarded them as his by right. In the above record Ratfred did not merely seize the property but he asked for, and received, sureties from the abbot; this was unusual procedure for a grant, although it was common in transactions of pledge, sale and exchange, and it suggests that Ratfred may have been more concerned to observe the proper forms of behaviour than the record at first indicates. The outcome is common for cases of this type – restoration of the disputed property to the 'rightful' owner and provision of guarantees; very occasionally, however, the *princeps* went further by making a personal visit to the area in question or by imposing a monetary sanction.

The outcome of requests to *local* leaders was invariably an investigation and usually a court case, although disputes in the *plebes* were sometimes settled outside local courts, at informal assemblies, as in the Fomus case above. Disputes were settled on all days of the week and in all months of the year but there are no records of formal hearings on Sundays nor in January, March, April, October and November; most, in fact, were heard early in the week. Dispute hearings took

---

[21] Literally 'eternal monastic property'; the phrase is common in the Redon material and has echoes in the Celtic charter tradition; see my 'Latin charter tradition', pp. 276f.

[22] And also 'to machtierns' (sometimes Latinized as *tiarnus, tirannus*); a double-entendre is probably intentional – a play on the word is explicit in *CR* 247.

place at more than half of all known ninth-century *plebes* in this area and formal local proceedings were held in at least ten different *plebes* in the region near Redon. Informal settlements occurred in the same *plebes* and in other *plebes* too (see fig. 2). This is so high a proportion that it suggests that every *plebs* had its own meetings, meetings which might easily be constituted as courts. Most of the witnesses, as well as the major participants, were local to the *plebs*. In some cases, however, a couple of *plebes* may have been grouped together: it looks as if Caro business was done in Guer and Pleucadeuc business was done in Ruffiac. Within the *plebs*, courts might be held at a range of locations – in church, or on the land in question, or even at a machtiern's *lis*; and we know of at least three different court locations used in the single *plebs* of Langon[23].

There are some standard elements of procedure in local courts. Most parties seem to have spoken for themselves for advocates are only mentioned for two aristocratic cases[24]. Presidents are named for a high proportion of court cases although their status and 'office' varied. They acted singly and also in groups; they were usually drawn from local machtierns or from representatives of the *princeps* (*missi principis*) and sometimes from a combination of the two. However, one elder of the local community seems to have been used in Avessac in 836 or 842 (*CR* 61). In one very early case (*c.* 801) the presidents were *missi comitis*, presumably representatives of the Carolingian count; and in another, very late, case (892) the abbot of Redon was president, presumably as *seigneur** of the *plebs* of Bains, where the case was heard. Very occasionally the *princeps* himself appeared in the *plebs* and presided[25]. Local panels of judges, sometimes referred to by the characteristic Carolingian term *scabini** but at others by more general terms like *boni viri**, are also mentioned in at least half of the recorded court cases. It is implied that their presence was standard in formal procedure, although the number of them certainly varied between three and twelve (and on one occasion it may have been fourteen).

In local courts right could be established in a number of different ways. Most commonly 'evidence' was produced, although even this was done by various means; duel and ordeal did not feature. When they had heard an accusation, the judges sometimes asked local men, often on oath, to provide information about the past history of the disputed property and associated persons; the charters include at least one record which appears to be a statement taken from a sworn witness[26]. The witnesses who provided this information were clearly supposed to be impartial: effectively the judges were conducting a small-scale local inquest**. The judges might also direct that the case be resolved by the use of oath-helpers**, although this is not frequently recorded. In a case at Langon in 801,

---

[23] Cf. F. Estey, 'The *scabini* and the local courts', *Speculum*, 26 (1951), 120.

[24] *CR* 107, 108. Both appeared at *Lisrannac* (one of Nominoe's centres) in the 840s and both cases involved settlement of problems of direct interest to Nominoe himself.

[25] *CR* 191, 271, 47.   [26] *CR* 205; cf. 185.

Anau, accused of wrongly holding that *vicus* (village), had to establish his right by swearing to the truth of his position together with twelve 'suitable' men (*CR* 191); in another case, in Sixt, round about 850, the accused had to swear on an altar to the right of his possession, together with three others (*CR* 46).

At other times the judges heard evidence produced by one or both parties; this might take the form of documents detailing, witnesses to or guarantors of past transactions, or some combination of these. The following record from Ruffiac demonstrates the significance that 'evidence' could have; it took place on 17 June, in 860.

Notice of the way in which a man called Uuobrian accused another called Uuetenoc about an allod which Uuobrian had sold him a long time before. Uuobrian said that he had not sold him as much land as he was working. Thereupon, Uuetenoc raised a court case, gathering his supporters; these were called Fomus, Iacu, Rethuualart, Drehuuobri. When his charter had been read and his witnesses and sureties (*dilisidis*) had testified, it was revealed that all that he worked had been purchased from Uuobrian. Then Uuobrian, vanquished as much by the charter as by the witnesses and guarantors, confessed. This was done in Ruffiac church, on the fifteenth of the kalends of July, Monday, before Machtiern Iarnhitin and Hinuualart[27] and Litoc, the representative of *Princeps* Salomon, and before many noble men[28], whose names are Uuorcomet, Nominoe, Miot, Omnis, Tuduual, Hoiarn, Abbot Sulmin, Abbot Iuna, Comaltcar (priest), Adaluuin, and Eusor-chit (cleric); Eusorchit then read the charter in public, to the effect that all had been sold to Uuetenoc just as he had said from his own charter (*CR* 139). (App. XIII)

This is a very ordinary local occasion of dispute settlement, and Uuobrian and his family were normal, active peasants. Uuobrian certainly made frequent appearances as an ordinary witness in Ruffiac and his brother, at least, was a donor of lands to Redon (*CR* 248). The witnesses on this occasion were peasants drawn from the *plebs* and not far beyond, the abbots being local abbots of minor monasteries. Within five years the victor, Uuetenoc, had given the property to Redon (*CR* 44), which presumably explains the preservation of the record. In fact, the record of the original sale (*CR* 138) reveals that Fomus and his colleagues had been sureties, in Ruffiac church, in 846. The oral evidence of the original sureties was crucial to the resolution of this case, although it is interesting that the settlement stresses the importance of the documentary record.

Documents could be important in providing proof but they were not automatically regarded as decisive: round about 840 a man called Uurbudic accused the abbot of Redon of being in wrongful possession of a weir on the River Vilaine and he made a point of the fact that the charter held by the abbot was false. His efforts to deny the force of documentary proof failed, but the matter was only finally settled by the verbal testimony (and local knowledge) of the men of

---

27 A machtiern Hinuualart is noted in *CR* 248 and 265; this may be the same man, but he is not called machtiern in this record.

28 'Noble' here means 'men of standing, of proven worth', not 'aristocratic'; cf. K. Nehlsen-von Stryk, *Die boni homines des frühen Mittelalters*, pp. 251f.

Avessac and Bains on either side of the river (*CR* 195). In fact, documents were not always used when they existed: *CR* 92, recording a grant from Bains by a son of Uesilloc, substantiates the argument in the later case detailed in *CR* 271, recording the unsuccessful attempt of three sons of Uesilloc to claim that they were *not* heirs to that villa*; it was not apparently cited in the hearing.

Since settlements were sometimes made in court, and one party sometimes conceded the case or confessed to dishonesty, a formal judgement was not an inevitable part of all proceedings. When it did happen, it was made by the local panel of judges, either with reference to the 'evidence' that had been brought forward or to the local knowledge of the *scabini* themselves. It was never made in these records with reference to stated legal nor customary principles, whether oral or written, and notably it was never made with reference to anything described as *lex*[29]. The only factor determining the judgement seems to have been knowledge of past events, transactions and relationships in the locality.

Out of court the informal procedure for settling disputes was very similar, with public assemblies in which trusted local men gave evidence on past transactions and relationships, although there were neither presidents nor judges at these occasions. The material which led to settlement was very much the same as in formal court cases and sometimes mediators – named as such – were used. The meetings were held in the same type of place as formal courts, although within or in front of churches were favoured meeting points, and sometimes the same terminology as that used for formal cases was used to describe the proceedings, presumably because they were recorded by the same individuals. Charter 144 is very like the Uuetenoc case of *CR* 139, quoted above, in its detail of production of witnesses and charters, but there was no formal court case, merely a publicly announced dispute, followed in turn by argument, pressure and settlement: the donor, Uuordoital, succeeded in extracting a payment from the donee, Maenuueten, in order that the latter might have the power to alienate the property as he wished: 'seeing that Maenuueten was gathering together his witnesses, guarantors and charter, and not wishing to lose his former friendship, Uuordoital sent to Maenuueten suggesting that he should give him 4 *solidi*, and he would then confirm the grant; Maenuueten did so'.

Since a high proportion of the cases detailed in this material are about rival claims to property rights, there is not much information about 'criminal' areas such as sentencing and punishment. It is therefore not at all clear if there is any evidence of 'criminal' jurisdiction and of the way it operated; indeed, it is not at all clear if such notions are appropriate to judicial practice in this society. As far as we can see, law *enforcement* was normally achieved by the use of sureties. When agreement on a disputed issue was reached, either by a judgement or by a settlement, it was common for sureties to be named, who had to be acceptable to

---

[29] However, going to court might be described as going *in lege*. This is in stark contrast with practice in ninth- and tenth-century northern Spain; see Collins below, pp. 85–6.

both parties. These would either effectively guarantee that the victor would not suffer any financial loss – by paying themselves or by distraining* on the guilty man's property – or they would effectively resign any personal claims on the property assigned to the victor. Members of the family of the loser might therefore be named as guarantors, but other, unrelated, supporters might line up behind him. Acting as surety was part of a local, small-scale pattern of alliance-making that is largely hidden from the records. Very occasionally the function of some sureties is specified in detail: in the case of a cleric, Anau, who had assaulted one of Redon's priests, a grant was made to Redon in compensation for the attack and three sureties were named for the property; another three were then named, to act with the first group, to restrain Anau from any future assaults. If they heard that he was likely to do further damage, they were to stop him and warn the abbot; if they failed to stop him, they were then to pursue him to death and give his worth to the abbot (*CR* 202). Here the sureties had a policing and punishing, as well as a distraining, function and punishment was administered by using the purely private machinery for guaranteeing obligations[30].

Apart from the sureties, evidence of enforcement and of punishment machinery is limited. In a case involving the machtiern Alfret and Redon, the *princeps* Salomon imposed a sanction of 5,000 *solidi* to be paid in the event of a contravention of the judgement (*CR* 247). This was exceptional, and a sum far larger than the stated value of any property. A sanction of double the value of the stated price was usually attached to records of sale, but there are no indications of *who* administered it nor of the destination of the sum. Anau himself, in the sureties cases quoted above, was at first condemned to lose his right hand for his assault but it is not absolutely clear if Redon sentenced him, exercising either public or seigneurial jurisdiction, or if someone else did. In the few recorded cases of killing and their consequences, compensatory land grants were made to the associates of the injured party: Nominoe was given land for the death of his injured vassal (*CR* 107); land and a serf were given to Redon in compensation for the killing of one of Redon's own serfs (*CR* 163); another serf was given to Redon in compensation for a range of depredations (including theft of cattle) (*CR* 32). All of these seem to have been arranged between the interested parties and were not the subject of judgements. The grants made to Nominoe as a substitute for

---

[30] See further my 'Suretyship'. Cf. the Irish *Cáin Adamnáin*, ed. K. Meyer, ch. 33, where the punishment for killing a woman was maiming (right hand and left foot) followed by death; after this the kindred were to pay compensation, rather than the appointed sureties, as here, where private agreement not family obligation is the enforcing machinery. The statement of a monk travelling in the late ninth century that Breton 'law' required anyone who had seen an injury done to take action against the injuror is puzzling; it would be difficult to work in practice. Perhaps the monk confused the onlooker with an agreed third party (that is, a surety); 'Itinerarium Bernardi', ch. 23, *Descriptiones terrae sanctae*, ed. T. Tobler. I owe this reference to Julia Smith, to whom I am very grateful.

payment of render are described as being done *pro fraude*; this could merely have been compensation for default in payment of the render but the transaction may conceal something more complex (*CR* 108)[31]. It is therefore clear that a notion of punishment and/or penalty was attached to certain sorts of offence, as well as compensation to the injured bodies; it is also clear that sometimes the penalty was administered by private machinery; it is *not* clear if the 'state' had responsibility for any stage of the process (or benefited financially) other than in the particular circumstance of the Breton ruler's dealings with the aristocracy. That might have been as much a matter of crude power politics between the individuals concerned as of evidence of 'state' responsibility.

In a princely court it was the *princeps* himself who presided, judged and sentenced. 'State' interest in the village processes was minimal either from the highest (Carolingian) level or from that of the Breton *princeps*, whether dependent or independent. Formal and informal occasions often had no representative of government noted – neither *missi principis* nor *missi comitis* – although the Langon case, of the very early date of 801, did show comital intervention (*CR* 191)[32]. Otherwise, representatives of 'state' only appeared when *principes* intervened personally at a local level on receipt of complaints or appeals. Even in these cases decisions tended to be thrown back to the local community of farmers who were permanent residents.

Who were the people of the *plebes* called on to act as judges and impartial witnesses? The *suitability* of individuals to give testimony – their legal competence or law-worthy status – was essential to the provision of effective evidence, and the judges are sometimes recorded investigating or pronouncing upon it; everyone's evidence was not equally admissible. What constituted 'suitability' was not usually specified in these texts, although an Avessac record of 892 comes very close to a definition: good behaviour, good character, an unbribable nature and a love and knowledge of justice, right and truth were essential requirements. People with local knowledge and free from conviction or suspicion of offence were presumably in mind here[33]. We can also observe that law-worthy people were male and not servile. But, given the unusual detail of this material, we can go further and investigate the circumstances and range of interests of many individual impartial witnesses, and of judges too.

The terms used to refer to the judges are several: *scabini, boni viri, principes* and *iudices**[34]. No regional or temporal distinctions in the usage are apparent. The

[31] Conceivably the inquiry at Langon involving the other Anau was some sort of criminal case, since it was conducted by representatives of the count (*CR* 191). The travelling monk (see n. 30 above) reported that Bretons imposed a death penalty for theft of goods worth more than 4 pence.

[32] Although machtierns were sometimes *used* by *principes* they were not appointees of state; see further my 'Distribution of political power', pp. 96–8.

[33] *CR* 271. Cf. Estey, '*Scabini*', 122, and see further my 'Disputes', 298f.

[34] Cf. La Borderie, *Histoire de Bretagne*, vol. 2, pp. 136, 150f, 161f; see also Estey, '*Scabini*', 121–4, for

twenty-five judges that are investigable (that is, those who appear on several occasions) were more often than not demonstrably propertied; they were donors, vendors and purchasers in other transactions, and sureties for the participants in yet more[35]. Their property interests were not vast but their own property did not always lie in the *plebes* in which they served as judges, sometimes lying in the immediately neighbouring *plebes*. So, for example, Framuual served as judge in Guer, was a donor of property in Caro and was surety for property in Guer – he owned property in Caro and performed services for the community and for individuals in the next *plebs*, Guer; Iarndetuuid was judge in Ruffiac, purchaser of property in nearby Pleucadeuc and often surety for property in Ruffiac; and Tiarnán acted as judge in Langon, was the donor of an unlocated property, and was surety for properties in Bains and Brain (Plaz) (see fig. 4a)[36]. They were not normally office holders; although Huuori was *mair* of Pleucadeuc and Riduuant was a priest, these cases are unusual: since priests normally featured prominently in all village business, their absence from the panels of judges is notable[37].

Although they did not usually serve as judge in more than one *plebs*, people from the panel of judges were often ordinary witnesses to ordinary transactions of sale or grant in several neighbouring *plebes*. Now, the total range of places where some might appear extended to Carentoir and Guer, or to Ruffiac and Carentoir, or to Ruffiac, Guer and Augan; however (after 832) others consistently and frequently appeared in all four *plebes* near Redon – Renac, Langon, Bains and Brain (in fact a *plebicula*), or this combination with the addition of one of the neighbouring *plebes* of Avessac or Peillac. The range of locations of the properties in relation to which they witnessed tends to be the same as the range of places where they appeared in person; it is again strikingly consistent in the *plebes* near Redon, with the addition of Avessac, often, or of nearby Massérac or Alarac (see fig. 4b). Further, unusually, many of these men also served as judges in *several* of the *plebes* in the block: Bains men served in Renac and Langon, and so on. Behaviour therefore markedly differed in this Redon zone from behaviour in the surrounding *plebes*. In the outer areas, a judge might serve in one *plebs* and appear in two or three, and one man's range was unlikely to be the same as another's; in the *plebes* near Redon, judges operated *throughout* the area and might additionally appear in one *plebs* outside it; so, for community and judicial purposes, this zone was treated as a single *plebs*.

comparably mixed terminology in other parts of Francia; and Nehlsen-von Stryk, *Boni Homines*, for an exhaustive survey.

[35] Sureties must have been propertied. For full discussion of the suretyship issue see my 'Suretyship', pp. 81–3.

[36] Tiarnán: *CR* 53, 58, 71, 124, 181; Framuual: *CR* 8, 25, 152, 177, 178, 179, 180, 194; Iarndetuuid: *CR* 130, 147, 148, 153, 174, 196, 255.

[37] Huuori: *CR* 12, 146, 147, 151, 155, 156, 196, 205, 267; Riduuant: 192. It is not clear what distinctive functions the *mair* performed; whether the term is a Breton borrowing from Latin *maior** or is the same vernacular word as Welsh *maer*, someone's deputy is implied – perhaps the machtiern's.

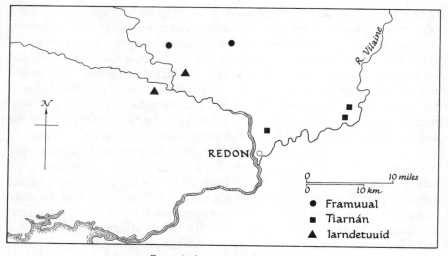

4a Some judges in the *pays de Redon*

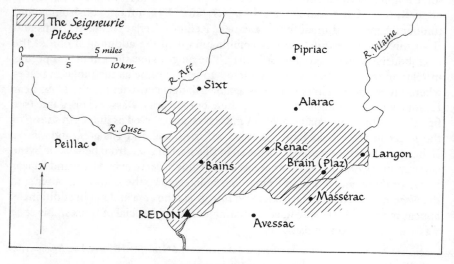

4b The Redon *seigneurie*

The texts refer to the impartial witnesses as *franci, nobiles viri, idonei viri, idonei testes, seniores* (especially), *seniores et nobiles* and *seniores et optimates*. The circumstances of the investigable impartial witnesses (fifty-six in number) were a little different from those of the judges; as might perhaps be expected their geographical range was more limited. In fact twenty-eight of them are explicitly associated with – respectively – the *plebes* of Renac, Sixt, Peillac or Bains, by being termed *senior* (elder of) Bains, *senior* Renac and so on; presumably this indicated residence in those *plebes*. They constitute only a small proportion of all the people who – in a decade – featured as ordinary witnesses to transactions in their *plebes*; this suggests that impartial witnesses tended to be chosen from a *limited* sector of the free, male, propertied population, although we can only guess at but we do not know the nature of the limitation[38]. Within their *plebes* it was not uncommon for men who were impartial witnesses to hold specific office: two held the office of *mair* and several were priests. A few were demonstrably propertied persons, but their property interests were usually in the *plebs* in which they appeared as impartial witness and their property dealings are not so evident as those of the judges[39]. A few of the impartial witnesses also served as judges but most had no other public rôle than ordinary witness of transactions. Hence, Arthuuiu, elder of Bains, was judge in Langon, impartial witness in Bains, had property in Bains, stood surety in Brain and was a frequent ordinary witness in these places. Catlouuen, elder of Renac, was impartial witness in Bains, and surety in Renac and Brain; but Uuetenuuoion was impartial witness in Avessac and had property there; both were also ordinary witnesses. The range of places at which they appeared was more limited than that of the judges but the distinctive quality of the zone near Redon is again clear. Many appeared within its limits only (Bains, Renac, Langon, Brain); several, including men who were explicitly termed *seniores* of Bains and Renac, appeared in the zone together with one neighbouring *plebs* (especially Avessac, but also Pipriac, Peillac and Sixt). By contrast, the Sixt *seniores* tended to appear in Sixt only, apart from the occasion when Nominoe called them to Bains; an Avessac group appeared in Avessac, or Avessac and Allaire, or Avessac and the Redon zone; a single man appeared in Ruffiac and Pleucadeuc[40]. The properties that were the subject of their evidence were comparably located except that men of Bains tended to witness to a wider range than the others. (This presumably reflects the fact that general Redon business was often performed in the church of Bains, using local Bains witnesses, even if the donation concerned a distant property.)

The distinctiveness of the behaviour of men from the Redon zone and the consistency of the group is very interesting. The four *plebes* of Renac, Bains, Langon and Brain were those 'given' to Redon by Carolingian rulers soon after

---

[38] Where meaningful statistics are possible the proportion of impartial witnesses to ordinary witnesses is in the order of a fifth or less. Of the nine *seniores* of Bains (*CR* 106, AD 841–51), four witnessed a lay sale pertaining to Bains in 846 (*CR* 121), as did two from Renac and one from Sixt; the remaining seventeen witnesses who were not actors in the transaction did not feature in special rôles in other cases in the locality.

[39] There is one exception to this pattern: Cadalun gave evidence in Avessac and had properties in two or three *plebes* to the south in St Étienne de Montluc (*CR* 59, 97, 162, 195).

[40] *CR* 62, 106, 161.

its foundation. These 'gifts' gave Redon proprietary rights over a whole territory without affecting the ownership of individuals within the *plebes*; in practice this probably meant rights to certain dues (including tolls), rights over vacant properties and some rights of jurisdiction; effectively it also created an area of immunity* from state intervention, as the monks were well aware and sometimes stated[41]. Other *plebes* were later given to Redon too but, with the exception of Massérac, which lay beside the original four, the others were scattered. The existence of the block of four (later five) around Redon gave a territorial coherence to the monastery's political powers in the neighbourhood; and the grants clearly marked the inauguration of the *seigneurie** of Redon. It is very striking that the territorial range of the judges and the impartial witnesses of this area coincides with the *seigneurie*, underlining the juridical significance of the territory, and marking it off from the ordinary *plebes*.

The dispute material in the Redon cartulary is of considerable interest in the context of ninth-century political and social development in Europe. It clearly indicates that there was local machinery in eastern Brittany at village level for the settlement of disputes, as well as for the recording of transactions and keeping of records. This machinery was in existence and well established at least a generation before the foundation of Redon and clearly cannot be a consequence of the establishment of the monastery itself. Dispute procedure differed fundamentally at this peasant level from procedure at aristocratic level for, in the latter case, the *princeps* himself carried out a range of functions that were performed by several different bodies in local courts; most strikingly, he both presided and judged, rôles which were always separate in the local courts, where judgement was never made by machtierns or other officials. Each village and its surrounding territory, the *plebs*, held its own meetings for dispute settlement, and a high proportion had courts; business relating to one *plebs* was normally heard in the *plebs*, with people of the immediate locality in attendance. 'State' interest in the proceedings was either minimal or non-existent; hence, many 3–10 km units effectively operated as autonomous judicial units. Each *plebs* had its own panel of 'suitable' men who could be called on to act as impartial witnesses and thereby

---

[41] Charles the Bald granted immunity from secular jurisdiction to the men living on Redon's lands, thereby theoretically putting Redon outside local process (*CR* A28); he ordered that no-one should enter the monastery's estates to hear cases and give judgement, and no-one should distrain upon nor take sureties from the men living on the monastery's lands ('iubentes . . . ut nulli fidelium . . . liceat praescripti monasterii ingredi villas vel agros sive silvas . . . ad causas audiendas . . . aut iudicium saecularia diffinienda; neque praesumat quislibet iudiciarum exercentium potestatem homines eorum . . . super ipsius monasterii terram commanentes distringere aut inquietare, vel fideiussores tollere'). This seems to have happened in some respects (see *CR* 32, 124, 185, 201 for the abbot taking action against 'invaders') although local courts continued to function within the *seigneurie* of Redon. The immunity may also have given the monastery a right to hold a court, although there are also cases of others presiding within the *seigneurie* (*CR* 124). Certainly in Bains, in 892, the abbot presided at a local court (*CR* 271).

provide the repository of local knowledge on which virtually all decisions were based. These people were certainly male, free and propertied but they were not wealthy men and their property interests were in most cases limited to the *plebs* in which they resided. Their reputations as trustworthy, knowledgeable men often seem to have stretched to more than their own *plebs* and normally they might be expected to attend business in an adjacent community as well as in their own – but no farther. The local men called to serve on panels of judges had essentially the same characteristics, but the range of their reputations tended to be wider, sometimes as much as three or four *plebes*, 20–25 km, and they therefore attended business over a larger area than either impartial or ordinary witnesses. There is nothing that explicitly suggests that this greater range of the judges depended on wealth, although it may have done. Behaviour in the *seigneurie* of Redon differed from that in the surrounding countryside for here four *plebes*, rather than one or two, served as a basic unit within which judges and impartial witnesses performed their judicial rôles and it looks as if the 'panel' from which they were drawn was a panel for the whole block.

In the absence of seventh- and early eighth-century evidence it is impossible to comment convincingly on the origins of these practices. They are unlikely to be of Carolingian origin for practice deviated from that recommended in Carolingian legislation more than might be expected for a recent introduction: the smallest unit to have a court was really very small and panels of law-worthy men tended to serve one or two village communities rather than some wider community of hundred or county. Judgement was certainly found by people called *scabini*, but also by others, including *boni viri*; these *scabini* give no indication that they were skilled in 'law', as required by the legislation and perhaps suggested by the well-known charter from Digne, and they were not usually priests; they did not go on tour[42]; and all available judges were not used for every case, as the Renac meetings demonstrate, so they were not in that sense 'permanent'. Moreover, plaintiffs did not travel long distances to go to court, as the Carolingian bishop Theodulf implied, and courts were often held in or near churches[43]. On the other hand, there is nothing especially Celtic in these Breton practices and there are some obvious points of contact with practice in other parts of Francia. It is therefore more likely that the machinery was of pre-Carolingian origin, and indeed this material may provide a glimpse of the late Roman heritage – much devolved – or at least of the continuation of the *in pago* justice evidenced by the formularies for sixth- and seventh-century Francia[44]. Whether this area of Brittany was distinctive in its rich provision of judicial machinery for peasant

---

[42] *Cartulaire de l'abbaye de Saint-Victor de Marseille*, ed. B. Guérard, vol. 1, pp. 43–6; for doubts about touring see also Estey, '*Scabini*', 125f.

[43] Theodulf, 'Versus contra Iudices' in *Poetae Latinae Aevi Carolini*, ed. E. Dümmler, vol. 1.

[44] See Wood above, pp. 20–2; and see Nehlsen-von Stryk, *Boni Homines*, pp. 256–344, for a thorough examination of the relationship between *boni homines* of early medieval Francia and those of late Antiquity.

communities in the ninth century is difficult to ascertain, but it was not necessarily so. *Centenarii** courts, which were presumably smaller than county courts, are mentioned in Carolingian sources and the 16–20 km range of the Mâcon and Nimois *scabini* is comparable to the range of judges from the Redon area[45]. East Breton practices could well have been paralleled in other well-worked parts of continental Europe, and the vociferous peasantry and strong sense of community so well evidenced by the Redon cartulary may have had their counterparts in other regions.

[45] Cf. Estey, '*Scabini*', 123–6. Estey's comments about the Redon material need some revision, and the significance he attributes to the property qualifications of these men is questionable – a high proportion of peasants owned property and so a property qualification does not in itself imply social distinction from the majority of the community. However, Estey's suggestions for the limited geographical range of *scabini* in southern France are strikingly consistent and his observations about the *local* interests and knowledge of these people are surely right.

5

Visigothic law and regional custom in disputes in early medieval Spain

ROGER COLLINS

The Visigothic *Forum Iudicum* enjoyed quite exceptional longevity as a code of law put to practical application. Although the geographical range of its authority steadily declined after the eleventh century, it remained the sole comprehensive work of legal codification with more than local relevance from its promulgation in the mid-seventh century to its final replacement by Alfonso X's *Siete Partidas* in the late thirteenth: a span of over six hundred years. Even in its final phase it is its intended practical applicability that is most striking: Alfonso X's father granted the use of the vernacular version, the *Fuero Juzgo* as the local law and privilege of recently reconquered Córdoba and Seville. It is as if the Laws of Alfred were still enjoying validity in the reign of Henry VII[1].

Admittedly, by this stage the *Forum* had ceased to be enforced in Castille and in Catalonia, and was generally elsewhere supplemented and modified by the proliferation of local *fueros**[2]. But for a code devised so long previously and in so distant a society the survival and continuing authority of the *Forum* (also known as *Lex Visigothorum*) is remarkable. The processes of its modification were also, as far as the evidence can now show us, of relatively recent date, beginning only in the middle of the eleventh century. Indeed the two hundred years before that may well be described as the hey-day of the *Forum Iudicum*, particularly in terms of our knowledge of how it was applied in practice.

In both the kingdom of Asturias–León, which also encompassed Galicia, and in the Frankish March in Catalonia the *Forum* was the code according to whose principles and procedures law was administered, disputes settled and documents drawn up[3]. The existence of a relatively substantial corpus of texts from both regions provides the basis for the understanding of the practical application of

---

[1] For a history of Spanish law in the middle ages see R. Gibert, *Historia general del derecho español*, vol. 1.

[2] A. Iglesia Ferreirós, 'La creación del derecho en Cataluña', *Anuario de Historia del Derecho Español*, 47 (1977), provides a substantial account of the development of law in Catalonia in this period, though not all his interpretations may be acceptable; see, for example, his treatment of *evacuationes* as documents of compromise.

[3] M. Zimmerman, 'L'usage du droit wisigothique en Catalogne du IXe au XIIe siècle', *Mélanges de la Casa de Velazquez*, 9 (1973).

Visigothic law, something effectively denied us for the seventh century as a result of the almost total loss of its charters* and administrative documents[4]. Furthermore contrasts between practices and documentation found on the one hand in León and on the other in Catalonia can give some indication of the way in which the mutual isolation of the two regions gave rise to independent developments and variations in their legal procedures, although both stemmed from a common Visigothic original[5].

In the area of dispute settlement this manifests itself most patently in the citations, sometimes with the provision of specific references, of relevant passages of the Code found in some of the existing documents[6]. Procedures were similar in that panels of judges, with responsibilities for defined geographical areas, met regularly under the presidency of the local count and/or bishop (in León at royal command) at various sites within their regions of jurisdiction to hear cases, together with panels of local *boni homines**. In both areas the judges rather than their presidents conducted interrogations, made rulings on procedure, and finally gave judgement. These judges may be called 'professional', although nothing is known of their training, in that when their periods of activity are traceable they are found to extend over several years, and furthermore when detected in other documents, such as deeds of gift or sale, in which they are fulfilling no judicial function, they are still characterized by the title of *iudex**; they were office holders and not merely local *potentes* occasionally called upon to act as judgement finders. The same may be true, if to a lesser extent, of some of the *mandatarii* or *assertores*, the advocates found conducting cases 'in voce' of one of the contesting parties. Similarly, there are indications that the relatively copious documentation created by the complex hearings was written down by professional notaries; however, in Catalonia, by the second half of the tenth century, it looks as if most texts were by then being enscribed by the beneficiaries, rather than the court notaries envisaged by the *Forum Iudicum*[7].

The basic principles by which disputes, generally concerning land ownership though occasionally also social status and therefore people as ownable property, were resolved were similar in both regions. Great importance was attached to written title, the possession of charters, but by itself this was never allowed to be sufficient, and, whenever possible, had to be corroborated by the production of witnesses, whose veracity and right to testify could be impugned by the opposing party. In both León and Catalonia witnesses' testimony after first being delivered

---

[4] See A. Canellas López, *Diplomática Hispano-Visigoda*, nos. 119, 119a, 178, 192, and 229, for the fragmentary remains of Visigothic charters.

[5] R. Collins, 'Law and Charters in ninth- and tenth-century León and Catalonia', *Eng. Hist. Rev.*, 100 (1985).

[6] See Iglesia Ferreirós, 'La creación del derecho', App., for a full list of such citations.

[7] For example, F. Udina Martorell, *Archivo Condal de Barcelona*: the scribe of the legal text, no. 35, was the principal scribe of the monastery of S. Joan de les Abadesses in the early tenth century; see p. 501 for a full list of the documents he drew up, including another *evacuatio* (no. 53).

in court was then formalized at a second delivery of it under oath, taken in a church on a subsequent date under the direction not of the judges but of an officer called the *saio**. What then followed marks a clear divergence in procedure between the two regions: in the Leonese kingdom one of the witnesses was obliged to submit to the ordeal of the *pena caldaria* in order to confirm the veracity of the oath they had all just taken. This too was supervised by the *saio*, and involved the witness who had volunteered in extracting two or three stones from a cauldron of heated water and then having his hand bandaged. Delivered into the custody of someone nominated by the opposing party, he was brought back three days later before the *saio* and another set of independent witnesses to show whether or not his hand was 'clean' (*limpidus*), that is unmarked. In Catalonia no such process of ordeal was employed other than in criminal accusations, the only rôle envisaged for it in the *Forum Iudicum*[8].

In general, Leonese dispute texts, of which there are fewer extant than those of Catalonia, indicate that a greater variety of documents was created by their hearings. Obviously the records of the ordeal, of which only a small number survive, mark a genuine difference, but some other apparent Leonese peculiarities are quite lacking in the Catalan evidence. For instance, Catalan documents neither record a prior hearing at which the complainant first states his case to the court, nor two concluding sessions, one before the judges at which the losing party submits his *pactum* – acknowledgement of defeat and renunciation of claim – to the victor via the *saio*, and another one with the *saio*, held on the disputed property, to carry out the formalities of restitution. The procedures themselves, though, may have been common to both regions, and merely the recording of their occurrence a Leonese peculiarity. Certainly the writing of the *pactum*, usually there called the *evacuatio*, was a standard feature of Catalan dispute settlement[9].

Leaving aside those types of document distinctive of Leonese procedures, there are three classes of text created by dispute settlement that are common to both León and Catalonia. These are, firstly, the *conditiones sacramentorum*, a formal record of the oath taken by the witnesses that notes their names, the place and particulars of the oath taking, what it concerns and on what it was sworn, and generally the date; secondly the *evacuatio, pactum* or *manifestum*, the recognition of the invalidity of the claim by the losing party, usually witnessed; and thirdly some form of account of the hearing, often presented in passages of direct speech[10]. It is by no means certain that every case inevitably produced three such

---

8 Collins, 'Law and Charters', 498–500.
9 For some of the Catalan examples see Udina Martorell, *Archivo Condal*, nos. 16, 35, 38, 53, 181; C. Baraut, 'Els documents, dels anys 981–1010, de l'Arxiu Capitular de la Seu d'Urgell', *Urgellia*, 3 (1980), no. 252; P. de Marca, *Marca Hispanica*, App., nos. 21 and 34.
10 For Leonese examples of *conditiones* see C. Sánchez-Albornoz, 'Documentos para el estudio del procedimiento judicial en el reino asturleonés' in *Homenaje a don Agustín Millares Carlo*, vol. 2, pp. 143–56, nos. 1 and 4; for *manifesta* see *ibid.*, no. 8, and also *Cartulario de Santo Toribio de Liébana*,

texts, but it can be shown that some did[11]. In Catalonia from roughly the middle of the tenth century onwards there was a marked tendency for a case to be recorded by just one document that combines elements of all three classes of text and blurs the formal distinctions[12]. This may be related to the parallel tendency at this time for the beneficiaries to be responsible for the writing of documents resulting from a hearing. Citations of Visigothic law appear in the third class of document, that which may be called the transcript of the hearing, but they are also retained in the mixed texts of Catalan origin.

Both the Leonese kingdom and the Catalan counties also employed similar procedures in the resolution of boundary disputes, based upon principles enshrined in the Visigothic code[13]. In both cases panels of judges perambulated the boundaries, either taking evidence by inquest* from the older inhabitants as to their memory of estate divisions or by searching for and restoring lost or hidden boundary markers. The former procedure was more generally employed in Catalonia and the latter in León[14].

All of these processes are well attested in the surviving evidence, which consists in large part of original documents preserved in the voluminous Catalan archives, or in later cartulary copies of lost originals, which is the case with most of the Leonese texts. The survival of large numbers not only of dispute settlement documents but of charters of all sorts, many of which also make reference to or follow procedures derived from the *Forum Iudicum* further substantiates belief in the importance of written title to property and of codified law for these societies; in form and even in points of particular detail this links them through their Visigothic heritage to a more distant Roman past[15].

Virtually all extant Leonese and Catalan dispute settlement documents can be divided up generically into the various categories previously mentioned, and the application of generic criteria can help in the elucidation of texts that are at first sight disorderly and chaotic, giving the impression of being the products of less sophisticated drafting and of more primitive procedures than have here been described. Thus, to take one example, a recently printed text from the twelfth-

---

ed. L. Sánchez Belda, nos. 17 and 66; for Catalan *conditiones* see *Marca Hispanica*, App., nos. 39–41; for *evacuationes* see n. 9 above.

[11] Collins, 'Law and Charters', 492–4, 498–502.

[12] For some Catalan examples see Udina Martorell, *Archivo Condal*, no. 181; Baraut, 'Els documents', no. 203; J. de Villanueva, *Viage literário a las iglesias de España*, vol. 12, App., no. xvi bis.

[13] R. Collins, 'Charles the Bald and Wifred the Hairy' in M. Gibson, J. Nelson, D. Ganz (eds.), *Charles the Bald: Court and Kingdom*, pp. 178–9; for Visigothic law on this topic see *Leges Visigothorum*, ed. K. Zeumer, x. iii, *MGH LL in quarto*, sectio 1, vol. 1, pp. 396–9.

[14] For a Catalan boundary case see *Marca Hispanica*, App., no. 143, in addition to those cited in Collins, 'Charles the Bald and Wifred the Hairy', n. 52. For Leonese examples see Justiniano Rodríguez, *Ramiro II Rey de León*, App., no. 10, and the cases in AHN Madrid, Codex 986B, 'Cartulario de Celanova', fols. 162r–v and 173v.

[15] W. Kienast, 'La pervivencia del derecho godo', *Boletín de la Real Academia de Buenas Letras de Barcelona*, 35 (1973/4); see also Zimmermann, 'L'usage du droit wisigothique', and Collins, 'Charles the Bald and Wifred the Hairy', with different perspectives.

and thirteenth-century cartulary of Celanova is a very long document which appears to be curiously repetitive and poorly structured[16]. It relates to a dispute between certain named inhabitants of the villa of Zacors and the abbot and monks of Celanova. As it stands the text begins with a lengthy recognition of the villagers that their claim to a portion of the 'villula' of St Felix by gift of the late bishop Rudesind was false and unjust. This had been proved by the testimony of many before a panel of named judges. The villagers were, therefore, making this written *placitum** so that neither they nor their descendants should resurrect the claim. As in standard Leonese procedure this document was to be handed over 'per saionem', and was dated fifth of the Ides of May, Era* 1025 (11 May, AD 987). It was signed by the five named villagers. However, the document is far from finished at this point as it proceeds without break to turn itself into a brief *manifestum* by Ordonio (here identified as the spokesman of the other villagers, who are also described as being his heirs – *heredes*), in which he acknowledges the injustice of the claim. It should be noticed that his hand was also put to the general renunciation immediately preceding. Then follows what is called a *placitum* or written promise by Salvator (identified early on in the opening *pactum* as the *mandator* or advocate of the monks of Celanova in this case) and by Ordonio to appear before the judge Abbot Abraham four weeks hence to go to law ('pro ad lege') over the disputed portion of the villa* of St Felix. This is addressed to the *saio* Gudesteus and signed by the two parties. Immediately after follows another promise by Salvator and Ordonio to the *saio* that they will present themselves before the judge Froyla Nunnizi five weeks hence on penalty of the payment of a fine of 100 *solidi** for non-attendance. This too is signed. Finally, there comes a *placitum* in the name of Ordonio and his heirs, the four other villagers of Zacors mentioned throughout the text, in which they assign the disputed villa to the *saio* for him in turn 'sicut veritas et lex gotica docet' to transmit to Salvator, the victorious *mandator* of the monks. (App. XIV, XV)

As a whole this document looks topsy-turvy: for one thing the agreement to go to law appears in the middle of it, although it has opened with the formal renunciation by the defeated side. Chronologically, then, its structure is irrational. Similarly the promises to appear before two separate judges on two different occasions appear baffling. However, sense dawns if the document is not treated as a unity and is split up into its component parts. It thus becomes in its current order: (1) the *pactum* or *evacuatio* of the losing party of villagers; (2) a separate *manifestum* or submission by their spokesman, who seems anyway to be their *paterfamilias* or some form of senior relative; (3) a promise by the spokesmen of the two sides to meet for judicial resolution of the dispute before Abbot Abraham; (4) a similar promise to appear before the judge, Froyla; and (5) the written surrender of the formerly disputed property by the losing party for its

---

16 Sánchez-Albornoz, 'Documentos', no. 9; printed below, pp. 252–3, corrected from the MS, AHN Madrid, Codex 986B, fols. 38v–39r.

handing over by the *saio* to the victors. The correct chronological order should be: 3, 4, 1, 2 and 5.

The apparent repetition or confusion between the third and fourth items, the two promises to appear, may result from one or both parties having failed or having been unable to do so, and a second date for the hearing having had to be made. This may be confirmed by the inclusion in the second of the texts of a penalty for non-appearance, something that the first one lacks. Particularly interesting is the final section, which, uniquely, indicates that the concluding process of restitution was also carried out by means of a document. Also noteworthy is the fact that the principal of the losing party was required to sign a personal renunciation, as well as putting his hand to the collective one. This, it is specified, was at the request of the *mandator* of the victorious Celanovan monks. It is likely, therefore, that such documents and procedural additions were available on request. It is conceivable that all of the records depended upon the beneficiaries asking for them, though *Lex Visigothorum* does stipulate that renunciations of lost claims should be drafted and given to the victors[17]. It certainly looks, though, as if Celanova was particularly scrupulous in collecting and preserving the numerous documents created by the dispute settlement procedures: it would seem that the text, now presented as a unit, is composed of five quite separate pieces, rather inexpertly put together by a later scribe. Such a view is supported by the existence in the cartulary of yet another detached document relating to this case: it is another version of the opening section of this one, the *pactum* of the vanquished villagers, but contains some interesting differences in wording and in the provision of the *mandator*'s patronymic, which would suggest that it was not just a later copy[18]. The end product of a Leonese case, it thus appears, might produce a plethora of documents: written agreements to appear before the judges, transcript of the proceedings, record of the oaths taken by the witnesses, record of the ordeal, one or more renunciations by the losing party, and a written document of restitution. It is also conceivable, on the Celanova evidence, that multiple copies of some of these texts might be produced. As with the formulaic elements employed in their composition, so such multiplication of specialized documents argues the existence of fairly considerable bureaucratic skills, and a belief in their value.

What then of those parts of Spain where by the ninth century, if not before, the Romano-Visigothic hold was weakened or non-existent – in other words, the Arab-controlled South, the Basque regions of the western Pyrenees, and, more controversially, Castille? Of these three, it is Castille alone that has received any significant treatment: the judicial procedures of the Christians under Muslim rule and of the Basque states of Navarre and Aragón remain untouched for this period. For all of these regions before the mid-eleventh century the evidence for

17 *Leges Visigothorum*, II. v.
18 AHN Madrid, Codex 986B, 'Cartulario de Celanova', fol. 54r; printed below pp. 253–4.

such an inquiry is pitifully small, consisting of no more than half a dozen texts each for Castille and Navarre, to be compared with fifty or more each for León and Catalonia.

The traditional view is that Castille was fundamentally different from León, even when only a frontier march of that kingdom under a subordinate count[19]. This difference is held to manifest itself not only in social and economic structures – the Castillians as free men unburdened by the complex ties of dependancy that shackled their Leonese neighbours – but also in other areas such as language[20]. Here the Castillians are presented as developing new and expanding vernacular usages, whilst the Leonese remained tied by the constraints of an archaic Latin, whose hold was being reinforced by the migration into their territories throughout the tenth century of increasing numbers of Mozarabic fugitives from the South, remnants of a Visigothic past long isolated from the march of development of the rest of western Europe.

Such distinctions must inevitably be expected to manifest themselves in the field of law: the Leonese are seen as being bound to the anachronistic rulings and savageries of the Visigothic code, a dependence also held to be reinforced by the rising tide of Mozarabism, whilst the Castillians rejected its principles and social divisiveness, to depend instead upon their ancestral customary law, meted out to them by their own democratically elected leaders, the village councils, under the benevolent supervision of a line of hereditary counts, held to have secured the effective independence of Castille from Leonese overlordship by the middle of the tenth century[21]. Some of these interrelated arguments have already come under attack, the linguistic ones in particular[22]. But only a beginning has been made. The idea of the judicial peculiarity of Castille remains firmly entrenched.

Some strength might appear to have been given to these arguments by the existence in Castille of the earliest sets of local *fueros*: special rules of law, privileges and exemptions granted to local communities by their lords, notably the tenth-century counts of Castille. Unfortunately, some of those most firmly relied on by traditionalist historians can and have been shown to be forgeries of the twelfth century or later[23]. Others, whilst not outright forgeries, only survive in much later versions. Thus the relatively early *fueros* of Castrojeriz (974), which provide the only Spanish evidence for oath-helping* in this period, exist solely in the form that they received in the reign of Alfonso VII (1126–57) and even that is in the form of a confirmation of the text by Fernando III in 1234[24]. The genuinely critical study of the *fueros* is still in its infancy, but in no instance can it be said that the existing text of a set of *fueros* takes us directly to the tenth century. Nor, even if

[19] See, for instance, J. Pérez de Urbel, *Historia del Condado de Castilla.*
[20] R. Menéndez Pidal, *Los orígenes del Español*, pp. 454–60, 472–6.
[21] M. Márquez-Sterling, *Fernán González, First Count of Castile*, pp. 28–32.
[22] R. Wright, *Late Latin and Early Romance in Spain and Carolingian France*, pp. 165–73.
[23] G. Martínez Díez, *Fueros locales en el territorio de la Provincia de Burgos*, pp. 21–2.
[24] *Ibid.*, pp. 119–22.

this reservation is waived, do any of the early *fueros* lead us to a rule of law other than that of the *Forum Iudicum*, although they modify its application, for example, by guaranteeing freedom from arrest for homicide during the harvest season[25].

Within the field of dispute settlement the problem can obviously best be resolved by recourse to the handful of documents from Castille that relate to its practical workings. These consist of three texts in the twelfth-century *Becerro Gótico* of San Pedro de Cardeña, and one from the *Cartulario* of San Pedro de Arlanza of like date, both monasteries in the vicinity of Burgos, the main comital centre[26]. To these can be added a 'pseudo-original', though early, copy of a document from San Salvador de Oña, in the north of Castille, and also four cartulary copies from the monastery of Valpuesta in Alava, a generally uneasy frontier zone between the kingdoms of León and Navarre[27].

With so small a sample it is hard to talk of 'representative' texts, but one of the Cardeña documents is particularly illuminating:

In the presence of the lord, to be named with the greatest veneration, our count Férnan González, together with many other men, I García Refugano declare, at the requirement of the lord Auriulf, who speaks for Abbot Recesuinth, the truth that I do not seek to deny; which concerns the Church of SS Peter and Paul, situated at the place called Tobiella, which I recognize as proved to have been given by my brother the priest Oveco, together with himself, both body and soul, to the Lord and to the Holy Apostles Peter and Paul, and to Abbot Stephen and the congregation of Cardeña; from there I later evicted your brothers [monks], that is to say, Fortún the confessor and the priests García and Gemellus, together with their companions. Subsequently the priests Dominic and Rapinatus came there together with the count's *saio*, Sarracino Ovecoz by name, and put the monks in possession of the church again by order of the count; and we made an undertaking on the fourth day after Christmas that if I did not appear before the count with my charters whereby my brother the aforementioned priest had given me the church, in the presence of many witnesses and of Alfonso Sendiniz, then I should pay 300 *solidi* to the count through the intermediary of a *fideiussor**; but I could not prove it and in my pride I was in contempt of you, and in the judgement before the count and before the lord Abbot Sebuld, and for my sin I have denied that charter of donation of the church and that document, because my brother did not make a charter, unless it was for the rule and chastity of eleven monks ('nisi pro gubernio et continentia de undecim fratres'), and I could not prove otherwise. Hence I recognize the evidence and affirm that this statement is true, and in this statement there is nothing that I have that I should add.

This statement (*manifestum*) was made on the nineteenth of the Kalends of February (14 January) in the Era 995 (AD 957), with King Sancho ruling in León and Count Férnan González in Castille.

I, García, who wished this statement to be made and have heard it read out, have made a signature with my hand.

[25] A *fuero* for the inhabitants of 'Urdaspal', AHN Madrid, Clero, Carpeta 1405, doc. 19.
[26] The Cardeña cartulary is edited in *El Becerro gótico de San Pedro de Cardeña*, ed. L. Serrano, and that of Arlanza in *El Cartulario de San Pedro de Arlanza*, ed. L. Serrano.
[27] The Oña text is *Colección diplomática de San Salvador de Oña*, ed. J. del Alamo, vol. 1, no. 3; as this has been discussed in detail in Collins, 'Law and Charters', 508, it will not be considered again here. For the Valpuesta cartulary see L. Barrau-Dihigo (ed.), 'Chartes de l'Église de Valpuesta', *Revue Hispanique*, 7 (1900).

Munnio Didaz – Beila Didaz – Sarracino – García witness –Velasco witness – Sancho witness[28]. (App. XVI)

There are substantial difficulties with the text of this document that must reflect scribal confusion in the original if not also in the understanding of the cartulary copyist, but the outline of the proceedings seems clear: the dispute concerned a church, of which the author of the *manifestum* claimed ownership, on the basis of a non-existent charter of donation made to him by his brother. It looks as if he were the respondant, and that the monastery of Cardeña, deprived of its property by his eviction of their monks, brought the issue before the count, with the result that the *saio* was ordered to repossess them and García Refugano was instructed to produce his charters on penalty of a fine. His recognition of his inability to do so, because the document in question did not exist, followed just two weeks later, and he was required to make this statement acknowledging the monks' right and the injustice of his actions.

In all but its lack of scribal sophistication this document is a straightforward *pactum* or *evacuatio*, and mirrors what one might expect from a Leonese case of similar character. It proves the existence of at least two hearings and is itself proof of the drawing up of documents. An *assertor* speaks for the monastery, and a *saio* fulfils functions identical to those of his Leonese or Catalan counterparts. There is, admittedly, no reference to the presence of judges other than the count and probably Abbot Sebuld. This does not necessarily prove that there were no other judges there, but it does indicate a more active comital rôle in the judicial process than is to be found in the Catalan counties[29]. This is, however, paralleled in the records of hearings conducted in the presence of some of the Leonese kings. The imposition of fines for non-appearance or the non-production of evidence is also a feature common to both Leonese and Castillian texts.

Basically similar conclusions can be drawn from the other Cardeña documents relating to legal disputes. Both of them are *pacta* or *manifesta*. One of them records the final resolution on 26 February 972 of a case concerning a vineyard in the villa of Gonzalo Telliz, the modern Villagonzalo Pedernales, some 6 km south of Burgos[30]. The sense of this text as it now stands is even less clear in parts than that of the Tobiella document, and its formal structuring lacks the clarity generally to be found in Leonese charters. But it is clearly the renunciation of a false claim, and has, moreover, the unique element of the admission of previous perjury. The two individuals making the recognition had at an unspecified earlier date obtained judgement in their favour and against the monk Argemir by the means of a mendacious oath, thus, as they now admit, rendering the judges and

---

[28] *Becerro de Cardeña*, no. 210. The witnesses all have Basque names.

[29] In Catalan hearings presided over by counts, the active rôle in questioning the litigants and witnesses and in making judgement is ascribed to the panel of judges. In several cases counts are the losing party in hearings over which they preside; see, for example, *Marca Hispanica*, App., no. 34.

[30] *Becerro de Cardeña*, no. 97.

boni homines wrong in their judgement as to the truth of the issue. How the perjury subsequently came to be detected is, unfortunately, not revealed. This document, as well as providing another Castillian example of a *manifestum*, also shows the important rôle of oath-taking in the judicial procedures of the county; it is similar again, therefore, to those of León.

The general impression is not contradicted by the third of the Cardeña texts, dated 15 February 941, which is very akin to the first one. It is a recognition by a priest called Gonzalo, made before Count Férnan González and unspecified others, that the claim of Cardeña to a certain church at Pesquera de Ebro was justly based upon a written deed of gift made to them by his uncle. In the document he pledged himself to return it to the monks 'per manus sayone', following the restitutory procedure to be found recorded in various contemporary Leonese texts. In both this and the previous document future challenges to the validity of the monks' title will incur the payment of penal fines of 300 *solidi* to the 'Dominus terre', in both cases probably the count of Castille. This is also a feature of the single relevant Arlanza document, though the penalty included in the minatory clause is specified as being 'one talent of gold'[31]. This text is also an *evacuatio* or *manifestum*, though here it is called a *dimissio*, resulting from a hearing held before 'iudicem nostro Nunnum Sonac' and in the presence of the council of Gostiace. Unusually, the document has a scribal signature. The victor in the case is a lady Fronildis, who employed an *assertor*. Women are never recorded as speaking 'in their own voice' in any Spanish case, but there were no restrictions on their initiation of litigation.

Before drawing general conclusions about Castillian practices, it is worth considering the four documents from Valpuesta, from the remoter though neighbouring county of Lantarón. Two of them are *conditiones sacramentorum*, records of oaths taken by witnesses, which are dated 911 and 919[32]. In both instances the procedures followed are those to be encountered in the Leonese texts of this class, involving the swearing of an oath by the Trinity, on various relics, by the Apostles, and on the Four Gospels. In the second text it is formally noted that this was recorded by the *saio* Peter, whilst in the first one the *conditiones* run directly into a brief *recognitio* by the losing party. In neither case is there any reference to an ordeal. The first hearing was conducted by the count, named Gonzalo Telluz (as was the villa in the Cardeña text of 972), who ordered the taking of the witnesses' oaths, but that of 919 was held before the judge Vigila 'and many other judges'. The general impression seems to be that in the presence of a count in both Castille and Lantarón other judges did not sit, or their rôle was deliberately not recorded, but that at least individual judges could be found conducting hearings within the counties. There is insufficient information to say whether they operated over a large or a small geographical area, but despite

---

[31] *Ibid.*, no. 265; *Cartulario de Arlanza*, no. 18.
[32] Barrau-Dihigo (ed.), 'Chartes de Valpuesta', nos. 11 and 12.

references to 'many' judges, there are few indications of the functioning of large panels of judges such as existed in León and Catalonia.

Two judges, probably brothers, oversaw the next hearing from the Valpuesta cartulary, which is recorded in the form of a brief *recognitio*[33]. Quite unprecedentedly, four *saiones* are recorded in the list of witnesses, evidence at least of their existence in Lantarón as well as in León, Castille and Catalonia. The minatory fine for any future impugning of the abbey's title to the disputed church, that of St Cyprian at Pando, is set at twelve cows, payable to the abbot-bishop of Valpuesta rather than to the count. A pledge of cows features in the final document, a *cauto* by a certain Vermudo, who was required to present two *fidiatores** to the abbot in case he should commit any further offences (of a kind unspecified) against the abbey[34]. In none of these texts is there any suggestion of the count benefiting from the profits of justice, which is a marked feature of the Castillian texts but not to be found in any of the other dependent counties of the Leonese kingdom. In León proper and in Galicia such fines were probably payable to the king[35].

Overall the character and classification of the documents and the procedures they describe indicate that Castillian practices were virtually identical to those to be found in contemporary León and Galicia. The occasionally baffling or hybrid quality of some of the texts would seem to suggest that notarial traditions were not strong in Castille, hardly surprising in a frontier region, and it is quite conceivable that all of these texts were written by the beneficiary. The first of the Cardeña documents makes it clear that it was enscribed on the spot at the end of the final hearing. Some of the cases may originally have been represented by more than one deed and it is possible that chance alone has restricted them to their present small number. Certainly the way in which some of the issues turned squarely upon the possession or otherwise of charters is indicative of the importance vested in the holding of written evidence of title.

Although it falls within the framework of the Visigothic legal tradition, the more rough and ready character of the Castillian documentation is hardly a cause for surprise. Burgos, only founded in 884, was by no means yet comparable to León or even Astorga and Zamora in size and importance, and none of the other settlements in Castille would yet be worth dignifying with the title of town. The frontier, not only *vis-à-vis* the Umayyads in the south, but also in respect of the Banu Hud in Zarogoza and other Arab and *Muwallad* marcher lordships in the upper Ebro Valley, kept Castille permanently open to incursion from several directions throughout the two centuries[36]. It is hardly surprising that, in such circumstances, its judicial organization was not as consistent or as sophisticated

---

[33] *Ibid.*, no. 33. [34] *Ibid.*, no. 39.

[35] *Becerro de Cardeña*, no. 98, for payment to the 'Dominus terrae' (in AD 972); from 974 such payments are said to be due 'ad regiam partem', *ibid.*, no. 55.

[36] R. Collins, *Early Medieval Spain: Unity in Diversity, 400–1000*, pp. 190–200, 238–44.

as that of the Leonese heartlands, but that it derived its principles and practices from León and the tradition of Visigothic law seems impossible to deny. That there are no instances of the specific citation of the *Forum Iudicum* in the Castillian texts is easily explicable in that the only classes of document we have in the small corpus of surviving evidence are *conditiones* and *manifesta*, in neither of which would such references be expected to appear.

If, then, Castille, despite certain practical limitations, really belongs to the broad spectrum of the Visigothic legal world, what may be said of the Christian communities of Al-Andalus, Muslim Spain? The general conservatism of the Mozarabs towards the Visigothic past is well known, and it is significant that in 1085 Alfonso VI confirmed the *Forum Iudicum* as the law to be applied in newly conquered Toledo, just as Fernando III was to do in Andalucia in 1236 and 1248. The Visigothic law was the law the Mozarabs knew and must have used, not least as the only alternative was Koranic law, which, because of its religious character, they would not have been entitled to use in disputes amongst themselves, nor would its use have been desired[37]. Unfortunately, a lack of documents makes the question of the practical application of Visigothic law in Islamic Spain almost impossible to approach; there is, however, one text that provides at least a glimpse of it.

This comes from the frontier region of the Ebro valley, in the vicinity of Lérida, which explains the chance of its survival when virtually all other administrative records of Al-Andalus have been lost: the document was preserved in the archive of the Pyrenean see of Roda, probably because the land in question subsequently came into the possession of the bishopric[38]. It survived long enough to be copied in the nineteenth century, but has now, unfortunately, disappeared.

In the name of the Lord God Eternal. The men of Kastro Aquilanido and the men of Jonsedh gathered on account of an altercation that occurred amongst them over that inheritance which they had sold one to another; and afterwards, as a result, the men of Aquilanido made an oath to the men of Jonsed. These are their names: Fortún son of Aberla, and Ferruz son of Hecca, and Guisandi son of Christopher, and Nunnus son of Hondemar, and Endura son of Ramio, and Exipio son of Ramio, and Altemir son of Axenci, and Rechesendi son of Oriulf, and Albin son of Hichila, and Uddi son of Savila, and Rechesendi son of Altemir. And these aforementioned men made their oaths in the Church of St Sebastian, the Martyr of Christ, that they had the third part in that salt pan by inheritance, and that they had not bought any inheritance from the men of Jonsed, neither field nor vineyard, after Azeka fell upon them. And they made these oaths by order of Fertun the priest, judge for all of the Christians of Lérida, under the rule of Zamega the Vizier. And those who heard their oaths were Comparati son of Aquila, and Exebi the priest son of Bia, and Bonofilio son of Omar. And it was the Kalends of April in the Era 1025 (1 April AD 987). (App. XVII)

---

[37] *Ibid.*, pp. 206–18; F. J. Simonet, *Historia de los Mozárabes de España*, cc. 13–17.
[38] *Catalunya Carolíngia III: Els Comtats de Pallars i Ribagorcca*, ed. R. d'Abadal, no. 270; see below, p. 235.

This then is a form of *conditiones sacramentorum*. It is much sparser than its Leonese or Catalan counterparts, though clearly generically related to them. There is no record of what the oaths were sworn on, and only the barest reference to the previous hearing at which the judge had ordered the *sacramenta* to be taken. The starkly monotheistic opening formula is notable, and may represent some form of Islamic pressure on the drafting of Christian documents of a public character, whilst the reference to the priest Fertun acting as judge of all the Christians in Lérida is clear evidence of the existence of such officials, doubtless to be found in all the main regional centres of Christian population in Al-Andalus. The mention of the depredations of Azeka is obscure, though may conceivably refer to a civil war of 975 between the governor of Lérida and a rival *Muwallad* lord, in which the Christians are recorded as supporting the losing side[39]. Though hardly a sample, the only extant judicial document from Islamic Spain thus supports the view, which might have been defended on theoretical grounds anyway, that the Visigothic legal legacy was alive in Al-Andalus, subject possibly to minor modifications as a result of the Muslim control of the state.

This just leaves the Basque-populated regions of the western Pyrenees as the only other part of the peninsula in which some alternative system of law might have existed before the eleventh century. In practice this means a search amongst the documents of Aragón. This small area in the mid Pyrenees first emerges as a county under Frankish control in the very early ninth century, but after the second battle of Roncesvalles in 824 and the creation of an independent Basque kingdom around Pamplona, Aragón seems to have been drawn quickly into the orbit of its neighbour, to which, despite the latter disappearance of the language in the region, it was also tied by bonds of racial and linguistic unity[40]. However, although the kingdom of Pamplona was both larger and generally more important than Aragón, it appears to have been slower in developing monastic institutions (or at least ones that have left records) and in assigning importance to charters; though an exception must be made in these respects for the area of the Rioja[41]. That region apart, no diplomatic of any sort can be securely assigned to the kingdom of Pamplona proper until the last quarter of the tenth century, and even then there is little of it. Aragón is in this respect slightly but significantly better.

It is able for one thing to offer us a genuine original document of judicial importance from the tenth century, the interpretation of which can be assisted by the study of some half a dozen other dispute settlement texts from cartularies.

---

[39] R. Pita Merce, *Lérida Arabe*, pp. 56–8.
[40] R. Collins, 'The Basques in Aquitaine and Navarre' in J. Gillingham and J. C. Holt (eds.), *War and Government in the Middle Ages*, pp. 3–17; J. M. Lacarra, *Aragón en el pasado*, cc. 1 and 2.
[41] For the limited number and suspicious character of the earliest Navarrese charters see J. Goñi Gaztambide, *Catálogo del Archivo Catedral de Pamplona*, vol. 1, nos. 1–7; *idem*, *Catálogo del Becerro antiguo y del Becerro menor de Leyre*, nos. 1–13; compare this with the substantial collection of charters from San Millán in the Rioja: *Cartulario de San Millán de la Cogolla*, ed. A. Ubieto Arteta, contains 119 pre-eleventh-century charters.

The original is preserved in the archive of the cathedral of Jaca, and has been twice edited, although only on the basis of a second-hand transcript and of a photograph[42]. The first and more accessible edition has been shown up by the second to contain serious omissions and misreadings, though it is also possible that the later edition has been over optimistic in its filling of what its predecessor recorded as *lacunae*. On the basis of the fuller and more accurate version it reads:

In the name and grace of God. This is the charter of corroboration concerning the allod of Gausa and its boundary, which Bishop Fortún and his brothers held as an allod from their parents, with no heir unless God; a boundary highly esteemed for more than a hundred years and with no one disputing it. After this they gave the land to the men of the villages round about to be worked. When the bishop died these men denied that these were the lands that they held. Therefore free men (*barones*) and the count and judges (*judiciales*) and abbots came together about that boundary, and they adjudged that they [the men] should validate their lands and boundary, and should they lose their lands and boundary they should pay in law whatever the judicial assembly commanded, and the lands be taken into possession. Thus, I Bishop Atto and my brothers presented as witnesses good old men from the vicinity, and they testified and wished to validate and to swear. [But] it was pleasing to Count Fortún Jiménez and to Abbot Bancio and to other men that they should not swear, and they divided that boundary and made a compromise (*cominenza*), as is the law concerning land, and we left the decision as the good men (*boni barones*) had seen it, so that neither should they have any complaint, nor I against them. And after this had been done and Fortún Jiménez left Aragón, those men (*homines*) broke the agreement and sent Sancho Jiménez a [or perhaps 'as'] Galiffa, and entered a plea before the king, Lord Sancho, and his men (*barones*), and those men (*homines*) could not through any relative have any part [in the estate]. After this they went to King García Sánchez, when he was coming from the partition of Enneco Sánchez, and he judged them in that road, at St Stephen of Binaqua, at which they claimed that allod and could not produce witnesses. After this had been done, King García Sánchez and his son commanded that Oriolus Galíndez, the father of Bishop Atto, should pace out the boundary and should swear on the altar, and this he did in St Vincent of Larbesa, that no one else should have a share other than the sons of the lady Inchulzata; when the lady Inchulzata handed it over to her son the lord Fortún, bishop in Sesave, she gave that Monte Besauni to St Adrian, and her husband thus gave . . . [the document is mutilated here] free of sons and daughters and of all other relatives other than those who served in St Adrian. On account of this Oriolus Galíndez validated it, and there were there as witnesses Abbot Bancio, and Dutisforti, Asner Hundrisculi, Enneco Donati the priest, Bradila Belascus, García Tolluz, Ato Banzonis, García Bradilanis, Lope Enneconis, Galindo Banzoniz, Psalla Asnari with his brothers, Belasco Sancionis with his brothers, García Jiménez and his brothers, and many others whom it would be long to write down. And whoever wishes to disrupt that which has been done, first let the anger of God descend upon him and may he have his portion with the traitor Judas in the lower inferno. Amen. This charter was made in the Era 996 (AD 958). Peace be to all hearers and readers. Amen.

García Sánchez validating ✠ Sancho Garcés son of the aforementioned king validating ✠ Salvus unworthy Abbot of Albelda, I have signed this testament of the kings with my hand ✠. (App. XVIII)

---

[42] Edited firstly in R. del Arce, 'El Archivo de la Catedral de Jaca', *Boletín de la Real Academia de la Historia*, 65 (1914), 49–51, and secondly in M. Serrano y Sanz, 'Un documento del obispo aragonés D. Aton' in *Homenaje a D. Carmelo de Echegaray*, pp. 42–3.

The most obvious thing about this document apart from its lack of clarity, some of which has had to be glossed over in the translation, is that it does not fit into any of the standard classes of text that can be established by study of the Leonese and Catalan deeds. It makes reference to witnesses and to oath-taking but is not a set of *conditiones*; there is no element of *evacuatio*, and, aside from a brief piece of direct speech on the part of Bishop Atto, makes no attempt to be a transcript of any of the several hearings that it describes. It is basically a narrative that sums up the final result of a complex set of judicial processes.

The first hearing was held in the presence of *barones* (who would seem to play a rôle equivalent to the Catalan *boni homines*), judges (?) and the count, and in the course of it Bishop Atto, whose relationship to Bishop Fortún is never specified, produces witnesses, who are prepared both to testify and to take an oath, thus so far following a pattern familiar to us from Leonese and Catalan texts. But the count and Abbot Bancio, who appear in this as the presidents of the court, were unwilling for things to go so far, and preferred that the parties should reach a compromise, or *cominenza* (a rare synonym of *conveniencia*) as the document calls it, 'sicut est lege de terra'. Both this particular term and specific injunctions to seek mutually acceptable agreements feature in several other of the Aragonese dispute settlement documents of the tenth and also eleventh centuries[43]. This is in marked contrast to the Leonese and Catalan texts, which virtually always contain decisive adjudications for or against the contending parties; any element of compromise there may have been in practice is kept hidden, as far as the documents are concerned.

In the end the villagers' persistence seems to have lost them the case absolutely, and with it any benefit from the *cominenza* it might have been better to have left unbroken. It may have been their refusal to remain satisfied with that agreement that led to the full resolution of the dispute, as the evidence in the final hearing was hardly weightier than that offered in the first one. This was the oath sworn by Bishop Atto's father and his perambulation of the boundaries of the estate, probably to define them. He testified that only the heirs of the lady Inchulzata, mother of Bishop Fortún, should have any rights to the property, and not, it would seem, just any heirs of the body. The following passages come from the most damaged part of the document but the indications are that Inchulzata gave the property to the monastic church of St Adrian at Sasave, which was also the bishop's see, during the course of her son's episcopate. Other relatives are excluded from claims on it. Why does Bishop Atto's father feature so prominently in all of this? One solution that might clarify this and some of the other problems would be the supposition that Oriolus Galíndez was himself the husband of Inchulzata and thus father of both bishops. Otherwise it is hard to see how the family property of Bishop Fortún and his brothers (called *germanos* not *fratres*)

---

[43] Amongst other examples see two from San Juan de la Peña: AHN Madrid, Clero, Carpeta 701, no. 16, and Carpeta 709, no. 15.

also became the property of the next bishop and his brothers, whose father also had the crucial rôle to play in defining its boundaries and inheritance rights.

There are elements in this text that are reminiscent of Frankish procedures or terminology, others that seem in a legal sense Visigothic, and yet others that may be related to neither and might be considered to be local and customary. Amongst the 'Frankish symptoms' may be included the classification of the disputed estate as alodial. Admittedly, the concept of the *alodium* was not in principle alien to Visigothic law, but this term for a freely heritable and unencumbered piece of landed property was a Frankish peculiarity[44]. It had, however, spread to the Frankish March south of the Pyrenees, and is to be found widely used in Catalan charters[45]. Catalan influence might account for the appearance of the term in this text; it would not, however, explain the use of *barones*, indicating here both freemen and royal vassals. Both of these usages feature in Frankish legislation and in later Aragonese texts, but neither can be found in Visigothic, or later Spanish, ones[46]. It is true that the word *barones*, with the implication of freemen, also appears in the Lombard Edict of Rothari, but the relatively widespread employment of the term in Frankish codes, and its apparently total absence from Leonese and Catalan documents, must make direct Frankish influence seem the most plausible explanation in this case[47].

Features more suggestive of Visigothic legal procedures might be the walking of the boundaries and the employment of an oath in the processes of verification. However, it must be remembered that all too little is known of the settlement of disputes in Francia other than in the presence of the king, and that such pacing out of controverted boundaries appears to be a Europe-wide phenomenon, probably, therefore, with Roman roots[48]. Thus neither of these items could safely be claimed to be exclusively Visigothic in origin, any more than could the existence of a documentary record of the proceedings. On the other hand, although most extant Spanish early medieval dispute settlement documents record decisive adjudications between rival claims, there is an emphasis on compromise in the laws of *Lex Visigothorum* that is not to be found in *Lex Salica* and other Frankish codes, especially in cases where written evidence was not forthcoming[49].

Alternatively, the search for a *cominenza* or accommodation between the parties may be more a reflection of customary norms. It is interesting that this was

[44] S.v. *Alodis* in J. F. Niermeyer, *Mediae Latinitatis Lexicon Minus*, pp. 36–8.
[45] To take just a few examples from one small Catalan county: C. Baraut (ed.), 'Els documents, dels segles IX i X, conservats a l'Arxiu Capitular de la Seu d'Urgell', *Urgellia*, 2 (1979), nos. 32, 39, 40, 49, 65, 68, 70, 84, 88, 95.
[46] S.v. *baro* in Niermeyer, *Lexicon*, pp. 85–6; for the later use in Aragón see C. Dufresne Du Cange, *Glossarium ad Scriptores Mediae et Infirmae Latinitatis*, vol. 1, p. 487.
[47] *Edictus Rothari*, ch. 14, in *Leges Langobardorum*, ed. F. Beyerle, p. 20.
[48] For the limitations of the Frankish evidence see the paper by Fouracre above pp. 26–7; for boundary walking in the Byzantine Empire see Morris below, pp. 135, 146.
[49] *Leges Visigothorum*, VII. v. 7.

the aim of the judges at the earliest and most localized phase of the proceedings, and that a decisive determination between the claimants only became the object when the case was brought before the kings; though this may have been conditioned by the refusal of one of the two parties to abide by the agreed compromise. The key phrase is obviously 'sicut est lege de terra', which might be translated as 'according to the law relating to land', or conceivably as 'following the custom of the land'. The use of the term *lex* does generally indicate written law, which in this case, for the reasons just mentioned, must be that of *Lex Visigothorum*[50]. However, in the absence of *any* comparable texts with similar usages from this region at this period it is dangerous to be too categoric. As has been seen, both in terminology and in the structuring of the document, local conventions here appear to be at some variance with those of the rest of the peninsula. It must be said, though, that when a sufficient corpus of Aragonese texts is available, that is, from the second half of the eleventh century, forms and procedures are generally congruous with those encountered elsewhere in northern Spain[51]. It is possible, therefore, that what we have in this Jaca document is an early Aragonese experiment in the use of written record, influenced by both Frankish and Visigothic legal norms, and with still some elements of local custom in the procedures being recorded, including perhaps the holding of the hearing in the open on the (king's) road.

There are one or two other minor issues that need clarification. Serrano y Sanz, the second editor of the text, thought that the king Sancho of the second hearing was Sancho I Garcés (905–25)[52]. This is impossible: both Count Fortún Jiménez and Abbot Bancio feature in the initial hearing, which, by Serrano's argument, must have been held before 925; but Bancio also signed the final document of 958. According to Serrano's dating, Bishop Fortún of Sasave would therefore have had to have been dead before 925, but can be shown to have been still living in 947. The only solution is that the 'King Sancho' is Sancho II Abarca (970–94), who during the lifetime of his father, García Sánchez I (933–70), served as subordinate king in Aragón, and who also signed this *testamentum regum*[53]. This would also indicate that the sequence of hearings was probably quite close in time, with Bishop Fortún still living in 947 and the whole issue being resolved in 958.

It is notable that this case, with all its ramifications, did not involve any written evidence, but at the end of it someone felt it necessary to have a record made of it.

---

[50] P. Wormald, '*Lex Scripta* and *Verbum Regis*' in P. H. Sawyer and I. N. Wood (eds.), *Early Medieval Kingship*.

[51] For later Aragonese texts see the collections in *Colección diplomática de la Catedral de Huesca*, ed. A. Durán Gudiol; *Colección diplomática de Pedro I de Aragon y de Navarra*, ed. A. Ubieto Arteta.

[52] Serrano y Sanz, 'Un documento de . . . D. Aton', pp. 43–4.

[53] For another document referring to Sancho ruling in Aragon under his father see *Cartulario de San Juan de la Peña*, ed. A. Ubieto Arteta, no. 18. On Sasave, *idem*, 'La diócesis Navarro-Aragonesas durante los siglos IX y X', *Pirineos*, 10 (1959).

Several of the other Aragonese texts seem to indicate the rise at this time of a growing awareness of the need to create and preserve documents. One of these also provides us with evidence as to how boundary disputes could be settled in the region: it is dated 928, but comes from a cartulary copy in the eleventh-century *Libro Gótico* of San Juan de la Peña.

⨎ In the name and grace of Christ.
    Notification and explanation of the boundary of St John.
    In those times when Fortún Garcés was ruling in Pamplona, there was a dispute over the boundary between neighbouring villages, one of which was called Banassa and the other of which was called Katamesas. And King Fortún Garcés came with his sons and the noble men of his land and abbots and priests, and he held a hearing concerning that boundary, and the king came with a multitude of men and imposed a boundary. The king himself on his horse went ahead pacing it out and the other men came after him. A great multitude validated this, he (the king) preceding all.
    With this finished and after much time had passed, he having lived until then, God set up King Sancho Garcés, the lord and governor of the land and defender of the people, and he ruled in Pamplona and in Deia. He ruled for twenty years and died.
    And after his death came the lord bishop Galindo, and in order to validate it again he gathered together other men, who knew that boundary. And abbots and priests perambulated it; just as they had seen the king go round it, so they went round it, and they went from the line of that stream which descends from St Vincent in the direction of the vineyard of Enneco Asnari and comes to the bad ford on the eastern side and to the canal of Banassa on the western side, just as the water turns. And they wrote this charter so that there should be no disagreement between us and the others.
    And concerning this these named witnesses swore: the monks (*fratres*) Isinarius, who was Master of the Horse to Fortún Garcés, and Sancho Centulli the priest, and Enneco Sánchez the priest; and these three swore in St John as to what they had heard with their ears and seen with their eyes, in the presence of King Jimeno Garcés and his ward, the Lord García, son of King Sancho Garcés. And the lord bishop Galindo presented as witnesses the named abbots and priests: [there follows a list of four abbots, nineteen priests and thirteen *seniores viros*].
    This charter was made in the Era 966, when Jimeno Garcés was ruling with his ward the lord García in Pamplona and in Deia, and the lord bishop Galindo was ruling similarly in Pamplona and in Deia and in Castro Sancti Stefani[54]. (App. XIX)

It is notable that no one thought at the time of the original settlement of the boundary dispute by King Fortún Garcés (*c.* 880–905) of providing a written account. The proceedings in 928, with the attendance of so many abbots, priests and secular *seniores*, could have formed part of some form of diocesan council; otherwise it is hard to understand why so many of them should be interested in what appears to be a village boundary dispute. It seems that only three witnesses of the original creation of the boundary still survived, and this may have prompted the making of the record. It is not explained, and perhaps no one any longer knew, on what basis King Fortún made his division, whether it was to some degree arbitrary or was dependent upon the existence of earlier boundaries. But the

---

[54] *Cartulario de San Juan de la Peña*, no. 14.

procedures followed for the confirmation carried out by Bishop Galindo are effectively identical to those employed in Catalonia in the resolution of boundary disputes, in that evidence is taken on oath from witnesses and, moreover, the salient physical features of the boundary are then recorded in the document, something not usually done in León[55].

The basic difference again lies in the form of the document rather than in the procedures it seems to describe. The narrative and anecdotal quality of this text is very marked, and this is generally true of all of the Aragonese dispute texts of this period. It looks as if the concept of the charter is only just beginning to take hold in the region, and this may explain the somewhat experimental character of these documents, and the need to compress the previous history of an estate or of a dispute into a single text. A full study of all forms of Aragonese and Navarrese diplomatic would be necessary to substantiate this impression, but it may be given some confirmation by the high rate of forgery to be encountered amongst the documents and cartularies of these regions, a problem hardly to be encountered elsewhere in the substantial corpus of Spanish early medieval *diplomata**[56]. It is usually possible to detect such forgeries and to trace their origins, generally to territorial and jurisdictional disputes of the twelfth and thirteenth centuries. The history of Navarre and Aragón in the ninth and tenth centuries is not appreciably more turbulent than that of the rest of Christian Spain, and so it is reasonable to suspect that the low survival rate of their charters is not just accidental. They probably did not exist in anything like the quantities that were being created in León and Catalonia. The lack of such records necessitated the later large-scale forging. Such a view cannot but be reinforced by the dispute settlement evidence, which is clearly indicative of a lack of concern or expectation for the use of written testimony, and the emphasis on *cominenza* would also militate against the employment of such hard-and-fast titles of ownership as provided by charters. From the middle of the tenth century there appears to have been a slow pressure towards change, resulting possibly from greater Navarrese involvement in the Rioja and Castille, where the use of charters was well established and whose monasteries had benefited from the receipt of written titles to property from the Leonese kings and lesser lay patrons. Similarly, the thoroughly Catalan traditions of Ribagorza must have exercised some influence over at least eastern Aragón[57].

In terms of *Lex Visigothorum* Navarre and Aragón may look out of step with the rest of the peninsula; and to a certain extent they were. There are no *assertores* or *mandatarii* to be found in the documents; no evidence of notaries, and it may be

---

[55] For boundaries see nn. 13 and 14 above.

[56] For Navarrese forgeries and a context for their composition see J. Goñi Gaztambide, *Historia de los obispos de Pamplona*, vol. 1, pp. 441–54; on those of Aragón see *Cartulario de San Juan de la Peña*, vol. 1, for the editor's verdicts – though he has in general been a little too lenient.

[57] For an instance of such influence compare the eastern Aragonese text of *Colección diplomática de Obarra*, ed. A. J. Martín Duque, no. 82, with its equivalents from Pallars and Ribagorza, such as *Catalunya Carolíngia*, vol. 3, no. 297.

doubted if a class of professional judges existed at least before the early eleventh century. We hear of counts 'judging in Aragón', and cases of no apparent importance are heard before the kings. However, for all of that, the procedures that we see, and even the unusual emphasis on compromise, which may indicate the greater limitations on enforcement in this society, can be tied to the Visigothic judicial tradition. It may be noticed too that the very conception of *lex* here had to derive from Romano-Visigothic roots; there being no indigenous Basque word for 'law' any more than there is for 'king'[58]. It is also worth recalling that the two finest manuscripts of the *Forum Iudicum* ever made were written within the confines of the kingdom of Pamplona, and in a full-page illumination parallel the Visigothic legislators Chindasuinth, Reccesuinth and Egica with the three contemporary rulers of Navarre: Sancho II Abarca, his wife Queen Urraca, daughter of the Castillian count Férnan González, and his brother Ramiro, king of Viguera (d. 991)[59].

Whether the conventions of the Visigothic law were themselves but newly introduced into Navarre and Aragón, paralleling the rise of interest in written records and reflecting recent influences from the Rioja, Castille and the eastern Pyrenees, cannot be now determined, but they were being applied and enforced in the kingdom of Pamplona and county of Aragón in the eleventh century, if not earlier. Thus in terms of the documentary evidence, the whole of the Iberian peninsula reflects fidelity to the jurisprudence and judicial norms of the Visigothic law, even in areas hardly touched by the Visigothic monarchy of the seventh century. Allowances must be made for some variations in scribal training and conventions and for a quite limited measure of regional divergence and development as well as for some possible vestiges of custom, but it looks as if the grip of the *Forum Iudicum* and Visigothic judicial *formulae** was even stronger by the end of the first millenium AD than it had been at the time of the first compilation of the code, some three hundred and fifty years previously; and it still had nearly three centuries of active life ahead of it.

[58] S.v. 'Errege' and 'Lege' in Resurrección M. de Azkue, *Diccionario Vasco–Español–Frances*, vol. 1, pp. 265, 537; it is conceivable, though highly unlikely, that these loan words could have ousted earlier indigenous terms.

[59] M. C. Díaz y Díaz, *Libros y librerías en la Rioja altomedieval*, pp. 63–70, 155–62; for a colour illustration of this full page illumination see P. de Palol and M. Hirmer, *Early Medieval Art in Spain*, plate VI, p. 30.

6

Land disputes and their social framework in Lombard–Carolingian Italy, 700–900

CHRIS WICKHAM

There are about 150 court-cases surviving from the eighth- and ninth-century kingdom of Italy, mostly as originals, in archives throughout the kingdom. Most of them are formal *placita**, public hearings held by state officials. The fifteen or so others, so-called 'informal' cases, were heard under the aegis of unofficial judges which in our documents in practice always means the church. These are often indistinguishable from *placita* in their procedural norms, and can in large part be assimilated to the public judicial system – they show, that is, the church standing in for the state, rather than the church exercising private judicial powers over its own properties. We can thus use these cases, too, as examples of normal judicial procedures. Churches were the preservers of all the judicial documents we have, in fact, in Italy as elsewhere in Europe. We cannot help this, and it would be scarcely worth mentioning, except in that it explains why churches are almost invariably parties to the cases we have, and almost invariably win: there was no incentive to keep cases they lost. At least one can say that a wide range of churches kept *placita*; but this general ecclesiastical imbalance must be kept in mind during what follows[1].

Let us first look at a case of 847, which survives as an original in the archiepiscopal archive in Lucca.

[1] Lombard court-cases begin in 673. Those up to 774, less than twenty in all, are all in *Codice diplomatico longobardo*, vols. 1 and 2, ed. L. Schiaparelli (henceforth Schiaparelli, cited by no.); *Codice diplomatico longobardo*, vol. 3, pt 1, ed. C. R. Brühl (henceforth Brühl, cited by no.); and *Regesto di Farfa*, ed. I. Giorgi and U. Balzani (henceforth RF, cited by no.). The major edition of cases (*placita**) after 774 is *I placiti del 'Regnum Italiae'*, ed. C. Manaresi (henceforth Manaresi, cited by no.): vol. 1 goes up to 945 (no. 144). Manaresi missed some, now edited by R. Volpini, 'Placiti del "Regnum Italiae" (Secc. IX–XI)' in P. Zerbi (ed.), *Contributi dell'istituto di storia medioevale*, vol. 3, pp. 245–520 (henceforth Volpini, cited by no.). He also excluded cases not run by state officials, of which I know about fifteen for the period to 900 (although there must be others) and many more after 950 or so: I will cite these in their editions when relevant. R. Hübner lists most of them in his checklist of Italian court-cases, 'Gerichtsurkunden der fränkischen Zeit, pt 2', *ZRG*, *Germ. Abt.*, 14 (1893), appendix; he also includes cases outside the Italian kingdom, from Benevento, Salerno, and Naples (about fifteen, from 740 to 900), which come from areas of varying judicial practice, and which I will mostly set aside. The best introductory critical survey of the Italian *placitum* as document, with extensive bibliography, is H. Keller, 'I placiti nella storiografia degli ultimi cento anni' in Istituto storico italiano per il medioevo, *Fonti medioevali e problematica storiografica*, vol. 1, pp. 41–68.

In the name of the Lord. While Adelbertus most illustrious duke [of Tuscany], together with Ambrosius venerable bishop of this city of Lucca, were sitting here in Lucca in the ducal court in judgement, with us Aron the gastald*, and the *scabini** Ardo, Petrus, Andreas and Gherimundo, to deliberate about the lawsuits of individual men; there were also with us [17 other named men] and many others. And there came there before us Andreas, the advocate of the baptismal church of S. Giulia, built at Controne, as well as the brothers Draco and Walperto, who were having a dispute. Andreas said to us: 'These brothers Draco and Walperto unjustly hold the properties of S. Giulia, whose advocate I am, which are to be found at *Filectule* near Granaiola; whence I seek that you give judgement between us'. Draco and Walperto replied: 'We do not know the property you are talking about'. When this was said, Andreas by our judgement gave *wadia** [a judicial pledge] to the brothers that he would show them the property, and we had the brothers give Andreas *wadia* that they would be ready to receive this demonstration on the spot, and put the property to judgement. Then they named guarantors for the pledges [*fideiussores**] and we ordered [a day] to be agreed between them.

On the agreed day both sides returned to us in judgement, and Andreas said to us: 'I have shown to the brothers Draco and Walperto the aforesaid properties in *Filectule*; I wish you to give me the right, for they are seen to hold them unjustly'. Draco and Walperto replied to this: 'We have this property, but not unjustly, for we bought it from Flaiperto son of the late Pino, and we have here the charter* in our hands, and according to the text of the charter we wish to offer as its authors* and defenders Fraimanno son of the same Flaiperto and his other heirs'. We, hearing this, had the charter read out, and among other things it contained what the brothers had asserted. And according to the text of the charter they gave *wadia* to Andreas to give him the author, and we had Andreas give *wadia* that he was prepared to receive the author from them. They placed guarantors between them and agreed [a day].

On the agreed day both parties, Andreas, Draco and Walperto, returned before us, the above-named Petrus and Andreas *scabini*, and with us were present [13 named men, mostly different from before], and others. Then Walperto and Draco according to their *wadia* presented to us Fraimanno their author and said to Andreas: 'Here is our author, deal with him'. This Fraimanno narrated against Andreas: 'I reckon myself author for the property of these brothers, because my father Flaiperto who sold it to them, more than thirty years ago, was its owner'. This said, we asked Fraimanno if he could prove what he said with witnesses. He said: 'I cannot'. Then Andreas proclaimed: 'I can prove by witness that this property was held in full ownership by the church of S. Giulia during the last thirty years'. Fraimanno said: 'What you say is false'. And, since the argument flared up so much between them, we judged that Andreas should give *wadia* to Fraimanno that he would prove what he said, and that Fraimanno should give *wadia* to him that he was prepared to receive this proof. They placed guarantors between them and agreed a day.

On the agreed day we the above-named Aron the gastald, Petrus, Andreas and Gherimundo the *scabini* were sitting in the same ducal court, and sitting with us were Iohannes and Adelperto *scabini* and Ambrosius and Iohannes bishops [of Lucca and Pisa] and Heriprando and Cuniperto royal vassals, and there were also present [17 named men] and many others. Then Andreas brought out his witnesses, Cunimundo and his brother Iohannes and Wito, and when they were presented we asked Fraimanno if he had anything to say against these witnesses. He said: 'I have nothing to say against the acceptability of the brothers, but about this other called Wito I say the truth, that he does not have property worth 150 *solidi**; therefore I wish you to hold testimony about this'. Then Gherimundo the *scabinus* and Adelperto and his brother Appo each witnessed singly saying: 'We know truly, that this Wito has more than 150 *solidi*'s worth between [landed] property and movables, and can certainly give evidence'. And when Wito had been witnessed by these men, we the above-named judges took the witnesses separately and began to inquire of them diligently one by one. First Cunimundo said: 'I know that property in *Filectule*, whence there is dispute between Fraimanno, and Andreas for S. Giulia, and I know that S. Giulia has held it in ownership during the last thirty years'. Iohannes and Wito said the same. We then had them led to the holy gospels, and each witness we had affirm their testimony on the gospels. Furthermore, Andreas the advocate swore on the gospels that the testimony the witness offered for this case was said truly. And when all this was done before us thus, it seemed right to us, together with the nobles and others present, that we judged that the church of S. Giulia should have the property, according to the proof that was made before us, without the opposition of Fraimanno, and that Fraimanno should remain content and without rights in it. And at once we had Fraimanno return this property to Andreas on behalf of the church. And then by our judgement Fraimanno gave *wadia* to Andreas that he should return the crops that he had taken from the property since the beginning of the case, on oath, according to the law. And as the case had been set out and discussed before us, we enacted that a record of our judgement be made out for the church of S. Giulia for security [there follow the notary's name, the date, 25 June 847, and nine signatures: three of the four *scabini* among them sign their own names][2]. (App. XX)

This case is fairly typical of Italian formal *placita*, if fuller than most. We will go through it to see what was going on, looking in detail at both the usual and the less usual in it, as a guide to what could happen in an Italian court in the ninth century.

The Controne case is a good representative of the natural style of Italian court records. It is colloquial, with lots of *oratio recta*; it is narrated by the judges in the first person. It might lead us at first sight to imagine that the dialogues in the text had actually been spoken by the participants, until we notice the recurrence of formal phrases all the way through. Parties probably spoke along the lines of the statements that are recorded, though much that was not germane to the case in question, or to how it ultimately came out, may not have been set down. Really atypical events may, indeed, have been recorded exactly; we have several apparent examples of it, at least, as we shall see. But a fixed template for how a normal case should be set down by public notaries and scribes, with its own prescribed set of formularies*, seems to have existed in every city. Indeed, we can identify the differences between such templates in some of the best documented centres, like Lucca and Milan; the different way cases proceeded in different areas certainly owes much to such formulaic differences. When such regional variations ceased, it was only because of the steady expansion of an even tighter set pattern, introduced at the end of the ninth century, that came to dominate court records everywhere after 900 or so. How different cases really ran we can, then, only guess at. But, at least before the 880s, no two cases are exactly alike, even when they come from the same court; such differences are likely to have been real, and they are illuminating.

The first thing the parties to the Controne case did was to appear before the public court of Lucca (see fig. 5). (Whether they did anything informally before this, to try to come to terms, we cannot say – I will come back to the issue later.)

[2] Manaresi 51. Controne and Granaiola are some 25 km north of Lucca into the mountains.

- - - Boundary of the kingdom
        of Italy, *c.* 900
—·—· Boundary of the area under
        the control of the Katepan
        of Byzantine Italy
□   Capital of an independent
        territory
o   City
+   Rural monastery
·   Other location

0 _____ 100 miles
0 _____ 100 _____ 200 km

Balerna
Vimercate
MILANo ·Cologno Monzese
        VERONAo
PAVIA□   oCREMONA
PIACENZA
VENICE

Pieve
Fosciana
        ·Granaiola   oRAVENNA
        ·Controne
LUCCAo   oFLORENCE
SIENA   oAREZZO
o

SPOLETO
o

Farfa +Casauria
+

□ROME

                BENEVENTO□   ·BARI
CAPUA□   □
    □NAPLES   ·Acerenza
            Tolve· ·Tricarico
SALERNO   ·Pietrapertosa

SICILY
(Arab after 902)

N

5 Italy in the eighth to eleventh centuries

The normal president of a court was the count of the city, but in Lucca the duke of Tuscany presided, there being no count. The count sat in judgement with lesser officials, most notably *scabini*, small aristocrats with some legal expertise, but also gastalds, *locopositi** and others; in practice it was they who tended to control the business of the court, often in the absence of the count, and they are often simply termed *iudices**, judges, in the texts. They were flanked by *adstantes**, local notables varying in status according to the location and political importance of the court concerned, who were there to make the court as authoritative and as public as possible. Other dignitaries sometimes presided – the local bishop, or even the king/emperor, but these rarely took an active part in the case. We can see at once from our case that the *placitum* must have been a common occurrence in Lucca, for it is unlikely that all these people would turn up specially, four times, for a case about a not very important property in nowhere very much, between people who (despite the very extensive Lucchese documentation) are not attested elsewhere; the court was in regular session, that is, and Andreas, Draco and Walperto simply agreed to turn up to the next session whenever their case was adjourned. How often it met is harder to say: probably more often than the two or three times a year that is commonly stated[3].

Once the parties to the Controne case appeared at the court, the defendants Draco and Walperto insisted on being shown the disputed property. This may have been a standard delaying device; it is paralleled elsewhere, in similar terms. The process was carefully set in motion by the pledging of property, and such pledges, *wadiae*, punctuate the whole of the rest of the case. Pledging was a crucial part of all judicial proceedings; one sometimes has the sense that only continuous pledging could ensure the end of any successful legal action, and one's *fideiussores*, the guarantors for such pledges, were in practice one's main legal support. They were, too, the supporters that were particularly responsible for making sure that legal obligations and even final judgements were carried out, for otherwise they would themselves be liable for the sum pledged[4].

Once the Controne case had properly started, it moved along well-established lines, initiated, as in other cases, by the presentation of documents. In this case, the church of S. Giulia had no document to set against the charter of sale produced by Draco or Walperto, but instead made its claim to land on the basis of long possession, backed up by witnesses, the commonest way a valid charter could be got around. The defendants had no other proofs and the case ended.

---

[3] G. Salvioli, *Storia della procedura civile e criminale*, vol. 1 (henceforth Salvioli) in P. del Giudice (ed.), *Storia del diritto italiano*, vol. 3, pt 1, pp. 47–76 for general Frankish-period court organization; pp. 62–4 for *placitum* dates. Salvioli is the most recent general survey of early medieval Italian procedure, and is for the most part the most detailed; I shall refer to him rather than to his predecessors.

[4] Other examples of disputants showing the property: Manaresi 24, 29, 60, 62, 73, 94. *Fideiussores* as responsible for execution: *RF* 44–5, Manaresi 1, all Spoletan examples; cf. also the rather later Manaresi 191 (AD 981), also from the duchy of Spoleto, an exceptionally informative text.

Cases normally ended when one side had no other proofs to offer; the judges' decision was then usually pretty self-evident. Judges had considerable control over how cases ran, intervening often to ask for extra evidence, to criticize documents, or to interrogate witnesses, but they seldom had to make a judgement based on contradictory proofs of superficially equal validity. Indeed, in legal theory they had no power to adjudicate at all; they were merely supposed to preside over courts and to decide who was to offer proofs and how. In practice, nonetheless, judicial decisions can be found often enough in our texts, and the opinions of judges can still, and obviously could then, be clearly seen; the limitations on their powers have been overstressed. In this case, however, there were no problems, and the rôle of the judges was restricted to making sure that the parties kept to the correct procedures, and to closing the case at the end[5].

The case may not have been problematic, but it does have some unusual features. The first of these is the calling of Fraimanno. Most private charters of the period have a *formula** by which the author of the document, that is to say the alienator of the land, promised to defend the land from any claimant, and committed his heirs to do so too, an obligation directly inherited from Roman law; it is, however, comparatively rare for such men or their heirs to be actually called as participants in any subsequent case[6]. But, in this case, not only was Fraimanno called, but he took over the case himself, and found himself facing direct accusation as a defendant; Draco and Walperto dropped out. Their charter had been accepted by the court; but, for them to win the case, it had to be shown that its author had previously owned the land legitimately. So, once Fraimanno became the defendant, he had to prove his own (or, rather, his father's) rights. The implication of his claim to the land is that his father had held the land undisturbed for over thirty years, for such a period of uncontested possession established ownership in law, as it had done ever since the fourth century. Long possession was an important basis for any stable proof of right to own land, and is present, explicitly or implicitly, in most of our land cases. Earlier documentary evidence was seldom invoked in them except for rhetorical purposes; it was enough for one to have occupied land for thirty years in any case, as long as one could establish it in court[7].

This is where the problem lay for Fraimanno. Not only did he have no

---

[5] For the legal theory that Lombard–Frankish judges were not adjudicatory at all, but merely presided over the case, see Salvioli, pp. 301–7; F. Sinatti D'Amico, *Le prove giudiziarie nel diritto longobardo*, pp. 25–30, 144–76, 372. *De facto* judicial power over the *conduct* of a case and its procedures, often so close to adjudication that the difference between the two is invisible, is clear in Manaresi 25, 36, 42 and others.

[6] Other examples of authors, *auctores*, being called or produced as participants: Manaresi 29, 43, 45, 48, 59.

[7] Basic Lombard law for thirty-year rule**: Grimoald ch. 4; cf. Liutprand ch. 54 (in *Leges Langobardorum 643–866*, ed. F. Beyerle, pp. 96, 124). Roman origins: E. Levy, *West Roman Vulgar Law. The law of property*, pp. 176–94. Rhetorical use of early documents: Manaresi 36, 42. Manaresi 44, 59, 104 show charters too old to be accepted as proof; but see n. 19.

documents, but he could find no witnesses to his long possession either. But Andreas, on behalf of S. Giulia, did have witnesses, and he could easily produce them; if their testimony favoured the church, it would win without opposition. They did; S. Giulia had, they said, owned the land during the last three decades. Witnesses generally favoured the people who called them, but not invariably: the normal requirement of swearing on the gospel inhibited some from perjury, with some unexpected results, as we shall see. Fraimanno's only recourse was procedural; he tried, although without success, to contest the rights of one of the witnesses to testify, on the grounds that he did not have 150 *solidi* in property. This was an even less common thing to do, but it sheds light on a major criterion for rights to witness, that the witness concerned should have enough property to be able to pay his wergeld* if he were fined for perjury: 150 *solidi* was the wergeld of an ordinary freeman in the seventh- and eighth-century laws[8]. Witnesses thus had to be men of a certain standing (women had no legal standing in Lombard courts, and had to be represented by others), which doubtless affected the sort of justice courts dealt out; only judicial inquests*, that is to say the calling and interrogating of sworn witnesses by the judge, could include other free men. Anyway, Fraimanno could not impugn the standing of the witnesses against him (indeed, one of the judges corroborated it), and lost. He had not failed to fulfil any of his *wadiae*, and incurred no direct financial penalty from that, but he had to return any crops he had taken from the land since the case began. Cases could last a long time, and, once a plea had been made, *de facto* possession no longer allowed an illegal owner to enjoy the fruits of a property.

The interest of this case is above all as a guide to the major procedural elements of an average Carolingian court-case in Italy. Some of its features are less than usual, but none are unparalleled, or even problematic; they generally appear because the case is recorded in more detail than most. It is a pity that we know nothing about its background; as we shall see, cases are at their most illuminating when they can be put in a social context. But on the face of it it looks reasonably fair, although Fraimanno's inability to prove his right could quite easily have been because his supporters were too intimidated to appear, and, similarly, the intervention of a judge as witness against him over Wito's eligibility could well show a less than unbiased court. At any rate, both of these phenomena can certainly be seen elsewhere, even though court records usually filtered out evidence that would have undermined the apparent justice of the verdict[9].

The procedures of the case look reasonably logical, too. This is an abiding feature of Italian legal records: they *make sense* as records of hearings. We can, usually, understand why one party wins and not the other. We should not be naive about this; eighth- and ninth-century Italians were not 'like us' in more than

---

[8] Liutprand ch. 62, *Leges Langobard.*, ed. F. Beyerle, p. 128.
[9] Biased courts are most visible in cases where peasants claimed against lords: see n. 24.

trivial ways; but they had recognizable attitudes to the nature of legal evidence and how to use it. This was true of much of Carolingian Europe, but in Italy it was perhaps older, and certainly longer-lasting. It can be linked to a considerable level of at least practical literacy among the Italian landowning classes, and, as can readily be seen in the case we have just looked at, to the institutional weight and coherence of public administration, at least on the surface; and these two can, in turn, be linked to the professionalization and legal expertise of the lay notariate, the identifying feature of Italian local (and central) government under the Carolingians as, later, under the Communes. One should not overstress the differences between Italy and Europe north of the Alps; much of the Frankish world shared very similar patterns in the ninth century. Only in the post-Carolingian world would it be different, for public institutions survived much better in Italy than they did elsewhere. But my first concern is with the Carolingian period. Against the background of a procedural system like that outlined above, I will concentrate on two aspects of Italian dispute settlement: the exact rôle of the written word, the charter, in court cases; and the purpose of disputing, as seen, in particular, in the ways that people achieved settlements.

It is possible to use the numerous and detailed provisions of the Lombard laws and the Carolingian capitularies that followed them, together with the tenth- and eleventh-century elaborations of the legal schools of Pavia, to work out a highly complex legal system for Lombard–Carolingian Italy. The most substantial monument to such attempts is Salvioli's 1925 account of civil and criminal procedure up to 1150, some 400 pages of systematic analysis[10]. Nor are such attempts out of place in Italy. The law books were a quarry for notarial expertise. Between 800 and 1100, they were glossed, cross-referenced, given concordances, associated with sample court-cases, expounded and argued over, contrasted and equated with Justinianic law, by generations of experts centred on Pavia, the capital of the kingdom of Italy[11]. The legists worked out formularies for the recording of *placita* in the late ninth century that caught on so fast that they covered nearly every formal *placitum* by 920, except in non-Carolingian southern Italy. (When the formulaic *placitum* becomes dominant, in fact, the usefulness of the formal court-case for social historians drops dramatically.) The legists certainly took law seriously; and people took the legists seriously, too. Even among laymen, law was widely known in Italy. Charters and *placita* sometimes cite phrases or whole texts of royal enactments. But even in Italy, the invention by modern scholars of a coherent legal system and set of procedures that covered every eventuality and was universally followed is fantasy. The major realization

---

[10] Salvioli, *passim*. There is pertinent criticism in Sinatti D'Amico, *Prove*, pp. 15–16, 203–6.
[11] Texts are edited by A. Boretius in *Liber legis langobardorum Papiensis dictus, MGH LL*, vol. 4, pp. 289–585. An introduction to them can be found in E. Besta, *Fonti: legislazione e scienza giuridica* in P. del Giudice (ed.), *Storia del diritto italiano*, vol. 1, pt 1, pp. 257–330.

one takes away from a reading of Salvioli is that things did not and could not work like that. Italian case-law, even at the height of the Lombard–Carolingian kingdom, was more muddy, inconsistent, regionally different, than most legal historians have recognized.

The 'spirit of Lombard law', the 'Germanic legal mentality', the traditional presuppositions of the *Rechtsschule**, are the main problem at issue here. The first and greatest code of Lombard law, the Edict of Rothari of 643, assumed that law-cases would only be ended by judicial duel or by oath-helping*, the so-called 'irrational' proofs, and set out elaborate rules for the latter. The alterations to the code made by Liutprand (713–44) and Ratchis (744–56), as well as by the Carolingians later, assumed the presence of other, more 'rational', means of proof – the charter, witnesses, the inquest – even though oath-helping and the duel remained in theory, of determinant importance for the ending of a dispute. These changes have fairly consistently been seen as Roman (and sometimes ecclesiastical) influences on the 'primitive mentality' of the German judicial system. Franca Sinatti D'Amico has set this argument out most fully and in the most scholarly manner: she shows how the legal system of the Lombards gradually came to accept these newer elements of proof, while maintaining its traditional oath-oriented structure until at least the Carolingian conquest. (No court-case records the judicial duel in our period at all[12].) Some of the presuppositions of such arguments are less than convincing. The idea that traditional Germanic law was essentially irrational can certainly be argued against. The idea of the Lombards cautiously welcoming Roman elements into their still-Lombard legal system is, however, quite likely; Liutprand and his successors certainly did this in other areas of law. Eighth-century procedures were almost certainly coming to be different from those of the time of Rothari. We can say nothing about how seventh-century procedures really worked, for we have no documents, but the steady increase in documents from 710 onwards must itself have had an effect on law. Kings mentioned them more and more in their legislation, and gave them more and more weight in the presentation of evidence, requiring only that they be backed up by oath-helping. The possession of charters came to be a major element in the decision by judges as to the terms by which one of the parties could clear himself by oath. King Ratchis in 746 enacted that the terms of a charter of sale could not be impugned by oath-helping, as long as the charter witnesses would testify to its authenticity[13]. Oath-helping became more and more a formality after 750; after 790 it virtually disappeared.

As far as it goes, this picture is credible. But the way that changes in the rules of evidence entered legal *practice*, as seen in the court-cases of the eighth-century,

---

[12] Salvioli, pp. 252–68, 288–301; see Sinatti D'Amico, *Prove, passim*, with full bibliography of previous work, for this and what follows.

[13] Ratchis ch. 8 (AD 746), *Leges Langobard.*, ed. F. Beyerle, p. 189. See below, pp. 149–50, 228–9, for arguments against the 'irrationality' of primitive Germanic law.

does some harm to the idea of Lombard law as a fully coherent system, governing procedure all over the kingdom. No king ever extended Ratchis's law of 746 for charters of sale to other types of document. In theory, oath-helping remained a legal necessity, even after 790. It was, however, in practice almost totally abandoned; the only examples of its use thereafter are a Veronese case of 806, where oaths were sworn because the relevant documents had been burnt, a Lucchese case of 840, where neither side had recent charters or any witnesses, and a few instances in the consciously traditionalist non-Carolingian South[14]. Practice clearly ran ahead of legislation, here. But even in the Lombard kingdom before 774 oath-helping was not universal. One of the numerous boundary disputes between the dioceses of Siena and Arezzo, from 714, only the second earliest case that survives from Lombard Italy, ended with a simple judicial decision, based, it would seem, on an inquest. A case heard in Pavia in 762, the legal centre of the kingdom, hung directly on the authenticity and legality of the provisions of rival charters, not on anyone's oath. One must not underestimate the attachment of early medieval Italians to written legal norms; but if judges even in Pavia were prepared to accept procedural rules that are not sanctioned in Lombard law, we must accept that procedure in Italy was reasonably flexible; *de facto* practices were of considerable importance. And in the eighth century, when more and more people were becoming familiar with documents, it must have seemed reasonable to many judges to recognize them as the straight-forward, direct evidence that most people already probably accepted that they were. It is these *de facto* practices that need to be emphasized. In the ninth century, indeed, they were probably even more important than under the Lombards, for Carolingian legislation was often rather remote from the day-to-day problems of law-cases, and the body of case-law and practical legal expertise available to any given court must have steadily increased[15].

In these ninth-century cases, and even in the eighth century, written evidence was of supreme importance. Two-thirds of the contested cases that survive between 700 and 900 hang directly on charters. The first point that one draws from them is that the wording of charters mattered. Charters were read out in court; they had to be authentic, with witnesses and a notarial signature; they had to be legally valid, conforming to the norms of written law; they had to be earlier than rival charters; they had to deal explicitly with the issue in dispute. Charters that did not conform to this fell[16]. Certainly, some idea of checking the possibility

---

[14] After 774, cases which involve oath-helping are Manaresi 3, 7, possibly 19, 44, and 104 for Benevento and *Codice diplomatico veronese*, ed. V. Fainelli, vol. 1, no. 71 (806). For later examples from southern Italy, see Manaresi 201 (983), and Salvioli, pp. 258–63, although the latter tends to confuse sworn witness with oath-helping.

[15] Schiaparelli 17, 163. This issue is seen differently in Sinatti D'Amico, *Prove*, pp. 180–97, 391–405, following and developing discussion by G. P. Bognetti in *L'età longobarda*, vol. 1, pp. 321–8, both of whom want to see Lombard cases as conforming very closely to legal norms, even if these norms came to be changed. I hope to discuss their arguments elsewhere.

[16] Invalid texts: Manaresi 96; *RF* 25 (AD 750) with 31 (751). Cases that hang on the relative dates of

of forgery existed, too; a case of 854 from Piacenza partially hung on a charter of the 620s, which was read out, and accepted because it was set out *propter barbarico exempla*. By 1000 in Rome it was even normal to use other charters to verify the handwriting of notaries, if they were dead and could not come forward themselves to testify. But these things are rare; even after Otto I in 967 introduced into Lombard law the idea of impugning authenticity by duel, such accusations were uncommon[17]. If the author of a charter or its notary or its witnesses were living, one or more were liable to be called to bear witness to its validity; if not, charters could normally be accepted as they were. They were, after all, always originals or authenticated copies.

The classic way that a charter could be defeated was on the issue of who held the original right to the land. I began with a Lucchese charter to that effect, and such cases do seem to be a feature of Lucchese political life more often than elsewhere. A church wished to establish its right to land occupied by X. X claimed ownership, and, in support, could show a charter showing he was sold it by Y. But how did Y have right to the land? If the church could prove that Y did not have rights to the land, it would win. The possession of earlier charters made this easiest, but sworn witnesses that confirmed long possession by the church were equally good. In the Controne case, the church's case looks strong enough on the face of it; but in several of these Lucchese cases it looks decidedly weaker. So many of them show bishops and priests using this technique that one is reminded that, after all, unscrupulous witnesses could claim thirty-year possession against any text; and in two cases, from 815 and 873, the church produced no evidence at all, contenting itself with impugning the defendant's charter because its author and witnesses were dead, and still won the case. We might conclude that written evidence had less power in Lucchese courts than elsewhere, at least if it was used against the bishop. Lucchese bishops themselves, on the other hand, happily used the small print in their own charters against, for example, lessees whose leases they wished to reclaim[18].

Charters could, then, be got around. But cases of this kind are rare outside Lucca. Charters had force, and people felt it. Charters far older than the thirty-year limit were accepted without trouble in courts when actual possession was not an issue. They looked good. In another Lucchese case, from 865, Audiprando of Pieve Fosciana had gone to the trouble to sell disputed land to a

---

gifts include *RF* 45 (761), Manaresi 14, 22, 48, 90; cases that hang on the precise wording of charters, often with very interesting results, include Schiaparelli 182, Manaresi 8, 15, 32, 42, 65, 71, Volpini 4, and *Memorie e documenti per servire all' istoria del ducato di Lucca*, vol. 5, ed. D. Barsocchini, pt 2, 225 (henceforth Barsocchini, cited by no.).

[17] Manaresi 59; for Rome, *RF* 658; cf. p. Toubert, *Les Structures du Latium médiéval*, pp. 1,249–50. Otto I and the duel: see *Liber Papiensis*, pp. 568–80, 589, A. Vismara, 'La Legislazione di Ottone I', *Archivo storico lombardo*, 53 (1925), and (for the tenth century) Manaresi 170, 236, 250, 254.

[18] Manaresi 29, 73, 94, for apparently tendentious judgements from Lucca (94 has been redated to 869 by Keller, 'Placiti', pp. 53–4); Manaresi 36 and 43 for the Po plain. Lucchese bishops void leases in Manaresi 57 and 71 for non-fulfilment of the conditions laid down in the charter.

friend, Eriprando, and to get Eriprando to sell it back to him, so that he could
have a charter; in this case, at least, the brisk uncovery of the collusion by the
ecclesiastical plaintiffs looks convincing[19]. Conversely, if one had a charter that
was inconvenient, one might burn it. The most striking example of this is a case of
786 from Lucca, concerning a certain Deusdona, a priest of S. Angelo *ad
Sgragium* in the city's suburbs, who was accused by his named successor
Deusdedit of stealing the charter by which Deusdona named Deusdedit
successor, and expelling him from the church. The text is a long one, but an
extended part of it deserves quoting, for its intrinsic interest, and for some other
reasons to which we shall return. We start from the end of Deusdedit's
accusation.

Deusdona the priest replied: 'Certainly it is true, as you say, that I confirmed to you S.
Angelo and its property by charter in the time of King Desiderius, and what I confirmed to
you I have nothing against; but the charter I never stole, nor did it ever come back to me'.
And when Deusdona began to state thus before the lord bishop Johannes [of Lucca] and
we judges, Bishop Johannes had him come before the gospels, so that Deusdona should
know that he should tell the certain truth about everything. And when the gospels were
placed before him, Deusdona the priest professed before us: 'Certainly I tell you the truth,
that I did not steal that charter nor that it returned to me, but I said to Alpert the cleric, who
was the servant of the priest Deusdedit: "Go, if you can, take that charter which I made to
Deusdedit, for my church S. Angelo and its property, and destroy it, and I will confirm you
in the church", as I have done. Thus afterwards Alpert his servant stole his charter and
brought it to me and said to me: "Here is the charter which you told me to take; now
confirm me in the church". But I said to him: "If you do not destroy the charter, I cannot
confirm you in the church". And when I had said that, Alpert in my presence gave that
charter to a British pilgrim, who had come there [presumably to spend a night at the
church; Lucca was on the major pilgrim route to Rome], and in our presence that Briton
[*Britto*] put it in the fire and burnt it there.'

There are unusually good grounds for doubting that Deusdona was fully sane.
He had, in still surviving charters (all later than the burnt charter would have
been), given the church to at least three other separate people, the bishop,
another Deusdedit and (perhaps another) Alpert. It was, in the end, the last
named that got the church, not the first Deusdedit, as a charter of 807 shows,
though we cannot say how this occurred; indeed, one alarming possibility is that
Alpert the cleric, villain of the above-quoted text, was the Alpert who got the
church in the end[20]. The whole framework of the case is so odd that we must be
careful about using it as typical. But the vision of these two crooks haggling over
who was to destroy the charter, and finally handing it to a man no one would ever
see again, is striking. Alpert did not escape a fine for destroying the charter, for it
was destroyed at his command; but he did not wish to do it himself, and nor did

[19] Old charters are mentioned in, for example, Manaresi 46, 81, 90. Audiprando: see Manaresi 70.
[20] Manaresi 7; cf. Barsocchini 177, 205–7, 340. Another example is Manaresi 5 (cf. 3). Oaths could
have force; in AD 777 (Manaresi 3) oath-helpers explicitly state that they do not dare to swear for
fear of perjury.

his patron. Contrary charters were dangerous, even if they were in one's own possession rather than one's opponents', but their destruction was not to be undertaken lightly. Charters were special. As the tenth-century formularies called the *Cartularium Langobardicum* show most explicitly, they had a ceremonial function in the process of the transfer of property[21]. This function fits with a respect for the charter as an entity in itself, not just as a record. But it never in Italy interfered with the use of the content of the document *as* record.

In the end, possession of documents came to be the overwhelmingly dominant mode of proof in the formal *placitum*. Opponents, increasingly, did not bother to continue the case once a charter was read out. It is possible that some were deterred by the financial penalty charters contained for molestation; in a Spoleto case from 814, losing parties tried to claim, in the face of such penalties, that they had never claimed the land at all[22]. But the tendency, however derived, for opponents not to contest the case culminated in the introduction in *c.* 880 of a set formulaic pattern for court-case recording, linked closely to *formula* 17 in the *Cartularium Langobardicum* formulary of the following century: X appears in court, reads out his charter, is asked why, states that he does so because it is opposed by Y (or, in a variant, because it might be opposed by persons unknown), Y says he does not oppose it, and the case ends. This pattern, known as the *ostensio cartae**, accounts for the great majority of all tenth- and eleventh-century formal *placita*. There has been a considerable argument about what it means. Many have assumed that all or most of such cases were fictitious, set up so as to produce a public notification of a transaction, for they often follow the sale of the land to X *by* Y, sometimes the same day or a few days later. Manaresi in the 1940s, however, showed that many such cases could be proved to be real, and he claimed that they all were – indeed, he proposed that the formulary was so dominating as a recording template that some of the charters shown at the start of some cases were themselves fictitious, having been concocted subsequently to fit the pattern, perhaps as a result of deals between the parties. As the *placitum* itself is usually the only text we have for each case, these arguments can seldom be proved either way. Manaresi is certainly sometimes right, but not always[23]. But the formulary

---

[21] *MGH LL*, vol. 4, p. 595, *formula* 2. Charters could only be destroyed legally if they were false, or, sometimes, if they were unsuccessful in court; see, for good late examples, Manaresi 294 (AD 1017), 314 *bis* (1022), and *RF* 658 (1012); for the latter cf. Toubert, *Structures*, p. 1,256.

[22] Manaresi 28. There are only about ten undefended cases in Manaresi until the mid-870s, when their number is suddenly augmented by a series recorded in the Casauria cartulary, Manaresi 74–5, 79–80, 82–6; that this is not, or not entirely, a local recording *formula* is shown by the details in 86 (AD 878). But the examples closely prefigure the *Cartularium Langobardicum formula*, *MGH LL*, vol. 4, p. 600.

[23] *Ostensio cartae formula*: *MGH LL*, vol. 4, p. 600. First examples, all from Piacenza: Manaresi 91, 99, 105–7. See, above all, C. Manaresi, 'Della non esistenza di processi apparenti nel territorio del regno', *Rivista di storia del diritto italiano*, 23 (1950), and *ibid.*, 24 (1951), with full reference to opposing views. There is a discussion in English of some aspects of these cases in J. N. Sutherland, 'Aspects of continuity and change in the Italian *placitum*, 962–72', *Journ. Med. Hist.*, 2 (1976), not using the Italian secondary literature.

clearly came into existence to fit a trend, that of the increasing tendency for opponents of charters to renounce the case without going through the rest of the procedures of the *placitum*. It spread fast: first represented in Piacenza charters, in three decades it was normal everywhere, clear witness, as I have noted, to the influence of legists in Italian legal life. The formulary, once accepted, expressed the real supremacy, in normal circumstances, of the charter as a means of proof. And it represented one further thing, too: it was the crystallization, the formalization, of *placitum* procedure as adversarial, that is, of every case having an outright winner and an outright loser. This, on the face of it, should not be a problem; all the instances we have seen so far show court-cases as very adversarial. But the issue is not as simple as that; in the concluding section to this chapter, we will look at some of the reasons why.

Disputes occur at all levels of social interaction. Why do they ever come to court? The only answer can be that there is no other means by which a party can get his way. But getting one's adversary to court is only one step in a long line of complex transactions. The average Italian court-case tells us little about these, in sharp contrast, for example, to the tenth- and eleventh-century Anglo-Saxon cases, despite their tiny number, or to the sociological wealth of the ninth-century Breton material. They had to be there, however. Even in a modern judicial system cases are settled out of court, sometimes halfway through a case. In criminal cases, there is plea-bargaining. In civil cases, a plaintiff knows he or she can twist a defendant's arm by the threat of a prolonged suit, and the defendant can in many cases bargain with the threat of difficult enforcement of a judgement, or of a lasting enmity brought about by legal defeat. And so it was in Lombard–Carolingian Italy, just as, more explicitly, in Anglo-Saxon England.

Italian cases are restricted in subject-matter. A dozen concern the status of tenants[24]. Rather fewer deal with ecclesiastical issues: adultery, the marriage of nuns, tithe. A group from Cremona are concerned with who gets the tolls from the city's river port. There are no directly 'criminal' cases at all[25]. All the rest deal with land. We are left, that is to say, with land disputes as the bases of all our generalizations. In some respects, our conclusions about these cannot be extended to other types of dispute. They certainly stress written evidence more than other types of case would, for documents are almost always about land; my discussion of the rôle of charters would only be valid for cases about land. But land was a crucial resource, one of the principal bases of all status, wealth, and power; as a type of *dispute*, such cases are likely to be as good a guide to social processes as any other.

The desire and need for peace and harmony in any small-scale society is a

---

[24] C. Wickham, *Studi sulla società degli Appennini nell'alto medioevo*, pp. 18–28.
[25] Some cases related to 'crime': *RF* 44–5 (cf. 56); *Codex diplomaticus langobardiae*, ed. G. Porro-Lambertenghi, 249 (henceforth Porro, cited by no.).

commonplace. Equally commonplace is that it is never achieved. Passions ran high in early medieval dispute, and were not easily appeased. A legal system had to be institutionally very strong to secure the agreement of powerful (and even, often, relatively weak) losers to the result of the case as it had been decided in court, and Italian institutions were by no means necessarily as strong as that. We do, indeed, have some indications that enforcement of legal decisions could be more troublesome than the firm ending of Italian cases as they appear in the documents might let one suppose. Teutpert of Vimercate and his son held Balerna in canton Ticino, a property claimed by S. Ambrogio in Milan in 844, with a charter showing how they had got it from Bruning of Magliaso (near Lugano). But S. Ambrogio had an earlier charter from Bruning. Bruning appeared at the *placitum* as author and supported S. Ambrogio, who won. Teutpert held on to the land, however, across two hearings of a new *placitum*, claiming Bruning had supported *him*. Bruning had to be brought in again, and stated that after the first case he had been ordered by the local count to coerce Teutpert to cede the land, but could not. Even in the text we have, Teutpert's son and co-defendant did not turn up, and the hearing was adjourned again[26]. This case shows more clearly than any other not only how difficult it was to enforce suit against a recalcitrant loser, but what processes were commonly used. The local count was in theory responsible; in practice he tended to leave it to concerned parties, such as to winning parties, legally liable authors like Bruning, or *fideiussores*, to sort it out themselves, and they could not always do so. In another example, Anspert of Milan (a future archbishop, and presumably an influential man in his own right) had to seek justice from the emperor Louis II in 857 because his brother's murderer would not pay the fine Louis's father had himself set. Louis did nothing more than confirm the fine, with a higher penalty for non-compliance. It is not surprising that court-cases put some weight on the explicit renunciation of rights by the loser, although over a quarter do not include it, and it is sometimes clear that the loser has renounced unwillingly. Losers who did not turn up in court, and so lost for contumacy as well as (or instead of) for having a weaker case, were even more likely to cause trouble: most notably the fifty-nine separate sets of defendants who held different lands claimed by the bishop of Lucca, none of whom turned up to hearings held in Florence in 897[27].

The standard remedies available to a court could do nothing about these problems. Counts could deal with them, in the last resort, but, even in the politically coherent kingdom of Italy, counts could not be everywhere; they had to hope that losers would cede without too much difficulty. And maybe, mostly, they

---

[26] Manaresi 48. The count had some personal links to Bruning: Porro 235. (See, for the family, D. A. Bullough, 'Leo, *qui apud Hlotharium magni loci habebatur*', *Le Moyen Age*, 67 (1961).)

[27] Anspert: Porro 201. Unwilling renunciation: *RF* 56 with 45; Manaresi 77, two years after the original case; and see n. 32. Contumacy: Manaresi 1, 48, 102 (the 897 Florence case), and 101, where the eventually successful party did not appear in the original case for fear of political persecution by the emperor Arnulf.

did. But the normal procedure of the *placitum*, with its adversarial pattern, was not subtle enough to include the negotiations and inducements that could be needed for such cessions to be obtained; and, in particular, the ways *placita* were normally recorded do not show us when these things occurred at all. After 900, with the growth of the formularies, the problem became even greater. The formal *placitum* of the tenth and eleventh centuries may have made victors feel good, but it may often, in practice, have had even less effect. So at this point we must grapple with the submerged levels of compromise, both inside the court and outside it, that can be dimly discerned in our evidence[28].

One type of simple compromise, an inducement to a loser, is the remission of fines for the illegal occupation of land. We have a couple of explicit instances of this in Farfa cases; and compromise may well be implicit in the fact that such fines are not very commonly mentioned at all in cases, even though, when they are, they seem to be normal, and could be high[29]. A second type of compromise, even cruder, is the leasing back to the loser of the land he has just lost. There are examples of this from Farfa and Lucca, for instance, and there must have been others – we only hear of the process at all as a result of the chance survival of subsequent documents[30]. In this second category, there is one instructive case of 859 from Milan, which deserves a closer look. It concerns Lupus of *Sclanno*, who held S. Ambrogio's estates at Cologno Monzese illegally. Lupus claimed he had it as a benefice from Archbishop Angilbert of Milan, and had gone to the archbishop and asked him to act as author. The archbishop refused, and Lupus ceded the case. Then the judges themselves went to Angilbert to clarify the situation; Angilbert charged his predecessor with irresponsible enfeoffing of lands owned by several monasteries, and said he was opposed to it. One need not doubt that Angilbert, while not deigning to come to the hearing (though he was technically presiding over the case) set this meeting up for his own political purposes, with useful results for historians. But what interests us here is Lupus. A month later, we have another charter concerning him and S. Ambrogio, explicitly as an aftermath to the Cologno case.

Thereto Lupus said that he had agreed with the monastery by *wadia* that the abbot should issue a *precaria** so that they should make an agreement together. Abbot Petrus and the same Lupus agreed among themselves, and so in the presence of all, first they 'diswadiated' and voided all the *wadiationes* they had between themselves, which they said they had made formerly concerning that *precaria* and agreement. [Then they offered new

---

[28] Thus J.-P. Delumeau, 'L'exercice de la justice dans le comté d'Arezzo (IXe–début XIII siècle)', *Mélanges de l'École française de Rome*, 90 (1978), 593–601.

[29] Remission of fines: *RF* 56 (AD 764), Manaresi 28; a later example is Manaresi 314 *bis* (1022). Cf. S. D. White, '*Pactum . . . legem vincit et amor judicium*', *American Journ. Legal Hist.*, 22 (1978), 296–7; this paper is the best general discussion of compromise I have seen. Imposed fines for property cases: Manaresi 4, 23, 57; *Codex diplomaticus Amiatinus*, ed. W. Kurze, vol. 1, no. 106 (828).

[30] *RF* 25 with 31 (AD 750–1); Manaresi 52 with Barsocchini 662, 668 (AD 848–9).

wadiae for the lands the abbot was proposing to grant to Lupus in *precaria*, in effect as another benefice.]

I translate verbatim to show the caution, the pledging and counterpledging, that surrounded a peacemaking agreement of this kind. The situation must have been tense. Lupus may have been influential; the issue was certainly highly political. Interestingly, part of the land Lupus got was a Balerna estate, almost certainly the one S. Ambrogio had failed to get back in 844 from Teutpert of Vimercate. Lupus's future may not have been as easy as it looks[31].

This case shows us something of how compromises out of court were reached. It also points to the importance of local politics, and not only (although most visibly) in disputes on the aristocratic level. This importance can be shown in some detail in the complex case of the Frank Sisenando, one of the most influential figures in south-central Adriatic Italy in the 860s–70s, participant in about twenty transactions recorded in the Casauria cartulary and vendor of land to the emperor himself (see fig. 5)[32]. Before 872, Sisenando had married a rich widow, Gundi, only to find out that she had previously become a nun. The marriage thus being adulterous, he lost her property, and was fined 600 *solidi*, in a court-case of 873. He refused to pay, and had had his own property confiscated by the time of his death in 875. His brother Fulerad contested this in 877, and came to an agreement with the monastery of Casauria, which had got the land from the fisc, to get some of it back in return for a horse and 100 *solidi*. This was not a very favourable compromise, in fact, and it did not last. Fulerad contested the issue again in 878 and had to concede fully in court.

Only two of the numerous documents that deal with Sisenando are *placita* (there is a third, of 877, that deals with the division of lands made by Gundi's sons by her first marriage as part of their penalty for Gundi's crime), but it is clear that the case is incomprehensible without the other texts. Sisenando's downfall may well have something to do with his property transactions, almost all of which show him buying up the property of local widows. One would like to think that he imposed himself on one widow too many; at any rate, he got caught in a trap that none of his local associates had any desire to help him get out of, least of all Casauria, newly founded by Louis II, and a rising acquisitive power in the zone. Sisenando's local influence, which had been considerable, must have vanished, for, without such a weakness, it is doubtful how far he could have been made to concede. Full discussion of the Sisenando cases would be out of place here, but

---

[31] Manaresi 64 with Porro 208 (both AD 859). Lupus did have links with Balerna himself, one should note: Porro 179 (852). Context: G. Rossetti, *Società e istituzioni nel contado lombardo durante il medioevo. Cologno Monzese*, vol. 1, pp. 81–8.

[32] For what follows, see Manaresi 76, 82, 84 for *placita*, and, for other texts, Instrumentarium Casauriense (Paris BN MS lat. 5411) fols. 13v, 17r–v, 41v, 87r, 88v–90r, 92r–v, 96v–97r, 106v. (I am grateful to Professor Alessandro Pratesi for letting me see a typescript of his edition of this text, to be published shortly, and to Laurent Feller for discussions on Sisenando.) The interpretation of Manaresi 82 in Wickham, *Early Medieval Italy*, p. 128, is mistaken.

they are important. They show, more than any other cases of the period, how our understanding of *placita* depends on the content of our *other* evidence about the people concerned, when we have it. Cases did not happen in a void; they happened between people who had lived together before and would live together again. Whether on a local or a national level, cases were political activities, and should be seen as such. They were part of the continuous processes of social interaction[33].

This issue takes us outside the bounds of this article, but it will be developed further in the conclusion: it is arguably the most important that court-case analysis involves. Unfortunately, the precise context of most cases is lost to us. But surviving records do give us some indications of the environment in which disputes made sense. And that brings us back to compromise. We have seen that much compromise happened out of court; the formal *placitum* did not, in theory, involve it. It may be that some plaintiffs entered into *placita*, got a quick compromise, and called off their action, without ever obtaining a court record; we do have informal renunciations that may fit this picture. One *placitum*, from 890, does stop abruptly halfway through, with the plaintiff waiting for the defendant to produce his charters, because the judges take it upon themselves to obtain a friendly compromise (*amica pactuacione**) between the parties, having considered God's mercy; and there is a similar text from 832 where a case about labour services turns into an agreement, based again on *amica pactuicio* (*sic*). Both these cases are from Piacenza, and perhaps express local practice; but there are no other explicit examples from there or anywhere else in Manaresi[34]. But most strikingly, as soon as we move into less formal cases, ones not held by royal officials, compromises suddenly become much commoner, even though informal cases are still far less numerous. At Lucca in 801, at Rome in 813, between Farfa and the bishop of Spoleto in 820, at Farfa in 838, at Milan in 863, men came to terms, often using the same *amica pactuacio formula*[35]. Outside the framework of the formal *placitum*, compromise was fairly normal. We may guess that many more *placita* cover such *de facto* activities than we could ever have evidence for, and might have ever thought[36].

If we want to understand the social context of Italian courts in the early middle ages, we must look at them above all as the result of two fairly constant sets of practices. First, the continuing survival of public institutions and public ideology,

---

[33] Cf. A. L. Epstein, 'The case method in the field of law' in *idem* (ed.), *The craft of social anthropology*, pp. 205–30, especially p. 230.

[34] Manaresi 97; Volpini, *compositio* I (pp. 447–51) for compromise inside the court. (Cf. Volpini I for a parallel in Byzantine northern Italy.) Discontinued suits may well be represented by, for example, Barsocchini 243–4, 259 (AD 793, 797). Discontinuance and compromise: see comments by S. Roberts and J. A. Sharpe, among others, in J. Bossy (ed.), *Disputes and settlements*, pp. 23, 173–7.

[35] Barsocchini 298, *RF* 199, 247, 282, Porro 226. From as early as 753 (*RF* 34) there is also an instructive case where a losing plaintiff gets 8 *solidi* from Farfa for not forcing the monastery to offer the formal oath, and for agreeing not to reopen the case again.

[36] Cf. Delumeau, 'Arezzo', 598–603.

not only in the Lombard–Carolingian period, but also well beyond it, coupled with a general knowledge of a certain basic set of procedural rules and legal norms, allowed people to continue to recognize the possibility of an adversarial victory, and to press for one where they could get one; even arbitration in Italy was carried out inside that framework of norms. Second, compromise in some form was regarded as a necessity, for without it cases could not easily be concluded. Nevertheless, we must understand that compromise was not seen as antithetical to abstract justice, and not even as antithetical to the outright victory of one party. A striking feature of cases in later periods, when compromise is even commoner, is that, in a number of them, the *formulae* for it cover the apparent complete defeat of the losing party and his surrender of all the property in dispute[37]. And this is indeed, perhaps, the point. Although formal and informal cases came to diverge in the nature of their written record very substantially after 900, what characterized nearly every finished case, perhaps even more insistently than in the ninth century, was a *renunciation* by someone, of at least some, and usually all, of his original claim; a (theoretical) preparedness by the legally weaker party to stop litigating. It was this that court-cases were for, in Italy as elsewhere, and either victory or compromise was satisfactory as a result.

It is generally thought that effective legal institutions in west-central continental Europe in the early middle ages depended on the power of the Carolingians, and that they declined as the Carolingian state declined, as it devolved to more local, less public, political structures in the tenth century and onwards. I do not believe this for Italy. In part, this is because public institutions survived in Italy rather better than in most of the rest of post-Carolingian Europe; but it is also because the issue of the effectiveness of courts has often been misunderstood. In early medieval Italy, as elsewhere in Europe, this effectiveness was dependent less on the coercive powers of officials, than on the preparedness of parties to accept the procedures of the court, and on their willingness to accept court judgements or to come to terms informally. The dominance of documentary evidence in land disputes and the impressive regularity of the court procedures we have in Italy indicate a general recognition of the rules of court among participants in cases; the rules actually became *more* stable and predictable in the tenth and eleventh centuries, not less. Conversely, however, what evidence we have shows that, even in the ninth century, disputes very often ended as a result of informal negotiation outside the theoretical terms of reference of the court; indeed in reality, the formal and informal were always inextricably mixed. There was no reason why this should change after 900, and there is no reason to think that it did. The powerful and the obdurate were less easy to deal with, but they always had been. If there was any change after 900, it was not because of the history of the state; it was because the very rapidity and

---

[37] For example, *RF* 483 (*c.* 1010), which still uses ninth-century terminology: 'pactum et bona convenientia et amica pactuatio'.

predictability of formulaic *placita* probably lessened their capacity to encompass less formal proceedings, and indeed lessened their dramatic impact as a whole. It was this, not their institutional backing, that led to their decline. The Italian Communes had to work out a new set of procedures, more or less from first principles, as a result[38].

[38] I am grateful to Cyril Wickham for reading this text, and for his helpful comments.

7

Dispute settlement in the Byzantine provinces in the tenth century

ROSEMARY MORRIS

It is an irony of history that so few administrative documents have survived from Byzantium, one of the most bureaucratic states of the medieval world. We know from existing documents that instructions were given to file duplicate or even triplicate copies in the offices of governmental bureaux, yet most of these originals have disappeared without trace. We possess only those documents of concern to the monastic houses which survived the onslaughts of westerners and Turks (such as the protected houses on Mount Athos) or those which found their way into ecclesiastical archives, such as the southern Italian documents to be discussed later. Everything else, including the entire imperial and governmental archives of Constantinople and the provinces has, with very minor exceptions, been lost[1].

But whilst much of the documentary flesh has decayed, the administrative skeleton of the middle Byzantine state has been successfully reconstructed and its guiding principles of centralization, order (*taxis*) and secularity established. Such principles were, in their turn, derived from two pervasive influences in Byzantine society: tradition, and its practical aspect, precedent[2]. These two criteria were most clearly expressed in the Byzantine legal system. It was descended from the tradition of Roman jurisprudence and legislation and, in theory, provided an all-embracing system of regulating criminal and civil justice. Custom certainly played a part in Byzantine legal activity, but it was a custom either long since subsumed into codified legislation or self-consciously referred to as an external element of which the law had to take account[3]. Byzantine law

---

[1] Such administrative documents as we possess are almost all copies or enquiries sent to the parties concerned and it is from them that the archives of the central government can be reconstructed. The archives of the monasteries of Athos provide a rich seam of this material.

[2] See. H. Ahrweiler, *L'idéologie politique de l'Empire byzantin*, pp. 129–47. *Taxis* was not only expressed by the existence of the imperial order, but also by the hierarchy of imperial officials.

[3] For the absorption of non-Roman customs into Roman law, see J. Crook, *Law and life of Rome*. L.-R. Ménager, 'Notes sur les codifications byzantines et l'occident', *Varia*, 3 (1958), discusses the question of possible Slav or Germanic influence on Byzantine law. In those parts of Italy where Lombards were present in large numbers, elements of the existing Lombard law *corpus* were incorporated into essentially Byzantine practices. See C. Mor, 'Considerazioni minimi sulle

was, above all, a written law. The great codifications of the Empire had themselves been gathered into the Justinianic *corpus* and there was no doubt about the source or the location of the law. The emperor was *fons legum*; the law books provided not only texts of imperial edicts (the Novels) which had the force of law, but also the accumulated wisdom of the Roman state since its foundation. Though criminal law was also codified, it is the great mass of civil legislation which stands as a lasting monument to Roman concepts of regulated behaviour[4].

By the side of this mountain of legal material stood the machinery to enforce it. The administrative organs of the Byzantine state were, again, directly descended from Roman prototypes. Law enforcement remained, in the first instance, the prerogative of city or provincial officials, though the emperor stood as the final court of appeal. Though the unrecorded activities of local village elders or other 'wise men' cannot, of course, be discounted, the interpretation and practice of the law was, in the main, the task of trained professionals. Alongside the written declaration of law evolved a complex charter* form by which its application was noted[5].

In the Byzantine state, as in any other, law did not remain static. It evolved in response to the needs and attitudes of contemporary society. But the amount and variety of Byzantine law in existence by the tenth century is a testament to the value placed on the Roman legal tradition as a means of social regulation. Indeed, the very practice of the law formed part of that tradition of which the Byzantines (or *rhomaioi* – 'Romans' – as they called themselves) were always aware.

The Justinianic codification overshadows the development of Byzantine law after the sixth century. But its very size and comprehensiveness – which has rightly been recognized as a major landmark in legal history – meant that for most practical purposes it was impossible to use. Legal practitioners could not assimilate it and even for theorists, the *Corpus* became a mine of information to be quarried and shaped rather than a manageable legal resource. A continuing theme of Byzantine legal literature in the following centuries was its prolixity and difficulty. This was most clearly expressed in the *prooimion* to the *Ekloga*, a code issued by the iconoclast Emperors Leo III and Constantine in 741[6]. Not only, it

istituzioni giuridiche dell'Italia meridionale bizantina e longobarda' in *L'Italia meridionale nell'alto medioevo, 3° congresso internazionale di studi sull'alto medioevo*.

4 There is no modern study of Byzantine law. The main developments are sketched by H. Scheltema, 'Byzantine Law' in *Cambridge Medieval History*, vol. 4, pt 2, but two nineteenth-century works remain indispensable: K. Zachariae von Lingenthal, *Geschichte des griechisch-römischen Rechts* and J. Mortreuil, *Histoire du droit byzantin*. Important new research is now being carried out in Frankfurt under the direction of Professor D. Simon. P. Pieler, 'Byzantinischer Rechtsliteratur' in H. Hunger (ed.), *Die hochsprachliche profane Literatur der Byzantiner*, vol. 2, provides an indispensable guide to Byzantine legal texts.

5 For the administrative system of the Byzantine state in the ninth and tenth centuries, see N. Oikonomidès, *Les listes de préséance byzantines*. F. Dölger and J. Karayannopoulos, *Byzantinische Urkundenlehre*, is a useful introduction to some Byzantine diplomatic forms.

6 *Ekloga* in *Jus graecoromanum*, ed. J. and P. Zepos, vol. 2. See now the new edition by L. Burgmann, *Ecloga. Das Gesetzbuch Leons III und Konstantinos' V*.

was said, was Justinian's legislative collection difficult to comprehend in itself, but there was also such a dearth of copies of useful commentaries that the compilers of the *Ekloga* had been forced to make a personal collection of reference books. It was also remarked that some legal literature was completely unknown 'especially outside the God-guarded and imperial City'.

The *prooimion* to the *Ekloga* marked a further stage in a process which had begun immediately after the Justinianic *corpus* had been issued: the use, for example, of Greek rather than Latin texts of the legislation, the evolution of a body of explanations of the texts (based on indices prepared by legal commentators and teachers, the *antecessores*) and the probable concentration on the study of the *Codex* and the *Novels* rather than the *Digest*[7]. One common thread runs through all these developments: the attempt to make the Justinianic legislation more accessible and relevant to the needs of contemporary Byzantine society. But it is by no means clear how far these developments in the study of law had any practical effects, especially in the provinces. The *Ekloga*'s statement of legal ignorance outside Constantinople might seem somewhat bald, but the undoubted upheaval inflicted on the provincial cities of the empire by Slavonic, Persian and Arab invasions, undoubtedly displaced many of their civilian élites, including the lawyers and their teachers. From the late sixth century onwards, it is virtually impossible to ascertain how much legal training went on in the provinces[8].

Little legal activity has survived from the seventh century but by the beginning of the eighth, two contrasting types of compilation had emerged which came to represent the major strands of Byzantine law. The *Ekloga* was a law-code; other compilations were simply private manuals of law which did not have binding force, but were clearly intended as guides for the practitioners of law. This development has sometimes been characterized by German legal historians as a 'decay' or 'vulgarization' of the Justinianic tradition. But it should rather be interpreted as a further attempt to make the *Corpus* usable by epitomizing or adding to it in ways which reflected the changing ethos of the empire. The final acceptance of Christianity as the official religion of the ruling and administrative élites of the empire, for instance, had a profound influence on the law. The institutions, and to a large extent, the doctrine of the Church had been defined and protected by Justinian. Now, however, Christian morality was brought to bear on the classical law and where the two were incompatible – as in the case of

---

[7] Pieler, 'Rechtsliteratur', p. 435. For the *antecessores*, see H. Scheltema, *L'enseignement de droit des antécesseurs*.

[8] For the effect of the sixth- and seventh-century invasions on the Byzantine provinces, see C. Foss, 'Archaeology and the twenty cities of Byzantine Asia', *American Journ. of Arch.*, 81 (1977). Theodore Balsamon, writing in the twelfth century, also discussed the problem of legal ignorance in the provinces. See Theodore Balsamon, 'Responsa ad interrogationes Marci patriarchae', *Patrologia Graeca*, vol. 138, col. 956.

marriage, divorce and, importantly in the present context, the taking of oaths –
the law was adapted to accord with Christian teaching[9].

The eighteen short sections of the *Ekloga* dealt almost exclusively with civil law,
particularly property rights in marriage, inheritance and wardship, and different
kinds of possession, but it also contained a passage on witnesses. The code
remained officially in force until the end of the ninth century, but with it arises a
problem which is common to all subsequent Byzantine legal codes. There is no
direct evidence that it was ever put to *practical* use. All that can be said of this and
other compilations, is that the number of surviving manuscripts of the original
texts and the use made of them as a source for later law books, indicate both a
lively scholarly interest and the distinct possibility that they were used in the
training of lawyers[10]. At this point, another short legal text should briefly be
mentioned. The *Nomos georgikos*, or 'Farmers' Law', dates from the end of the
seventh century or the beginning of the eighth. It is important for our purposes
because it contains fragments of eminently practical regulations about boundary
disputes[11].

With the *Procheiros Nomos*, the next code to be issued (at the end of the ninth
century), there begins a new and better documented era of legal activity[12]. There
has been considerable debate, for a century or more, whether this code and the
others that soon followed – the *Novels of Leo VI* and the vast compilation of the
Basilika – mark a return to legal classicism on a par with the so-called
'Macedonian Renaissance' in the arts[13]. But it has become increasingly clear that
Justinianic law was never rejected in the period between the sixth and tenth
centuries; it was simply excerpted into small, practical handbooks or epitomized
in new codes. What was of concern to the jurisprudents of the late ninth century
was, certainly, a renewal of interest in legal principles, but also a strongly
expressed wish not only to establish the panoply of the 'old' law, but also to teach
what was current. The *Procheiros Nomos*, was, in reality, a political rather than a
legal milestone. The emperor, Leo VI, was far more concerned with ostensibly
replacing a code issued by iconoclast (and therefore, in his eyes, non-Christian)

9 Pieler, 'Rechtsliteratur', pp. 432–4.

10 Pieler, 'Rechtsliteratur', pp. 438–43, deals with the use of the *Ekloga* as a source for later law books.
Ménager, 'Notes', 242–5, discusses the problematic Italian manuscripts.

11 *Nomos georgikos* in *Jus graecoromanum*, ed. Zepos, vol. 2; also ed. and Eng. trans. W. Ashburner,
'The Farmers' Law', *J. Hell. Stud.*, 30 (1910) (Text); *J. Hell. Stud.*, 32 (1912) (Commentary and
trans.). See Pieler, 'Rechtsliteratur', p. 441. For similarities with early Visigothic law, see R.
Collins, *Early Medieval Spain*, p. 28.

12 *Procheiros Nomos* in *Jus graecoromanum*, ed. Zepos, vol. 2. English translation is by E. H. Freshfield,
A manual of Eastern Roman law: the Procheiros Nomos. See Pieler, 'Rechtsliteratur', p. 446, and
Ménager, 'Notes', 245–7.

13 *Les Novelles de Léon VI le sage*, ed., and Fr. trans., P. Noailles and A. Dain. The new edition of the
Basilika was unavailable to me at the time of writing: *Basilicorum libri lx, series A, Textus*, ed. H.
Scheltema and N. Van der Wal and *Basilicorum libri lx, series B, Scholia*, ed. H. Scheltema.
References are to the old edition of C. Heimbach, *Basilicorum libri lx* (hereafter *Basilika*). For the
Basilika and its literature, Pieler, 'Rechtsliteratur', pp. 462–4.

emperors, than with making a major contribution to legal studies, though the preface to the new code again emphasized confusion and ignorance as reasons for a 'new' compilation. The compilers had taken great care 'to avoid tedium and to make the study of law easier to grasp'. The existing laws were to be examined and provisions which were 'necessary, useful and in constant demand' were to be extracted from them. Useless clauses were to be purged and new legislation added where necessary.

The *Procheiros Nomos* duly appeared in forty chapters, of which the second half rested firmly, if unattributed, on the *Ekloga*[14]. It was envisaged as the introduction to and synopsis of a larger work, intended for students and professional lawyers. The *Book of the Eparch*, a series of regulations concerning the trade and professional corporations in Constantinople probably dating from the early tenth century, declares that the notaries (*taboullarioi*) must show a knowledge of the forty titles of the *Procheiros Nomos* and, in addition, familiarity with the sixty books of the *Basilika*, a massive compilation probably issued in the last years of the ninth century[15]. This work has been described as 'a firework display, whose light did not last long'[16] and, certainly, the vast amount of material contained in it was mainly made use of by practising lawyers in the so-called *Synopsis major* of the *Basilika* and a series of commentaries upon it. Apart from evidence that, even in the capital, the *Synopsis* itself was found to be too unwieldy, in the provinces lawyers still, apparently, referred to other compilations including the *Ekloga*. Two legal streams flowed on, both fed from the same Justinianic source. One provided repertories, commentaries, glosses and *scholia* on the *Basilika*; the other, mixtures of the *Ekloga*, *Procheiros Nomos* and their derivatives[17].

Within this legal jungle, there is one small clearing in which we can glimpse the law in action. At some point in the mid-eleventh century, a judge in Constantinople gathered together a series of *hypomnêmata* (legal opinions) and *semiômata* (verdicts or decisions) delivered by himself as well as by other legal luminaries, including the celebrated judge, Eustathios Rhômaios. These real-life cases were interspersed with teaching examples and short references to relevant legal material. The work was arranged in sections which were clearly aimed to assist students to gain a knowledge of case law on a particular topic and is thus known as the *Peira* ('rulings'), a title which reflects its practical character. The collection is of tremendous importance because it conveys an impression of the judicial activity of the secular courts so that, in Professor Dieter Simon's phrase, 'the social effectiveness of dead norms can be tested, and Byzantine law

---

[14] Ménager, 'Notes', 145.
[15] *Eparchikon biblion* in *Jus graecoromanum*, ed. Zepos, vol. 2. For English translation, E. H. Freshfield, *Roman law in the later Roman Empire*. For the date of the *Basilika*, Pieler, 'Rechtsliteratur', p. 455. [16] Ménager, 'Notes', 247.
[17] See N. Svoronos, *Recherches sur la tradition juridique à Byzance: la Synopsis Major des Basiliques et ses appendices*, and Ménager, 'Notes', 249–50.

6 Mount Athos and its environs in the tenth century

LAVRA

MOUNT ATHOS

ZYGOS RIDGE

+KOLOBOS

+ST CHRISTINA

HIERISSOS

+ORPHANOU/
GOMATOU

REBENIKA

NEOCHÔRION

STRATONION

RODOPE MTS

THRAKE

CONSTANTINOPLE

Strymón

THESSALONIKA

Peristerai

Basilika

Hierissos

MT ATHOS

Lavra

CHALKIDIKE

100 miles

150 km

50

100

50

50

N

20 miles

30 km

10

20

10

20

0

0

.... Boundary of Mount Athos

□ City

o Village

+ Monastery

gains an historical dimension'[18]. The only practical legal touchstone for this period is, therefore, the *Peira*. It is unsatisfactory in the sense that it is a later compilation, but nevertheless relevant because the cases it discusses often reach back into the tenth century. But there is an important underlying question which must continually be faced, and which a study of the *Peira* brings into focus: how far, in the resolution of the cases about to be discussed, can any legal code or maxims be seen to be put into practice? Professor Simon has suggested that, far from applying the letter of the law, Byzantine judges and lawyers merely used the law codes as a quarry from which to mine their rhetorical arguments. When it came to judgement, other factors – common sense, local custom, even expediency – might come into play[19]. There is some evidence that this may have been so in our tenth-century cases.

The issues in the two cases about to be discussed centre on the question of the involvement of state officials in the affairs of local communities. We can observe in what circumstances they intervened and what their motives were for doing so. The cases also provide an opportunity for deciding the extent to which the participants and practices contained in the Byzantine legal codes and hand-books were actually adhered to. The two cases chosen are both disputes about boundaries – the most common type of dispute in the surviving texts. One covers the problem of the definition of the Holy Mountain of Athos with its lay neighbours[20]; the other is a conflict about rights between two neighbouring districts in that part of southern Italy still controlled in the tenth century by the Byzantines[21].

The documents concerned with the Athonite dispute and its aftermath cover a period of about two years. They concern a period when the monastic communities had already permanently established themselves on the peninsula of Athos, land which, until the early years of the tenth century, had provided unquestioned common grazing and refuge for the settlements of the south-eastern Chalkidike (see fig. 6). It was now being claimed by the monks as part of their monastic seclusion and attempts were being made to exclude the

---

[18] *Practica ex actis Eustathii Romani* in *Jus graecoromanum*, ed. Zepos, vol. 4 (hereafter *Peira*); see Pieler, 'Rechtsliteratur', p. 469. This text, though much quoted, has not yet been the subject of a full-scale study, but see D. Simon, *Rechtsfindung am byzantinischen Reichsgericht* for a short introduction and S. Vryonis, Jnr., 'The *Peira* as a source for the history of Byzantine aristocratic society' in D. Koumjian (ed.), *Near Eastern Numismatics, Iconography, Epigraphy and History*, pp. 279–84.

[19] Simon, *Rechtsfindung*, p. 17. See now M. Angold, *The Byzantine Empire*, p. 42.

[20] The early history of Athos is discussed in *Actes du Prôtaton*, 1 (*Archives de l'Athos, 7*), ed. D. Papachryssanthou (hereafter *Prôtaton*; page reference is to Papachryssanthou's commentary; documents are cited by number). For this dispute, *Prôtaton*, nos. 4, 5, 6 and pp. 56–9. The *Prôtaton* is still the administrative centre of the Holy Mountain and is, therefore, the natural place for documents concerning the community, rather than those of individual houses, to be kept.

[21] For this dispute and related documents, see A. Guillou and W. Holtzmann, 'Zwei katepansurkunden aus Tricarico', *Quellen und Forschungen*, 41 (1961) (reprinted in A. Guillou, *Studies on Byzantine Italy*, pp. 12–20) for text and commentary on the case.

laity. To complicate matters, the imprecise designation of the boundaries of sales of land abandoned some time previously, had led to further conflict between lay and monastic communities. The official responsible for the government sales of this abandoned land, the *epoptês**, plays an important rôle in the dispute under discussion.

The three surviving documents dealing with this stage in the hostilities come from various stages of the resolution of the dispute and it is only incidentally that they reveal its cause. The first, dating from May 942, is an agreement between the two parties: the monks of Mount Athos and the inhabitants of the region centred on the neighbouring settlement of Hierissos (present day Ierissos). The document reads as follows:

SUPERSCRIPTIONS:

Signa of Gregory, *hêgoumenos** of Orphanou; Methodios, *hêgoumenos* of St Christina; Andrew, *hêgoumenos* of Spelaiôtou; John of Rebenika; Constantine Laloumas; Basil Garasdos; Michael *apokentarchos* [retired army officer]; Demetrios Nepribasdos; John, *hêgoumenos* of Athos; Bardas, Athonite monk; Paul, Athonite monk; Theodore Goireutos, Athonite monk.

TEXT:

In the Name of the Father, Son and Holy Ghost. We the aforementioned signatories, who have made the sign of the holy and life-giving Cross with our own hands[22] confirm the present written agreement (*engraphon asphaleia*) and final settlement (*teleia dialysis*) to you, Thomas, *basilikos prôtospatharios*, *asêkrêtês* and *epoptês* of Thessalonika[23]. We are, on the one side, the *hêgoumenoi* and peasants of the village commune (*koinotês tês chôras*) and, on the other, the Athonite monks, that is, the monks of the mountain of Athos.

When, some time ago you [the *epoptês*] sold some *klasma** land to the inhabitants of the *chôrion* [rural commune], you did not establish the boundaries of what should be controlled by the purchasers and what by the Athonites[24]. Because of this, we came to Thessalonika and to the presence of the most honourable *stratelatês** [military governor], Katakalôn, and of our most holy archbishop, Gregory; Thomas Tzoulas, the *basilikos prô-tospatharios*; Zoêtos, the *basilikos prôtospatharios* and *kritês** [judge] and you, yourself, the aforementioned *epoptês*[25]. We made a request (*enklêsis*) that the property of Athos should be divided off from the land which had been sold. We of the *chôrion* maintained that our control (*despoteia*) stretched as far as the Zygos ridge and that from there the land belonged to the Athonites[26]. But we, the Athonites, countered that a larger share of the land which

22 The names are written round the four 'arms' of a Cross and doubtless appeared in such a way in the original.
23 Thessalonika was the chief city of its eponymous theme (administrative district) which may have been in existence in the early ninth century; see Oikonomidès, *Les listes*, p. 352.
24 The land was probably abandoned because of Bulgar raids earlier in the tenth century. If by 'recently' in the text it is implied that the *klasma* land had been sold within the previous two years, then, since by law it had to have been abandoned for thirty years, the cause of the abandonment could be placed about 911–12. For Bulgarian campaigns from *c.* 912–27, see R. Browning, *Byzantium and Bulgaria*, pp. 61–9. Other *klasma* lands in the Chalkidike had already been bought by monastic houses *c.* 883; see *Prôtaton*, p. 47.
25 *Prôtaton*, p. 190, for a discussion of their identities. Katakalôn, though he is here qualified with the description of *stratelatês* (Oikonomidès, *Les listes*, p. 332), is given his correct title of *stratêgos** in *Prôtaton*, nos. 5 and 6. The *epoptês* was probably called Thomas Môrokoumoulos; see *Prôtaton*, p. 200.   26 See fig. 6, p. 130.

had been sold belonged to us. After a great deal of argument, both sides came to an agreement and both declared as follows:

That the boundary should run from coast to coast from the lands of the Lord Methodios in the vicinity of the Zygos, and that all the lands from there towards the Zygos should come under the control of the Athonites, and from the boundary towards Hierissos, all should be under the control of the purchasers and the monastery of Kolobos[27]. And we, the Athonites, have no rights from the boundary in the direction of Hierissos, neither do you, the inhabitants of the *chôria* have any rights from the boundary towards Athos.

Having agreed to these things and wishing them to be confirmed, we came to you, the *epoptês*, so that you could confirm them and come to the place and mark the division we have agreed. Whoever challenges and is not satisfied with the above agreement, is firstly a denier of the Holy and Undivided Trinity and alien to the faith of the Christians and to the calling of a monk, and then should be condemned for laying claim to the share agreed in the present agreement. We place the *kathedra tôn gerontôn* outside [the terms of this agreement][28].

In order to confirm all these things, we have superscribed the holy and life-giving Crosses, the text having been written by the hand of Demetrios, cleric, *kouboukleisios* [church official] and *orphanotrophos* [head of a state orphanage], in the month of May, in the fifteenth indiction[29]. (App. XXI)

There follows a list of witnesses: Gregory, Archbishop of Thessalonika; Thomas, a *basilikos prôtospatharios* and *notarios tou kommerkiou* (officer responsible for levying the sales tax); and Basil Skrinarês, Gregory Phouskoulos and the cleric Michael 'of the Great Church' (in this case, Haghia Sophia in Thessalonika)[30].

The next document, dating from between May 942 and August 943, provides an account of the dispute from another point of view, for it is the report of the *epoptês* himself[31]. Again we hear of the sale of the *klasma* land to the Hierissiotes and of other land transactions in the vicinity including gifts of land to the nearby monastery of Kolobos. The boundaries between these various parcels had been established but:

the boundary between them and the monks of Athos had not previously been fixed, in order to show how far the monks' holding extends or from which point the klasmatic land held by the village or by the other monasteries begins.

[27] For the monastery of Kolobos, see *Prôtaton*, pp. 36–8.
[28] There is some controversy about the precise nature of the *kathedra tôn gerontôn* ('old mens' seats'). It was once believed that it was a meeting place for the early hermits on Mount Athos, but Papachryssanthou, *Prôtaton*, pp. 111–14, makes a convincing case for it to be understood as a small holding once possessed by monks but by the 940s absorbed firstly by the monastery of Kolobos and then by the Athonites.
[29] The fifteen-year cycle of the indiction was the most common method of dating of Byzantine official documents. The year began on 1 September each year. Since the same *epoptês* is mentioned in other cases from Athos in 941, it can be firmly stated that the fifteenth indiction in question ran from September 941 to August 942. See *Prôtaton*, p. 189.
[30] *Prôtaton*, p. 190, for what is known of the witnesses. The *notarios tou kommerkiou* was a notary in one of the customs bureaux, probably in Thessalonika.
[31] *Prôtaton*, no. 5. For dating, p. 196.

The reason for this uncertainty is now far more clearly stated than in the first document: there had been no formal ratification of the boundary by the *epoptês*:

Nothing concerning the purchased klasmatic land and that of the monks of Athos was particularly examined by us, or taken any trouble over in the matter of the boundaries, because no strife had arisen about them.

Why had the paperwork not been done? The *epoptês*' remark may have been prompted by the wish to divert attention from a personal failure to act with the requisite speed, or it may simply have been that he did not anticipate any problems concerning the fisc (his prime responsibility) arising from the sale[32]. In any case, his lack of action, whatever the cause, should warn against the assumption that, even in a bureaucratic state, paperwork was always efficiently and promptly completed.

At this point, the local dispute was given a far more significant dimension:

After this, the monks of Athos went and asked the help of the Holy Emperors and [as a result] both the *stratêgos* [military governor] and Thomas Tzoulas undertook to separate their landed rights from those of the *kastron** [fortified settlement] and to request from the said inhabitants a written guarantee that they would no longer importune the monks[33].

At imperial instigation, both parties were summoned to Thessalonika. Their arguments are summarized and it emerges that the Athonites' case was based on a fine piece of fiscal and legal argument. The monks firstly claimed control over the entire Athos peninsula, since they had been assigned it 'in the old *klasma* lists'[34] and they also produced a *chrysoboullon* (imperial document) of Basil I, which gave them possession 'from the *enoria* (district) of Hierissos beyond' – that is, towards Athos[35]. The next stage was to argue that the *enoria* was *not* that of the settlement and its associated lands (the *chôrion*), but that of the *kastron*, that is, simply the area within the fortifications of Hierissos. If the Athonite interpretation had been accepted, it would, of course, have meant that they gained more territory. The *epoptês*' report relates how the inhabitants of Hierissos 'stood their ground' and maintained that their land extended as far as the Zygos ridge. This view prevailed, for 'after a great deal of argument, it was established

---

[32] Each party's purchases should have been noted in *libellika* and the boundaries delineated. Perhaps the area sold was indeed specified, but the precise establishment of the boundary remained to be done.

[33] There were four emperors in 942–3: Romanos Lekapênos, who held supreme power; his son-in-law, the deposed Constantine VII and his two sons, Constantine and Stephen Lekapênos, *Prôtaton*, p. 186. Romanos had already begun to take an interest in the fortunes of the Athonite monks as he had already made a grant to them in 934 (*Prôtaton*, no. 3) and made an annual money grant (*roga*). See *Theophanes continuatus, Chronographia*, ed. I. Bekker, pp. 418–19.

[34] These *kôdikes* were the official records of the sales of *klasma*. See *Prôtaton*, pp. 46–8, for other sales in the ninth century.

[35] The grant of Basil I is preserved as *Prôtaton*, no. 1 (June 883). It gave the Athonites freedom from interference by imperial officials and other civilians and recognized the right of the monastic groups to lands in the peninsula. It did not specifically grant lands, but it did, significantly, mention the 'nuisance' of the flocks of Hierissos.

by both parties where the boundary was to be traced'. The *epoptês* somewhat ironically commented that 'they made peace because of their dislike of strife and, more importantly, because of confusion and ignorance surrounding the bone of contention'.

The *epoptês* was instructed by the *stratêgos*, the archbishop and the *basilikos prôtospatharios*, Thomas Tzoulas, both to mark out the boundary on the site and to give documents (*libelloi*) to both parties confirming this action. They were to swear oaths that they wished the boundary to be in the agreed place, a precaution against 'fickleness' and after they had done so, the *asphaleia* (confirmation) was ratified by the signature of the archbishop and the rest of the dignitaries. The *epoptês* then formally established the boundary by walking it with representatives of the two parties as well as his own officials. This did not, however, mark the end of the matter, for the Hierissiotes complained that the agreement did not allow them to take refuge on the mountain in time of 'barbarian' attack as they had been wont to do[36]. This point seems to have been appreciated, for the *epoptês* granted them the right to flee to Athos, but only with the consent of the monks. He banned them, however, from establishing wattle sheep-folds or bee-hives there, because of the damage the animals might do.

At this point, it might be justifiable to consider the matter closed. But the existence of yet another document (dated to 2 August 943) shows that this was not the case[37]. It was issued by the *stratêgos* of Thessalonika, Katakalôn, himself and was in response to the earlier imperial instruction. In it, the *stratêgos* reported that he had gone with Gregory, the archbishop of Thessalonika and a number of other lay and ecclesiastical dignitaries and marked out the boundary again. This time we are given the *periorismos* or detailed description of the boundary. The details need not detain us, but the references to *existing* cairns and marked trees indicate that the *stratêgos* was following the boundary which the *epoptês* had already laid down: 'thus dividing and fixing the boundaries *just as the epoptês had fixed them*, and, giving written confirmation to our deed, we gave each party their share'.

Here this particular dispute seems to have ended, but the friction caused by the increasing economic and political power of the Athonite houses was a constant issue throughout the tenth century. By the year 1000, monastic superiority on the Chalkidike was well established and the houses began to accumulate lands even further away from the peninsula and to enjoy ever more lavish imperial protection and patronage.

The involvement of powerful officials and the interest taken by the emperor himself in the Athos case is certainly striking, but this is not an unusual feature of

---

[36] Another reference to Bulgar, or possibly Slav, attacks. See. F. Dölger, *Ein Fall slavischer Einsiedlung im Hinterland von Thessalonika im 10. Jahrhundert, Sitzungsberichte der Bayer. Akad. der Wissen., phil.-hist. Klasse*, 1952, pt 1.

[37] *Prôtaton*, no. 6 (2 August Ind. 1 = 2 August 943).

Byzantine charters and can be observed in our second, south Italian case, again about boundaries[38]. Although we have only one document to deal with, it was again delivered by an important governmental official: the katepan* Gregory Tarchaneiôtês. It dates from the year 1001–2. It also relates, in a somewhat clumsy style, the history of this dispute concerning the boundaries of the lands of two neighbouring fortified settlements.

> Since in the time of Luke the kaffir and apostate, he who seized power in the *kastellion* [fortified settlement] of Petrapertousa, and, not content with perpetrating many acts of tyranny and raids throughout Italy, not only took for himself unsettled places, but also, like a brigand, grabbed lands and territories. Amongst these he took all the places and lands subject to the inhabitants of the *kastron* of Trikariko, which those who dwelt in the aforementioned *kastron* of Trikariko had controlled for a long time and he did not allow them to enter into these lands, nor to cultivate their own properties. Since now the aforesaid Luke has been driven out of the aforesaid *kastellion* of Petrapertousa together with his men and fellow apostates, the inhabitants of the *kastron* of Trikariko brought a complaint (*enklêsis*) concerning the boundaries and the control of their town[39].
> So first we sent the *taxiarchês* Constantine Kontos who, acting together with the inhabitants of the *kastellion* of Toulba and with the agreement of the two parties, established the boundaries and the property which came under the control of the inhabitants of Akerentza and the inhabitants of Trikariko, just as either side had held them long ago.

This visit corresponds with that of the *epoptês* in the Athonite case, though the official concerned was a military man, rather than a fiscal official[40]. Again, however, further action was necessary, though it was probably undertaken to bring matters to a satisfactory conclusion rather than as a consequence of objections from any of the parties or interference from elsewhere. Let the katepan take up the account once more:

> A short time afterwards, we ourselves, wishing to take a hand in this affair, sent, in the December of the fifteenth indiction, our representative (*proximos*) Romanos, with the *magistros* [court official] Argyros of Bari and Myron ex- *chartoularios* of the Scholai[41]. They took with them inhabitants of the *kastron* of Trikariko and inhabitants of the *kastellion* of Toulba and made enquiries concerning the boundaries.

---

[38] The best narrative history of Byzantine Italy remains J. Gay, *L'Italie méridionale et l'empire byzantin*. But see also V. von Falkenhausen, *La dominazione bizantina nell'Italia meridionale*, her chapter 'I bizantini in Italia' in G. Cavallo, *I bizantini in Italia*, A. Guillou, *Studies on Byzantine Italy* and *idem*, *Culture et société en Italie byzantine*. For George Tarchaneiotês, see Guillou and Holtzmann, 'Katepansurkunden', 17.

[39] For the location of the places see fig. 5, p. 108. Petrapertousa is the present-day Pietrapertosa; Toulba is the present-day Tolve and Trikariko/Tricarico and Akerentza/Acerenza are easily recognizable. To avoid confusion, I have used the Byzantine spelling throughout. All these settlements were fortified. The brigand Loukas' epithet of *kaphiros* ('kaffir', literally 'one who practises a religion alien to Islam'), here indicates a Greek apostate from the Orthodox faith. See Guillou and Holtzmann, 'Katepansurkunden', 12–13 and notes.

[40] Constantine Kontos is not otherwise known. See von Falkenhausen, *Dominazione bizantina*, p. 126.

Again, the processes in the two cases are very similar. We hear that five inhabitants of Toulba were asked to give evidence. They took a leading rôle because they belonged to the settlement in the jurisdiction of Akerentza nearest to the boundary with Trikariko (see fig. 5). Like the Hierissiotes on Athos, the people of Toulba were keen to preserve the mutual rights of entering neighbouring territory to pasture or gather wood. They also gave a full description of the boundaries. But in this case, the rights of one community were clearly established at the expense of their neighbours:

So we maintain that, from this time, the inhabitants of the *kastron* of Trikariko have the *exousia* [control] over these places in full ownership (*teleia authentia*) and irremovable control from now until the end of time. Accordingly, from now on, neither the inhabitants of the *kastron* Akerentza, nor those of the *kastellion* of Toulba, nor any others, have the right to cross the boundaries of the aforementioned *kastron* of Trikariko and to take control of any of these places. (App. XXII)

The document itself was given to the inhabitants of Trikariko as proof of their rights and it remained in the episcopal archives of the town until the eighteenth century at least.

Though the Athos dispute was primarily concerned with the placing of a boundary, about which there was no argument in the Italian case, both were concerned with the rights of neighbours to pass across boundaries. Both, too had arisen in the aftermath of raiding and disorder. In the Athonite case, the same raids which had led to the declaration and subsequent sale of *klasma* land were clearly responsible for the Hierissiotes' concern for a safe refuge for their flocks. In southern Italy, the activity of the Muslim convert, Luke, provided a similar background of danger from which the communities concerned were struggling to recover. The officials of the state were playing their part in returning the rural settlements to some semblance of peace and order. But apart from the intrinsic similarities of the cases, there are many other parallels to be drawn.

In both cases, the involvement of imperial officials is noticeable and it is clear that, even in the case of provincial boundary disputes (such as the Italian example) the representatives of the central government expected to become involved and the inhabitants of the areas concerned expected to involve them. Unlike Constantinople, where professional judges of various kinds sat to deal with cases, the provincial 'judiciary' reveals what at first sight appears to be a remarkably amateur aspect[42]. For until the mid-tenth century, the courts were

---

[41] December of the fifteenth indiction nearest to the year of the world given (6510) has been established as December 1001, Guillou and Holtzmann, 'Katepansurkunden', 16. For Romanos, Myron and Argyros see von Falkenhausen, *Dominazione bizantina*, pp. 129, 133, 188–9. The *magistros* Argyros may be identified with the *tourmarch* (military commander) Argyros mentioned in another document issued by George Tarchaneiotês in December 999. In addition to von Falkenhausen, see J.-F. Vannier, *Familles byzantines: les Argyroi*, p. 58.

[42] In Constantinople the *koiaistôr* concerned himself with forgeries, successions to property, wills, matrimonial affairs and the conduct of provincials in the capital. The Judges of the Hippodrome

usually presided over by the *stratêgos*, or in the case of southern Italy, the katepan. As the official who commanded both the military and civilian government of a region, he was most unlikely to have received any formal legal training. However, like all *archontes* (leading men), he was expected to be literate. But the *stratêgos* was not abandoned helpless to judge the cases that came before him. As in Roman times, he sat with a panel of *symponoi* or assessors, referred to in the Justinianic *corpus* as *adsessores* or *consiliarii*, some of whom, at least, had received legal training[43]. In the Athos case, one of those who sat in court, the *kritês* Zoêtos, was a professional judge, and two others, the *basilikos prôtospatharios* Thomas Tzoulas and the *epoptês* Thomas, may well have had some kind of legal training. In the latter's case, a grounding in fiscal regulations and practice would have been necessary. In the Trikariko case, the complaint was brought to the katepan by one only of the parties and it is not clear whether there ever was a hearing at which the representatives of Akerentza and Toulba were also present. None of the officials involved in this case can be positively identified as having legal expertise. Suffice it to say that the *taxiarchês* Constantine Kontos may, as a military man, have possessed some elementary knowledge of surveying[44]. But it is unlikely that either he or the *magistros* Argyros or the former *chartoularios* of the Scholai, Myron, had any formal legal training. The only possible candidate, the *proximos* Romanos, is nowhere identified as a legal official. We can only conjecture that the katepan took such legal advice as he needed from unnamed officials in Bari.

The lack of legal expertise on the part of those who were in charge of legal matters in the provinces did not strike the Byzantines as odd. For them, justice was not a separate, specialized sphere of activity. It was part of the administration of a region granted to an individual for reasons which often had more to do with military prowess, social influence or even corruption than with intellectual excellence[45]. One salutary example from Constantinople may make the point. About the year 902, one Podarôn, after acquitting himself nobly in various naval engagements, was appointed *prôtospatharios* of the Basin, a post which involved overseeing the imperial oarsmen and the palace harbour. 'But as he was unlettered (*agrammatos*)', a tenth-century text informs us, 'by order of the emperor, a judge (*kritês*) from the Hippodrome used to go down there and take

---

and their seniors, the Judges of the Vêlon, seem to have heard mainly civil cases. Under the Eparch, the *praefectus Urbi*, who may himself have heard appeals from the provinces, sat local judges for the districts of Constantinople. More work needs to be done on Byzantine legal officials, but for the above, in respective order, see Oikonomidès, *Les listes*, pp. 32, 323, 319–20, and Guillou, *Civilisation byzantine*, pp. 150–1.

43 Guillou, *Civilisation byzantine*, p. 149. For the Justinianic period, see H. Jolowicz and B. Nicholas, *Historical introduction to Roman Law*, 3rd edn, pp. 449–50. A man acting as a judge had, at least, to be able to sign his own name; see *Novelles de Léon VI*, p. 181.

44 For Byzantine surveying techniques, see E. Schilbach, *Byzantinische Metrologie*, esp. pp. 233–63.

45 The eleventh-century retired general, Kekaumenos, warned against the habit prevalent amongst *kritai* of 'taking gifts'; see *Cecaumeni Strategicon*, ed. B. Wassiliewsky and V. Jernstedt, pp. 6, 59.

his seal with him to the Basin and judge the oarsmen.'[46] This was an extreme instance of a circumstance which seems to have persisted. As the twelfth-century canonist, Theodore Balsamon commented:

The high officials who preside over the courts are not obliged to have precise knowledge of the law, because they have other duties. As a consequence, if some of their findings are due to incompetence, they are excused[47].

There seems to have been little change in attitudes since the days of Rome, when it was the duty of each provincial governor to try a case by whatever means he saw fit, but not necessarily to reveal any legal expertise himself. As J. A. Crook has pertinently put it, 'jurisprudence was an amateur activity just as much as being a historian or an agriculture expert'[48]. The Byzantines, too, only saw the need for expert *advice* to be provided to the presiding officials, not for expert *knowledge* to be shown by them. For, as Balsamon added, the leniency shown to the *archontes* was not to be extended to their *symponoi*, who faced serious consequences if their advice were subsequently shown to have been mistaken or wrong.

But there was, in the person of the *kritês*, at least one official in each theme whose duty it was to concern himself with legal affairs. During the tenth century, the *kritês'* power began to increase. More and more campaigns mounted on Byzantium's eastern and northern frontiers meant that the *stratêgoi* were increasingly away from base. As a result, not only the settlement of cases, but also the administration of the theme itself, seems increasingly to have fallen into the hands of the *kritai*. When the future emperor, Nikêphoros Phokas, sought information about the whereabouts of St Athanasios of Athos (958), he directed his enquiry to the *kritês* not the *stratêgos* of Thessalonika and a *scholion* to the *Basilika* envisaged two heads to the thematic organization at this time – the *kritês* and the *doux* (military leader). By the eleventh century, the *kritês* was no longer simply a judicial official; he had a number of financial officers also under his command[49]. In the Athonite case, however, we see the *kritês* playing his old rôle of legal adviser to the *stratêgos* and this very fact helps to establish the chronology of the change in the status of the *kritês*. He was joined by other figures also, surely, acting as *symponoi*: the most important churchman of the region, Gregory, archbishop of Thessalonika; the *epoptês* Thomas and another imperial official, Thomas Tzoulas. The 'bench' thus consisted of five members.

[46] Constantine Porphyrogenitus, *De administrando imperio*, ed. G. Moravscik, trans. R. Jenkins, ch. 51; Const. Porph., *Admin.*, vol. 2, *Commentary*, ed. F. Dvornik *et al.*, p. 201.

[47] As quoted by Guillou, *Civilisation byzantine*, p. 149. See G. Rhalles and M. Potles, *Syntagma tôn theiôn kai hierôn kanonôn*, vol. 3, p. 339.

[48] Crook, *Law and life*, p. 89.

[49] Oikonomidès, *Les listes*, pp. 323–5, discusses the changes in the duties of the *kritês*. See also, H. Ahrweiler, 'Recherches sur l'administration de l'empire byzantin aux IXe–XIe siècles', *Bulletin de correspondance héllenique*, 84 (1960).

There does not seem to have been any fixed number of judges who could hear a case[50]. Indeed, a discussion in the *Peira* about whether majority or individual verdicts should be returned in cases of disagreement took as an example a case involving ten judges[51]. As for the verdict, the same *Peira* discussion reveals a state of uncertainty about whether a majority vote should prevail. Questioned on this point, a 'most learned *magistros*' declared that it depended on the circumstances. If, in the case of ten judges, six were of the same opinion and four of another, then the majority view should prevail. If, however, ten different views were expressed, then each should be noted. In practice, it seems safe to assume, majority verdicts prevailed, with the *archôn* concerned taking due note of the expert opinion of his *symponoi*. In all circumstances, however, as the *Peira*, following both the *Basilika* and a Novel of Leo VI, clearly stated, 'all those giving judgements . . . should state their view clearly *in writing*' and 'a sentence verbally delivered is not valid until it has been set down *in writing*'[52].

The recording of cases and judgements was thus of paramount importance and it was undertaken by a variety of officials. Although there is no mention of a scribe in the Trikariko case, it is unlikely that the katepan wrote it himself, though he did sign his own name and affix his own lead seal[53]. Of the Athonite documents, the first agreement between the two parties was written out by a churchman, Demetrios, the administrator of the orphanage (*orphanotrophos*) in Thessalonika[54]; the report of the *epoptês* was presumably drawn up by one of his officials or even by himself, and the final document issued by the *stratêgos* was doubtless drawn up by a member of his suite. The same scribe who wrote the copy we possess of this last document also provided the official copies of the previous two, implying that he was a member of the theme notariat.

It is likely, though unfortunately never explicitly stated, that these scribes were members of a group usually referred to as *nomikoi* or *taboullarioi*. These notaries are well documented in Constantinople, where they formed one of the corporations described in the tenth-century *Book of the Eparch*[55]. We do not have evidence for such associations in the provinces in the tenth century, but by 1097 a *primikêrios* (head) of the *nomikoi* in Thessalonika, one Stephen Argyros, cleric of Haghia Sophia in the city, could draw up an act of sale, though the text was actually written out by his *notarios*, the priest Michael Katzikês[56]. He was acting as a *tabelliôn* or *symbolaiographos* who did not compose the document, but simply

---

[50] *Pace* Guillou, *Civilisation byzantine*, pp. 153–4, who maintains that three judges heard a civil case.

[51] *Peira*, li. 16.

[52] *Peira*, li. 20. See also *Basilika*, IX. i. 66.

[53] The seal is mentioned at the end of the text: 'Signed by our own hand and sealed with our lead *boullon* in the year 6510.'

[54] *Prôtaton*, no. 4, line 37. The preserved copy was not written by him.

[55] Freshfield, *Roman Law*, pp. 3–10.

[56] *Actes de Lavra*, vol. 1 (*Archives de l'Athos*, vol. 5), no. 53, ed. A. Guillou, P. Lemerle, N. Svoronos, D. Papachryssanthou.

wrote it out[57]. The scribe of the first agreement between Athonites and Hierissiotes, Demetrios, was also a cleric, and it is probable that the church provided the majority of the *taboullarioi* and scribes in the countryside. Italian evidence confirms this view. A grant of rights to a fishpond made in 981 to the monastery of SS. Peter and Paul in Taranto was written by Gregory the representative (almost certainly the *tabellion*) of the *prôtopapas* (senior priest) Kortikês, the *taboullarios* of the town. The same *taboullarios* later appears in a document of 984[58].

Paperwork was, then, of prime importance and documents needed not only to be correctly drafted, but also correctly copied, sealed and witnessed. A *scholion* to the *Basilika*, dating from the reign of Alexios Komnênos (1081–1118) or after, commented on the need for the state to preserve correct records of transactions and in the process gave a helpful list of the documents that should be produced: the *prôtotypon*, the state's copy, the individual copies belonging to the parties concerned (*idika*) and summaries of transactions (*schêdaria*)[59]. If the *prôtotypon* should be missing, then two identical copies such as those which are frequently referred to in the Athonite documents, could provide authenticity[60]. The correct formulation of documents was paramount and in the cases under discussion it is clear that diplomatic norms (invocations, penal clauses and dating clauses, for instance) were both known and adhered to. In addition, the documents are clearly identified by their official type: an *asphaleia* and *dialysis*, a *praxis* and *diachôrismos* and, in the Trikariko case, a *hypomnêma*[61].

Although written records of disputes were kept, not all parties to them were literate. All the witnesses to the Athos–Hierissos agreement signed their own names (*idiocheirôs*). However, the lay parties to the dispute, whose names are written round the *signa* of the Cross at the head of the document, probably only marked the simple sign. We cannot know for sure because we only possess a copy. It cannot even be assumed that the clergy were able to write their own names, and even if they were, handwriting in Athonite documents of this period often leaves a great deal to be desired. The final proof of authenticity was, of course, the official seal. The agreement between the two Athonite parties and the *stratêgos'* confirmation of the boundary were both sealed, the latter with no less than three lead seals. The katepan's document in the Trikariko case was also sealed with a *molybdoboullon* (an official lead seal)[62]. The diplomatic ramifications of the Athonite case are almost overwhelming (some sixteen documents are mentioned,

[57] For the *taboullarioi*, see Guillou, *Civilisation byzantine*, p. 153. There has been much debate about the precise meaning of the terms *tabellion*, *taboullarios*, *nomikos*, etc. See G. Ferrari, *I documenti greci medioevali di diritto privato dell'Italia meridionale*, pp. 9–11, 79–82.

[58] *Syllabus Graecarum membranarum*, ed F. Trinchera, nos. 8 (981) and 9 (984).

[59] *Basilika*, XXII. i. 31.   [60] *Basilika*, XXII. iv.

[61] Ferrari, *Documenti greci*, pp. 23–39, 86. The terms mean, respectively, 'confirmation', 'act', 'land division' and 'memorandum'.

[62] *Prôtaton*, pp. 189, 197–8. See n. 53, above, for the katepan's seal.

most of them now lost), but the plethora of parchment was undoubtedly due to the imperial interest taken in the fortunes of the Athonite monks which galvanized the local officials into action[63]. But even the Trikariko case warranted two interventions by imperial officials after the first request to the katepan.

All pervasive state interference? It would be tempting to think so. To the time involved in reaching a source of justice (Athos to Thessalonika and Bari to Trikariko were possibly ten days' journey each) must be added the effort of the previous Athonite appeal to Constantinople and the numerous journeys of the imperial officials. The law itself envisaged long delays between stages in a legal process. The *Peira* reproduced the *Basilika*'s instructions about the intervals to be left: twenty days for a defendant to make a deposition after the initial complaint by the plaintiff: three, six and nine month delays for the deposition of evidence and counter-evidence and a further period of three one-month periods during which the right might be granted to the plaintiff to submit yet more evidence[64]. It is not surprising that the time limit for raising claims to land was usually thirty years, though the *Procheiros Nomos* indicated that claims involving religious houses might be received up to forty years after the issue had arisen[65]. But in spite of all the potential time and effort involved, the parties concerned clearly envisaged no firm end to their disputes unless the settlement has been ratified by geographically distant, but *politically* ever-present, authority.

The tradition of state involvement in such local legal affairs was a long one. Even if the *stratêgos* Katakalôn had not been pressurized to summon the parties by men in high places, the case might well have ended up in a similar level of court as that of the south Italians. The Roman law on boundaries envisaged that such disputes would involve either a hearing by a *iudex*, or the inspection of the *vetera monumenta* which marked the boundary by one of the *agrimensores*[66]. The *Farmer's Law* also envisaged judicial involvement:

If there is a dispute about a boundary or a field, *judges* find in favour of territory with longer possession, unless there is a landmark, for this must not be questioned[67].

Whilst there must have been cases which were settled by discussion between the parties concerned, the records of disputes which have survived naturally involve recourse to the agents of the central Byzantine government. They demonstrate the applicability, in the Byzantine context, of Roberts's suggestion that in some societies 'order is only conceivable if there are strong men in

---

63 The dossier of documents has been painstakingly reconstructed by Papachryssanthou, *Prôtaton*, pp. 190, 194–5, 201.
64 Zachariae von Lingenthal, *Griechisch-römisches Recht*, vol. 3, p. 394 and n. 1434.
65 *Procheiros Nomos* in Freshfield, *Eastern Roman Law*, pp. 150, 152.
66 The *actio finium regundorum* is discussed by A. Watson, *The Law of property in the later Roman Republic*, p. 111. For the rôle of the *agrimensor*, O. A. W. Dilke, *Roman Land Surveyors*, pp. 105–6.
67 Ashburner, 'Farmers' Law', 88 (Text); 85 (Commentary).

positions of authority to tell others what to do'[68]. Byzantine political philosophers made much of the concept of *taxis*; its practical application can be seen in these cases.

What the central government could not control, however, was the selection of representatives by the parties concerned and it is here that we can see, at last, some traces of local activity and inclination. In both cases, the lay participants acted communally and there was nothing in Roman law to prevent this. It was evidence of that strong sense of commonality (*koinôsis*) which was a feature of Byzantine social and fiscal organization[69]. The monks of Athos, too, had formed some sort of organization by this time. The parties combined in themselves the rôles of litigants and witnesses and both the numbers concerned and their identities are worthy of comment. Five inhabitants of Hierissos, three *hêgoumenoi* of monasteries near Athos and four Athonite monks ratified the agreement; it can be presumed that they were the parties which set off for Thessalonika since the document was signed there. The *hêgoumenoi* were acting with the laity because a mutual interest was involved: that of preventing the Athonite monks from encroaching on lands which they maintained to be theirs. Each, however, formed a separate party and this is probably why a party of five Hierissiotes was allowed. Three of them were designated by forenames and surnames; one by his, or his family's place of origin and one – the ex-*kentarchôn* – by the military rank which he had once held[70]. The delegation from Toulba which gave evidence to the katepan's officials in the Italian case was also five in number; some Byzantine legal codes, indeed, declared that this was the most suitable number of witnesses to have[71].

It would be interesting to know the social status of these representatives since Roman and Byzantine legislation continually emphasized the need for witnesses to be of reasonable standing. According to the *Procheiros Nomos*, 'paupers' could not testify and the definition (a very problematic one!) was that of 'a person who

---

[68] S. Roberts, 'The study of disputes' in Bossy (ed.), *Disputes and settlements*, p. 10.

[69] For the *koinotês chôriou*, see P. Lemerle, *Agrarian History of Byzantium, passim*; Guillou and Holtzmann, 'Katepansurkunden', 14, n. 21.

[70] *Prôtaton*, p. 191. The Hierissiotes were Basil Garasdos, Michael *apokentarchos*, Demetrios Nepribasdos, John of Rebenika and Constantine Laloumas; the other *hêgoumenoi*: Gregory of Orphanou (or Gomatou), Methodios of St Christina, Andrew of Spelaiôtou. Their lands and houses lay in the region between Hierissos and Athos (*Prôtaton*, pp. 40–1). The Athonites were John, the *hêgoumenos* of Athos, and three monks, Bardas, Paul and Theodore Goireutos (or Gyreutês). The title of *hêgoumenos* of Athos is problematic. Papachryssanthou suggests that it referred to the head of a house on Athos, not to the chief *hêgoumenos* of the mountain, later known as the *Prôtos*, *Prôtaton*, pp. 61–4. For the rank of *kentarchês*, Oikonomidès, *Les listes*, p. 341. He commanded a hundred men, possibly the personal guard of the *stratêgos*. If so, this would have made Michael an important figure in local circles.

[71] The Toulba witnesses were: Charzanitês, Sikenoulphos (Sikenulf, a Lombard name), John of Kara, Goïandos (Guinantus, another possible Lombard), and John Barsianon. See Guillou and Holtzmann, 'Katepansurkunden', 14, nn. 17–20. For the number of witnesses, see *Basilika*, XXII. iv. When the participants were illiterate or semi-illiterate, five witnesses were advised by a *scholion*. For very small-scale cases involving sums of less than 2 *nomismata*, two witnesses were sufficient.

does not possess 50 *nomismata* (gold coins)'. Witnesses had to be over twenty years of age and 'not wholly ignoble' – not slaves, perhaps[72]. The presence in the Hierissos delegation of a retired military man (who had perhaps been posted there to help guard the *kastron*) associated with the three *hêgoumenoi* meant that the opposition to the Athonites was of some social standing. It can be suggested that the delegation from Toulba similarly comprised the chief men (women, of course, being precluded in Roman law from giving evidence)[73].

The Athos documents indicate that each party made its case in turn; the Trikariko document indicates the kind of detail which was to be supplied. Here, the villagers gave details of presumed rights of entry into each other's lands. The Athonites and their opponents will have entered into detail about previous sales of *klasma* land and fiscal definitions. It is not surprising that the documents report a 'great deal of strife about these things'. The evidence was noted. In the Trikariko case, it seems to appear *verbatim*, whereas in the Athos case the arguments are summarized, doubtless from fuller accounts of the evidence taken at the time. Although it is nowhere explicitly stated, the use of such phrases as 'thus spake', 'we maintained' and 'we countered' strongly indicates that the parties were questioned by the tribunal. There is no sign of professional cross-examination. The parties spoke for themselves; there were few lawyers to be had outside Constantinople. Lawyers (*synegoroi*) had never, in any case, been the source of information about the law and its application. Their task had been to present an argument, deploying all the weapons of logic and rhetoric as best they could[74]. But their non-appearance in these tenth-century documents must suggest two important considerations: firstly, that formal rhetorical training was difficult to come by in the provinces and, secondly, that access to courts was straightforward enough for 'lay' Byzantines to order their affairs themselves. In the Athonite case, indeed, the two parties eventually made a settlement 'out of court'. The process by which this was achieved is obscure. Two documents mention 'a great deal of discussion', but did this involve the tribunal as well as the litigants? Although a process (the *compromissum*) was available by which two parties could come together before and accept the arbitration of an arbiter, we have no indication (unlike the Trikariko case) that any *ruling* was passed by the court[75]. But the taking of an oath (*orkos*) did indicate a willingness (somewhat short-lived!) to accept the agreed boundary of Athos. The making of such an agreement was obviously of benefit to both parties, but it was also another example of a phenomenon commented upon by Nicole Castan in another

[72] Freshfield, *Eastern Roman Law*, pp. 117–18. I have discussed the problem of the legal definition of poverty in 'The powerful and the poor in tenth-century Byzantium', *Past and Present*, 73 (1976).
[73] See J. Beaucamp, 'La situation juridique de la femme à Byzance', *Cahiers de civilisation médiévale*, 20 (1977).
[74] Crook, *Law and life*, p. 87.
[75] For the *compromissum*, see J. Thomas, *Textbook of Roman law*, p. 320.

context: 'the duty of all Christians to seek peace and love their neighbours'[76]. The monastic interests were probably all too well aware of the damage to their spiritual reputation, if not their property, from prolonged litigation, though this did not prevent them from attempting to get the agreement altered in their favour.

The moment at which the oath was taken is of some importance, for it illustrates the reluctance of Byzantine courts to use oaths for any but confirmatory purposes; not, that is, as an intrinsic part of the process of proof. A passage from the *Basilika* dealing with this question included a long *scholion* quoting St John Chrysostom's opposition to the taking of oaths based on Christ's abjuration in the Sermon on the Mount: 'Let your speech be "Yea, yea!" or "Nay, nay!" and whatsoever is more than these is of the Evil one' (Matthew 5: 37)[77]. Whilst in Justinian's time, witnesses had to be sworn before their testimony could be heard, by the eighth century, self-consciously orthodox rulers, such as the empress Irene, were discouraging the administering of general oaths at the start of a case[78]. A novel of Leo VI acknowledged that there did seem to be some contradiction between Christ's precept and the old civil law, but added, with some sophistry:

It is accepted that the civil law did not make its decision in order to set itself against religious law, but that it attempts, on the contrary, to achieve by the taking of an oath that which the Divine Law wishes to achieve when it orders us not to swear[79].

In addition, the novel continued, the Lord's Commandment had not been made entirely to regulate temporal affairs, but 'to take to that state of perfection those who aspire to raise themselves up to these happy summits, just as other Precepts were made'. Thus legislation still allowed for the forms of oaths 'established by ancient legislators', but there is little sign of them in our tenth-century documents. Zachariae von Lingenthal's suggestion that, by the end of the eleventh century, oaths were most usually made to *confirm* depositions or agreements already made seems borne out at this earlier date[80].

As we know, the oath that they took to adhere to the first agreement did not prevent the Athonite monks from trying to break it and to restrict the movements of their neighbours and their flocks. The untidy aftermath of the Athos–Hierissos agreement of 942 should act as a warning against assuming that all parties obediently went home to obey the law. Certainly the officials of the state then came into their own. The action of the drama shifted to the places actually in dispute. In southern Italy, Constantine Kontos established the boundaries of

[76] N. Castan, 'Arbitration of disputes under the *ancien régime*' in Bossy (ed.), *Disputes and settlements*, p. 334.   [77] *Basilika*, XXII. 5. i.
[78] Pieler, 'Rechtsliteratur', p. 434 and n. 47; Zachariae von Lingenthal, *Griechisch-römisches Recht*, vol. 3, pp. 397–8.
[79] *Novel* xcvii, *Les Novelles de Léon VI*, pp. 317–19.
[80] *Novel* xcix, *Les Novelles de Léon VI*, pp. 327–9.

Akerentza and Trikariko on behalf of the katepan and the later delegation found them being adhered to. The process of tracing a boundary line is clearly revealed in the Athonite documents, although in this case it had to be done twice. Firstly the *epoptês*, in his own words, 'went to the place and established the boundary according to the written *asphaleia*'[81]. The reason for his presence was that *klasma* lands were involved. The text does not mention any other dignitary accompanying him, but he will doubtless have had with him assistants to erect the cairns and mark the trees, and members of the parties concerned to show him the local landmarks upon which the boundary was to be based. He must have resembled the late Roman *agrimensor* of Cassiodorus's charming description:

The *agrimensor* is entrusted with the adjudication of a boundary dispute that has arisen . . . he is a judge, at any rate of his own art; his law court deserted fields. You might think him crazy seeing him walk along tortuous paths. If he is looking for evidence among the rough woodland thickets he doesn't walk like you or me, he chooses his own way . . . like a gigantic river. He takes areas of the countryside from some and gives them to others[82].

In our case, the *epoptês* was conducted by the locals, but when the *stratêgos* visited the boundary he led a much more high-powered delegation. It consisted of three chief members: the *stratêgos* Katakalôn, the archbishop and Zoêtos the *kritês*, all of whom had formed part of the court which had first heard the case. In addition, there were numerous representatives of administrative, clerical and local monastic interests – a surprising assemblage of influential people[83]. Why were they there? It can only be suggested that after the affair had begun to cause such discord in the region and had attracted imperial concern, the leaders of the local community had to be brought in to put an end to the matter. It is another example of a process familiar in Byzantium as elsewhere: the strengthening of legal decisions by the participation of those influential in local society in the rituals which enforced them. By this means the disputing parties were shown that there was a more important consideration than their own claims, that of the right of the local community to peace and the observation of law.

In the strictly legal sense, the establishment of the boundary of Athos marked the end of that particular dispute. It is generally agreed that the present-day frontier of the Holy Mountain runs along the same path and there are no later

[81] *Prôtaton*, no. 5, line 46.   [82] Dilke, *Roman Land Surveyors*, p. 45.

[83] The members of the delegation were: the *stratêgos* Katakalôn; Archbishop Gregory of Thessalonika; the *kritês* Zoêtos; Anastasios, *basilikos spatharokandidatos* and *kômes tês kortês* of Thessalonika (a military man, see Oikonomidès, *Les listes*, p. 341); Andrew, *basilikos spatharokandidatos* and *chartoularios* of the theme; Parilos, *basilikos spatharokandidatos* and *epi tôn oikeiakôn* (as was Zoêtos, see Oikonomidès, *ibid.*, pp. 297–9); Stephen, *basilikos spatharokandidatos*, *engestiarios* and *epi tês oikeiakês trapezês* (official of the imperial private table, *ibid.*, p. 306); Stephen Bardanopoulos, *basilikos spatharokandidatos*; Michael, *prôtomandatôr* (*ibid.*, p. 341); Demetrios, domestic of the *vestiaritoi* (for the *vestiarion*, *ibid.*, p. 305). There were two officials of the church of Thessalonika: Constantine the *kouboukleisios* and Theodore the *oikonomos* as well as another bishop, John of Herkoula. Three *hêgoumenoi* were there, all with lands in the region concerned: Euthymios of Peristerai, Gregory of Orphanou (Gomatou) and Andrew of Spelaiôtou.

documents in the archives of the *Prôtaton* concerning the boundary. But in the social and economic sense, the matter was by no means closed. By the end of the tenth century the Athonites were extremely active in the land market. With their liquid resources of ready cash continually augmented by imperial donations, they were in an admirable position to encircle the lands of the other monastic and lay communities. We are less well informed about the aftermath of the Trikariko affair. But it does appear that the boundary established in 1001 continued to be observed and that subsequent disputes about territorial supremacy were conducted not by the neighbouring communities, but by ambitious bishops[84]. But the fact remains that here, too, the Byzantine authorities were concerned to establish a firm and lasting peace.

The extent and pervasiveness of the activity of state officials is one of the strongest impressions left by a study of these two cases. The disputes, though minor in the geographical sense, were deemed worthy of regional and even imperial attention. Was there, then, no stone left unturned by the attentions of Byzantine bureaucrats? It would be rash to make such an assertion, for the cases were begun by the decision of ordinary Byzantines to resort to law. The people inaugurated the process. They were able to do so because there existed a uniform legal system of which they were aware. The similarity in procedures visible between northern Greece and the most 'byzantinized' part of southern Italy indicates that the same legal tradition flourished and that the same imperial 'writ' ran in the most inaccessible and far-flung regions of the Empire. Both individuals and communities had access to the imperial legal system and whilst they may on many occasions have chosen not to use it, they knew that it existed and, more significantly, how they could gain access to it.

A note of caution must, however, finally be sounded. The working of the machinery of the law always depended on the realities of the political situation. In southern Italy, the Norman incursions of the eleventh century and the establishment of Latin rule meant that although the Roman legal tradition remained paramount, the administrators of that law ceased to be the representatives of the emperor in Constantinople. In provinces retained by the empire, the problems were of a different order. Local, powerful interests usurped the governmental rôle of the imperial officials and, to combat them, investigating magistrates came out from the centre to dispense that justice which the provincial *archontes* had once given. By the end of the eleventh century, the relationship of capital to provinces in the judicial sphere, as in many other aspects of Byzantine social life, had altered leaving the local communities at the mercy of those with economic power and social prestige[85].

[84] Guillou and Holtzmann, 'Katepansurkunden', 7.
[85] I would like to thank particularly Paul Magdalino and Ruth Macrides for their criticisms and comments and J. C. Morris for invaluable assistance with German material.

8

Charters, law and the settlement of disputes in Anglo-Saxon England

PATRICK WORMALD

The extant records of Anglo-Saxon dispute settlement and judicial procedure have received remarkably little attention from historians either of English law or of early English society. Just one attempt has been made to assemble and discuss a corpus of cases, exactly a hundred and ten years ago; these 'select' thirty-five include three post-dating 1066, two pairs relating to the same disputes and one that would be more properly labelled political melodrama (if, indeed, it ever happened at all); and the relevant residue constitutes less than twenty per cent of even the more informative records[1]. This collection received the most cursory acknowledgement from Maitland in the classic history of early English law[2]. It was more fully used, and to some extent expanded, by Liebermann in the relentlessly learned *Sachglossar* to his *Gesetze der Angelsachsen*, but its evidence was always subsidiary to that of the *Gesetze* themselves[3]. The orthodoxy thus established over forty years has remained substantially entrenched throughout the subsequent seventy. In this article, I shall argue that full analysis of the whole range of specific and descriptive evidence, largely drawn from charters*, compels radical reappraisal of the conclusions drawn from prescriptive law codes about Anglo-Saxon litigation. But more must first be said of what 'orthodoxy' is, and how it came to subsist[4].

It is best epitomized by a series of quotations from Maitland himself:

It suffices to know that, in its general features, Anglo-Saxon law is not only archaic, but offers an especially pure type of Germanic archaism... So far as we can say that there was

---

[1] J. Laurence Laughlin, 'The Anglo-Saxon Legal Procedure' and 'Appendix: Select cases in Anglo-Saxon Law' in H. Adams *et al.*, *Essays in Anglo-Saxon Law*; the post-1066 cases are nos. 31–3, the pairs, nos. 8 and 9, 19 and 25; the melodrama, no. 29. See below, n. 9.
[2] F. Pollock and F. W. Maitland, *History of English Law*, vol. 1, p. 41 and n. 6.
[3] *Gesetze der Angelsachsen*, ed. F. Liebermann, vol. 2, p. 625, s.v. *Rechtsgang*, with cross-references in section 2; see also under *Anefang, Beweisnähe, Bocland, Eid, Eideshelfer, Gerichtsbarkeit, Grafschaft, Grafschaftsgericht, Hochverrat,* Hundred, *Mord, Rechtssperrung, Schiedsgericht,* Sheriff, *Strafe, Unzucht, Urteilfinder, Vermögenseinziehung.*
[4] This paper owes much to advice and criticism from Professor Nicholas Brooks, Dr Simon Keynes and Dr Michael Clanchy; in the nature of this book, it also owes a great deal to my co-authors and editors, but I would wish to acknowledge an even more special debt than usual to Dr Jenny Wormald.

any regular judicial system in Anglo-Saxon law, it was of a highly archaic type... The staple matter of judicial proceedings was of a rude and simple kind. *In so far as we can trust the written laws* [my italics], the only topics of general importance were manslaying, wounding and cattle-stealing... As to procedure, the forms were sometimes complicated, always stiff and unbending. Mistakes in form were probably fatal at every stage. Trial of questions of fact, in anything like the modern sense, was unknown. Archaic rules of evidence make no attempt to apply any measure of probability to individual cases. Oath was the primary mode of proof, an oath going not to the truth of specific fact, but to the justice of the claim or defence as a whole... Inasmuch as the oath, if duly made, was conclusive, what we now call the burden of proof was rather a benefit than otherwise under ancient Germanic procedure... The king has judicial functions, but they are very far removed from our modern way of regarding the king as the fountain of justice. His business is not to see justice done in his name in an ordinary course, but to exercise a special and reserved power which a man must not invoke unless he has failed to get his cause heard in the jurisdiction of his own hundred... In Anglo-Saxon as well as in other Germanic laws we find that the idea of wrong to a person or his kindred is still primary, and that of offence against the common weal secondary, even in the gravest cases[5].

It is not surprising that these views have commanded near universal acceptance. Wise historians think at least twice before dissenting from Maitland, who was here supported by Liebermann's erudition. But it is important to identify the source of such ideas. Something has already been said, in the Introduction and elsewhere, about the *Rechtsschule** and its preconceptions of Germanic law. Partly because the Anglo-Saxon codes, unlike most other Germanic legislation of the period, were in the vernacular, scholars were easily convinced that here above all they could find a uniform and time-honoured procedure, with its roots and most of its foliage in the 'Forests of Germany'. This was Laughlin's approach in his 1876 essay on Anglo-Saxon legal procedure. Subsequently, Maitland was persuaded by Brunner (co-dedicatee of the third volume of Liebermann's *Gesetze*) that the judicial inquest*, and so, in effect, the English Common Law*, was Franco-Norman, not Anglo-Saxon, in origin[6]. The argument thereafter became circular: Anglo-Saxon evidence was quarried (if at all) for whatever was *not* found in later ages, and was thus 'irrelevant' to the history of English law. Little or no attention was paid to whatever pre-Conquest procedure may have had in common with that of Henry II's reign. At best, early English legal processes were treasured as charming archaisms[7].

At the same time, it must be admitted that the documentary evidence on which

---

[5] Pollock and Maitland, *English Law*, vol. 1, pp. 44, 38–9, 40–1, 46; cf. T. Plucknett, *Concise History of the Common Law*, pp. 88, 105, etc.; Laughlin, 'Legal Procedure', pp. 185, 259, 275, 296, etc.

[6] H. Brunner, *Die Entstehung der Schwurgerichte*; cf. Pollock and Maitland, *English Law*, vol. 1, pp. 138–50.

[7] For honourable, if partial, exceptions, see N. D. Hurnard, 'The Jury of Presentment and the Assize of Clarendon', *Eng. Hist. Rev.*, 56 (1941), and the works cited in n. 72 below. Since this article was first drafted, Dr Susan Reynolds has breathed an invigorating blast of common sense (not to mention learning) into the whole subject: *Kingdoms and Communities in Western Europe, 900–1300*, esp. pp. 12–38.

reappraisal must be based has serious limitations. Records of Anglo-Saxon cases have no sort of *placitum** format (the very word *placitum* was apparently never used before the Conquest)[8]. In Professor Sawyer's invaluable handlist of Anglo-Saxon charters, they are classified as royal charters, as charters of laity, bishops and other ecclesiastics, as 'miscellaneous texts' (significantly the largest proportion), as wills and as 'lost and incomplete texts'; while a fair number do not appear at all because they are not in any sort of charter form. Their heterogeneous character can make them very uninformative about the processes involved. Indeed, it is often unclear whether a given dispute can helpfully be called a legal suit, whereas superficially straightforward transactions may conceal evidence of conflict. Elsewhere, I hope to publish a handlist of Anglo-Saxon cases, together with discussion of the criteria for selection. At present, I have found 100 cases, distributed over 89 documents and another 75 in what can loosely be called narrative sources; of these 175, at least 30 say little about legal issues[9]. A second, more obvious, drawback is thus the relatively exiguous size of the sample, compared to Hübner's 616 Frankish cases (to 1020) and 815 from Italy (to 1066), or to the 665 assembled in Professor van Caenegem's forthcoming re-edition of *Placita Anglo-Normanica*[10].

But the third, and perhaps most important, defect of such evidence is that it is unbalanced and uneven. In England, as almost everywhere in early medieval Europe, nearly all known cases were resolved, directly or indirectly, immediately or eventually, in favour of churches, and this is *why* they are known. One apparent exception makes the point. A case heard before the Hereford shire* court in Cnut's reign was of no obvious interest to the Church, yet the winner had it recorded in a Hereford cathedral gospel book, and one wonders whether it is wholly coincidence that the cathedral canons owned one of the two properties at stake when the Domesday Book was compiled (1086)[11]. Moreover, especially before 899, a high proportion of cases come from the archives of Kentish churches, particularly Canterbury cathedral, or from the West Midlands, overwhelmingly Worcester; while some of the best evidence in the later period is in the cartulary-chronicles of the Fenland abbeys, Ely and Ramsey. There are obvious problems in compiling a general picture from so few (perhaps exceptional) areas. Finally, the evidence 'peaks' at certain periods: the latter years

---

[8] The nearest approximation is the phrase *placiti sunt* in a record of a series of disputes before a council of 803: P. H. Sawyer, *Anglo-Saxon Charters*, no. 1431. (References to Anglo-Saxon charters henceforth by number in Sawyer's handlist (S), except when it is pertinent to cite views or editions published since 1968.)

[9] This list should appear in *Anglo-Saxon England* before the end of the decade. Many of my arguments, especially from p. 164, will be expanded in my forthcoming *Kingship and the Making of Law in England: Alfred to Henry I*.

[10] R. Hübner, 'Gerichtsurkunden aus der fränkischen Zeit', *ZRG, Germ. Abt.*, 12 (1891) and 14 (1893); R. C. van Caenegem's re-constitution of M. Bigelow's 1879 *Placita Anglo-Normannica* should be published by the Selden Society in 1989; I am grateful to the author for this foretaste.

[11] S 1462.

and aftermath of the reigns of Offa of Mercia (757–96) and Alfred of Wessex (871–99), the reign of Edgar (957–75) and above all that of Æthelred II (978–1016). Foreign invasion could be one reason for this, and the aggressive behaviour of powerful kings another. The relevant point is probably that both factors hurt many churches at once, and so produced many recorded disputes. Different legal rhythms could have prevailed in less traumatic times.

Reappraisal must thus begin by acknowledging that 'typical' Anglo-Saxon dispute settlement (if there was any such thing) remains elusive. Our records may be quite unrepresentative of more mundane circumstances, or, indeed, of aristocratic feuding (Maitland ignored them for precisely that reason)[12]. It still seems best to accept the situation as it stands, and to select for detailed analysis two cases which are indeed exceptional in that we know so much about them. Both, almost inevitably, concern the fortunes of churches, respectively Worcester and a Kentish house. Their value is that they expand the range of possibilities in Anglo-Saxon dispute settlement to unexpected extents and in neglected directions. They show that, at least on one social and cultural level, more was at stake than 'manslaying, wounding and cattle-stealing'. Further, in that one dates to the first quarter of the ninth century and the other to the last quarter of the tenth, they hint at the major changes that came over English law as a result, not of the Norman Conquest, but of the creation of a kingdom of 'the English'.

My first case is a judgement made in October 824. It is one of a series during the reigns of the Mercian kings, Offa, Cenwulf (796–821) and Beornwulf (823–6) which apparently involved a council of the whole ecclesiastical and political 'establishment'[13]. The witness list of the charter which records it included not only King Beornwulf and Archbishop Wulfred of Canterbury (805–32) but also nearly all the southern English bishops, four abbots, a papal legate, the king's brother, nine of the prominent Mercian ealdormen*, two priests and four others, one a 'toll-collector'. The document begins by dating and describing the assembly of these 'wisest men'. It goes on to tell how, 'among other discussions, a certain dispute was brought forward between Bishop Heahberht (of Worcester) and the community of Berkeley, concerning the inheritance of Æthelric, son of Æthelmund, i.e. the monastery which is called Westbury'. It then says simply that the bishop 'had the land with the title-deeds (*libris*), just as Æthelric had ordered that it was to revert to the church of Worcester'; it was 'stated and decreed (*statuta est... atque decreta*) by the archbishop and all the holy synod, that the bishop, who had the monastery and the territory with the deeds, was to swear the land into his own possession with an oath of the servants of God... And when the dispute had been thus concluded and written down (*finita*

12 See n. 2.
13 For a list, see P. Wormald, 'Bede, the *Bretwaldas* and the Origins of the *Gens Anglorum*' in P. Wormald, D. Bullough, R. Collins (eds.), *Ideal and Reality in Frankish and Anglo-Saxon Society*, n. 118.

et proscripta illa contentione), that oath was given thirty days later at Westminster' (i.e., Westbury itself, the property at issue). There follows an anathema, the date 30 October, the aforementioned witness list and the names of the fifty-six priests who took the oath[14]. (Appendix XXIII)

The first point to note is the nature of this text. Like many others from this period, it is a Latin account of a council, said to have discussed a variety of business, which concentrates on just one decision[15]. A council of the same year found in favour of Archbishop Wulfred himself; and in 825, similar assemblies heard pleas not only from Worcester and Canterbury but also from Selsey[16]. The significant thing about these sets of records is that, while there are several indications that each were proceedings of the same 'synod', their diplomatic suggests that each was drawn up by the victorious church in question[17]. Thus, the phrase 'factum est pontificale conciliabulum' in the Westbury document was a *formula** used elsewhere by the Worcester *scriptorium*, whereas Canterbury texts tend to talk of a *sinodus* or *concilium* 'congregating' or 'collecting'[18]. Here, as with other charters in Worcester's interest, the subscribing verb of witnesses is in the past tense, but with those of Canterbury's it can be present or future. A perhaps decisive point is that the text's anathema uses *'ceastre'* to mean Worcester, something unlikely – when there were so many other episcopal 'chesters' – except in the mind of a Worcester scribe. Thus, not only did the Church alone preserve judicial records; in this period, churches alone wrote them up, and the virtual absence of formulaic prescription gave scribes the freedom to be as biased as they liked.

Secondly, we should observe what this document does *not* tell us. But for the further evidence to which I shall return, the causes of the dispute would be as obscure as they are in most such texts. We are not told who really decided the case, except that it was the 'archbishop and all the holy synod', the king apparently restricted to a 'presiding' rôle; nor do we know *why* they did so, apart from the repeated references to Bishop Heahberht's 'title-deeds'. Much the same goes for Canterbury's disputes in the same period[19]. Above all, there is scant evidence of 'stiff and unbending' formalism. Nothing is said of how Heahberht actually pleaded. Before the same council, Wulfred 'expounded the whole order and truth of the affair, offering the text of the gift . . . to be read'[20]. Preconceptions that, in Anglo-Saxon procedure, 'mistakes in form were . . . fatal' might perhaps suggest that the archbishop presented a formulaic plea, and that

---

[14] S 1433; the date may be either that of the assembly or of the oath.

[15] S 1431 is a good example: it was almost certainly the same assembly as that which transacted S 1260, and it is explicitly said to have judged two other cases 'eodem die'.

[16] SS 1434–7.

[17] Cf. N. Brooks, *The Early History of the Church of Canterbury*, pp. 168–70, and his Oxford D.Phil. thesis, 'The pre-conquest charters of Christ Church Canterbury', pp. 133–85.

[18] For example, SS 1433, 1436.

[19] SS 1434, 1439.   [20] S 1434.

even his charter could have been invalidated if he stuttered or sneezed; the evidence indicates only that he put a strong and documented case eloquently.

Thirdly, therefore, the Westbury case challenges traditional assumptions about proof. It is obvious from the kite-like tail of 'servants of God' borne by the document that the oath they swore in the bishop's support was important. It certainly concluded proceedings; but this does not mean that it was 'conclusive', or that 'the truth of specific fact' was irrelevant[21]. The implication of the text is rather that what made up the council's mind were the bishop's 'title-deeds'; and we are actually told that the suit was *finita*, and indeed *proscripta, before* the oath was taken. Oaths are in general surprisingly rare in early judicial records. Archbishop Wulfred's 824 case was allegedly decided by *libris* and by witnesses who, 'truthfully and *viva voce*', vouched for the documents; they are not said to have sworn their evidence, nor is it suggested that they were oath-helpers* rather than witnesses to fact (in so far as the distinction exists)[22]. The 825 council heard a Worcester plea where there was apparently no written evidence, and bishop and clergy were again obliged to swear their claim; but there is again no oath-taking in Canterbury's dispute of that year, and it is surely significant that the victorious archbishop insisted that his opponent delete all records of the property at stake from her family archive[23]. Of three earlier Worcester disputes, one was decided by 'the testimony of . . . writings'; one, lacking in written evidence, was won by 'witnesses'; and the third, also undocumented, resulted in a compromise which the bishop insisted on having in writing[24]. On the other hand, in a later Canterbury suit, charters failed to impress the opposition, and four religious communities took an oath in the archbishop's support[25]. The most one can therefore say for the oath in this sort of dispute is that it could be important for conflicts irresolvable by other means, and that it may have been the formal means of ending litigation – so formal that it was often unmentioned. By contrast, a high proportion of such cases *do* seem to have involved an 'attempt to apply [a] measure of probability', and there was a premium on the written word.

We may now turn to the dispute itself, obscure as the 824 record stands, but illuminated by a second text, the will of Westbury's donor, Æthelric[26]. This tells how, after the death of his father, Æthelmund, he was summoned before another

---

[21] Cf. D. Whitelock's comment on this case in her *English Historical Documents*, vol. 1, p. 516; and the significant remarks of Laughlin on the Ely case (below, p. 160 and n. 53): 'Legal Procedure', pp. 252, 380.   [22] S 1434. Cf. below, pp. 220–3.

[23] S 1436. Cf. W. Levison, *England and the Continent in the eighth century*, p. 252, and the seminal discussion of Brooks, *Church of Canterbury*, pp. 175–97.

[24] SS 137, 1430, 1431.   [25] S 1439.

[26] S 1187. It seems likely that 804, the date borne by the document and indicated by the witness list (Archbishop Æthelheard died in 805), was that of the council which originally tested Æthelric's rights rather than that in which he proclaimed his will. Æthelmund was almost certainly the ealdorman of the Hwicce killed in 802 (Whitelock, *English Historical Documents*, pp. 183, 512), and the 'paucos annos' which intervened between the first council and the second, and which included Æthelric's pilgrimage, were surely not as 'few' as two.

great 'synod', and appeared 'with the title-deeds of the estate, i.e. Westminster', which his kin had previously granted him; the synod (the archbishop, again, to the fore) scrutinized his documents and judged that he was free to dispose of his land and deeds as he wished. He then went to Rome, entrusting his rights to his 'friends', and receiving them back on his return, having repaid 'the price we previously agreed that we might be mutually at peace'. He later reminded yet another synod of his 'former privilege', and publicly distributed his patrimony. Among his bequests were Westbury, and also Stoke, to his mother, Ceolburh, for her lifetime, with reversion to the church of Worcester, 'that . . . she may . . . have there protection and defence against the claims of the Berkeley people'. Failing Worcester's support, she could appeal to the archbishop, and, failing his, she could 'choose what protection she liked'. Further dispute was forestalled by giving copies of his dispositions to another bishop and to two 'faithful friends' (apparently laymen). Anathema and witness list follow. (App. XXIV)

Though this document explains how Worcester and Berkeley came to be in dispute, it still leaves much unexplained. What claim had Berkeley on Westbury? It is possible that Berkeley (where Ceolburh died as abbess) was her 'family' monastery, while Westbury became Æthelric's (hence West*minster*); so, while willing to give her a life-interest in his own house, he wished to exclude the claims of her kin, even at the cost of its eventual reversion to Worcester[27]. But was it Berkeley or another party that challenged him at the first council? With whom did he reconcile himself before his pilgrimage, at a 'price'? Was it perhaps Worcester itself, whose bishop, like Archbishop Wulfred, was campaigning to reform the proprietary monasteries of his diocese[28]? Is it significant that Æthelric envisaged Ceolburh *not* being helped by either Worcester or Canterbury? At any rate, he was right to foresee trouble, and Worcester was by 824 on the receiving end. Its part in proceedings emerges from two other documents, with very important implications.

Æthelric's right to the lands at Westbury and Stoke, which he bestowed on his mother, and which were thus at issue in 824, was vested in two charters for his father, Æthelmund. Both exist in alternative versions, one significantly more favourable to Worcester than the other. As regards Westbury, we have a grant by Offa of fifty-five hides to Æthelmund (793–6), which is extant as an original, and a cartulary text, of apparently similar date though with a different witness list, whereby Offa gave *sixty* hides to *Worcester*[29]. These are what diplomatists usually consider suspicious circumstances. Offa was admittedly cavalier with church property, and the cartulary text derives credit from the fact that, unlike

---

[27] As I have suggested in J. Campbell (ed.), *The Anglo-Saxons*, p. 123.

[28] Brooks, *Church of Canterbury*, pp. 175–206.

[29] Respectively, SS 139, 146. The Anglo-Saxon hide, which Bede implied was the land necessary for the support of a freeman and his family, became the standard unit of assessment both in grants and in government demands.

Æthelmund's, it bears a heavy food-rent, which one would not expect forgers to invent[30]. However, even Offa did not revoke his *own* patronage in such short order; and other features of the text are dubious. One is the hidage: the difference between Æthelmund's fifty-five and Worcester's sixty could be explained by the fact that Æthelric later put Westbury and Stoke together, the latter assessed at five hides. Another is the witness list: Æthelmund's charter has Hygeberht, Offa's subsequently disgraced archbishop of Lichfield, before the archbishop of Canterbury, as one would expect from Offa's policy; but in Worcester's, he is wholly absent. There are thus indications that Worcester's scribes converted Æthelmund's charter into one for themselves, using another charter with food-rent and near-contemporary witness list to give it plausibility.

This could have happened at any time before the compilation of Worcester's cartulary in the eleventh century; it is the Stoke documentation that links it to the 824 dispute[31]. Here, both versions are grants to Æthelmund by the sub-king (under Offa) of the Hwicce, one dated 767 surviving only in an eighteenth-century transcript, the other dated 770 and generally considered original[32]. Dates aside, the texts have two significant discrepancies. In that of 767, Æthelmund had complete freedom of disposition, but in that of 770, he could leave the land only to 'two heirs after him' whereupon 'the land with the title-deeds is to be given back' (*sic*) to Worcester. So substantial a clause seems unlikely to have been overlooked by the 767 transcript, and the 824 controversy gives it sinister implications[33]. The other discrepancy darkens suspicion. On the dorse of the 770 charter, the scribe added three witnesses: Offa's queen and their children. Cynethryth rarely occurs in charters as early as 770, and Ecgfrith and Ælfflaed turn up only very much later[34]. Further, while there is little comparable material from the West Midlands, my palaeographical advisers are inclined to date the 770 text's script to the early ninth century[35]. Suppose that the original of the 767 transcript had survived, while the 770 charter was known only from eleventh- or eighteenth-century copies: the latter, with its anachronistic witness list and marked bias towards Worcester, would surely have been discounted as a pious

---

[30] S 146 also confirms Worcester's rights at Henbury; a lost charter to this effect could have been the source of the extant text's more plausible features.

[31] Worcester itself supplies several pre-1100 examples of charters converted into texts in its own direct interest; S 60 is one.

[32] SS 58–9. For radically different conclusions from mine about these texts, see D. Whitelock's personal comment, cited in S 58 (cf. her identification of the estate in her *English Historical Documents*, p. 512); see also A. Bruckner in *ChLA*, vol. 4, 274.

[33] The 770 charter's provision for *two* heirs before the reversion of the estate to Worcester could well reflect the fact that, by 824, it had passed through the hands of Æthelric and Ceolburh.

[34] Apparent exceptions, like S 50, can be explained as later confirmations by Mercian authorities: Wormald, 'Bede ... and the ... *Gens Anglorum*', pp. 116–17.

[35] These were Professor Brooks, Dr Mildred Budny and Mrs Michelle Brown – which is not to say that they would endorse my views *in toto*. A final point is that SS 58–9, though with different incarnational dates, have precisely parallel indictional errors – a curious case of lightning striking twice if the former were just a careless transcript of an original latter.

fraud. It has been trusted only because it survives in approximately contemporary script, and no one believed that the Anglo-Saxons, with their 'archaic rules of evidence' forged charters. But Professor Brooks has now shown that Archbishop Wulfred concocted an elaborate privilege at precisely the time of the Westbury dispute[36]. There can no longer be much doubt that Bishop Heahberht did the same.

Thus, while much remains unclear even about the well-documented Westbury case, its outlines are visible. Æthelric's inheritance was challenged by parties and for reasons unknown, and he defended it before a council of the kingdom's great men. Subsequently, in a similar arena, he provided that Westbury and Stoke were to go to his mother, with reversion to Worcester. As he feared, Ceolburh's community at Berkeley held on to the property. The bishop of Worcester, who conceivably had a prior interest in Westbury, had to defend Æthelric's bequest before another great synod, and his success was based on a partly doctored cache of charters. It was not an untypical case for the period, but it is irreconcilable with 'orthodoxy' on Anglo-Saxon legal process. It was heard by what one is tempted to consider a royal (and certainly not a local) court. It took nearly a generation to conclude. It vividly illustrates the determination of England's Carolingian prelates to challenge proprietary rights in religious communities by taking them under episcopal control[37]. The reversionary principle applied to Westbury was the only concession to the opposition, and there was no compromise in the eventual solution, any more than in other (if not all) early disputes[38]. Finally, it was decided by what *can* be considered 'rational' means – evidence of fact, and documents above all[39]. The smell of ink hovers over the whole story, from the multiple copies of Æthelric's will to the *libri* clutched by Bishop Heahberht to his chest. Perhaps most significant is the 'over-kill factor': the *libri* surely included Æthelric's will, but it was thought to need reinforcement. One does not fabricate superfluous written evidence if one expects to win by out-swearing or out-remembering one's opponents.

My second case is even better documented and even more complex – so complex that it is probably better to begin, not by paraphrasing the two main texts (Appendices XXV and XXVI), but by distilling a narrative from all the available evidence, which includes at least four other documents. At some date before 958, Ælfhere or his wife Æscwyn assigned an estate at Snodland, Kent, to St

---

[36] Brooks, *Church of Canterbury*, pp. 191–7. According to Bruckner, *ChLA*, vol. 4, 274, this was also the view of M. P. Parsons in her almost unknown Vienna Ph.D. dissertation (1937).

[37] Cf. SS 89 + 1411 + 1257; or SS 53 + 1177 + 153 + 1430 + 1260 + 1432; also Brooks (above, n. 28).

[38] Cf. SS 137, 192, 1257, 1429–31, 1437; the one (quite remarkable) case of compromise amounting to defeat is S 1446.

[39] A parallel (no less extraordinary than S 1446, but given its 897 date, perhaps affected by King Alfred's obsessions with the literacy of his judges, *Asser's Life of King Alfred*, ed. W. H. Stevenson, ch. 106, pp. 92–5) is S 1442.

Andrew's cathedral, Rochester[40]. However, some priests stole the title-deeds (*landbec*) and sold them to the donors' son, Ælfric, who then died. The bishop of Rochester brought a case against Ælfric's widow, Brihtwaru, before King Edgar and the same sort of great council as we met in 824. The stolen deeds (*bec*) were restored to Rochester, together with 'compensation (*bote*) for the theft'; further, 'the widow's property was forfeited to the king'. This included lands at Bromley and Fawkham, in which Rochester may already have been interested[41]. Faced with disaster, Brihtwaru made terms with the bishop: just as the royal reeve was about to seize her property, she surrendered the title-deeds (*boc*) to the king, and the bishop then bought them for a tidy sum, allowing her a usufruct. Then King Edgar died. Brihtwaru was persuaded by her kinsman, Brihtric, to seize her property outright: 'they applied to . . . the section of the public which was the adversary of God, and compelled the bishop to give up the title-deeds (*boca*) . . . nor could he . . . offer any of the three [modes of proof] formally granted to the whole people, namely statement of his claim, vouching to warranty* or declaration of his ownership (*tale ne teames ne ahnunga*)'. The first of the key records concludes with the witnesses to the bishop's purchases of Brihtwaru's lands; it does not disguise his resounding defeat so far[42].

But Brihtric was apparently smitten by conscience. His will provides that Snodland, Bromley and Fawkham should all revert to Rochester once Brihtwaru died[43]. But when Rochester should have realized its rights, King Æthelred made one of the interventions to which he was prone early in his reign: he attacked Rochester in 986, and a charter of the next year granted Bromley to Æthelsige, one of his *ministri*[44]. Ten years later, Æthelred repented, as with other victims of his 'youth'. Rochester received a (reduced) estate at Bromley, which settled that issue. Æthelsige, we are told, was a 'public enemy', in that he killed the reeve who obstructed his annexations, whereas Brihtwaru had merely outmanoeuvred the bailiff; 'wherefore . . . I decided that he deserved to be deprived of all status (*dignitate*), so that he who unjustly seized what was others' should now justly lose what was his own'[45]. However, Snodland had also eluded Rochester's claim. When Godwine acceded to the see of Rochester in 995, he 'found in the cathedral the very deeds (*swutelunga**) which his predecessor had had, and with which he laid claim to (Snodland)', and he took proceedings against 'Leofwine, Ælfheah's son'[46]. 'When the claim (*talu*) was made known to him, [the king] sent

---

[40] S 1511, recently edited in *Charters of Rochester*, ed. A. Campbell (henceforth cited as *Roch.*), no. 35.

[41] The 862 charter of King Æthelberht of Wessex, giving Bromley to his *minister*, was probably drafted at Rochester, and certainly preserved there: S 331 = *Roch.* 25; and see Campbell (ed.), *Anglo-Saxons*, p. 159. *Bot* was compensation to the injured party, *wite* the payment made over and above this to the king, in the Anglo-Saxon system of amendment for offences.

[42] S 1457 = *Roch.* 36.   [43] S 1511.

[44] S 864 = *Roch.* 30. Cf. Whitelock, *English Historical Documents*, p. 233.

[45] S 893 = *Roch.* 32.

[46] The name of Leofwine's father might suggest kinship with Snodland's original donors, but it was extremely common among the later Anglo-Saxon aristocracy.

his writ* and his seal (*gewrit 7 his insegl*) to Archbishop Ælfric, and gave orders that he and his thegns in east and west Kent should settle the dispute between them'. The archbishop and bishop, together with 'Leofric the sheriff* (*scyresman*) and ... all the leading men (*duguð*)' of Kent, assembled at Canterbury, where Godwine produced his evidence. He ultimately agreed to give Leofwine a life-interest in Snodland, provided that it revert to Rochester, that Leofwine surrender his own *swutelunga* and that something be given up at once. The relevant record, our second main text, then gives the names of those who 'negotiated this settlement', the witnesses to it, and an anathema[47].

The complexity of this dispute – or set of disputes – should not obscure its significance: it reflects as many aspects of later Anglo-Saxon proceedings as did the Westbury case earlier. Beginning once more with the nature of the records, it remains the fact that they all derive from an ecclesiastical source, the Rochester archive; and while Dr Keynes has shown that the royal charters creating, then destroying, Æthelsige's right to Bromley were not the work of Rochester scribes, the other three texts, including the two key narratives, probably were. The 'centralized production of diplomas' does not much improve our chances of viewing Anglo-Saxon justice from the centre[48]. What is new is the variety of the evidence. Whereas early records are nearly always Latin accounts of great councils, with at least pretensions to charter form, the Bromley–Snodland file includes three vernacular and largely informal documents. In the later period, royal diplomata* become important evidence for the punishment of alleged crime, as with Æthelsige. But most of our knowledge of dispute settlement comes from memoranda in Old English. Apart from texts of the Bromley–Snodland type, we have chirographs*, entries in liturgical books and incidental references in wills and writs[49]. To these can be added post-Conquest histories of individual churches which blend, in varying proportions, concern with property and miracles. Such material is even more open to suspicions of prejudice than charters. But two sources, the *Liber Eliensis* and the *Chronicon* of Ramsey, are, in one case demonstrably and in the other almost certainly, based on vernacular records, and their information is precious[50].

Alongside laymen's language comes better evidence than hitherto of the 'archaic' procedures which historians have considered characteristic of society at large. The bishop of Rochester was prevented from defending his claim by methods open to the 'whole people', and 'tale ne teames ne ahnunga' sounds splendidly formulaic. In Rochester's other great suit of this period, Archbishop Dunstan (959–88) is said to have 'proved possession [*ahnunga*] ... in the

---

47 S 1456 = *Roch.* 37.
48 S. D. Keynes, *The Diplomas of King Æthelred*, pp. 39–153, esp. pp. 89–90, 103.
49 Among cases discussed elsewhere in this paper, see SS 1454, 1462, 1511; also, e.g., S 1077.
50 *Liber Eliensis*, ed. E. Blake (henceforth cited as *El.*), esp. p. xxxiv; *Chronicon Abbatiae Ramesiensis*, ed. W. Macray (henceforth *Ram.*).

presence of [named witnesses] . . . and all the men of east Kent and west Kent; and it was known in Sussex and Wessex and Middlesex and Essex that [he] with his own oath had secured possession of the estates . . . with the title-deeds [*bocan*] on the Cross of Christ. And Wulfsige the sheriff [*scirigman*], as king's representative, accepted the oath . . . and there were . . . a good thousand men who gave the oath'[51]. We have cases decided without mention of written procedure[52]. A remarkable suit in *Liber Eliensis* finds the 'wise and old men' of Cambridgeshire, who 'well remembered' the time of Edward the Elder (sixty years before!), declaring that a claim against Ely was 'frivolous': first, those making it had 'lied' about the past, and second, 'he ought to be nearer [i.e. more entitled to take the oath] that he have the land who had the charter than he who did not'; Ely's would-be benefactor then adduced more than a thousand 'faithful men' who took the oath (refused by his opponents), and 'all stated [*statuerunt*]' that he had won[53].

Yet there is no real reason to modify the impression of Anglo-Saxon procedural priorities already made by 824. In the first place, oaths are no more evident in the Bromley–Snodland saga than in many cases of the Westbury period. As before, they may have concluded proceedings and been to *that* extent 'conclusive'. But in an interesting, if partly obscure, dispute before the Berkshire court in 990, the oath was dispensed with, because (for reasons we shall see) it could have got the loser into serious trouble; this did not affect the almost outright victory of the other party, based on a powerful team of witnesses[54]. It is hard to see how oath-taking in thousands could be more than (no doubt solemn) ratification of decisions already taken or foreseen. Secondly, the criteria for reaching such decisions look no less rational than earlier. Whatever their formulaic ring, the words *talu, team* and *ahnung* mean no more than 'statement of claim' (as when Bishop Godwine approached the king about Snodland), 'vouching to warranty' (a logical way of tracing claims to their source, consistently evident in Domesday Book), and (proof of) 'ownership' (as in Rochester's other contemporary case). 'Realistic' evidence is implicit in all three. One of the two reasons for thinking Ely's benefactor 'nearer to the oath' was that people, however remarkably, remembered what *had* actually happened[55]. *Liber Eliensis* is generally less interested in oaths than in the substantial basis of pleas, usually oral but sometimes, as here, reinforced by charter[56].

Hence a third point: written evidence is at least as prominent in later as in

---

[51] S 1458 = *Roch.* 34.
[52] Like the Herefordshire dispute, S 1462.
[53] *El.*, pp. 98–9. For more multiple oath-taking, see the full text of S 1497, now published as *The Will of Æthelgifu*, ed. D. Whitelock *et al.*   [54] S 1454.
[55] The (contemporary) text of the *Anglo-Saxon Chronicle*, s.a. 917 (Whitelock, *English Historical Documents*, pp. 215–16), shows that King Edward did, as the Cambridgeshire court averred, occupy Huntingdonshire before Cambridgeshire.
[56] For example, *El.*, pp. 80–2, 86–7, 100–1, 107, etc.

earlier judicial records. The Bromley–Snodland cases began with the theft of charters and ended when the bishop discovered them in his archives. As Archbishop Dunstan's oath echoed round the Home Counties, he was, like Bishop Heahberht, brandishing *bocan*. There are two further reasons for thinking documents important, one old, one new. First, they were forged to win disputes. Rochester itself probably did so. Extant in late tenth-century script is a charter of Edgar granting Bromley to the see. It may not be wholly invented because, like Worcester's Westbury charter, it involves counter-obligations. But its date (955) is impossible, and its witness list implausible then or later. And the bounds of the estate thereby conveyed are not those that stood in the ninth century, nor even those of what Æthelred gave his crony in 987, but they suspiciously correspond with the shrunken limits of what Rochester got in 998. It seems that Edgar's charter was concocted, for an implicit price, to remind the now penitent king of his father's revered example[57]. There are several contemporary parallels[58]. Secondly, from the early tenth century, charters have anathemata which envisage the rivalry of variant texts: in one case, we hear that people 'falsely usurped a hereditary schedule for themselves against right, only afterwards discovered and annulled'[59]. Awareness that even written evidence was at risk implies a degree of 'charter inflation' in later Anglo-Saxon society[60].

The paradox that increased reports of 'archaic' procedure accompany indications of proliferating parchment may be only apparent. Oral process (in which ritual did not preclude rationality) remained important[61]. But Bishop Godwine's determination to have Leofwine's *swutelunga*, even when waiting for the relevant property, is among other signs that many later Anglo-Saxon laymen were as careful of their muniments as Æthelric had been in the early ninth century[62]. Thus, precisely those most accustomed to pre-literate transactions were exploiting the implications of literacy. This may explain why judicial records were now so much less formal, so often in the vernacular: they could be read to, if not by, the laity[63]. It is perhaps significant that chirographs were more often used in dealings involving laymen than in those between clerics alone: their

---

[57] S 671 = *Roch.* 29.

[58] Brooks, *Church of Canterbury*, pp. 240–3; Keynes, *Diplomas*, pp. 98–102. See also H. P. R. Finberg, *Early Charters of Wessex*, pp. 214–48; and, for Westminster's early steps in its notorious life of crime, SS 670, 1450, 1451.

[59] S 884; cf., e.g., S 1242. As against three such *formulae* before 900, I have found over seventy in the period 900–1066.

[60] As Archbishop Lyfing of Canterbury vigorously complained, if S 985 (1017–20) can be trusted; cf. P. Chaplais, 'The Anglo-Saxon Chancery', *Journ. Soc. Archivists*, 3 (1965–9), 174.

[61] Hence the collection of oaths known as *Swerian* in *Gesetze*, ed. Liebermann, vol. 1, pp. 396–9.

[62] Another vivid illustration of this (and further) important aspects of later Anglo-Saxon litigation, to which there is not room to do justice here, is S 1447.

[63] In some of Æthelred's charters, Old English was used not only for the boundary clause but also for accounts of the 'crime' for which the land had been forfeit – an obviously relevant consideration if the dispossessed sought to re-open his claim: e.g. S 877.

authenticity could be tested by illiterates with a practised eye[64]. In other words, we find new evidence of supposedly traditional methods because lay customs were being sucked into the procedural orbit of the Church[65].

We should next consider the arenas of dispute settlement (that is, the courts), where there was again both continuity and contrast between earlier and later periods. The bishop of Rochester began his suit before the sort of council that decided the Westbury case. But it all ended at Canterbury before the 'thegns' and 'leading men' of Kent: that is, in the Kentish shire court. Robertson's prosopography shows that those who arranged and witnessed the settlement were local worthies[66]. And while we encounter other instances of decisions taken by the royal court (meeting curiously often at London[67]), much the greater number of later Anglo-Saxon cases were heard by courts of the shire, sometimes of several shires (the hundred*, sub-division of the shire, also had a judicial rôle, but its judgements are not recorded as such in the extant documents). This was true of all the cases so far compared with Bromley–Snodland: of that where Dunstan took his mighty oath, of the Ely dispute turning on a sixty-year folk-memory, of the Berkshire suit in 990, and indeed of the Herefordshire clash alluded to earlier. It would be possible but pointless to multiply examples.

What needs emphasis is that the nature of these assemblies has been consistently misconceived. Partly, no doubt, because in the light of twelfth-century developments royal and county courts came to seem antitheses, and partly because of romantic notions of ancient Germanic 'moots', pre-Conquest local courts have been seen as essentially popular institutions, convened on local initiative and purveying local justice. For Maitland, there was no royal justice in the 'modern' sense; the king was only a last resort. Yet, whatever their origins, shire courts by the tenth century *were* royal courts. Royal legislation decreed that they should meet twice a year, that bishop and ealdorman preside, that each large borough (and shire?) should have thirty-six chosen witnesses, each small borough and hundred twelve, who were to swear to the truth of what they saw and heard[68]. The laws of Edgar and Cnut which persuaded Maitland of a limited royal rôle were designed to establish a judicial hierarchy: only when litigants had failed to get justice at successive local stages could they 'seek the king'. This need mean no more than that English kings disliked being pestered[69]. The 990 Berkshire case began when one party approached the king with formidable

---

[64] Out of my estimated total of sixty-four chirographs and similar documents, just five are of exclusively ecclesiastical interest.
[65] To this extent, I retract what I wrote on this theme ten years ago: P. Wormald, 'The uses of literacy in Anglo-Saxon England', *Trans. Royal Hist. Soc.*, 5th s., 27 (1977).
[66] *Anglo-Saxon Charters*, ed. A. J. Robertson, p. 385.
[67] Cf. S 877, and *El.* pp. 85, 110.
[68] III Edgar, cl. 5–5ii; IV Edgar, cl. 3–6ii in *Gesetze*, ed. Liebermann, vol. i, pp. 202–3, 210–11.
[69] III Edgar, cl. 2–2i; II Cnut, cl. 17–19ii in *Gesetze*, ed. Liebermann, vol. i, pp. 200–1, 320–3.

support; it was in precise accordance with Edgar's law that her opponent insisted successfully that the plea be referred to the shire; and Æthelred, so far from withholding his hand, sent his seal, as in the Snodland case, to the meeting[70]. The offices of bishop and ealdorman were, potentially at least, in the king's gift, and there is no reason to doubt that, at least in theory, they acted on his behalf. Legislation was never actually quoted in the cases we know of, but their proceedings corresponded closely with official directions.

Above all, judicial records give considerable emphasis to the rôle of the sheriff. Leofric, *se scyresman* (the shire man), was prominent in the resolution of the Snodland dispute. If there is no specific evidence here that he was the king's representative, his predecessor is said to have accepted Dunstan's oath in Rochester's other case 'to the king's hands'. In the 990 Berkshire suit, Ælfgar, 'the king's reeve' was among those who witnessed the settlement, and in the Herefordshire dispute of Cnut's reign Bryning, *scirgerefa* (shire-reeve), was present, as was Tofi, 'there on the king's business'. Sheriffs do not appear in all later Anglo-Saxon records of dispute settlement, and the word itself remains relatively rare. But there is still reason to believe that the king's interest was regularly represented in judicial proceedings[71]. As against the constant sounding of this 'public' note, there is no clear instance of the 'private' justice by then prevalent across the channel[72].

This is not to say that the 'people' had no place in legal process. The question of *who* passed judgement and of how it was enforced remains as obscure in later as in earlier records; the most informative sources, the Fenland abbey chronicles, come from the 'Danelaw', and may reflect Scandinavian customs rather than English norms. It is only in potentially Danish-influenced areas that we find professional *iudices**, though these might be equivalents of the select witnesses prescribed by Edgar[73]. Only here do we hear anything (and it is not much) about the rôle of sureties* in property disputes, though public surety was fundamental in later Anglo-Saxon 'criminal' law[74]. And here alone is there even a hint of the

---

[70] S 1454. Whether, as with Snodland, he also sent a writ has been doubted: Chaplais, 'Anglo-Saxon Chancery', 170–1. For different conclusions on royal courts to not dissimilar effects, see A. Kennedy, 'Disputes about *bocland*', *Anglo-Saxon England*, 14 (1985).

[71] S 1458 = *Roch.* 34; S 1454; S 1462 (note that Abbot Ælfhun may have been special king's representative in the Snodland case – *AS Charters*, ed. Robertson, pp. 384–5 – while Abbot Ælfhere of Bath brought the king's writ to the Berkshire court – *ibid.*, p. 380). See also S 1497 = *Æthelgifu*, ed. Whitelock, and *Ram.*, p. 79; and on reeves in general, P. Stafford, 'The Reign of Æthelred II' in D. Hill (ed.), *Ethelred the Unready*, p. 29. See also Campbell (ed.), *Anglo-Saxons*, pp. 237–8.

[72] Much of the criticism that Maitland *has* received challenges his view of the extent of seigneurial justice before the Conquest: J. Goebel, *Felony and Misdemeanour*, pp. 339–78; N. D. Hurnard, 'The Anglo-Norman Franchises', *Eng. Hist. Rev.*, 64 (1949); H. Cam, 'The evolution of the Mediaeval English Franchise', *Speculum*, 32 (1957).

[73] On these problems, see F. Stenton, *Anglo-Saxon England*, pp. 510–13.

[74] III Edgar, cl. 6–7iii in *Gesetze*, ed. Liebermann, pp. 202–5.

sworn inquest in 'civil' procedure, though there are signs of its general application against those of 'ill-repute'[75].

But of the three generalizations that are possible, the first is that in nearly every text the judging, decreeing or settling verb is in the plural: the rhetoric of Anglo-Saxon process remained participatory and communal. Secondly, the expertise required was essentially amateur. One would *have* to be 'old' as well as 'wise' to remember events sixty years before, but generally in England it was the opinion of men of standing, whether by birth, knowledge or expertise, that counted for most: the word *duguð* in the last document on the Snodland case has, in the Old English poem *Beowulf*, connotations of long and worthy service rewarded by royal patronage[76]. *Liber Eliensis* usually defers to the views of *viri legales* or even 'the better sort'[77]. Thirdly, however, the court president was also important. It is well known that Stevenson, at the beginning of this century, reluctantly excepted the last chapter of Asser's *Life of Alfred* from his endorsement of the text as a whole, on the grounds that the king's expectations of his judges were irreconcilable with what was 'known' about Germanic law; and it is now common ground that his reservations were misplaced. Kings would not have made the laws they did about the responsibility of reeves to be knowledgeable, impartial and incorrupt unless they thought they could influence proceedings[78]. Litigants, as we shall see, thought likewise.

If doubts still linger as to how far later Anglo-Saxon justice was directed (though devolved) from above, they should finally be dispelled by the outcome of cases. Leofwine was able to come to the same sort of terms over Snodland as had opponents of the bishops of Worcester earlier. But there would never have *been* a case about Bromley if Edgar's court at London had been content to restore the stolen *landbec* with a sweetener for the widow, as often – though not always – happened previously. Instead, Brihtwaru had to pay 'compensation' as at least an accessory after the fact, and, as if that were not enough, her property was forfeit to the king: only when the king's reeve was about to confiscate Bromley and Fawkham did she make her pact with the bishop. Similarly, Rochester eventually got Bromley after all on the ostensible grounds that Æthelsige was a 'public enemy' who deserved to lose his 'status'. While compromise remained a possible solution to Anglo-Saxon disputes, the verdict, as before, could come down

---

[75] *Ram.*, p. 166; cf. R. C. van Caenegem, *Royal Writs in England*, pp. 69–71. For other possible Anglo-Saxon applications of at least the principles of inquest, see P. Wormald, 'Æthelred the Lawmaker', in Hill (ed.), *Ethelred*, pp. 66–9.

[76] D. Whitelock, *Audience of Beowulf*, p. 90.

[77] *El.*, pp. 81, 88, 89, 99, etc.

[78] *Asser's Life of King Alfred*, ed. Stevenson, ch. 106, pp. 92–5, and notes pp. 342–3, but see Whitelock's introduction to the reprint, pp. cxlv–cxlvii. See M. Rintelen, 'Die Urteilfindung im angelsächsischen Recht' in M. Krammer (ed.), *Historische Aufsätze Karl Zeumer . . . dargebracht*; and note that there is an Anglo-Saxon tract on the duties of judges, which we now know to have been a translation from Alcuin: *Eine altenglische Übersetzung von Alcuins De Virtute et Vitiis*, ed. R. Torkar.

heavily on one side; and there was once more a new factor inasmuch as the consequence of being 'in the wrong' could be serious.

This point, perhaps the most important of all, needs extended treatment elsewhere, but some of its ramifications must be faced now. It seems that the critical factor was the oath – not Maitland's procedural oath, but the public statement of loyalty whereby all those aged twelve or over were pledged, on pain of life and forfeiture, not only that they would abstain from treason or harbouring the king's enemies, but also that they would not be a 'thief or a thief's accomplice'[79]. The implications both of theft and perjury were widely extended in later Anglo-Saxon England. Flagrant theft had always been subject to instant vengeance; so now was proven theft, and at the hands not of the victim but of the state. Perjury by definition imperilled the soul; for tenth-century legislators, it logically precluded Christian burial. Thieves could thus be seen as traitors and perjurors, with their prospects foreclosed in this world and the next[80]. Even those who lost their pleas in cases of property dispute were in danger of being regarded as thieves, and so traitors, and liable to condign punishment, temporal and eternal; and if they tried to defend their claim under oath but still lost, they aggravated their position. Of all Maitland's observations, perhaps the most misleading is that the 'Anglo-Saxon idea . . . of offence against the common weal [is] secondary'. On the contrary, perceptions of unamendable crime extended from whatever could be construed as treason through witchcraft to marital offences and tax evasion[81]. The early English kingdom had an ambitious and aggressive idea of its public responsibilities: there was an ideological continuum between treachery and unproven cases.

On the evidence (even if supplied by the opposition), it was perhaps not unreasonable to regard Brihtwaru as a criminal. But let us return to the 990 Berkshire case: it was decided that 'it would be better for the oath to be dispensed with rather than sworn, because thereafter friendship would be at an end, and [the loser] would have to return what he had robbed and pay both compensation and his wergeld* to the king'. The reference to 'friendship' suggests the sort of sunny compromise normally thought to have terminated Anglo-Saxon proceedings, but the rest of the sentence shows that perjured losers stood to pay their life's value[82]. In a Ramsey case of the same period, the oath was again avoided, but the abbey's opponent was still 'adjudged at the mercy of the king for all his land

---

[79] II Cnut, cl. 20–1; and cf. Alfred, cl. 1, 4; II Edward, cl. 5–5ii; III Edmund, cl. 1; *Swerian*, cl. 1; all in *Gesetze*, ed. Liebermann, vol. 1, pp. 322–5, 46–51, 142–5, 190, 396–7. See J. Campbell, 'Observations on English Government from the tenth to the twelfth century', *Trans. Royal Hist. Soc.*, 5th s., 25 (1975), 46–7.

[80] IV Æthelstan, cl. 6 and II Æthelstan, cl. 26 in *Gesetze*, ed. Liebermann, vol. 1, pp. 172, 164. Note the clear implications of SS 1447, 883, that the souls of those who breached their oath were at stake.

[81] SS 1377, 901; and see M. K. Lawson, 'The collection of Danegeld', *Eng. Hist. Rev.*, 99 (1984), 723–6.   [82] S 1454.

and chattels, because of his false calumny and unjust vexation of religious men'
(though in the event he was less harshly treated)[83]. One of the notes most often
sounded in Domesday Book is the king's right to *forisfacta*. The word of course
means 'forfeiture', but in Henry I's Coronation Charter it meant 'amercement' –
the payment due to the king for his 'mercy' – and, by the time of *Magna Carta*,
amercements were heavy, widespread and capricious[84]. What needs emphasis is
that, on Henry's own evidence, they existed before the Conquest, the difference
apparently being that they were fixed rather than arbitrary. Henry may well have
been referring to the principle that loss of one's case (especially when involving
perjury) put one at the king's mercy, because it implied that one was a thief and a
traitor; such mercy could be had (literally) at the price of one's life. However this
may be there is a wealth of evidence from Alfred's time, and especially in
Æthelred's, that lands were forfeit for what was seen as crime[85]. This could be
why we begin to find reference to rival charters: with land changing hands at the
king's *fiat*, it was all too likely that there would be more than one extant title to
property.

If the state could play a powerful part in later Anglo-Saxon justice, this does
not mean that it was always either 'fair' or effective. In the first place, regarding
theft as treason implied that theft, like treason, could be a 'political' offence. The
substance of the Bromley–Snodland dispute, like that over Westbury, was the
understandable tension between a family's perception of its rights and New
Testament pressures on its system of values; the Ramsey chronicle has a
memorable passage on the litigious consequences of such tensions[86]. But
Æthelsige's fate has further implications. It is possible that he *was* an inveterate
bandit, especially if he can be identified with the Æthelsige elsewhere accused of
stealing pigs. But Dr Keynes is reluctant to accept this and provides important
evidence that Æthelsige's real 'crime' was to belong to the faction which led the
king 'astray' in the 980s, and which was displaced when Æthelred regretted the
'sins of his youth'. In due course, the succeeding faction met a similar fate, and its
offences are described in equally lurid terms[87]. In other words, Æthelsige was a
minister who first lost office, and then lost everything for his aggressive attitude to
the fruits of office.

Secondly, it took Rochester as long to realize its rights as it had taken
Worcester, and even a sympathetic king could be defied by local potentates[88]. If
politics could work in the Church's favour, they could also work against it. The

---

[83] *Ram.*, p. 80.

[84] W. Stubbs (ed.), *Select Charters*, p. 119; A. L. Poole, *Obligations of Society*, p. 80.

[85] It may not be coincidence that the very first references in Anglo-Saxon charters to the possibilities
of forfeiture occur in and just after Alfred's reign: SS 1441, 1445, 362.

[86] *Ram.*, pp. 46–7.

[87] Keynes, *Diplomas*, pp. 184–5. The most remarkable illustration of political influence on the
fortunes of a litigant is S 1211, the case of Queen Eadgifu, which lasted over six reigns and
changed radically with the advent of almost every new king.

[88] S 877 is a notorious example.

point is easy to miss because such documents as those recording Rochester's humiliations were obviously not often kept. But one of the objectives of the cartulary-chronicles was to preserve the memory of grievances. *Liber Eliensis* rounds off its vivid series of victorious suits with a (much briefer) sequence of failures, and among its villains was precisely the Ealdorman Æthelwine who was Ramsey's hero: it seems that his chief offence was to take bribes from Ely and then fail to keep his side of the bargain[89]. If this could happen to what was, by 1086, the second richest monastery in England, under the protection first of the formidable Bishop Æthelwold and then of Ealdorman Byrhtnoth, hero of Maldon, it is a fair bet that laymen were still more vulnerable to chicanery. While more is unclear about the Herefordshire dispute of Cnut's reign than even the average Anglo-Saxon law case, one thing is not: given that the winning party was the wife of the most powerful local magnate, the loser stood no chance[90].

My two main cases and those with which I have compared them lead me to five conclusions. The first is that what could be called the 'oral–formulaic' approach to Anglo-Saxon litigation is not borne out by the records of actual pleas. Oaths mattered, but so, to a much greater extent than hitherto appreciated, did what modern justice would consider evidence, and such evidence was preferably in writing. Secondly, the main difference between the Westbury and Bromley–Snodland cases is that, while the first was resolved by what it *might* not be anachronistic to consider the royal court, the second was decisively affected by the remorseless, if not always consistent, exercise of royal power. The Anglo-Saxon state came to play an aggressive and interventionist part in proceedings, which is not to say that, any more than other states, ancient or modern, it was always just and efficient. Thirdly, while the case-law evidence is confined to the social and intellectual élite, it may be wrong to regard what it implies as remote and unfamiliar for a wider swathe of society. On the one hand, judicial process involved men who had local standing but were not aristocrats; on the other, the conflicting claims of family and institutionalized piety need not have been confined to the rich, any more than they are today.

Fourth, one finds, as one would expect to find, that such tensions were at their height in periods of religious reform, like those of Archbishop Wulfred and King Edgar. But it is misleading to think that principles were all that was at stake. So too was power and patronage: the strength of Wulfred and the bishops of his time derived, at least in part, from the desperation of an increasingly vulnerable Mercian dynasty to secure support; Rochester was both victim and beneficiary of King Æthelred's politics: and, in *Liber Eliensis* as with Bromley–Snodland, it is unlikely to be coincidence that almost every case either began or was re-opened after the death of Edgar, who was not just a religious reformer, but who could implement the politics of patronage as ruthlessly as any later English ruler.

---

[89] *El.*, pp. 101, 104, 114–17, 126–7.　　　　[90] S 1462.

Finally, English justice by Edgar's time was therefore much more like that of Henry II's than so far supposed. Maitland himself once wrote: 'I try to cheer myself by saying that I have given others a lot to contradict'. This paper does contradict Maitland, but perhaps it also solves one of his problems. We should not just 'trust the written laws' (or not as Maitland's mentors did); and, if we do not, there was no 'marvellous suddenness' about the emergence of English Common Law. For, to judge from recorded proceedings, pre-Conquest dispute settlement was not 'archaic', but, in most senses of the word, 'medieval'[91].

[91] Since this paper went into proof, Mr John Hudson has drawn my attention to evidence that Pollock, not Maitland, was originally responsible for the view of Anglo-Saxon law criticized here: C. H. S. Fifoot (ed.), *Letters of Frederick William Maitland* (Selden Society), no 109. All the same, the generally accepted custom (encouraged by Pollock himself) is to attribute the opinions of the *History of English Law* to Maitland; and it is this that has ensured the lasting influence of what it says about pre-Conquest procedure.

9

Dispute settlement in medieval Ireland: a preliminary inquiry

RICHARD SHARPE

Ireland is different in very many ways from the other areas treated in this volume. That is not to say that it was isolated in the middle ages, or that its differences make comparisons an unprofitable study. Far from it – some of the differences are more apparent than real, and arise from the habit of assuming that Ireland is different in all respects, and that its history can be studied without regard to the interests of historians elsewhere. Conversely historians of England and Europe have often been indifferent to matters Irish (or, for that matter, Welsh or Scottish), so that where Carolingians are familiar territory, Uí Néill or Dál Cais have always to be explained. Scholars approaching Irish history and law from philology have devoted more study to archaic aspects of *troscad*[1] (distraint* by ritualized fasting) with its Indian parallels, though it was of very limited significance in the historic period, than to the nature and functions of the *airecht*, hesitantly translated 'court', an institution of central importance to the functioning of law in society[2]. The absence of any corrective interest from historians has allowed this approach to go unchecked. Some refocusing of attention is desirable, away from the search for 'primitive western institutions'[3], and on to the operation of the law in seventh- and eighth-century Ireland.

Nonetheless, Ireland is different from continental Europe. In considering procedure for dispute settlement, the two most important differences are these. Ireland lay outside the area of *Romanitas* as it is relevant to the legal historian[4].

---

[1] W. Stokes, 'Sitting dharna', *The Academy*, 28 (1885), 169; H. d'Arbois de Jubainville, 'La procédure du jeûne en Irlande', *Revue celtique*, 7 (1886), 245–9; *idem*, *Études sur le droit celtique*, vol. 2, pp. 220–2; F. N. Robinson, 'Notes on the Irish practice of fasting as a means of distraint' in *Putnam Anniversary Volume*, pp. 567–83; R. Thurneysen, 'Das Fasten beim Pfändungsverfahren', *Z. celt. Philol.*, 15 (1924–5), 260–75; M. Dillon, *Celts and Aryans*, pp. 118–20; D. A. Binchy, 'Irish history and Irish law: I', *Studia Hibernica*, 15 (1975), 23–7; *idem*, 'A pre-Christian survival in mediaeval Irish hagiography' in D. Whitelock, R. McKitterick, D. Dumville (eds.), *Ireland in Early Mediaeval Europe*, pp. 165–78.
[2] *Airecht* occurs as a gloss on Latin *curia*, but without context, W. Stokes and J. Strachan, *Thesaurus Palaeohibernicus*, vol. 2, p. 42, l. 5. See also D. Binchy, *Críth Gablach*, p. 73 and below, pp. 186–7.
[3] D. Binchy, 'Linguistic and legal archaisms in the Celtic law-books', *Trans. Philol. Soc.*, 1959, 15.
[4] The use of the term *Romani* in Irish contexts has provoked much discussion. Only one item seems to have any bearing on legal matters, namely the problematic canon requiring that 'omnes negutio

Roman vulgar law* made no impression in Ireland. Even after the establishment of Latin Christianity, the Irish church proved eclectic. There was no generation of Irish kings served by scholar-bishops trained in Roman law, and there were no Romano-Irish codes. Irish law, as we know it from the seventh century, resulted from the fusion of native customs and the teachings of Christian jurists more familiar with Biblical law and Irish practice than with the ideas of law held by European churchmen. Second, and very likely dependent on the first, there are virtually no documentary records of any kind of legal transaction[5]. Though it is now accepted that the charter – in a form close to that of the British–Latin charter[6] – enjoyed at least limited use in Ireland during the seventh century, extant sources suggest that written evidence of title to land never became widely accepted in Irish legal practice[7]. If so, it follows that there was no motivation to record the resolution of any dispute to title, and there is nothing resembling the *placitum** to use as evidence for procedure in dispute settlement.

Of necessity, therefore, this paper is pieced together from fragmentary evidence. For although legal treatises survive in abundance from the seventh and eighth centuries, there is none which specifically covers the topics here at issue. The legal treatises bristle with problems, to some of which I have devoted space for the benefit of the many not well acquainted with them. But until more of this evidence has been sifted, I aim only to discuss the little evidence for dispute settlement with a historical context, and then to offer some starting-points in the legal material, for which the context is more problematic.

I begin about 1100, roughly half way through the period between the composition of the earliest surviving law tract and the majority of the legal manuscripts. For the sake of comparison with foregoing essays, I have chosen to start with the only documentary record, such as it is, of an actual case. The document dates from the beginning of the twelfth century[8]. It was entered in a mixture of Irish and Latin on a blank verso in the Book of Durrow, a seventh-century gospel book[9]. No dispute is actually described, but one has to be assumed to lie behind the resolution indirectly recorded. The background to the case goes back 'a long time' before this, but it is not clear that the dispute itself was of long duration.

'Show us [thy mercy], O Lord, and grant us thy salvation' [*Psalm* 84.8]. A great agreement (*oentu*) between Comgan and Columcille. Comgan gave to Columcille a *reclés*, and [it was

subscriptione Romanorum confirmanda est', *Synodus Patricii*, cl. 30, in *The Irish Penitentials*, ed. L. Bieler, p. 196.

[5] Binchy, 'Irish history and Irish law: I', 27–31, discusses the reasons for this.

[6] W. Davies, 'Latin charter-tradition' in D. Whitelock *et al.* (eds.), *Ireland in Early Mediaeval Europe*, pp. 274–80.

[7] G. Mac Niocaill, 'Admissible and inadmissible evidence in Irish law', *Irish Jurist*, n.s., 4 (1969), 332–7.

[8] The closest date is between 1103 and 1116, as suggested by F. J. Byrne in Davies, 'Latin charter-tradition', p. 261n.; for argument, see D. Ó Cróinín, *The Irish Sex Aetates Mundi*, pp. 41–3.

[9] R. I. Best, 'An early monastic grant from the Book of Durrow', *Ériu*, 10 (1926–8).

left] for a long time in neglect without being claimed by the community of Columcille, that is by the community of Durrow. Then the community of Durrow came with their abbot (*appaid*) and their priest (*saccart*) to claim the *reclés*, and these are their names, Gilla na Nóem Ua hÉnlúain the abbot and Gilla Adamnáin Ua Cortén the priest, and very many others with them. But they did not obtain their own *reclés* because it had been given to the Dál Cais. So this is what the community of Killeshin did about it: they gave to the community of Durrow the equivalent both in length and breadth of their own *airlise*, that is, the *airlise* of Int Ednán was given to them instead of their own *airlise*. The persons of rank (*maithe*) in the community of Killeshin were guarantors (*i commairge*) to them for it from the erenach Cathasach Ua Corcráin.

These are the names of the guarantors (*slánta*): Dublittir Ua hUathgaile the master of the school, Dunchad Ua hUathgaile, Saírgaile Ua Suibne and his son Saírbrethach, Artgal mac Cuilennáin and his brothers, Mael Choluim mac Cortáin and his brothers, and Amalgaid Ua hAirudáin and his brothers.

It was given in the time of Muiredach mac meic Cormáin and Muircheartach Ua Briain king of Ireland. A blessing on the community who gave it and to whom it was given. Flannchad Ua hÉolais was the scribe. (App. XXVII)

First, some factual explication of the text. Comgan and Columcille were sixth-century saints, the founders of the churches involved in the dispute. It is normal practice for their names to be used on behalf of the communities they founded. Comgan's church of *Glenn Uissen*, now Killeshin, Co. Laois, was of little significance in Irish history, but in the eleventh century was noted for its school. The church was rebuilt after 1042, and has a fine Romanesque doorway of the twelfth century. This document may be said to date from its heyday[10]. It is noteworthy that the master of the school is the first guarantor: Dublittir was a scholar of repute, and author of the Irish treatise *De sex aetatibus mundi*[11]. The second guarantor is his kinsman, suggesting a very strong family interest in the church. Another kinsman, Conchobair Ua hUathgaile, who died in 1082, had also been master of the school. The church lay in the territory of Uí Bairrche, and the dating clause presumably refers to Muiredach mac meic Gormáin, lord of Uí Bairrche, who died in 1124 (see fig. 7). The monastery of Durrow, Co. Offaly, on the other hand, founded by Columcille (St Columba) in the sixth century, had always been a church of some importance. Its continuing place in the federation of Columban monasteries is demonstrated by the fact that Gilla Adamnáin – named in honour of the ninth coarb or successor of Columcille – here mentioned as *saccart* of Durrow, became coarb of Columcille in 1128. The distance between Durrow and Killeshin is over forty miles on the ground.

The central transaction was the conveyance of an item of property from Killeshin to Durrow. Durrow had neglected to take up possession of this property, which had instead been given to the Dál Cais, who in the eleventh and twelfth century were not only provincial kings of Munster but also the most powerful rulers in Ireland. Killeshin lies in a different province, Leinster, so we

---

[10] J. O'Hanlon and E. O'Leary, *History of the Queen's County*, pp. 257–66, collects the data on Killeshin.   [11] See above, n. 8.

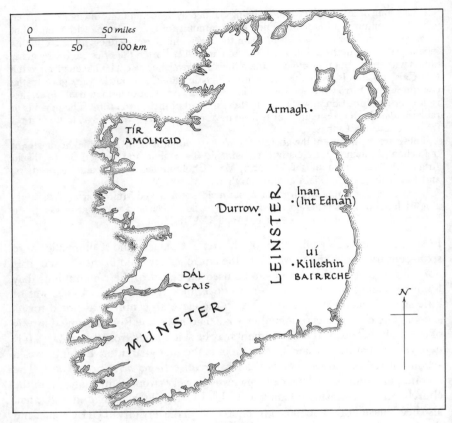

7 Ireland

may perhaps infer that, in saying that the *reclés* was given to the Dál Cais, the
document means that it was given to the political superior. At the date of the text,
the head of the Dál Cais dynasty was Muircheartach Ua Briain, king of Ireland
(1086–1119, though his position was not unchallenged during this period), who
was the third king of Ireland from that family in four generations. We have no
date for the relevant stage in the series of transactions, but it must surely have
been during the period of Dál Cais supremacy. Although it is interesting to note
the occurrence of such transactions, it is not apparent what motive lay behind
either of these acts of generosity on Killeshin's part.

What property was involved is also a matter of guesswork. The word *reclés*
normally means a minor church held as property by one of the larger churches
such as Durrow. It is used here as equivalent to *airlise* 'enclosure, precinct'. We
are not told the name of the *reclés* Killeshin first offered to Durrow but which in

fact went to the Dál Cais. The *airlise* which Durrow got, Int Ednán, was itself a church, several of whose abbots appear in the Annals of Ulster between 849 and 1024. Its location is uncertain, but it may be represented by the townland name Inan, near Clonard. This Inan is about twenty miles east-north-east of Durrow, and somewhat more than forty miles north of Killeshin (see fig. 7).

The part played by Durrow is curious, first neglecting to take up the property offered, and then claiming it when it was already in other hands. R. I. Best suggested that Durrow may have made its demand after 1095 when fire damaged the monastic buildings and library there, so there might have been a special need to muster resources in order to finance rebuilding[12].

It is unfortunate that there is so little indication of the legal steps taken in what happens. Durrow sent its abbot and priest to claim the *reclés*. This presumably means they came to Killeshin: though an ancient legal text required that claims be announced by entry on the disputed land, it would seem impolitic where the land was already held by a powerful third party. Nothing is said about arguments one way or another: whether, for example, Durrow's original claim might not be deemed to have lapsed and the *reclés* rightly reverted to Killeshin. But with or without argument or arbitration, Durrow won its point, and Killeshin agreed to provide an equivalent property to replace the original one. On behalf of their erenach (who controlled the properties of the church), the *maithe* (lit. 'good ones') or leading persons of Killeshin acted as guarantors that Killeshin would abide by the agreement to part with Int Ednán. The names of the guarantors are then listed. One may infer that the dispute never came to arbitration, but that Killeshin, for whatever reason, conceded to Durrow and gave sureties*. It is perhaps arguable that the document itself, which makes no attempt to record an equitable judgement, constitutes a kind of promise.

The record was made by Durrow, and can hardly have been an actual warranty document signed by the Killeshin guarantors. The story is told wholly from Durrow's point of view, and is recorded in Durrow's gospel book. Though the scribe Flannchad is not mentioned elsewhere, he was most likely a member of the community of Durrow. The fact that this is the only document so preserved at Durrow may have a significance. In form, this record is very like the ten charters entered in blank spaces in the Book of Kells, also a gospel book and belonging to another Columban monastery, during the period *c.* 1030–1160[13]. Incidentally, Gilla Adamnáin of Durrow here is also mentioned in one of the Kells charters of the early twelfth century. The only other documents of this type in the Irish-speaking world are the six grants entered in the Book of Deer, again a gospel book belonging to a monastery in Scotland also associated with St Columba[14]. These three sources are so similar in form, and sufficiently close in

---

[12] Best, 'An early monastic grant', 141.
[13] G. Mac Niocaill, *Notitiae as Leabhar Cheanannais 1033–1166*.
[14] K. H. Jackson, *The Gaelic Notes in the Book of Deer*.

date, for it to be possible that they represent a rather short-lived revival in the Gaelic areas of a form derived from the British–Latin charter[15]. The Columban connexion makes one wonder whether this revival was not even more limited. Though we have only a small number of Irish gospel books left, those from churches without Columban connexions have yielded no charters, while all three from Columban houses have. If this is significant, then one could infer that Int Ednán was the only one of Durrow's possessions acquired during this period of charter revival where there seemed enough risk of litigation to necessitate the record. But seen outside the Columban context, this record is quite exceptional.

It is no surprise, however, that the only surviving record should be directly associated with the interests of a church. The only other charter material from Ireland likewise survives in an ecclesiastical source, for it was appended during the eighth century to the work of Tírechán and copied with that work into the Book of Armagh in 807–8. These texts, not charters but apparently charter-derived, are in many ways comparable with Tírechán's own writings. His book was probably written about 670 to complement a lost Life of Patrick by one Ultán. But what Tírechán wrote is less a *vita* than a sort of historical cartulary, perhaps based to some extent on the same kind of charter material as that later appended to it[16]. His primary purpose was to catalogue the churches belonging to the coarb or successor of St Patrick, the archbishop at Armagh.

Tírechán tells us at some length a story of a dispute involving St Patrick, here seen as the founder of Armagh's interest in that church, and seven brothers, of whom one, Énde, established a church with which Tírechán was personally connected. The story assumes great importance for Tírechán, not merely because it establishes his own relationship with Armagh, and Armagh's interest in his native territory (*Tír Amolngid*, now Tirawley, Co. Sligo), but also because it represents the fulfilment of a passage in St Patrick's *Confessio* interpreted as a prophecy and a promise[17]. As Tírechán tells it, the saint hears two men talking, one of whom identifies himself as Énde son of Amolngid from the wood of Fochloth. This was the place to which Patrick had been called in his dream according to the *Confessio*, so he asks to go there with Énde. Énde requests Patrick to baptize his son Conall, which Patrick does, giving the boy into the custody of Bishop Cethiacus. Tírechán's narration of the sequence of events is then confused. Énde must have expressed his intention of making over to Patrick

[15] There is some evidence for the use of the British–Latin form of charter, and a vernacular equivalent, in the seventh century; see above, p. 170.

[16] Davies, 'Latin charter-tradition', p. 273; R. Sharpe (review of Bieler, *Patrician Texts*), *Éigse*, 18 (1980–1), 331; C. Doherty, 'Some aspects of hagiography as a source for Irish economic history', *Peritia*, 1 (1982), 306–7.

[17] Tírechán, cc. 14–15 in *Patrician Texts*, ed. L. Bieler (hereafter Tírechán); cf. St Patrick, *Confessio*, ch. 23 in *Libri Epistolarum Sancti Patricii*, ed. L. Bieler.

his share of the family estates, a permanent alienation which involved the whole kin group in loss. Énde's six brothers objected:

Six sons of Amolngid came before Loíguire for judgement, and against them came Énde alone and his young son and St Patrick before them [(?) as their spokesman]. They examined the case of their inheritance, and Loíguire and Patrick gave judgement to them, that they should divide the inheritance in seven parts between them. Énde said, 'My son and my share of the inheritance I give to Patrick's God and to Patrick'. Some say this is the reason why we are servants (*servi*) of St Patrick to the present day. Patrick and the sons of Amolngid with a host of laity and holy bishops made a covenant (*foedus*) through the hand of Loíguire.

Patrick and Énde then set out for the wood of Fochloth, marking the beginning of Patrick's first great missionary journey. They eventually reach this destination, and further stories involving the sons of Amolngid are told, concluding thus:

And behold Patrick proceeded to the land which is called the Meeting Hill of the Sons of Amolngid (*Forrach macc nAmolngid*) to divide it between the sons of Amolngid, and he made there a square earthen church of clay because there was no timber near[18].

The whole passage is historically very interesting. It provides one basis for the disputed location of the wood called *silva Vocluti* by Patrick, identifies Tírechán's background, and shows how a family might be conscious of its hereditary status as *servi* of a distant church. It is particularly important as evidence for the irruption of the church into a system of land ownership based on family property which was inalienable without the consent of the kin, and the problems this might lead to. As evidence for an approach to dispute settlement, it shows a family dispute with direct church involvement; the case is referred to secular judgement – the fifth-century king, Loíguire, a legendary figure whom Tírechán anachronistically portrays as king of Ireland; and the judgement appears to be based on an equitable partition. It is, however, not equitable: for it would preclude any benefit for the heirs of the six brothers from any redistribution affecting the seventh brother's share. The case seems to have been heard in public, in front of a crowd of laymen and bishops – practically a synod. The end result in legal terms is a *foedus*, a covenant or pact, presumably representing an Irish term[19], guaranteed by the king as surety, if that is the meaning of Tírechán's phrase *per manum*[20].

---

[18] Tírechán, cc. 42–4.

[19] Irish *cairde* is found as a gloss on *foedus* in the Milan glosses, Stokes and Strachan, *Thesaurus Palaeohibernicus*, vol. 1, p. 24, ll. 9 and 30, but the context there is a treaty of peace. Irish *cairdes*, also used as equivalent to Latin *foedus* and *pactum* means 'covenant, pact'. The term *cotach* 'covenant, treaty of friendship' (from the verb *contoing* 'swears jointly'), is, however, perhaps the most likely; cf. *Bethu Phátraic*, ed. K. Mulchrone, p. 94, on St Patrick's *cotach*.

[20] Bieler, *Patrician Texts*, p. 219, has a vaguely worded note, but see, for example, *Berrad Airechta*, sect. 51, ed. R. Thurneysen, *Die Bürgschaft im irischen Recht*, where each clause of the promise administered to the guarantor begins 'Gaib fort laim' or 'Gaib it laim' ('Take on your hand . . .'). Note that *Berrad Airechta* sections 1–43 are edited by K. Meyer, *Z. celt. Phil.*, 13 (1921) and translated by Thurneysen, *Die Bürgschaft im irischen Recht*.

Loíguire's dual rôle as judge and surety probably derives from Tírechán's wish to make him appear fully to support Patrick's interests; though this arrangement may have been common enough, we should not assume it to have been the norm.

But the case of the sons of Amolngid only indirectly involved St Patrick, though – as in the Durrow document – the saint's name stands for the interests of his church, Armagh. It was a dispute about one member of the kin group giving himself and his share of the family property into ecclesiastical control without the consent and cooperation of his kin. Such problems may have been frequent during the expansion of Christianity. But in his own day, Tírechán was openly concerned with disputes between Armagh and other great churches for the control of minor churches. He mentions several such disputes, and the statement of Patrick's historical claim is a major part of his purpose[21]. But even before Tírechán, some legally minded proponent of the claims of Armagh had set out in the *Liber Angeli*, in the mid-seventh century, the basis and implications of Armagh's position (as he saw it) of supremacy among the Irish churches:

Therefore by reason of the said authority it is not lawful for any Irish church to cast lots against Armagh nor for any bishop or abbot against the coarb of Patrick, but he has in law the power to overswear (*a se recte supraiuratur*) all churches and superiors, if the needs of truth (*vera necessitas*) demand it[22].

Tírechán takes up this claim, saying that the enemies of Patrick's church, who illegally occupy what should belong to Armagh, hate the *familia* of Patrick

because it is not lawful to swear against (*contra*) him nor over (*super*) him nor off (*de*) him, and it is not lawful to cast lots against him, for all the *primitiuae aeclesiae* of Ireland are his, and everything which is sworn is sworn by him[23].

MacNeill and Binchy have pointed out that Tírechán is here Latinizing technical terms from Irish law[24]. Two methods of settlement are involved, both belonging to the category of 'irrational' judgement finding.

First, the casting of lots (*consortem mitti* in *Liber Angeli*, *lignum mitti* in Tírechán, Irish *cocrann* or *crannchor*) is not so much a means of resolution as one of random determination between two parties. Its range of use tends to be limited to deciding who goes first among equals, or to the allotment of roughly equal benefits or penalties between persons of equal standing[25]. Armagh could not

---

[21] Tírechán, cc. 16, 18, 22, 25, 47, 51.

[22] *Liber Angeli*, ch. 20 in *Patrician Texts*, ed. Bieler. For discussion of date, see R. Sharpe, 'Armagh and Rome in the seventh century' in P. Ní Chatháin and M. Richter (eds.), *Irland und Europa. Die Kirche im Frühmittelalter*, pp. 60–4.

[23] Tírechán, ch. 22. Bieler emends the last sentence to read 'he overswears whatever is sworn'.

[24] E. MacNeill, 'Dates of texts in the Book of Armagh relating to St Patrick', *J. Royal Soc. Antiq. Ireland*, 58 (1928), 99; D. Binchy, 'Patrick and his biographers, ancient and modern', *Studia Hibernica*, 2 (1962), 62.

[25] See, for example, *Gúbretha Caratniad*, sect. 10 (allotment of shares in inheritance), and comments by R. Thurneysen, 'Die falschen Urteilssprüche Caratnia's', *Z. celt. Philol.*, 15 (1924–5), 316–17. Compare the Latin instances in the *Hibernensis* xxvi (*De sorte*), xviii. 5 (place of burial), xxix. 7

submit to the lot because (so it claimed) there was no church of equal standing. Its superior status also gave it the power to override by its oath any contradictory oath by an inferior (Irish *fortoing* 'to overswear', verbal noun *fortach*). This invocation of status – a fundamental principle in Irish law – appears to produce a deterministic result, for the person of higher status will always win[26]. But as *Liber Angeli* indicates, the litigant of superior status only wins if he swears in accordance with *vera necessitas* 'the needs of truth'. Status would not necessarily subvert justice. Otherwise, the law-tracts tell us, the superior oath is perjured and its swearer loses status entirely[27]. However, unless a witness demonstrated the perjury, it may have been difficult in practice to prevent overswearing as a means of 'force majeure', for the person whose oath was wrongly defeated may not have had access to one of even higher status than his overswearer, or other means of redress. The sanction is therefore again 'irrational': the litigant of higher status will not perjure himself for fear of divine retribution. The same legal claims are made in more detail by Tírechán, who says that it is not possible for anyone to take a legal oath (vb *imtoing*, verbal noun *imthach*) in a dispute with Patrick, nor to overswear him, nor to rebut or deny his case on oath (taking *jurare de eo* as equivalent to *ditoing*, verbal noun *díthech*)[28]. The greater detail is a logical development of what *Liber Angeli* says, for if Patrick overswears everyone, then it is pointless for anyone to attempt an oath against him. It is not hard to see why other churches disliked the claims of Armagh, but we may be sure they were not implemented. No litigant would challenge Armagh under such rules, nor agree to abide by them if Armagh initiated the case. Further, there is no evidence that Armagh was able to recover the churches which it held to have been misappropriated.

These two Latin texts, written in a sort of 'hagio-legal' style, portray the church as quite assimilated to the Irish legal system. Though Armagh tries to bend the rules, there is not here the attitude that the church must live by canon law rather than by secular law. Irish law applied among laity and church alike[29]. Indeed, the *Hibernensis*, a collection of biblical, patristic, and conciliar texts arranged by subject as a handbook of ecclesiastical law, includes many clauses attributed to Irish synods, which closely correspond to the vernacular law tracts. Many of the headings treated are matters of legal procedure, such as *De judicio, De sorte, De*

(nature of punishment), xxxii. 23 (division between coheirs), *Die Irische Kanonensammlung*, ed. F. W. H. Wasserschleben (hereafter *Hib.*).

[26] E. MacNeill, 'Ancient Irish law. The law of status or franchise', *Proc. Royal Irish Acad.*, 36 (1923) C, 265–316.

[27] *Corpus Iuris Hibernici* (hereafter *CIH*, cited by page and line), ed. D. Binchy, 1268, l. 4, 795, ll. 8–10, etc. But compare *Hib.* xvi. 6 which suggests that the laity were willing to perjure themselves in overswearing (*superiurare*) even when they had no knowledge of the facts.

[28] These types of oath are defined by Binchy, *Críth Gablach*, pp. 99–100.

[29] Though the legal sources distinguish different kinds of law – see, for example, P. Mac Cana, 'The three languages and the three laws', *Studia Celtica*, 5 (1970), 62–78 – there was considerable overlap in their application.

testimonio, De juramento, De debitis et pignoribus et usuris, and *De fidejussoribus et ratis et stipulatoribus*[30]. The relationship between this Latin compilation and the contemporary vernacular tracts is one beset with problems, but it is certain that each can illuminate the other on particular points[31].

Turning now to survey the vernacular sources, two sets of questions must be borne in mind. The first concerns the nature of the texts and the form in which they survive, the second the problems of establishing what tracts are preserved in a usable state and what subjects they usefully cover.

On the matter of form and survival there are some introductory studies[32]. The texts present many difficulties. What survives is the bulky detritus of centuries of study, annotation and abridgement by the legal profession in Ireland between the seventh and the sixteenth century. Most of the manuscripts date from the fifteenth and sixteenth centuries. Some texts survive in full, often accompanied by commentaries and glosses ranging in date from the ninth century to the date of the manuscripts; other texts survive incomplete, some merely as incoherent fragments quoted in the commentaries; in some cases we have a continuous text which differs from or is inferior to that available to the medieval commentators, whose quotations can supplement the text. All of this material is printed, but with minimal interpretation and no attempt at an analytical table of contents, in *Corpus Iuris Hibernici*[33]. The question of what early tracts survive intact, and what can only be glimpsed through later commentaries, is not easily answered. The best introductory account surveys the contents of one early eighth-century collection, *Senchus Már*, and makes little comment on other tracts[34]. At least one other collection or 'school' is known to have existed, to which some tracts may be attributed[35]. Some texts are independent of any such grouping. A serious attempt at an interpretative listing of the extant material is long overdue[36].

---

[30] For discussion of *Hib.*, see references in M. Lapidge and R. Sharpe, *A Bibliography of Celtic–Latin Literature*, no. 612.

[31] See most recently D. Ó Corráin, L. Breatnach, A. Breen, 'The laws of the Irish', *Peritia*, 3 (1984); and L. Breatnach, 'Canon law and secular law in early Ireland', *Peritia*, 3 (1984).

[32] Most of the problems are aired by D. Binchy, 'The linguistic and historical value of the Irish law-tracts', *Proc. Brit. Acad.*, 29 (1943), and some in a paper written in 1920 by E. MacNeill, 'Prolegomena to a study of the *Ancient Laws of Ireland*', *Irish Jurist*, n.s., 2 (1967). Bibliographies are provided by Binchy, 'Ancient Irish law', *Irish Jurist*, n.s., 1 (1966), and more fully by L. Ronayne, 'Seandlithe na nGael: an annotated bibliography of the ancient laws of Ireland', *Irish Jurist*, n.s., 17 (1982).

[33] *Corpus Iuris Hibernici*, ed. D. Binchy.

[34] R. Thurneysen, 'Das keltische Recht', *ZRG, Germ. Abt.*, 55 (1935), 85–99. For a more detailed account of *Senchus Már*, see R. Thurneysen, '*Ancient Laws of Ireland* und Senchas Már', *Z. celt. Philol.*, 16 (1927), and 'Zum ursprünglichen Umfang des Senchas Már', *Z. celt. Philol.*, 18 (1929).

[35] D. Binchy, '*Bretha Nemed*', *Ériu*, 17 (1955); *idem*, 'The date and provenance of *Uraicecht Becc*', *Ériu*, 18 (1958).

[36] This applies to commentaries as well as to texts: if we are to understand the development of Irish law in law schools of the later middle ages, their books should not be treated merely as quarries for occasional help with the older texts.

The critical period in the development of the laws was the seventh century, a century during which many changes seem to have affected Irish society and one which is peculiarly well represented in the surviving evidence. There was already a complex legal system, and a flourishing legal profession which had probably been responsible at a much earlier date for the transmission of the legal maxims and verse in which Irish law was preserved. But during the seventh century this legal material changed dramatically.

First of all, the traditional legal material consisting largely of highly allusive, aphoristic verse began to be revised and in part written down, probably a consequence of the church's use of the written word. These verse texts, called *fénechus*, rarely survive continuously, so that one can hardly say they were committed to writing. For the most part only occasional quotations of *fénechus* are found in prose tracts on a wide variety of legal topics. Linguistic study of the prose texts, however, has shown that many of them are not later than the seventh century, and some perhaps before 650, though few can be given precise dates[37]. Few texts are homogeneous in style or content, tending to move in short bursts, sometimes with little real connexion of thought or even matter[38]. Two styles of writing are distinguishable in the prose texts which Dr Charles-Edwards has characterized as 'plain prose' and 'text-book prose'; the latter style, influenced by Latin text books, came into use at a slightly later date, but both continued in use together[39]. The mixture of these two styles and verse quotations requires more than a stylistic or linguistic criterion for separating the strata. As Professor Binchy observed, almost all tracts contain several legal strata, and the antiquity of the legal ideas need not correspond to the age of the style or language[40]. But the reluctance to omit old rules, and the retaining of them alongside later rules, does allow the legal historian to attempt analysis of changes in legal practice.

A major question, however, is the status of the tracts in relation to the practice of law. Some texts, particularly the well-known tract on status, *Críth Gablach*, 'Branched Purchase', dated to a little after 700, have been castigated as schematic and idealized, not corresponding to real life[41]. This criticism applies much more to the law of status than to any other, and there is a danger of making too much of it. At an early date, the law tracts had become the school books of a legal profession, and the written law shows signs of artificiality in describing how a lawyer's ideal society might be regulated. But this artificiality is only the surface – presumably the latest – layer. The greater part of the laws record custom,

---

[37] Binchy has argued that *Cáin Fuithirbe* was written between 678 and 685, 'Date and provenance of *Uraicecht Becc*', 53, and that *Críth Gablach* dates from soon after 700, *Críth Gablach*, p. xiv.

[38] Thurneysen, 'Das keltische Recht', 90.

[39] T. M. Charles-Edwards, 'The *Corpus Iuris Hibernici*', *Studia Hibernica*, 20 (1980). Thurneysen, 'Das keltische Recht', 93, thought that a jurist might compose in verse or prose as different registers, without chronological distinction.

[40] Binchy, 'Distraint in Irish law', *Celtica*, 10 (1973), 31.

[41] Thurneysen, 'Das keltische Recht', 91.

however incompletely, though we cannot know how much this had been transformed by the activities of the legal profession. In their written texts, however, the lawyers did not intend a complete guide to the law[42]. Many tracts do not attempt to deal with *how* the law operates, but discuss areas in which legal problems frequently arise.

Take as an example the relatively homogeneous tract *Coibnes Uisci Thairidne*, 'Kinship of Conducted Water'[43]. The leading of water for a mill across several persons' land, causing benefits and nuisances to the several parties, was a fruitful source of dispute, and the jurists have attempted to organize the customs which regulated this into a set of rules. Among other rulings, it is allowed that fixed compensation should be paid for new lades, but those established for two generations enjoyed a right of *aquaeductus*. 'For,' the writer adds:

there are three rules which heirs are not capable of altering if their father and grandfather have acknowledged them throughout their lifetime: the rule of a watercourse, the rule of a river mouth, and the rule of a bridge. For these are the three burdens which heirs cannot dispute if their father and grandfather have acknowledged them throughout their lifetime. If they have been acknowledged, they are to remain so for ever, whether they be gratis or whether a fee is due according to the decision of a judge[44].

The writer is recording accepted law, and does not explain his allusion to the rules of river mouth (for fishing) or bridges. Customary regulations of this kind abound in any settled agricultural society, and many people would know their rights. The jurist puts it on a more formal basis. Disputes will occur, and it is mentioned here that a judge may be called in to decide the level of compensation appropriate. If one were to collect all such slender references to disputes and their settlements, one might see how social harmony was maintained and learn a great deal about social organization.

The legal capacities of every individual depended on whether he was free or unfree; if free, on his status, defined in terms of honour price based on property and inherited status. His legal responsibilities were framed within a kin-group structure, to which he was responsible, but which would represent him in his dealings with other kin groups of the same *tuath*[45]. The *tuath*, usually translated 'petty kingdom', was the largest social unit for legal purposes, though in scale it was rather smaller than a county. In dealings outside his own *tuath*, the freeman was represented by his king (*rí tuaithe*). Within the *tuath*, a great many social obligations were seen in terms of contract, and most contracts were secured by an elaborate system of sureties.

The purpose of this was to insure against any breach of contract, and to help provide a ready means of resolution, should dispute occur. Much of Irish law is

[42] C. Plummer, 'Notes on some passages in the Brehon laws: I', *Ériu*, 8 (1915–16), 127.

[43] D. Binchy, 'Irish law-tracts re-edited: I. *Coibnes Uisci Thairidne*', *Ériu*, 17 (1955).

[44] Sect. 9.

[45] The legal framework of society is discussed in general terms by K. W. Hughes, *Early Christian Ireland: Introduction to the Sources*, pp. 43–64.

framed in such a way as to anticipate, and contain if it could not prevent, the kind of disputes which might interfere with essential cooperation in society. In the event of any breach of contract, a plaintiff and his sureties could take private action to enforce the contract, through a formal procedure of distraint. This procedure moved step by step, with an interval between each stage, a formal 'cooling off period' to prevent a dispute from getting out of control, and to allow maximum opportunity for private agreement. If the defendant maintained that he was not at fault, the dispute would require independent adjudication. The tracts deal separately with the procedures for distraint and surety, and from the treatment of these topics we may infer how the Irish law of contract aimed to anticipate disputes and provide a basis for settlement.

It may have been the case, as Binchy argues, that in its earliest form the taking of distraint allowed justice to be done on a purely private basis[46]. A triad specifies 'the three occasions on which there is illegal enforcement in Irish law: an unjust distraint, an unlawful entry, a duel without contracts'[47]. Three methods of procedure are here distinguished: distraint of chattels, entry as a means of distraint against real property, and duel[48]. The last method of settlement, duel between two contending parties, was only valid with the consent ('contracts') of the parties' kindreds, but has little place in the extant tracts. Formal procedure for 'entry' (*tellach*) is described in an early tract, largely in verse, with an example in a ninth-century commentary[49]. But 'entry' was a ritualized statement of claim, persuading the claimant to go to arbitration rather than leading directly to settlement. Though distraint of chattels might in principle provide self-help justice, the tract on the subject regards it rather as a procedure leading to a settlement by arbitration or agreement.

In the historic period, all distraint procedures were regulated to a high degree of formality, and must almost invariably have involved a professional, judicial rôle[50]. As *Cetharslicht Athgabálae* says:

He is not capable of taking distraint who is not able to bind it, unless an advocate (*suí thengad*) watch over him, who shall buttress the court (*airecht*), so that it can be verified in his sight. For in Irish law no-one witnesses a thing of which he is not eye-witness. He who has not acquired knowledge of it [i.e. the court] is prevented from prosecuting suits in court[51].

---

[46] 'Distraint in Irish law', 23–5, 56–65.

[47] *CIH*, 213, ll. 27–9. Cf. Binchy, 'Distraint in Irish law', 30.

[48] These topics are discussed by H. d'Arbois de Jubainville in 'Des attributions judiciaires de l'autorité publique chez les celtes', *Revue celtique*, 7 (1886), 2–37, and *Études sur le droit celtique*.

[49] *CIH*, 205, l. 22–213, l. 26, cf. extracts at 907, l. 36–910, l. 34, where the commentary includes the illustrative story of Nin. The text is briefly discussed by T. M. Charles-Edwards, 'Boundaries in Irish law' in P. H. Sawyer (ed.), *Medieval Settlement: Continuity and Change*, pp. 83–4.

[50] *Berrad Airechta*, sect. 32, implies that resolution can be achieved through 'binding' (*naidm*) by sureties and witnesses without recourse to law (*dliged*).

[51] *CIH*, 358, ll. 1–4 etc. For translation, compare *Dictionary of the Irish Language*, ed. E. G. Quin and others, s.v. 1 *airecht*, and Binchy, 'Distraint in Irish law', 31–2.

Furthermore, many of the procedures for contracts or dispute hearings have a communal aspect. The casting of lots, for example, is considered a public procedure in the early tract *Berrad Airechta*, 'Shearing (?) of the Court', quoting from *fénechus*[52]. The same passage, discussing the need for witnesses, excludes the testimony of a friend: justice could not be a matter to be settled privately between two sides, therefore, but required an impartial, communal dimension[53]. This communal procedure would require the swearing of oaths by the parties involved, and the tract says that an oath is not valid unless it is ordered, presumably by a judge[54]. Another passage of *fénechus* quoted in the tract says:

> Do not lend unless you take sureties,
> so that you should not swear to that which you have not given.
> There is no judgement on what is not within one's control.
> Consideration precedes judgements (*mesu*).
> He who does not acknowledge tradition is no supervisor.
> He who does not supervise an oath is not a guardian of tradition.
> There is no oath without casting of lots.
> There is no casting of lots without persons of equal status[55].

Interpreted, the sequence of ideas runs: if a person puts himself in the position of creditor, he should ensure that the contract is secured by sureties, oaths and witnesses. Otherwise, he cannot seek judgement to recover the debt in the event of default. A judgement can only be made by one learned in the law, who will insist on the casting of lots and the taking of oaths, but who will also inquire into the facts of the case. The need for sureties and pledges in the vast majority of minor obligations shows that, even if default was not frequent, normal procedure always sought to anticipate it. In a brief aside on contracts, the author of *Coibnes Uisci Thairidne* observes:

No adoption [of a watercourse] is legally valid unless sureties from the adopter's kin group have warranted it and the head of the kin group has authorized it. For in Irish law every contract without surety may be dissolved[56].

This establishes a family context for contractual relationships. The universality of the last sentence, however, goes beyond the facts: *Berrad Airechta* lists many debts which need not be secured[57]. But the latter are exceptions to a general rule. *Berrad Airechta* goes on to specify who is or is not contract-worthy, so that no-one will engage in a contract which cannot be enforced[58]. The text discusses in detail the duties of persons acting as surety. But the basic requirement of security is positively asserted:

---

[52] *Berrad Airechta*, sect. 59, if the passage is correctly translated; this was accepted by M. A. O'Brien, 'Some questionable emendations', *Ériu*, 11 (1930–2), 155.

[53] Cf. Mac Niocaill, 'Admissible and inadmissible evidence', 334–6. *Hib.* xvi. 9f nonetheless quotes an Irish synod warning against the suborning of witnesses.

[54] *Berrad Airechta*, sect. 62.   [55] *Ibid.*, sect. 83.   [56] *Coibnes Uisci Thairidne*, sect. 6.

[57] *Berrad Airechta*, sects. 1–20.   [58] *Ibid.*, sects. 21–3, 35–7.

Refection does not take away debts – everything which was given should be given back. If it is no longer all available, it must be made good. He is a fool who does not have for every transaction (*cundrad*) a *naidm* and a *ráth* and a witness to confirm memory by testimony without which there is no knowledge. No-one is able to rebut on oath who does not see, who does not hear, without witness to the contractual obligations involved. A contract (*cor*) without *ráth*, without witness, without *naidm* is an unsure truth. For the *naidm* enforces, the *ráth* gives his pledge, the witness protects debts together with the contractual obligations of the other party. No debt and no contract is made known without witness[59].

If the debtor defaulted, the creditor could call on the debtor's sureties: his *naidm* ('binding surety') would force the debtor to meet his obligations, or his *ráth* ('paying surety') would pay instead and then recover the debt himself (together with compensation for his trouble), or, in special circumstances, a third type of surety, the *aitire*, would become hostage to the creditor until the debt was settled (again, claiming compensation from the defaulter for his pains)[60]. *Berrad Airechta*, in quoting *formulae** for the oaths which sureties took, and those made during the prosecution of their duties, gives a rare insight into actual processes.

Where default occurred, the procedures of surety and distraint were designed to bring the parties in dispute to accept a settlement by independent adjudication. But such adjudication must have been called for in many disputes where no contracts or sureties were involved. We have seen how, in a dispute over a long-established watercourse, a compensatory payment might be assessed by a judge. Similarly, we find a difficult passage in the *Hibernensis* about a land dispute:

About two churches disputing a piece of land. *An Irish synod*: The land should be looked up in the written evidences of the two churches; if it is not found there, inquiry should be made of elders neighbouring [on the property] as to how long it has been held by the present holder; if it has remained unchallenged for longer than the period of legal warranty, let it remain [with the holder] for ever; if no elders are found, they should divide the land between them, and the church nearer to it should pay a sum which judges will determine[61].

It is implied that the judges do not participate in the inquest or the division of the property, merely in fixing a sum to be paid presumably to the church losing part of what it held. This reticence about the rôle of the judge is characteristic. Though *Berrad Airechta* makes occasional reference to the judge who will order the oaths or decide the case, little is said of his part in the process. In fact, as a whole, very little is certain about the functions of this individual, the *brithem*. He was a specialist in law, a professional arbiter to whom the two parties would refer their dispute, and whose conclusions they bound themselves in advance by pledges to

[59] *Ibid.*, sect. 63.
[60] Sureties have been discussed in detail by Thurneysen, *Die Bürgschaft im irischen Recht*, *Abhandlungen der Preussischen Akademie der Wissenschaften, phil.-hist. Kl.*, 1928, pt 2, pp. 33–85.
[61] *Hib.* xxxii. 24, xlii. 8.

accept[62]. Though Thurneysen always rightly translated the word as 'Richter', the English translation has long been 'jurist', the word favoured by MacNeill, who argued that the *brithem* did not himself give judgement[63]. Binchy has now expressly rejected this[64]. It was the responsibility of the *brithem* to give judgement. What makes his position most unusual is that unlike the judgement finders of other countries, he did not serve out of public duty nor was he an official. His legal work was done in a professional capacity, and he was paid by the winner a sum contingent on the value of the award. Though some *brithemoin* combined this work with an ecclesiastical career, this was perhaps abnormal in the period of the law tracts[65]. Most would have trained in one of the law schools, and then worked up the legal profession from advocate, through adjudicator in a minor legal capacity to the full status of judge[66].

A difficult tract, *Cóic Conara Fugill*, 'the Five Paths of Judgement', deals with how a suit was brought to the *brithem*. Each party would have a legal counsel or advocate (*feithem*) with whom a 'path' should be chosen. The first four of these paths are designated by abstract nouns, truth (*fír*), law (*dliged*), right (*cert*) and due (*téchta*)[67]. Whatever the meaning of these distinctions, all come together in the fifth 'path', inquiry before a judge (*athchomarcc do brithemain*)[68]. The process involved eight stages: (1) the fixing of the time for the hearing, (2) the selection of the proper 'path' by the plaintiff's counsel, (3) the giving of pledges, (4) pleading, (5) rejoinder, (6) judgement (*breth*), (7) promulgation (*forus*), and (8) conclusion[69]. This seems rather to simplify the procedure of pleading and

---

[62] The verb *fogella* 'appeals to the judgement of' is formed from *fo* 'under' and *gell* 'pledge'. E. MacNeill, 'Ireland and Wales in the history of jurisprudence', *Studies*, 16 (1927), 612, optimistically noted that the tract *Bretha im Fuillema Gell*, 'Judgements about the Interest of Pledges' (*CIH*, 462, l. 19–476, l. 26), 'explains how such pledges operated'. The tract is in fact concerned with the value of each person's pledge, and his right to some interest from the third party who enjoyed the benefits of the pledge between its deposit and the case's coming to judgement.

[63] See below, n. 82.

[64] In his legal glossary, *Críth Gablach*, p. 79, Binchy follows MacNeill, and in 'Date and provenance of *Uraicecht Becc*', 45, he explicitly prefers MacNeill's 'jurist' to Thurneysen's 'judge'. But in 'An archaic legal poem', *Celtica*, 9 (1971), 152, and in '*Féichem, fethem, aigne*', *Celtica*, 11 (1976), 29, he has announced a change of mind and adopted the translation 'judge'.

[65] D. Ó Corráin, 'Nationality and kingship in pre-Norman Ireland', *Historical Studies*, 11 (1978), 14–15, lists those high-ranking clerics of the tenth to twelfth centuries described as judges in their annal obits.

[66] Cf. *Uraicecht Becc* and commentary, *CIH*, 1613, l. 38–1615, l. 3.

[67] Compare *Uraicecht Becc*, which says that *brithemnus* is founded on truth (*fír*), law (*dliged*) and nature (*aicned*); *CIH*, 634, l. 11, 1590, l. 1.

[68] *Cóic Conara Fugill*, in the composite recension RE sect. 23, ed. R. Thurneysen, *Abhandlungen der Preussischen Akademie der Wissenschaften, phil.-hist. Kl.*, 1925, pt 7. It appears that the later recension H sect. 133 may have misunderstood the passage, for instead of the two parties (*féichemoin*) bringing their case to judicial inquiry, it speaks of their questioning the judge on his judgements, though if this were the sense, one would want to read *feithemoin*. *Athchomarc* is discussed by Thurneysen, *ibid.*, 79–80.

[69] *Cóic Conara Fugill*, H sect. 16, and Binchy, '*Féichem, fethem, aigne*', 31.

judging to one of letting each side state its case and giving an equitable judgement based on ascertained facts. There was more to it than that, though the sequence of events is not clear. Each party will take his oath (*noíll, lugae*), the legal value of which corresponds to his status as defined by his honour-price. As *Berrad Airechta* says, 'There is no oath without casting lots', we infer that lots were cast to determine which side swore first, if both were of equal status. The insistence on witnesses to every contract shows that the judge will also want to make inquiry into the facts of the case. Everything that is said about witnesses (*fiadnaise, tuarastal*) suggests that they should be independent parties, having personal eye-witness knowledge of the facts. Hearsay is excluded. Witnesses gave testimony under oath. The tracts also provide for oath-helpers* (*arrae, noíllid*). But compurgation was a means of last resort if there were no witnesses for one or both parties[70]. Some questions were settled by ordeal[71]. The two parties' legal representatives (*feithem, aigne*) had the opportunity to plead[72]. These representatives may have been the heads of the parties' kin groups in the prehistoric period, though by the seventh century they were professional lawyers[73]. In giving his judgement, the *brithem* must bear in mind several factors: he is not simply to decide the equitable justice of the case, but must be guided by *roscada* – a word here referring to the maxims of *fénechus* – and by *fásaige* 'legal precedents'[74].

Where did all this take place? *Cóic Conara Fugill* at one point implies that both parties had merely to go to the house of the *brithem* along with their legal counsel and their witnesses[75]. Perhaps some minor cases were dealt with in this way, in chambers so-to-speak. But the regular answer seems to be that it took place at the *airecht*. As one later text asks, 'When does the law suit (*ai*) come to court (*airecht*)?'[76] The answer follows the steps we have already seen of suit (*toiched*),

---

[70] See *Tecosca Cormaic*, sect. 24, ed. K. Meyer in Meyer, *Instructions of King Cormac*, p. 40; cf. *Synodus Patricii*, cl. 24 and *Hib.* xvi. 14–15, xxxv. 14.

[71] See above, n. 47, for ordeal by battle; *Synodus Patricii*, cl. 24, for ordeal by fire; and for ordeal by cauldron, C. Plummer, 'Notes on some passages in the Brehon laws: III', *Ériu*, 9 (1921–3), 115, and references.

[72] *Cóic Conara Fugill*, RE sect. 25, H sect. 133; read *fetheman* for *fecheman*, with Binchy, 'Féichem, fethem, aigne', 24. The word for pleading (*tacrae* from the verb *doaccair* 'to plead') becomes transferred to mean 'law-suit', an indication that pleading formed an important part of the inquiry.

[73] Binchy, 'Féichem, fethem, aigne', 20–3.

[74] Binchy, 'Linguistic and historical value', 207, equates *fásach* with what he has called a leading case, an account of a decision by a legendary judge, usually to support a recent change of practice. *Cóic Conara Fugill*, H sect. 2, lists three such considerations, 'roscadh 7 fasach 7 testemain'; *Uraicecht Becc* mentions the same three, *CIH*, 634, l. 26, 1591, ll. 13–14. *Teistemain* comes from Latin *testimonium*. A short tract *Urchoillte Brithemon* (*CIH*, 2102, l. 31–2103, l. 32) adds two further criteria, 'roscad 7 fasach 7 testemain 7 cosmailius 7 aicned'; this text is edited by Thurneysen, 'Zum ursprünglichen Umfang', 362–4 (sect. 6), and by R. M. Smith in *Irish Texts*, vol. 4, pp. 24–7 (sect. 4). It is quoted in the commentary on the passage of *Uraicecht Becc* just cited, *CIH*, 635, ll. 13–14. For *aicned* 'nature' see above n. 67; *cosmailius* appears to mean 'comparison, analogy'.

[75] *Cóic Conara Fugill*, RE sect. 22, H sect. 26. Binchy, *Celtic and Anglo-Saxon Kingship*, pp. 16, 19, interprets this as signifying that all 'ordinary private suits' were held 'in the brehon's house'.

[76] *CIH*, 1149, ll. 7–35, 1921, l. 28–1922, l. 13; R. M. Smith, 'A tract on pleading', *Irish Texts*, vol. 4, p. 20.

interval (*rē*), choice of consent (*toga*), pledges (*airge*), leading to the court and the judgement seat (*diaigside*).

The *airecht* has been defined as 'the public assembly of freemen whose functions included the transaction of certain important legal business'[77]. It takes its name from the most widely used legal term for freeman (*aire*), and the involvement of all men of free status in its legal business is shown by a maxim quoted in *Críth Gablach*: 'the grades of the freemen (*Féne*) are reckoned by the measure of the court'[78]. These measures include his capacity to take oath in litigation (*imtoing*), to act as surety of the various types, or to give eye-witness testimony, or to offer legal protection (*snádud*). The law itself belonged to the freeman, and the formula meaning 'in Irish law' is *la Féniu* 'according to the *Féni*'. It is to the *airecht* as a court of law that the procedures of distraint will lead, and we should probably imagine this as a regular and accessible legal assembly in every *tuath*, though I know of no direct evidence on how often it met. It met in the open air, generally at the *forrach* or meeting hill, though some legal business was done at the burial grounds of the community[79].

In the last century, O'Curry believed that there had existed a hierarchy of *airechta*, rising from the petty courts to the court of the king of the *tuath*, and beyond that to interterritorial courts and a provincial court of appeal[80]. He based this on a short tract, *Cenéla airechta*, which purports to describe five categories of court in terms of the status of its personnel, and to list the sixteen members of the basic *airecht* and their functions[81]. It is highly schematic, and I hesitate to rest any interpretation on its testimony.

It is inherently likely that courts sat for legal business on a very local basis, but one must wonder how large a population was necessary before its litigation was enough to support a local *brithem* and several professional advocates. There cannot have been many *brithemoin* in each *tuath*. *Críth Gablach* mentions the *brithem tuaithe*, 'judge of the people', which led MacNeill to construct a thesis in which the *brithem* sat as 'legal assessor' alongside the *rí tuaithe*, 'king of the people', in a *Curia Regis* which he identified with the *airecht*, 'a regular court of law, with the king as president, in every *tuath*'[82]. Whether or not the king had any judicial power is a vexed question[83]. But MacNeill's desire to imagine a prototype

---

[77] Binchy, *Críth Gablach*, p. 73. Cf. *idem*, *Celtic and Anglo-Saxon Kingship*, p. 19, 'meeting of notables', 'court'.   [78] Sect. 5.
[79] On the *forrach*, see C. Doherty, 'The monastic town in early medieval Ireland' in H. B. Clarke and A. Simms (eds.), *The Comparative History of Urban Origins in Non-Roman Europe*, pp. 49–51. But some oaths, for example, were taken at cemeteries; see Plummer, 'Notes on some passages: III', 114.
[80] E. O'Curry, *On the Manners and Customs of the Ancient Irish*, vol. 1, pp. cclxii–ccxcv.
[81] *CIH*, 601, l. 20–602, l. 4; also edited by K. Meyer, 'Cenēla airechta', *Z. celt. Philol.*, 12 (1918), 359–60.
[82] MacNeill, 'Ireland and Wales', 608–13.
[83] N. McLeod, 'Parellel and paradox', *Studia Celtica*, 16/17 (1981–2), 36–9, overstates the case for the king as judge, which rests largely on the evidence of proverbial texts on the duties of a king. One

royal state led him to undervalue the judicial rôle of the *brithem*. Nor is there any evidence to support the notion that the *airecht*'s authority depended on any supposed royal presidency. Such authority as the court possessed depended rather on communal respect for legal processes, perhaps enhanced by a peculiarly Irish respect for the *brithem* as a specialist in one of the learned arts like the *fili* or the *ollam*. Only from the thirteenth century is it possible to see the local king or chief imposing any seigneurial authority on the process of law[84]. In the early middle ages, the procedure for the settlement of disputes depended on no public authority[85]. Settlement was in principle a private matter, but if the procedures for sureties and distraint did not lead to a settlement, a settlement at law was available for free individuals, in the sight of the local community and with the expert assistance of a professional judge.

In these pages, I have tried to collect some key pieces in the jigsaw but not to fit them together. Every element – lots, oaths, witnesses, ordeals, pleadings, advocates, judges, courts – requires detailed study. Of these, the procedural elements will bear comparison with those current throughout the West in the early middle ages, though it cannot yet be said how similar or different they were in operation. But three points stand out as distinctive of Irish practice: the degree of professionalism in advocacy and judgement, the power of decision of a single, expert judge, and the importance attached to inquiry after the facts rather than to the correctness of formality, oath-taking or other 'irrational' means of finding judgement. It is also apparent that the procedures of swearing in sureties and taking distraint, which serve both to bring a dispute to settlement and to enforce the judge's decision, are more formally regulated than any similar, non-public procedures elsewhere at this period. Though sureties and distraint have been studied individually, their relationship to the process of adjudication remains unclear. It is possible that examination of the law tracts will replace this sketch with a reasonably detailed picture of how the legal system operated about AD 700. But in view of the incompatibilities within and between the different tracts, and their detachment from a historical context, it may remain uncertain how the legal picture will square with, for example, the intentions of the *Liber Angeli* and Tírechán.

Still more imponderable is the question of how the Irish legal system may have changed after 700. What comparison is there, if any, between the legal background of the Durrow document and the procedures of seventh-century

---

legal text from the *Nemed* school lends some support to the idea, discussed by P. Mac Cana, 'The three languages and the three laws', 76–8. But Binchy argues that the king's judicial rôle ended in the prehistoric period, *Celtic and Anglo-Saxon kingship*, pp. 15–17. One might add that as early as the fifth century, St Patrick, *Confessio*, cc. 52–3, distinguishes between kings and judges, and incidentally shows the importance of the *brithem*.

[84] G. Mac Niocaill, 'Aspects of Irish law in the thirteenth century', *Historical Studies*, 10 (1976), 34–5.

[85] D. Binchy, 'Secular institutions' in M. Dillon (ed.), *Early Irish Society*, pp. 60–1.

law? It remains orthodox opinion that the canon of legal texts was closed at the beginning of the eighth century, and that the texts became frozen and immutable[86]. While it is true to say that there are apparently no major new tracts later than the eighth century, there is revision of some of the tracts, minor tracts are written, and there are commentaries of the ninth century which suggest no great change in the legal system to that point. Thereafter we are dependent on increasingly irrelevant glosses, from which it is rarely possible to perceive, still less to date, significant developments. During the tenth and eleventh centuries, new and greater political lordships emerged, capable of exerting something more nearly resembling government than Ireland had known before[87]. Though we see from the annals a corresponding change in the territorial descriptions of judges (in 908 Colmán, 'chief *ollam* of the jurisprudence of Ireland', in 1032 Ailill Ua Flaithim, '*ollam* of Munster in jurisprudence' or in 1095 Augustín Ua Cuinn, 'chief judge of Leinster'), this was not matched by any development in the law as an instrument in that trend towards government. In the twelfth and thirteenth centuries, the private measures of Irish law came up against the influence of English Common Law*, but little was borrowed and the two laws tended rather to coexist[88]. When Giolla na Naomh Mac Aodhagáin wrote his handbook of Irish law about 1300, the vocabulary used is very different from that of the ancient texts, but the principles had not changed in essentials[89].

As late as the sixteenth century, Irish law was still in use in many areas alongside Common Law. In 1584 Richard Stanihurst describes how on a set day the men of the neighbourhood assemble in an elevated place (the Meeting Hill) to bring their complaints at law to the *jurisperiti* or brehons (from *brithemoin*)[90]. If the books of the law schools are a true guide, the brehons were still studying (perhaps with little comprehension) texts nearly nine hundred years old. There even exists a copy of a law student's exercise, a draft speech to the court, filled with quotations from the early medieval tracts without regard to their relevance[91]. From this same period, when early modern records are available to document Irish dispute procedure, there survive a considerable number of arbitral awards, of which few have been published[92]. Professor Mac Niocaill has published a Latin warranty of the sixteenth century not wholly unlike the Durrow document[93]. But altogether there is too little information about the eleventh to fifteenth centuries for one to say how different this phase of late medieval Irish

[86] Binchy, 'Linguistic and legal archaisms', 16, says that once assembled at the beginning of the eighth century in *Senchus Már*, the form of the law was 'final and canonical', its text 'sacred and immutable'.

[87] Ó Corráin, 'Nationality and kingship in pre-Norman Ireland'.

[88] Mac Niocaill, 'The interaction of laws' in J. F. Lydon (ed.), *The English in Medieval Ireland*.

[89] *CIH*, 691–9.

[90] R. Stanihurst, *De rebus gestis in Hibernia*, pp. 33–8.

[91] *CIH*, 2204–8; Binchy, 'Distraint in Irish law', 67–70.

[92] Briefly discussed by Mac Niocaill, 'Notes on litigation in late Irish law', *Irish Jurist*, n.s., 2 (1967).

[93] G. Mac Niocaill, 'Meabhrán dlí ó mhuintir Eolais, 1497–1513', *Galvia*, 4 (1957).

law is from the law of the seventh to ninth centuries. It may be that the Durrow record belongs more to the later phase than to the earlier, and that the ninth and tenth centuries really did witness the passing of a whole social and legal order[94]. But in the eyes of the law schools, there was no major change from the seventh century until the eventual triumph of Common Law in the seventeenth century[95].

[94] Binchy, 'The passing of the old order' in B. Ó Cuív (ed.), *The Impact of the Scandinavian Invasions*.
[95] I am grateful to Dr Thomas Charles-Edwards for his helpful comments on a draft of this chapter. Since this chapter was written, an indispensable textbook has appeared: Fergus Kelly, *A Guide to Early Irish Law* (Dublin, 1989). Two articles print relevant passages of the law tracts with translation and discussion: Fergus Kelly, 'An Old-Irish text on court procedure', *Peritia* 5 (1986) [1988], 74–106 and L. Breatnach, 'Lawyers in early Ireland', in *Brehons, Serjeants, and Attorneys. Studies in the history of the Irish legal profession*, ed. D. Hogan and W. N. Osborough (Dublin, 1990), pp. 1–13.

10

An early modern postscript: the Sandlaw dispute, 1546

JENNY WORMALD

Late medieval and early modern Scotland was notoriously a feuding society, overstocked with overmighty aristocracy and therefore awash with bloodshed and civil disorder; so said a typically contemptuous English observer in the late sixteenth century, and a number of suitably Enlightened Scottish lawyers and historians of later times[1]. It was indeed a feuding society, in the sense that the word 'feid', as defined in an act of parliament of 1598, covered everything from the full-scale and classic feud which involved vengeance killing to civil dispute from which violence was entirely absent[2]. It was also a feuding society in that there were major, long-term and very bloody feuds[3]. But above all, it was a feuding society which strove for peace; historians have listened to what the wealth of documentation about the feud has to say about dispute and violence, but have been rather more deaf to what it tells us about the efforts to curtail violence and end dispute[4]. But the evidence is there, in great quantity. We can get a bird's-eye view of the settlement of dispute in sixteenth-century Scotland in a way which is not possible for the early medieval world. But there is much in common between the two; in both, the underlying principle that disputes should be settled and not prolonged, in the most effective way possible, was exactly the same. There is good reason, therefore, to bring the detailed analysis which can be made of a dispute settlement of the sixteenth century to bear on those of the early medieval period, which this book illuminates.

The case of dispute settlement which will be described here is not, of course, archetypal, for in practice there is no such thing. The process whereby disputes were ended, and the particular outcome, varied in any society and at any time according to the personalities involved, depending on whether they were prone to

---

[1] British Library, Additional MS 35,844, fols. 193r–198r. For examples of later comment, see A. McDouall, lord Bankton, *An Institute of the Laws of Scotland*, bk 1, ch. 2, sect. 85–6, and W. Robertson, *History of Scotland during the Reigns of Queen Mary and King James VI*, vol. 1, pp. 25–6.

[2] *The Acts of the Parliaments of Scotland*, ed. C. Innes, T. Thomson, vol. 4, pp. 158–9, cl. 1.

[3] Two such feuds are analysed by K. M. Brown, *Bloodfeud in Scotland*, cc. 4 and 6. I am very grateful to Dr Brown for allowing me to read his book in advance of publication.

[4] For an alternative view of feud, see J. Wormald, 'Bloodfeud, Kindred and Government', *Past and Present*, 87 (1980), and *idem, Lords and Men in Scotland*, pp. 115–36.

compromise or to fight, and varied also according to the strength and standing of those who arbitrated. But it may be called typical, in a way in which the great headline-hitting feuds were not. Despite Scotland's traditional reputation, such feuds were rare compared to the vast multitude of little feuds which involved individuals or small groups of people, and which were brought to an end by a well-understood procedure. It is important to stress that point. We may be too ready to contrast cases which came before the courts with private settlements, seeing in the first a formality and an authoritative quality which was lacking in the second. It is a false distinction. There was nothing casual about the private settlement, as the case of the dispute over the lands of Sandlaw and many others like it make clear. The point in common between the justice of the courts and of the private settlement is that both offered the chance to resolve dispute. The distinction, insofar as one can be drawn with any confidence, lay in the fact that the private settlement might be more effective. For the only certain way of ending a dispute lies in the ability to persuade both parties that the end has indeed been reached, and there is therefore no point in reviving and pursuing the quarrel; and in mid-sixteenth-century Scotland, that was still more likely to be achieved by the pressure brought to bear by the social *mores* of the locality than by outside intervention from above, by state or central court. It is this, more than anything else, which the case of Sandlaw illustrates.

The lands of Sandlaw lie three miles south of Banff, on the River Deveron (see fig. 8). They were good farming land – the farms of north and south Sandlaw still exist today – but their principal economic attraction was probably the fishing of the Deveron. In 1541, they were worth £1,000 Scots in outright sale[5]. They were an attractive property. Held by the Stewarts in the fifteenth century, they had ultimately fallen into the king's hands in 1505 because of the non-entry of James Stewart of Baddinspink (that is, the failure of the heir to pay his entry due, so that the rents of the property reverted to the superior, and could be granted by him as a 'feudal' casualty, like wardship and marriage). Two north-eastern families, the Ogilvies and the Bairds, now acquired an interest in them. In 1507, Thomas Baird of Ordinhuivis was granted the non-entry of the lands. Then in 1512 the Ogilvies came into the story, when James IV granted the lands themselves to Alexander Ogilvy of Deskford and his heirs. In the following year, Baird's widow Janet Maitland and their son George personally renounced all claim they might have to Sandlaw; the reason they gave was the formulaic one of 'good deeds and favours' done to them by Ogilvy, and while this phrase could often reflect reality, in this case it seems likely that 'good deeds' actually meant pressure put on the widow. Already a pattern in which the Ogilvies did better than the Bairds had been set[6].

[5] The pound Scots in the 1540s was equivalent to 4:1 sterling.
[6] For these incidents see *Registrum Magni Sigilli Regum Scotorum*, ed. J. Thomson and others, vol. 2, nos. 2133 and 3368; *Registrum Secreti Sigilli Regum Scotorum*, ed. M. Livingstone and others, vol. 1,

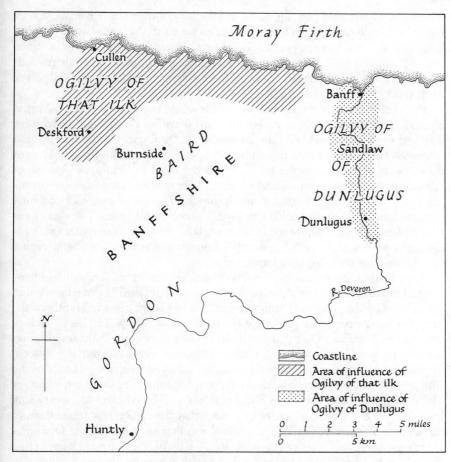

8 The dispute over Sandlaw

In 1532, the Bairds were given a second chance, when Ogilvy of Deskford –
now styled 'of that ilk', after the consolidation of his estates into the barony of
Ogilvy in 1517 – feued Sandlaw to George Baird of Ordinhuivis and his son
William; William was to have the sasine (that is, seizin – possession), George free
tenancy for life[7]. Both were probably dead by 1540, and certainly by 1541, in

---

no. 1413; Scottish Record Office (hereafter SRO), Abercromby of Forglen Muniments, GD 185,
   box 3, bundle 1.
[7] *Registrum Secreti Sigilli*, vol. 2, no. 1384; see also *Illustrations of the Topography and Antiquities of the*
   Shires of Aberdeen and Banff, ed. J. Robertson and G. Grub (henceforth *Aberdeen–Banff Illustrations*),
   vol. 3, p. 584. For the 1517 consolidation, *Registrum Magni Sigilli*, vol. 3, no. 166. Feu: a heritable
   grant in which land is given for a down payment (*grassum*) and an annual payment (feu-duty) for life.

which year Ogilvy sold both the lands and the superiority to his kinsman, Walter Ogilvy of Dunlugus. His grounds for doing so were that the lands had reverted to him because of the non-entry of the Baird heir, Alexander, who was then a minor under the tutelage of Thomas Baird of Burnside; and he provided Dunlugus with a letter of gift, giving him the non-entry and wardship of Sandlaw, and full power of distraint[8]*.

The problem was that this time the Bairds would not go away. On 16 August 1545, a signet letter to James earl of Buchan, sheriff of Banff, and his deputies directed them to enquire into the complaint by Dunlugus that he had warned Thomas Baird of Burnside, pretended occupier and tacksman (leaseholder) of Sandlaw, to remove from the lands, which belonged to Dunlugus because of Alexander Baird's non-entry, and which had been in his hands as superior for 'divers yeris bigane' (diverse years bygone); Thomas Baird had violently occupied the lands, and expelled Dunlugus's servants and goods. The sheriff was now ordered to take cognizance of the complaint, and if he found that the lands did indeed belong to Dunlugus, to expel Thomas and restore Dunlugus, paying him his lost profits[9]. Nothing happened.

For a further seven months, Thomas Baird held on in the lands of Sandlaw. Then a much more powerful figure than the sheriff of Banff became involved in the affair. On March 1546, Dunlugus and Thomas Baird came to Huntly castle, and there in the presence of George Gordon, earl of Huntly, and his two fellow arbitrators, Alexander Ogilvy of that ilk and George Gordon of Scheves, drew up a contract by which they settled their dispute over Sandlaw, and also agreed, apparently as a more minor matter, to end the enmity between them caused by the killing of Dunlugus's nephew Alexander and Sir John Christison, chaplain, by Baird and his accomplice James Baird of Forfalds. The contract was a very long and detailed document, which gives a somewhat contradictory statement about the settlement (App. XXVIII). The lands of Sandlaw were adjudged to Dunlugus on two grounds: first, a letter of reversion, given by Walter Baird to Ogilvy of that ilk, which has not survived[10]; and second, the non-entry. It was the letter of reversion which was used to put Sandlaw firmly into Dunlugus's hands. He was to act as assign for Ogilvy of that ilk, and require Alexander Baird and his tutor (legal guardian) Thomas to come to the parish church of Banff to receive 600 merks Scots – not much less than half the value of the estate – and a letter of tack and bailliery of Sandlaw for nineteen years[11]. Thomas Baird would then have to acknowledge that the lands were lawfully redeemed, and hand over to Dunlugus all charters*, instruments of sasine and other evidence of title made to William, George or Alexander Baird, and as Alexander's tutor give up all claims or title for

---

[8] SRO, GD 185, box 2, bundle 9.   [9] SRO, GD 185, box 2, bundle 11.
[10] A letter of reversion was one promising that, on certain conditions, the recipient of a grant of land would restore the land to the grantor.
[11] Tack and bailliery was a lease of land and office of bailiff.

the future. In return, Dunlugus would discharge him of all debts owed on the lands, in particular the 1,000 merks non-entry money due since the death of William Baird. Then came the final blow to the Bairds:

And therefore the said Thomas Baird, as tutor to the said Alexander and in his name, shall remit and give up the right and title of right that the said Alexander and Thomas Baird his tutor has or may have in and to the said tacks and bailliery of the said lands of Sandlaw for ever, so that it shall be lawful to the said Sir Walter Ogilvy and his heirs to labour the said lands of Sandlaw with their own proper goods in all times to come after the redemption to be made thereof as is said, or to set the same to tenants as they shall think expedient, notwithstanding the said letters of tack and bailliery for nineteen years, which letters of tack and bailliery in token of the said renunciation the said Thomas shall render, restore and deliver again to the said Sir Walter immediately after the said redemption.

By contrast to all this, the settlement of the murder got only a brief, almost casual reference:

And also the said Sir Walter shall remit the said Thomas Baird and James Baird of Forfalds all rancour that he has or in any wise had against them or any of them for the slaughter of the late Alexander Ogilvy his brother's son and Sir John Christison chaplain, and shall deliver a letter of slains in due form to them therefore for himself and all that he has control over, between this and the feast of Whitsun next; and shall from thenceforth stand in amity and kindness with the said Thomas and James Baird, and shall maintain and defend them as his special servants and men in time to come, in all their actions, quarrels and controversies lawful and honest against all men during their lifetimes as it accords a gentleman of the manner of Scotland to maintain and defend his man and servant, and therefore the said Thomas and James Baird shall become and by these presents become thrall men and servants to the said Sir Walter during their lifetimes, and shall make sufficient letters and bonds of manrent thereupon in the best form as the said Sir Walter will devise, the queen's grace the [public] authority and those who have alread infeft them only excepted[12].

What is lacking here is the kind of detail so carefully recorded in the settlement over the land. We are not told what compensation had been given. Normally there would be a monetary payment, or some other tangible form of compensation, as well as the making of bonds of maintenance and manrent which were designed to bring the former combatants into a close and peaceful relationship, but these things are not spelt out here[13].

In all, the curious thing about this contract is that it presents such a confusing picture. Such financial advantage as there was had been to Baird, paid 600 merks and relieved of a debt of a further 1,000 and more. At the same time, he was forcibly reminded of his position of weakness. The phrase 'thrall men and servants' is unique, suggesting a degree of servitude which was not in fact a

---

[12] A letter of slains was that given by the victim of crime or his principal kinsmen to the wrongdoer, stating that he was fully assythed (compensated), and enmity between them was at an end. 'Kindness' denotes kinship. 'Manrent' meant allegiance; for discussion of bonds of manrent, see Wormald, *Lords and Men*. 'Infeft' means legally put into possession of heritable property.

[13] For examples, Wormald, *Lords and Men*, pp. 127–9; *idem*, 'Bloodfeud', 73–4 and 89–90.

feature of the agreements of maintenance and manrent made among the higher and lesser nobility of early modern Scotland. The presumption must be that there was more to the settlement of the murder than the document bothered to say, and that Baird did not simply get off with nothing more than a humiliating phrase, but that it was felt unnecessary to spell out the whole agreement. What we are witnessing, in other words, is a little Banffshire example of a much wider phenomenon: that it is in civil rather than in what we would now call criminal matters that complexities arise, leading to a fuller documentation – and more lucrative business for the lawyers.

But the same impression of victory which was not total victory for Walter Ogilvy of Dunlugus emerges from other parts of the contract too. Dunlugus was firmly in the saddle. He could use the insulting term 'thrall men'. Elsewhere in the contract he could give the knife a further twist by dragging in a very touchy subject when he asserted that Baird should have to answer in his court when charged, and grind his corn at his mill. He could insist that the bond made by the Bairds should be drawn up according to his dictate. He could also insist that

the said Thomas Baird as tutor foresaid shall contract and by the tenor hereof contracts with the said Sir Walter Ogilvy in the most large and ample form the said Sir Walter or his friends can devise, and at the redemption of the said lands shall seal and subscribe letters of contract in the best form the said Sir Walter will devise to the effect above written, and shall be obliged and asked in the official's books of Aberdeen to fulfil the same under pain of cursing (excommunication) in the name of the said Alexander Baird pupil, and make faith before the said official that the same contract is made in evident utility and profit of the said Alexander pupil, and therefore desire the authority of the said official as judge ordinary to be interposed thereunto in the largest manner the said Sir Walter can devise.

And as if that amount of devising on Walter's part – and the amazing reference to the unfortunate Alexander's utility and profit – were not enough, the contract ended with yet more promises of proliferating documentation; both parties, having sworn on the gospels to observe the terms of the contract, promised that they

shall of new subscribe and seal each to the other the double and copies of the principal as often as they shall be required both in paper and parchment.

On the other hand, the cash payment and cancellation of the debt were not the only sweeteners given to Baird. The friars of Banff had leased the lands of Dalhauch to Baird, who had defaulted on payment of his rent. His position was further threatened because, since his lease was given, Dunlugus had become feuar of the lands. But not only did Dunlugus not use his position to get rid of Baird; he actually promised to allow him to enjoy his lease for its nineteen-year term, or even to give him a new nineteen-year lease, provided he paid what was owed to the friars, and kept up payments to Dunlugus[14].

[14] SRO, GD 185, box 2, bundle 11.

The immediate question which arises from this case is how fair was the judgement. At first sight, the arbitrators look suspect. The normal practice was for both parties to a dispute to nominate arbitrators, but there is no indication that it happened in this case. Ogilvy of that ilk may certainly be suspected of being partial; indeed, not only was he related to Dunlugus, but he had particular reason to please him. Relations between the two had not always been smooth; they had themselves been involved in a land-dispute in 1519. More immediately, Dunlugus and Ogilvy's heir James Ogilvy of Cardell had made a bond of friendship, promising mutual assistance, in 1543. Two years later, on 20 June 1545, Ogilvy had disinherited his son in favour of John Gordon, third son of the earl of Huntly[15]. Small wonder, then, that Ogilvy wanted to do what he could for a kinsman who, had he not been given support, might well support his disinherited son.

This was not Ogilvy's only contact with the Gordons. The families were linked by marriage; both Ogilvy's mother and his second wife were Gordons, and his daughter was married to another Gordon[16]. We get some hint of the closeness of the relationship between him and the earl from witness lists. Periodically he travelled south to Huntly from his seat at Deskford. The sale of Sandlaw to Dunlugus in 1541 was made in the presence of the earl. And among Gordon documents which he witnessed are two bonds of manrent, made on 10 and 12 May 1543, which suggest that he was on sufficiently close terms with the earl to be a guest at Huntly castle[17]. In one sense, Huntly was the most obvious man in the North East to be the principal arbitrator in a north-eastern feud. He was by far the most powerful magnate in the area, and therefore the most likely to impose judgement. But in another, even allowing for the fact that in what was a small local society the earl was likely to have personal contacts with parties at feud, the relationship between him and Ogilvy does make his presence appear very one-sided. And when one adds to that the fact that the third arbitrator, George Gordon of Scheves, was kinsman and dependant of Huntly, the cards look increasingly stacked against the Bairds.

The impression of obvious partiality changes, however, when the parties to the dispute are considered. Comparison of the relative positions of the Ogilvies and the Bairds reveals the surprising fact that the stronger family was forced to resort to calling in very powerful support indeed in order to obtain satisfaction from the

---

[15] For the 1519 dispute, SRO, GD 185, box 2, bundle 6, *Aberdeen–Banff Illustrations*, vol. 2, pp. 102–3, and *Registrum Magni Sigilli*, vol. 3, no. 215. For the 1543 bond of friendship, GD 185, box 2, bundle 10. The disinheriting of Ogilvy's son is described in J. Balfour Paul (ed.), *Scots Peerage*, vol. 4, pp. 21–5; the reasons why he so firmly threw in his lot with the Gordons can only be guessed at, for there is no record of the presumed quarrel between Ogilvy and his son. The son was eventually restored, in the aftermath of the Gordon rebellion of 1562, in a series of charters and agreements between 1562 and 1567.

[16] *Scots Peerage*, vol. 4, p. 22.

[17] SRO, Gordon Castle Muniments, GD 44 13.8.20 and 13.8.24, partly printed in *Miscellany of the Spalding Club*, ed. J. Stuart, vol. 4, pp. 208–10.

weaker. The map of Banffshire shows very clearly just how weak and apparently vulnerable the Bairds were, for their lands lay mainly in the forest of Boyne, surrounded on three sides by the lands of Ogilvy of that ilk and Ogilvy of Dunlugus (fig. 8). The lands of Ogilvy of that ilk lay mainly to the west in the area surrounding and stretching south of Cullen, the burgh itself being firmly in Ogilvy's control; and Ogilvy also possessed the lands to the north of the Bairds[18]. These were paralleled to the east by the lands of the rising and ambitious laird Ogilvy of Dunlugus, whose successive styles of Baddinspink, Monycabok and finally Dunlugus reflect his territorial acquisitions which were concentrated in the northern stretches of the valley of the Deveron, and which were erected into the barony of Dunlugus in 1536[19]. His family controlled the burgh of Banff; Ogilvies were provosts and parliamentary commissioners, Ogilvies got the best share of the burgh's fishings on the Deveron, Ogilvies were natural protectors of the friars of Banff[20]. All this makes Dunlugus's desire to obtain Sandlaw and also Dalhauch readily understandable, for both lay between Dunlugus and the burgh of Banff in precisely the area where the laird was so successfully establishing himself.

The Bairds are more shadowy figures, but the one thing which is clear is that they were always in the galling position of having to play second fiddle to the Ogilvies. They too had an interest in Banff, but they served as baillies under Ogilvy provosts, got less good fishings, got a lease from the friars where Ogilvy got a feu. Records show them, however, not just as underdogs, but in a bad light. George Baird of Ordinhuivis's major if unsubstantiated claim to fame is that he reputedly had thirty-two children; if this was an attempt to redress the dynastic balance with the Ogilvies, it failed. What is certainly known is that his tenure of the office of sheriff-depute of Aberdeen was distinguished only by a complaint which was upheld by the lords of council in 1539 against James earl of Moray, sheriff of Aberdeen, and his 'pretendit schireff deputis', Baird and others. His father Thomas is rarely mentioned, but in 1490 he turns up as the subject of an order by the lords auditor to pay to Alexander master of Huntly a last of salmon; and because he had been 'oft tymis callit and nocht comperit' (often called and not turned up), his lands were distrained[21]. And the Sandlaw dispute itself shows Baird of Burnside having murdered a relative of Ogilvy's, failing to pay for legal entry, and at the same time defaulting on payments for Dalhauch. While all these

[18] The burgh had given its bond of manrent to James Ogilvy of Deskford in 1472: *Annals of Banff*, ed. W. Cramond, vol. 1, pp. 20–1.

[19] *Registrum Magni Sigilli*, vol. 3, no. 1614.

[20] Banff, like Cullen, had made a bond of manrent to Ogilvy of Deskford in 1472 in return for Ogilvy's maintenance: *Annals of Banff*, vol. 1, pp. 20–1. But by the late 1520s, the dominant figure in the burgh was Ogilvy of Dunlugus, not surprisingly in view of the geographic distribution of the Ogilvies' lands: *Annals of Banff*, vol. 2, pp. 267, 247–8, 271; SRO, GD 185, box 2, bundle 13.

[21] For the 1490 incident: *Acts of the Lords Auditors of Causes and Complaints*, ed. T. Thomson, p. 138; and for the 1539 complaint: *Aberdeen–Banff Illustrations*, vol. 4, pp. 231–2.

things were no doubt common enough, the Bairds do seem to have made a particularly consistent habit of 'pretendit' claims and failure to appear and pay up, which can hardly have endeared them to those who had to deal with them, and particularly to the man whom Thomas Baird of Burnside had successfully kept out of the lands of Sandlaw for which he had paid £1,000, for five years.

And yet they were not without support. Huntly had no known hostility to the Bairds; in 1540 he had given the precept of sasine to George Baird as heir to his mother of lands in the forest of Boyne – and the witnesses had included both Ogilvy of that ilk and Ogilvy of Dunlugus[22]. If this relationship between Huntly and the Bairds may be regarded as perhaps neutral, the one between the Bairds and Ogilvy of that ilk had certainly been closer. Ogilvy had given the Bairds the lands of Sandlaw in the first place, in 1532; and in 1537, when the latter were disputing with George Mortimer of Auchlady over debatable lands and fishings between Sandlaw and Auchlady, they acted with the advice and counsel of their superior, Ogilvy, and used him as the principal of their chosen arbitrators[23]. It would be too simple, therefore, to see the Ogilvies as a united kin group in terms of their own activities, or – whatever the theory of kin solidarity – as a cohesive force, lined up with their backer Huntly to victimize the weaker Bairds.

The terms of the contract itself certainly do not suggest victimization, although they do reflect a certain human pleasure in emphasizing that the Bairds were the losers. Whether the decision that Sandlaw belonged to Dunlugus was strictly correct in legal terms, cannot now be known with complete assurance, not because the arbitrators were amateur laymen – for they had notaries to advise them – but because the evidence is incomplete; we may accept the argument about non-entry, even if it is known only from Ogilvy sources, but the letter of reversion issued by Walter Baird has not survived, and its terms are therefore not fully known. But the presumption must be that the decision was correct, and more than this, immense care was taken to ensure that it was; hence the use of two arguments where either one would have been sufficient. It may have been socially hard on the Bairds that Dunlugus chose to exercise his legal right as superior and demand his lands back because of their non-entry, rather than giving them the chance to pay up, but there is little doubt that he had the right, and was exercising it only after several years of defaulting. Equally, if there was a letter of reversion, then he could reclaim his lands when he could fulfil its conditions, and at least one of its presumed conditions, the payment of 600 merks, was indeed fulfilled, even if the other, the letter of tack and bailliery, was not, except in the most nominal sense. The fact that the 600 merks was paid in any case takes us away from the purely legal into that equally important area of dispute settlement, its social consequences. By invoking the letter of reversion, the arbitrators could ensure that although Baird lost the main battle, he did not lose everything.

[22] SRO, GD 185, box 2, bundle 18.   [23] SRO, GD 185, box 3, bundle 1.

Dunlugus had to make two substantial concessions, over this and over the lands of Dalhauch, which it would have suited him very well to take into his own hands. It was an attempt to ensure a point of fundamental importance: that the loser to a case should not lose so badly that he would not accept the settlement, but re-open the matter, thus provoking further dispute and possible violence. It is a point which would perhaps weigh more in a small society where men were deeply conscious of the dangers of rivalry and hostility between neighbours, than in one where the judiciary is increasingly cut off, by education and lifestyle, from the majority of those with whose cases it deals; and it provides the counter-argument to the assumption that where justice was personal, it was also necessarily partial.

The settlement shows concern with both physical symbolism and documenta-tion. 'And for the observing of the premisses', said the contract, 'either of the said parties is bound, obliged and sworn to the other by their great oath, the gospels touched.' We are not told what form the 'great oath' took, but this clause is entirely standard in Scottish agreements of the period. After the Reformation, the touching of the gospels was dropped, but it was replaced by the phrase 'in the most sure style of obligation that can be devised'. Both are a reminder that the mentality of sixteenth-century Scotsmen was still very far from that which would accept a lawyer's letter through the post, despite the extensive writing involved in the case. The same thing applies to the ceremony which finally ended the dispute, the meeting at the parish church at Banff on 30 April 1546. The six weeks between the contract and the meeting were used, by Dunlugus at least, to very good purpose. He sent his servant Bernard Stewart out into the locality to advertise the meeting in advance. Meanwhile, he himself went to the parish church of Banff on 21 March 1546, a week after the contract was made, where, as assign to Ogilvy of that ilk, he had the letter of reversion of the lands of Sandlaw read out, and cited and summoned 'with due intimation' Alexander and Thomas Baird to come to the church on 30 April and receive their 600 merks and letter of tack and bailliery, adding that the lands would be redeemed on that day whether the Bairds came or not; if they defaulted, the money and letter would simply be handed over to the curate of Banff for safe-keeping[24]. In fact, Baird of Burnside did come. The lands were duly redeemed, the letter of tack handed over – and, as its survival among the Ogilvy papers indicates, handed back.

The essential retention of physical acts and imagery can be paralleled by other cases of the same period. A resignation of tofts in Banff by the Bairds in 1537 was to be done 'per fustim et baculim ut more est'[25]. In 1548, David Barclay, deputy to the Steward of Fife, was badly caught out when he was required to hear a case concerning Alexander Spens, son and heir of Spens of Wolmerston, who successfully claimed to be tried by the ancient law of Clan Macduff; he had

[24] SRO, GD 185, box 2, bundle 11.
[25] SRO, GD 185, box 2, bundle 18: 'by rod and staff as the custom is'; cf. *festuca**, and Fouracre above, p. 34.

remembered the wand by which he gave Alexander the king's peace, but he had forgotten his seal, and therefore had to borrow his father's in order to produce his written testimonial[26]. To some, it seems, the new fashion of documentation had not yet become second nature. Even documents themselves still retained something of the aura of a symbol. Precepts of sasine had to be in Latin, because they had always been in Latin; and so, in 1540, Huntly's precept in favour of George Baird contained the provision 'latina ac in vernacula seu Scotorum lingua exponitura dictis ballivis'. Earl Warenne with his rusty sword in thirteenth-century England had his echo in mid-sixteenth-century Scotland[27].

On the other hand, the demand for documentation had reached an almost obsessional level – which is perhaps not inconsistent with the idea of the document as a symbol. The immense and sometimes repetitive detail of the contract, the requirement that it be registered in the official of Aberdeen's books, the provision for more and more copies, on paper and parchment, all testify to the care taken to leave nothing unwritten; in that sense, it begins to look very like a legal document of modern times. It was written on parchment, which testifies to its importance; the widespread use of paper since *c.* 1500 had so largely replaced parchment that the latter was now used only for particularly solemn and weighty documents. It was beautifully written, by the Banff notary James Currour; his name appears only in the list of witnesses, because this was not a notarial instrument, but the hand is identical to that in documents known to have been written by him. He was, it seems, associated with the Ogilvies; it was he who wrote the notarial instrument attesting Bernard Stewart's appearance at Fraserburgh to announce the forthcoming ceremony at Banff, and he turns up in other Ogilvy documents. More generally it is notable how much the Sandlaw case was surrounded by notaries. Every stage after the contract had its notarial instrument, including the grant made four years after the case had been settled, when Dunlugus gave Sandlaw to his son and heir George. Whereas the letter of tack and bailliery, given to and returned by the Bairds, was a truly horrible document, scribbled on paper, the notarial instrument recording the meeting at Banff was quite superb. The number of notaries involved was remarkable. The instrument of 21 March 1546 had three, all of whom put on their splendid notarial marks; that of 30 March, relating to Bernard Stewart, had two, one being among the witnesses; and that of 30 April no fewer than four[28]. It has been estimated that about 70 per cent of notarial instruments had one notary; only 2 per cent as many as three; and four was very unusual indeed, and unexpected in a

[26] *The Practicks of Sir James Balfour of Pittendreich*, ed. P. McNeil (henceforth *Balfour's Practicks*), vol. 2, p. 511.
[27] SRO, GD 185, box 2, bundle 18: 'Latin and in the vernacular or language of the Scots should be expounded by the said baillies'. On Earl Warenne, see M. T. Clanchy, *From Memory to Written Record*, pp. 21–8.
[28] SRO, GD 185, box 2, bundles 11 and 18; box 3, bundle 1.

case like this[29]. Great care was being taken to bring every possible formality to this settlement. It may have been because of a high level of tension between the disputants which was itself the product of their claustrophobic proximity. It may have been that Dunlugus, although he resorted to the private settlement rather than the courts, was a man of litigious cast of mind, with a taste for as much legalism as possible. It may have been, more generally, the result of the fact that Dunlugus and Baird were both examples of the new phenomenon, the literate laird, who was coming into existence in the late fifteenth and sixteenth centuries, and who would change the face of Scottish governmental and legal practice, and Scottish society with it. Both parties signed the contract with their own hands[30].

What, then, does this case tell us about dispute settlement in sixteenth-century Scotland, and how does it relate to the earlier dispute settlements analysed in this book? To begin with, it may provide a yardstick for assessing the complex and changing rôle of the state. We are seeing, in the Sandlaw case, the dispute settlement at a very highly developed stage of its existence, and one obvious contrast with at least some earlier forms is that it did not invoke public authority. In part, this was because public authority did not want to be invoked. Kings of fifteenth- and sixteenth-century Scotland did interest themselves in 'deidlie feids' (deadly feuds), those which were primarily of a criminal nature. In the first place, their rôle as justice-giver was linked mainly to the need to provide peace and security for their subjects' lives and livelihood. Secondly, even if some of them had to be bullied into fulfilling their obligations, and were criticized for lack of interest, there was a financial advantage to them in criminal justice when it was the subject of settlements whose procedures paralleled the procedures of the Sandlaw case and others which dealt mainly with civil matters. Letters of slains, given by the victims of crime or their kinsmen to the criminals, acknowledging themselves to have been assythed, were the preliminary to the royal remissions, by which they were restored to the king's peace and for which, of course, the king charged; kin and king co-operated in the justice of the feud[31]. But in property cases, there was no need to bring in the king; the local procedure was entirely adequate. Yet to say that, as the Sandlaw case reminds us, is to make too clear-cut a distinction; this whole subject is a good deal more fudged than historians – and particularly legal historians – might like. For Sandlaw involved a murder as well as civil dispute, and it is quite clear that violence, causing injury or death, was very often a part of property disputes before they reached the court or the arbitrators. It is not possible, in mid-sixteenth-century Scotland, to draw a dividing line between criminal and civil justice, precisely because the procedures for dealing

[29] I am indebted to Dr R. J. Lyall, University of Glasgow, for the statistics about notaries.
[30] For discussion of lay literacy, see G. G. Simpson, *Scottish Handwriting*, pp. 8–12; J. Wormald, *Court, Kirk and Community*, pp. 68–70; R. J. Lyall, 'Two of Dunbar's Makars: James Affleck and Sir John the Ross', *Innes Review*, 27 (1976), 99–109.
[31] Wormald, 'Bloodfeud', 78–86.

with both had not yet been entirely separated; compensation to the kin, imposed by the kin or by arbitrators, rather than punishment by public authority, was still an acceptable way of dealing with crime[32]. Involvement by the crown was therefore involvement in one area of dispute settlement, its violent side, and the crown came in not to exact retribution but to underwrite the settlement, where the violence itself was the principal matter of dispute. To discuss the rôle of the monarchy in this way is to remove the constitutional shroud which has clothed the high medieval and early modern English monarchy and has affected the perception of its Scottish counterpart, and to highlight instead its practical, rather than its theoretic rôle. What this suggests is that Scottish society by the sixteenth century had an extraordinary degree of confidence, both in public authority and in private arbitrators. The ruler did not have to emphasize his rôle as justice-giver; the arbitrators did not need to remind people forcibly of their sanction. There was now little conscious appeal to models of kingship or precedents of the past because there was no uncertainty about the established success of present procedures as they operated both within and outwith the courts, to cover both criminal and civil matters. We are looking at a very pragmatic society. This has made sixteenth-century Scotland appear under-developed, compared to both contemporary and earlier societies; and comparison with Carolingian Francia or later Anglo-Saxon England, let alone societies to the south in that period, may indeed suggest that the impression is valid. But this book has shown that most of Europe before the twelfth century had, on the one hand, surprisingly 'advanced' systems of state intervention in disputes, and, on the other, an understandable faith in more local assessment. The real point about this study of a characteristic Scottish dispute in the Renaissance period is its demonstration that the justice of kin, lord and locality could simultaneously become as sophisticated as that of the king, and that both could work together, without fuss or elaborate theory, with success and in harmony.

The argument may be taken further simply because Sandlaw, unlike much that is discussed in this book, was an out-of-court settlement. The emphasis in Scotland, like many but not all of the early medieval cases, was on the local settlement. This did not mean that no Scotsman would travel in pursuit of a case. They did, to Edinburgh, and even, for matters which came under the jurisdiction of the church, to Rome; distance will not deter determined, and dissatisfied, litigants. But on the whole, they sought justice close to home, and turned to what seemed to them the most effective way of getting it. Dunlugus began with public authority, found it dilatory, and so resorted to private arbitration. But in terms of its procedures, the dividing line between public and private authority was as blurred as that between criminal and civil justice. The procedure used in the

---

[32] *Balfour's Practicks*, vol. 2, pp. 511–18.

private settlement could very well mirror that of the courts, for arbitration was common in both, and had been at least since the thirteenth century. Scots lawyers, with their training in Roman and canon law, knew very well the rules governing the use of arbitrators and the more informal *amicabiles compositores*; and these rules, about the choice of arbitrators and the binding nature of the decree arbitral, could cover the private settlement just as much as the case which came before the courts[33].

There was, therefore, no conflict between public and private justice. King, courts and private arbitrators worked in a harmonious triangle. A crucial reason for this was that as yet it was the courts which might be the least effective, and that in itself indicates why, several centuries after the other cases in this book, the private settlement was still such a prevalent and effective force in Scottish justice. In the second half of the fifteenth century and in the early sixteenth, complaints and grievances were aired, in parliamentary legislation and literary works, not about the private settlement but about the corruption and lack of justice in the courts[34]. This was partly due to the fact that there was a real problem of competence. The only 'central' courts were parliament and council; the Session, set up in 1426, had at best patchy success and was, until the end of the fifteenth century, a peripatetic court which in effect behaved like a local one. Parliament was of course the supreme court. But the lords of council in their judicial capacity had very limited competence. They could try cases of possession; but cases of right still had to be referred back to the local courts. This was still the case when the Session was revived and re-established as the College of Justice in 1532. But gradually the lords of Session took unto themselves jurisdiction over cases of right, and were doing so by the 1540s[35]. Thus when Dunlugus asserted his right to Sandlaw, he did so at a time of legal flux. For it was not only the competence of the courts which was uncertain, but the law itself; the land law was still a jungle, for Dunlugus brought his case just before the beginnings of the great attempts to codify and rationalize Scots law, which were such a feature of the second half of

---

33 For further discussion of this point, see D. Maxwell, 'Civil Procedure' in *Introduction to Scottish Legal History*, pp. 414, 416; T. M. Cooper, *Select Scottish Cases of the Thirteenth Century*, pp. 49–50, 53–5; P. Stein, 'The Source of the Romano-Canonical Part of *Regiam Maiestatem*', *Scottish Hist. Rev.*, 48 (1969), 107–23. For rules about the use of arbitrators, see *Regiam Maiestatem*, ed. T. Cooper, bk 2, cc. 1–10, and *Balfour's Practicks*, vol. 2, p. 411–17.

34 See, for example, M. E. Rowlands, 'Robert Henryson and the Scottish Courts of Law', *Aberdeen University Review*, 39 (1962), and C. McDonald, 'The Perversion of Law in Robert Henryson's Fable of *The Fox, the Wolf and the Husbandman*', *Medium Aevum*, 49 (1980).

35 For discussion of the Session, see A. A. M. Duncan, 'The Central Courts before 1532' in *Introduction to Scottish Legal History*, pp. 329–39; J. J. Robertson, 'The Development of the Law' in J. M. Brown (ed.), *Scottish Society in the Fifteenth Century*, pp. 143, 146–7. Their increased jurisdiction is analysed by A. L. Murray, 'Sinclair's *Practicks*' in A. Harding (ed.), *Law-Making and Law-Makers in British History*, pp. 97–9, and H. L. MacQueen, 'Jurisdiction in Heritage and the Lords of Council and Session after 1532' in D. Sellar (ed.), *Miscellany of the Stair Society*, vol. 2, pp. 61–85.

the sixteenth century. Small wonder, then, that people still resorted to what was convenient, and offered a chance of a negotiated and practical settlement.

Yet this was the last great age of the private settlement in Scotland; and the final point about the Sandlaw case is that it shows not only the great strengths of such settlements, but the seeds of the decline that was shortly to come. These literate lairds Walter Ogilvy of Dunlugus and Thomas Baird of Burnside might remain in their locality, obsessed with their rivalries in Banff and Banffshire. But others like them did not so remain, but went off to Edinburgh and carved a place for themselves in central government and, above all, in the law[36]. The lay professional lawyer, who came from exactly the status group to which Dunlugus and Baird belonged, was the dominant figure of the very near future. Already the mass of documentation and the almost excessive use of notaries show how the private settlement was shifting ground. There were already clear signs of acquiescence in the greater elaboration and professionalism of the world of the lawyers and the courts; and as laymen, rather than clerics, became the lawyers, and as the Court of Session established its supremacy, so other laymen increasingly concurred in the need to turn away from amateur arbitrators like themselves, to the professional lawyers. This process was to coincide, in the late sixteenth century, with the heightened level of violence and disorder which accompanied the traumatic upheavals of Reformation, collapse of established authority in the reign of Mary queen of Scots, and economic hardship[37]. The change thus created was not the product of royal policy imposed from above. It was the result of a radical, even revolutionary change of attitude and expectation, in a changing world, among that massively influential group, the lairds – the lesser nobility – of sixteenth-century Scotland, who continued to use the justice offered by their own kind but now used it in the milieu which had formerly been virtually the exclusive province of churchmen.

Sixteenth-century Scotland has been characterized as an early medieval society with early modern evidence. That might seem to do little justice to the dispute settlement of early medieval or early modern times. But if it is seen as a comment on the strengths and sophistication of early medieval dispute settlement procedure, strengths which were to survive and flourish for centuries thereafter, then it makes very good sense indeed.

[36] G. Donaldson, 'The Legal Profession in Scottish Society in the Sixteenth and Seventeenth Centuries', *Juridical Review*, n.s., 21 (1976); Wormald, *Court, Kirk and Community*, pp. 151–9.
[37] The increased level of violence in the late sixteenth century is the finding of Dr K. M. Brown; I have benefited from discussion with him on this point.

Conclusion

THE RÔLE OF WRITING IN THE RESOLUTION AND RECORDING OF DISPUTES

As an alternative to papyrus or parchment, stone has certain obvious advantages as a medium in which records may be made and preserved. However, if the stonemason's skill is not necessarily less than that of the scribe, his rate of production is slower and the fruits of his labour more expensive and harder to store. Thus, it may be true, as asserted, that in Armenia under the rule of the Bagratid dynasty (861–1045) deeds of foundation and donation were recorded in the form of monumental inscriptions carved on stone, but if so such acts could only have been those of the highest and the wealthiest in the land[1]. Such a procedure would hardly be justified, if indeed possible, for the sale of a field, let alone of a pig. It is impossible to credit that a society, wedged between two such bureaucratic neighbours as Byzantium and the ʿAbbāsid Caliphate, and with such strong late Antique traditions of its own, did not make extensive use of written as well as carved records, the subsequent total disappearance of which its later history easily explains. The study of documents in the period with which this book has been concerned is the study of the accidents of survival.

This accepted, it would be little of an exaggeration to say that all of the successor states to the Roman empire are marked by their employment of writing in governmental and private transactions, and by their attempts, however circumscribed, to preserve the resulting records, and that for practical rather than antiquarian reasons. Such a generalization applies as much to the Islamic as to the Christian states that emerged in the former territories of Rome[2]. It is also indicated by the lack of such records and recording procedures in such areas as Ireland and the Basque regions, either outside or not fully integrated into the former empire, and also by the expedients that later had to be resorted to in those parts when the advantages of written title to property and accounts of transactions concerning it came to be appreciated[3].

[1] A. Ter-Ghewondyan, *The Arab Emirates in Bagratid Armenia*, tr. N. Garsoïan, p. 13.
[2] S. M. Stern, *Fāṭimid Decrees*, pp. 85–175.
[3] See Sharpe and Collins above, pp. 169–70, 103–4.

To a considerable degree the generic diversity and formal sophistication of documentary records stand in a direct relationship to a society's ability to preserve them. In the Roman empire, at least by the early second century AD, state archives existed in Egypt in the Temple of Hadrian and the Nanaeum, and a prefectural edict of AD 127 required copies of all contracts drawn up in the province to be deposited there[4]. This may be matched by the considerable variety of formally distinguishable classes of document that have survived from this period and the succeeding three centuries. In particular, in respect of the particular types of text that have been studied in this book, it is clear from Roman Egypt that any given dispute, if taken to law, would throw up a considerable quantity and range of documents, copies of which would be centrally preserved[5]. The beneficial effects of the climate and the penchant of the Egyptians for using papyri for the stuffing of mummified crocodiles, once their original value had been exhausted, have saved an incalculable number of such documents for posterity. The same is, unfortunately, not true of the rest of the empire, but there seems little reason to doubt that similar archives and records did exist elsewhere. These may well represent the earliest form of the town archive, known as *gesta municipalia*, whose existence in the later imperial period is well attested[6].

Some of these seem to have survived the periods of upheaval and often violent transition marking the end of Roman rule in the West. Gaul may have been particularly fortunate in this respect, but this is more likely to be a reflection of the accidents of the survival of evidence. The existence of the Ravenna papyri would alone alert us to the probability of continuity in parts of northern Italy, and Spanish urban institutions may have been considerably less disrupted than is often thought. It has also to be remembered that, considerable as the interests of the state or of the municipality might have been in the preservation of the records of the private legal transactions of the citizenry, such items lost their practical value with the passage of time and became so much clutter. Deliberate clearing out, as in the notorious nineteenth-century burning of the tallies of the medieval English exchequer, is not an improbability. In the case of Gaul survival of copies of documents that have been shown to have been taken from functioning early Merovingian *gesta municipalia* is due almost exclusively to the work of those compilers of formularies* who drew upon extant examples to provide the basis for their model texts[7].

In addition to such considerations, the erosion of much of the apparatus of

---

[4] *Oxyrhynchus Papyri*, vol. 1, ed. B. P. Grenfell and A. S. Hunt, no. 34, pp. 68–74; for examples of documents thus deposited see *ibid.*, nos. 68 and 70, pp. 127–9, 130–1.

[5] *Ibid.*, nos. 37 and 38 of AD 49, pp. 79–83, and no. 67 of AD 338, pp. 124–7.

[6] B. Hirschfeld, *Die Gesta Municipalia in römischer und frühgermanischer Zeit*; for some examples see *ChLA*, vol. 17, no. 653, pp. 23–59 (of AD 552/575), vol. 20, no. 712, pp. 99–111 (of AD 557) and vol. 21, no. 713, pp. 2–10 (of AD 572). Note the use of direct speech in the last.

[7] See Wood above, pp. 12–14.

central government in the post-imperial period restricted and ultimately terminated state interest, other than in Byzantium, in the preservation of local records. However, the later Roman empire also saw the appearance of new institutions, which increased in number in the succeeding centuries, with a very strong interest in keeping their own documents. These were the bishoprics and monasteries of the Christian Church. The greatest of the western dioceses, that of Rome, seems to have begun preserving its records at an early stage, although relatively few of these are now known, and not one is in its original state[8]. As its own rôle expanded so did the variety and sophistication of its documents, as well as their number, and as also did the size and organization of the notariate employed in creating them. Other dioceses may have been less interested or less successful, and in England the relative over-representation of Canterbury and Worcester in the realm of written records is striking, as is the preponderance of the charters of Lucca in the case of Italy prior to *c.* 850[9]. In Christian-ruled Spain, there is a fairly even distribution of the early records, whilst on the other hand St Denis is strikingly over-represented in the corpus of extant charters of the Merovingian period in Gaul[10]. The interest of such corporations as monastic houses in preserving their formal titles to the properties with which they were endowed, and also the records of disputes in which they successfully defended those titles, is obvious enough, and accounts for the survival of most of the known English, Spanish, French and Italian charters*.

With peripatetic courts, at least in the English kingdoms and Gaul, and the lack of fixed centres of government where the state could preserve its own records, assuming it wished to, churches and monasteries could also serve the interests of rulers and also of lesser lay patrons by functioning as their archives. At a very simple level this could involve the enscribing of lay charters in gospel books. More complex procedures must have lain behind the preservation of the documents of the royal house of Mercia in the monastery of Winchcombe. Whether this implies that copies of the documents drawn up for the Mercian kings were kept there is impossible now to determine, as these texts, together with the monastery's own charters, are long since destroyed, probably in the sack of 1151[11]. Other examples of such practices may exist. It is thought that the authoritative text of the *Forum Iudicum* was kept in a monastery under particular royal patronage in tenth-century León, which might also make a likely location for an archive[12]. However, it would be unwise to dismiss the continued existence of functioning royal archives attached to the court at too early a date. They still existed in late sixth-century Gaul, when that of King Chilperic, his *Regesta*, is

---

[8] R. L. Poole, *The Papal Chancery*, pp. 20–36.
[9] See Wormald and Wickham above, pp. 151, 107, 115–16.
[10] *ChLA*, vol. 14, *passim*, and review by David Ganz in *Speculum*, 59 (1984), especially 890.
[11] S 1436; W. Levison, *England and the Continent in the Eighth Century*, p. 252.
[12] J. Rodriguez, *Ordoño III*, p. 159.

recorded as being divided into different *scrinia*[13]. Such problems do not seem to have troubled the Byzantine state, in which the Roman traditions of the making and preserving of state copies of private documents apparently continued unbroken, and went hand in hand with close governmental interest in the overseeing and settling of citizens' disputes in the still fairly far-flung localities of its empire[14].

The survival of a developed bureaucracy and a substantial measure of lay literacy also enabled Byzantium to maintain a professional notariate. Moreover, a distinction could still be kept within it between those responsible for the formulation of documents and those whose humbler task it was merely to write them. Something of this was also able to survive, at least in the highest levels, in Merovingian Gaul, where in the royal charters the scribal act was performed by court notaries whilst the authentification of the document was the responsibility of the *referendarius*[15]. This system proved in practice to be effective in the detection of forgery. For Visigothic Spain, where the work of the royal writing office is now only represented by one fragmentary and palimpsested document, the evidence is insufficient for comparison to be made[16]. A professional notariate, and a largely lay one at that, seems to have continued to exist, or at least re-emerged, by the ninth century, in Italy[17]. In most of the other societies that have here been considered the scribes of documents were usually clerics. However, this in itself is not a valid point of distinction between two different forms of society. In Merovingian Gaul, for example, both lay and clerical scribes were employed in the writing of royal documents, whilst the Redon cartulary indicates that, in parts of Brittany at least, clerics and members of the religious communities could serve as scribes to the local population in drawing up documents of no immediate concern to their own house[18]. In Spain after the Arab conquest notaries, when named, were generally, though by no means exclusively, clerical, whilst the late Anglo-Saxon state, like its Carolingian neighbour, drew for its expertise in drafting documents entirely on the resources of its church[19].

It is also unwise to make too much of the fairly substantial variation in the forms of drafting and record making found between the practices of the different states that have been considered here, or even as between different regions of the same kingdom, and of which examples can be seen in the appendix of texts below. Differences of training and notarial tradition explain such discrepancies. Thus,

---

[13] Gregory of Tours, *Decem Libri Historiarum*, x. xix, ed. B. Krusch and W. Levison, *MGH SRM*, vol. 1; see also J. M. Wallace-Hadrill, *The Frankish Church*, pp. 47–8.

[14] See Morris above, pp. 126, 147.   [15] See Fouracre above, pp. 24–5.

[16] A. Mundó, 'Para una historia de la escritura visigótica' in *Bivium: Homenaje a Manuel Cecilio Díaz y Díaz*, p. 179 and pl. 3(a).   [17] See Wickham above, p. 112.

[18] D. Ganz, 'Bureaucratic shorthand and Merovingian learning' in P. Wormald, D. Bullough, R. Collins (eds.), *Ideal and Reality in Frankish and Anglo-Saxon Society*, pp. 62–3; also Davies above, pp. 68–9.

[19] S. Keynes, *The Diplomas of Æthelred 'the Unready' 978–1016*, pp. 19–28.

for instance, scribes writing documents for the Galician monastery of Celanova frequently cited in the preambles of the charters of donation the law in the *Forum Iudicum* permitting those without male heirs of the body to donate their property to the Church, whilst on the other hand none of the texts from the monastery of Sobrado in the same province make any reference to it[20]. Even formulary books were initially limited in the areas of their application, and in origin were probably no more than private compilations. There is little reason for surprise at the formal variation to be encountered between such geographically divergent texts as Frankish, Spanish or Celtic Latin charters; any more for that matter than there is to assume the existence of a prior uniformity in the drafting of such documents in the Roman period.

Where there is certainly an area of significant differentiation, and one for which notarial variations can provide a clue, is that between those societies in which scribes were employed by the courts to draw up records of the proceedings and other related texts, copies of which might be presented to the successful party in a dispute, and those in which the recording or otherwise of a case was left entirely to the latter's discretion. Although the second way of proceeding would usually involve attestation of the record by the judges and/or witnesses, it inevitably produced a simplification in the character of the records, a decline in generic sophistication, and a decrease in the standardization of the *formulae** employed in the documents. Leaving responsibility in the hands of the interested parties rendered the making of records optional and a process only likely to be favoured by those able to provide or to afford the services of a trained scribe. Ultimately an imbalance in the availability and employment of written records affected the judicial processes themselves. This is not just a question of geographical differentiation, although the northern fringes of the area encompassed in this book look more prone to beneficiary production of records than do the Mediterranean regions. Practices could change across a period of time. Thus, for example, Catalonia moved from the automatic court production of multiple and generically distinct documents in the mid-ninth century to exclusively beneficiary-produced records in the tenth, with an attendant decline in the quality and formal distinctiveness of the texts[21]. Such a process did not just occur in one direction only. This can be seen in comparing the very informal recording of disputes in those parts of the Gumay cartulary dating from the late Croatian period (*c.* 1080) with the stylized court reports drawn up by public notaries under Byzantine rule a century later, preserved in the same manuscript[22]. The character of the recording between the two is exactly

---

[20] R. Collins, '*Sicut Lex Gothorum continet*: Law and Charters in ninth- and tenth-century León and Catalonia', *Eng. Hist. Rev.*, 100 (1985), 508, n. 4.

[21] *Ibid.*, 491–2.

[22] *The Cartulary of the Benedictine Abbey of St Peter of Gumay (Croatia)*, ed. Edo Pivčevič; compare pp. 49–51 and 81–3 with pp. 89–91.

paralleled by the increasing emphasis on the rôle of written evidence in the cases of the later period.

For most of the societies considered here, and also the Islamic states of the Mediterranean, correctness of form in the drafting of nearly all documents was of crucial importance. In some cases, notably Merovingian Gaul, Spain and the Papacy, the survival of formularies, whose model texts can be compared with extant documents, confirms the value attached to formulaic drafting, and, as with some of the Visigothic slate documents, can even be used to identify the genre of some otherwise incomprehensible texts[23]. In general it is not difficult to detect the existence of standardized features in our legal records, even when, as with many of the Italian and Spanish texts, the use of direct speech seems to give a dramatic immediacy to the reporting – a Roman practice.

Contrary to a belief that such things are indicative of a high level of scribal incompetence, it could be argued that the existence of formularies, actual or implied, is a sign of the particular importance attached to the written word and its correct application: the more formulaic the drafting, the more sophisticated the notariate that is producing it. As the English common lawyers have long recognized, the more precisely drafted a document is, the harder it is to undermine it. In addition, complexity of drafting can be a useful first line of defence against forgery, and this can also extend to esoteric calligraphy that can only be read or written by a closed group of trained scribes; this is something that may well be as true of some of the early medieval cursives as of the English court hands of the seventeenth century[24]. In Italy, Spain, and Merovingian and Carolingian Gaul cases have been referred to in which one of the parties apparently attempted to pass off incorrectly formulated documents[25]. Perhaps in some of these cases, such as that from Tours in 857 involving the lady called Agintrude, justice may not always have been served, and amateurishness of draftsmanship became a convenient way to discredit evidence that was unacceptable for reasons less easy to make public. Certainly in Anjou in 1074 a case was lost because of a charter that had an 'i' in a place-name where it should have had an 'a'[26]. In general it looks as if those societies which displayed the greatest interest in the production of rigidly formal records were also those most suspicious of and best able to take steps to counter the existence of forged documents.

The overall importance of documentary evidence in the resolution of disputes has been emphasized by most of the contributors to this volume. Ireland here

---

[23] M. C. Díaz y Díaz, 'Los documentos hispano-visigóticos sobre pizarra', *Studi Medievali*, 7 (1966).

[24] M. Drogin, *Medieval Calligraphy*, p. 119; see also D. Ganz, 'Bureaucratic shorthand and Merovingian learning'.

[25] See Wickham, Collins, Wood and Nelson above, pp. 114, 92, 12, 56–7.

[26] Cartulary of St Aubin, Angers, no. 106; discussed in L. Halphen, 'La justice en France au XIe siècle' in his *A travers l'histoire du Moyen Age*, pp. 183–4.

proves to be the most obvious exception, with a society able to maintain a complex legal system that appears to have functioned satisfactorily without the use of written records. Even in this case, though, the picture is not uniform: the Columban houses at least look to have started to use a charter form that they may have borrowed from western Britain, and another type of record of endowment emerges with a number of instances of the writing of acts of donation into the contents of hagiographic texts, some of which may indeed have been devised principally for that purpose[27]. Likewise in Aragón, where a charter tradition is late in appearing, it is initiated by an experimental phase in which a variety of informal text forms are used before something close to the standard western European model emerges[28]. The same is probably also true of the earliest Dalmatian records, as preserved in the Gumay cartulary[29].

Even in societies and periods in which the written record predominated it was never allowed an exclusive rôle. Procedures existed to subject documents to testing, not only in terms of the internal soundness of their drafting but also by requiring support from evidence produced orally by witnesses and/or by the invocation of spiritual sanctions through oath-taking and ordeals. Inevitably, though, the greater the emphasis on the written record, the more determined could be the efforts made to circumvent or manipulate it. This could result in attempts by the stronger to force the weaker to draw up documents against their will and under duress, as reported in a late tenth-century case from Galicia[30]. It could also lead to attempts to take title deeds by force, as in the case from the other end of the period treated in this book of the 'Roasting of the Abbot', when in 1570 Alexander Stewart, Commendator Abbot of Crosraguel in Ayreshire, was apparently tortured by the Earl of Cassillis in order to make him hand over some of the abbey's charters[31]. In both these instances, the victims were able to secure the intervention of powerful protectors, and the notoriety of their deeds eventually led to the perpetrators of these acts of private enterprise losing their ill-gotten gains. There may have been other instances in which such actions paid off, about which we can know nothing because they were never the subject of complaint. The same applies to cases of the destruction of inconvenient documents, two Italian instances of which have been described above, which are again only known of because they proved unsuccessful[32]. This vulnerability of the

---

[27] See Sharpe above, pp. 173–4, and W. Davies, 'The Latin charter-tradition in Western Britain, Brittany, and Ireland in the early mediaeval period' in D. Whitelock, R. McKitterick, D. Dumville (eds.), *Ireland in Early Mediaeval Europe*; for an Irish hagiographic text see 'Do Macuib Úa Suanaig', *Bethada Náem nÉrenn*, ed. C. Plummer, vol. 1, pp. 312–16, vol. 2, pp. 303–7.

[28] See Collins above, pp. 103–4.

[29] *The Cartulary of Gumay*, pp. 41–87.

[30] Biblioteca Nacional, Madrid, MS 18387, 'The Cartulary of Samos', fol. 275r–v.

[31] *The Charters of the Abbey of Crosraguel*, ed. F. C. Hunter Blair, vol. 1, pp. l–li, vol. 2, pp. 7–15.

[32] See Wickham above, pp. 115–17; for a late tenth-century case from the French Pyrenees, in which a whole monastery was accidentally burnt down in the course of an attempt to destroy a charter, see *Instrumenta Ecclesiae Ausciensis*, XVI. 167, *Gallia Christiana*, ed. D. Sammarthani, vol. 1.

written word affected its utility in court, and in part gave impetus to developments in procedure, to the wider context of which attention must now be turned.

PROCEDURE AND PRACTICE IN THE SETTLEMENT OF DISPUTES

In Paris in the late twelfth century the scholar Peter the Chanter complained frequently and bitterly about the shortcomings of one aspect of traditional legal procedure: the use of ordeals. His observations on the visible unfairness of trial by ordeal have been used often to illustrate the dawning of a new and more rational attitude to the practice of law in the middle ages, and Peter's complaint continues to evoke an empathetic response in a latter-day mental climate in which obvious unfairness is instinctively condemned – one cannot but agree with him when, for instance, he points out that success in trials by the ordeal of hot water must be related to the state of the participants' hands: those with rough and calloused hands would always stand the better chance[33]. But ordeal, just one element in early medieval judicial procedure, has been treated all too often as typical of the whole mass of traditional practices, which have been accordingly characterized as arbitrary and irrational, as if they derived their form from custom developed so haphazardly that it is to us (or even to them) nigh on incomprehensible.

The studies in this volume present a very different picture – one showing that the particular forms of procedure used in the settlement of disputes do not represent arbitrary practices at all; they are, above all, historically comprehensible. Procedure in all our societies may be loosely described as customary, but the customs of each society reflect its particular historical development. There are, of course, common elements which influenced the development of all these European societies: most obviously they shared basic features in their social and economic structures; all of them were subject to the growing influence of an increasingly organized and self-aware religion, and in different ways all of them, except Ireland, were highly impressed with an idealized notion of a Roman past. But equally there is an infinite variety to the ways in which shared influences fared in the local context. It is in these terms that the background to developments in procedure will be discussed. We must then tackle our main theme: just how were disputes settled formally in these early medieval societies? We must look at the kind of people who ran the courts in which our cases were heard and we must try to see how judgement was arrived at and how it was made effective. Then, finally, we must survey briefly some of the basic differences in the ways in which procedure developed in our separate societies, before taking stock of the overall picture.

---

[33] For Peter the Chanter's observations on ordeals, see J. Baldwin, 'The intellectual preparation for the Canon of 1215 against ordeals', *Speculum*, 36 (1961), and for the hot-water ordeal in León, see Collins above, p. 87.

A recurring theme in our studies has been the impossibility of neatly separating early medieval judicial procedure into Roman and Germanic traditions, the two elements conventionally seen as its components. Instead we have seen procedures grow out of a pragmatic accommodation of traditional practices to present needs. Ian Wood's paper dealt explicitly with this process, for instance in the context of oath-taking in the Burgundian courts in the very early sixth century. This led to the use of trial by battle for those 'with an indecently frivolous attitude towards oath-taking'[34]. In view here (apart from the high profile of the church) is the development of vulgar law. To categorize its base as 'Roman' points usefully to the fact that its procedures developed with reference to practices which were likely to have been found in those areas directly controlled by the former Empire. To identify 'new' elements as 'Germanic', or at least 'non-Roman', is less useful because traditionally such an identification has been associated with a qualitatively different kind of law and legal procedure – a more primitive kind. But in the societies studied here such stark differences are not apparent in the ways in which people settled their disputes, not even in England, traditionally viewed as completely Germanic, nor in Ireland, viewed as if it were beyond comparison with other European societies in its legal development, nor, at the other end of the world, in Byzantium, the society which upheld Roman traditions most vigorously.

Of determinant importance to the development of dispute settlement procedures in all societies was the church. Churchmen appear in our case records as the presidents of courts, as judges, advocates, litigants and witnesses, and the case held in 857 in the ecclesiastical immunity of Tours shows the clergy running a court session just as if it had been a sitting of the count's court, the *mallus**[35]. This ecclesiastical involvement we can trace back, as has been suggested, to the post-Constantinian elevation of bishops as judges; and bishops as judges, and presidents, heavily influenced the development of judicial procedure in the use of oath-swearing and of the written word. In a more general sense too the influence of conventional religion on the courts was very marked: in all societies the practice of law was permeated with a sense of accountability to God. This served both to limit and to license the activities of courts.

The courts across Europe shared other features too. Nearly everywhere, they were, for example, organized around judicial tribunals rather than dominated by single judges. Generally courts had presidents, single, in tandem and occasionally in higher numbers, who certainly took a direct part in proceedings, but who shared judgement with others. The type of person to be president of a court was, most often, the local representative of a wider authority, be it the emperor's, king's, prince's or that of the holder of independent jurisdiction

---

[34] See Wood above, p. 17.
[35] For the Tours case, see Nelson above, pp. 56–7.

(immunity*)[36]. The president provided the link between local justice and higher authority, and his status can be related to the level at which cases were conducted. In Brittany, at village level, the president was often the local community leader, the machtiern*, but in Francia in cases held in the county court it was the king's representative, the count, who presided, and in the royal court the president was the king himself.

The nature of the links between president and wider authority varied according to the strength and activity of the latter. They are most visible, not surprisingly, in Byzantium, with the influence of the state 'all pervasive': at theme level the *stratêgos** in the Athos case intervened on direct imperial orders[37]. In tenth- and eleventh-century England links were strong enough to allow justice to be done in the name of the king in the shire courts, without the king putting in a personal appearance. In Francia, Merovingian legislation, following Roman tradition, fiercely upheld the memory of unfettered state control – in theory court-presidents could be executed for not following the correct procedure in court. But in practice, both in England and in Francia, the actual ability of the wider authority to direct proceedings through the president varied considerably from region to region and according to the fortunes of particular rulers.

The function of the court's president was to bring authority to bear on the judicial process. King, duke, count, bishop, *stratêgos*, katepan*, all, in person or by proxy, provided the facilities for dispute settlement – they 'held' the hearings. In this sense it did not matter whence their authority was derived, as long as in the immediate situation their power was sufficient to make defiance of the court's rules and rulings a risky business. The actual use of such power is not at all prominent in the cases presented here, but it is well to remember that the presidents who in these case records tend to appear as passive figureheads were, in other contexts, powerfully active: except in special circumstances, it is hard to imagine judgements being made against their wishes and interests.

In Ireland judgement was made by a single person, a professional known as the *brithem*. Elsewhere generally we have found collective judgement in an atmosphere of public witness. It was this, presumably, which encouraged people to use the facilities of the courts and to accept their decisions, and even in Ireland the forum for the *brithem*'s weighty decisions could be the *airecht* which supplied a communal audience for them. None of the societies studied here, Ireland apart, have provided clear examples of professional judges expressing judgement according to learned expertise. León and Catalonia come closest, with people called *iudices** functioning over several years across a whole range of judicial

---

[36] See Wormald above, pp. 197–9, for comment on the rôle of the president in the Sandlaw case, the one case in which we have detail on the person of the president and his relationship with the parties in dispute.

[37] For the Athos case, see Morris above, pp. 132–5. For discussion of the state and its rôle in dispute settlement, see below pp. 229–39.

activities and referring to a body of written law. In Byzantium, however, provincial court-presidents were generally amateurs. Italy, Francia and perhaps Brittany concur to a degree in having panels of judgement finders who were expected to be experienced in the practice of law but who cannot be described as professional judges. They range, without clear distinction, from *rachymburgi**, *scabini** and *boni viri* to *iudices*. Anglo-Saxon records do not allow such generalization, but we may observe that judgement was expressed in plural form, and judges were expected to be experienced and of good character. What emerges here is the impression that the tribunals were able to draw on a collective store of legal experience but that local standing was the major qualification for membership. In Byzantium status and expertise seem to have resided in different people in the *symponoi*, the panels of judges, with an *archon*, an amateur of high status, expected to take the advice of experts, the *kritai**. In Catalonia and León too the expert *iudices* were joined by local worthies, the *boni homines**, when judgement was made. Elsewhere status, expertise and function are impossible to separate, as K. Nehlsen-von Stryk has recently shown in an attempt to define the respective rôles of *boni homines* and *rachymburgi*[38]. In Francia the number of people joining in court decisions seems to have been infinite: in the seventh century the Amalbert case was held before at least fifty-six people and in the ninth century the panel for the Perrecy case included, apparently, 'all the noble men of the county, and many other men of the said county'[39]. The witness lists of some of the Anglo-Saxon records suggests that similarly large assemblies were involved in judgements in England too.

Given the collective nature of judgement in these societies it is natural that an important factor in arriving at judgement was discussion, between the judges themselves, and between judges, litigants and witnesses. The Byzantine legal handbook, the *Peira*, suggested that a rule of simple majority verdicts might operate amongst a panel of judges. None of our case records actually gives any indication of how the judges decided amongst themselves – the record simply presents any decision in plural form. What the records do show is that the accounts of what was said in court tend to make sense to the modern reader. In nearly all cases the litigants spoke directly to the president and tribunal, though in most societies women and churches were represented in court by advocates. Recorded speech always related to the matter of the dispute. The absence of rhetoric in early medieval court cases is very striking indeed.

Let us now look more closely at how the courts actually operated. Generally we can characterize their procedure as pragmatic – it followed logical sequences. If a litigant claimed to have a charter, he was told to produce it; if someone reckoned to be able to find supporting witnesses, the court would defer the hearing until

---

[38] K. Nehlsen-von Stryk. *Die boni homines des frühen Mittelalters*, pp. 83–92.
[39] For the Amalbert case, see Fouracre above, pp. 28–9, and for the Perrecy case, see Nelson above, p. 53.

they appeared; if a boundary was in dispute, members of the tribunal would accompany both parties to visit the area in question, and so on. Basic to the court's ability to act pragmatically was the way in which participants were bound to accept its rules once a case had been formally raised: what the courts asked them to do had to be done. Once the process had started, there could be no unilateral withdrawal without defeat and/or penalty. To ensure this there were various mechanisms, apart from a realization of the president's potential. In Italy people pledged themselves to carry out the court's instructions – that is, they 'wadiated'; and to step down both parties had to agree to 'diswadiate'. Breaking of pledge meant loss of property. In Francia and Spain the very formality of procedure was a vehicle for ensuring that people adhered to the rules. In León and Catalonia the hearing was divided up into stages, several of which had to be completed formally before a special officer, the *saio**, before the next stage was entered upon. In Merovingian Francia any abrogation of procedural norms halted the process, whereupon either the abrogation was acknowledged and punished, or the offender (or even both parties, despite any agreement to withdraw) lost the case.

Everywhere pressure from outside also played an important part in forcing people to accept the rules inside the courts. In Byzantium it was the public duty of officials to become involved in court proceedings, and once in train they doggedly followed the process until they were sure that it was complete. In England it was the king who ultimately guaranteed procedure in the courts, although active royal involvement may have been restricted to those cases in which particular kings had, or could be persuaded to take, a direct interest. In Brittany, the power of the *princeps* kept people in line in his own court. To the local courts in that region, however, there is a more informal aspect and here settlement of disputes could occur before the case reached judgement. The same social context also produced a significant number of informal, that is, out-of-court, settlements. But even in the latter area there were normative rules which people obeyed under pressure from the monitoring of community leaders. Throughout Europe, adherence to the rules of the court was further reinforced by a sense of agreement between disputing parties that they would stick to them: in all societies the acknowledgement of the necessity of abiding by the rules – as a prerequisite for a formal contest – underpinned all other measures employed to get people to accept set procedures[40].

This general acceptance of strict rules of procedure allowed the court to govern the way in which cases ran. It also produced a framework within which the

---

[40] Modern African parallels can be very instructive here. See F. Snyder, 'Colonialism and legal form: the creation of customary law in Senegal' in C. Sumner (ed.), *Crime, Justice and Underdevelopment*, pp. 90–121, and M. Chanock, 'Making customary law – women and courts in Northern Rhodesia' in M. Hay, M. Wright (eds.), *African Women and the Law: Historical Perspectives*, pp. 53–68.

disputing parties could approach each other as open adversaries in a legal battle witnessed and validated step by step. Although it is true that the formal dispute process could in practice produce compromise, any compromise tends to be hidden in the records behind statements of victory and defeat: the element of compromise becomes clear only when the record is very detailed, or when there is sufficient circumstantial evidence to show how a judgement worked out in practice[41]. Though courts could, and did, make judgements which produced compromise, most obviously in the realm of boundary disputes, compromise was nevertheless in the nature of a decision imposed by the court. As we have seen, the first step to dispute settlement was agreement to abide by the rules of the formal process, and what was attractive about the latter was its ability to produce a decision. It was to that end that its procedures had evolved. We must now examine this decision-making procedure.

Right in cases was usually established by reference to the past, access to which was sought through living memory or the written word. Although the written had no undisputed primacy over the spoken word, it is striking that the written word, in the form of charters, was regularly used as evidence in courts. Charters were presented to public view and for this there was a formal procedure, the *ostensio cartae** as the Italians described it, the English equivalent being the bishop who brandished his *bocan*. Italy, Francia, England and Brittany all supply cases which show that people readily challenged the veracity of charters: indeed there was a special procedure – *transpunctio* – for destroying invalid charters in court. This in fact shows just how useful charters were, and the general impression is that in all areas, bar Ireland, their use was increasing. We have already seen, in the previous section of the conclusion, how the recording of dispute hearings in itself produced charters. This process illustrates the link between charters and other forms of testimony: they were drawn up according to well-defined procedures and could encapsulate moments of sworn testimony, corroborated by public witness. On occasion courts would retrace the steps in the making of a charter, by going to the people named in it and asking them whether the written record faithfully represented their rôle in events stated to have taken place.

The Roman tradition was that all testimony was received by the courts under oath. The Hispanic regions laid very great emphasis on the taking of oaths before the *saio*. By the end of the fifth century Byzantine commentators, on the other hand, were not keen on the use of oaths in court, confining them to a confirmatory function. Generally it appears that oaths were added to testimony when the latter became a formal element on which judgement rested. Because the concept of perjury was inherent in the oath, it brought an element of the divine into court proceedings. The testing of witnesses before God is seen in an extreme form in Leonese courts which made selected witnesses undergo a hot-water ordeal, the

---

[41] The Sandlaw case is our clearest example of how compromise may be revealed when the record is more detailed. See Wormald above, pp. 199–200.

pena caldaria. Elsewhere witnesses were merely required to be 'suitable'. In our examples the clearest indication we have of suitability is from Italy, where in the Lucca case of 847, a witness was challenged on the basis that he did not have sufficient property to pay a fine (equivalent to his *wergeld**) should he be found guilty of perjury[42].

Amongst the qualified there were, however, different kinds of witnesses and there were also different kinds of oath-backed testimony. Witnesses were both partial and impartial. The former presented themselves in support of one of the parties in dispute; the latter came to the tribunal on a neutral basis. Partial witnesses, as in the Lucca case, had to be qualified to testify, but it seems likely that if their knowledge was especially useful, then their status might have been relatively less important. Impartial witnesses seem always to have been of relatively high local standing – though of course at village level this might mean no more than the leaders of a peasant community – and sometimes appeared in more than one case[43]. Their 'law-worthiness' approached that of the judges, and with the judges, their functions could extend beyond cases of dispute to public witnessing in general. Part of their public witness – if the *boni homines* of the Italian, Frankish, Hispanic and Anglo-Saxon sources are to be identified with the *nobiles viri, franci, idonei testes, seniores* of the Breton – was to observe that the procedure of the courts was correctly followed.

A separate form of partial witness was oath-helping*, when a party's supporters were asked to take an oath to demonstrate their support: in numbers of a dozen (or its fractions or multiples) supporters were required to recite *formulae* under oath, usually before relics, and with witnesses. In England numbers of oath-helpers could sometimes be spectacularly high – in two of the cases presented here there were over a thousand of them[44]. Everywhere it is clear that collective and public perjury was not chanced lightly. Although oath-helpers might do no more than demonstrate support, partial – like impartial – witnesses could also be asked to testify to the truth, or otherwise, of statements made by parties in support of their case. This could involve detailed questioning about the facts of a case, not just a request to deny or affirm statements. Searching inquiry into the facts of cases is seen too in the inquest* in which impartial witnesses were empanelled by courts to declare all knowledge relevant to a given case.

Traditionally much emphasis has been laid on the contrasts in basic legal principles underlying these different kinds of testimony: the simple request for a witness to be tested by oath is contrasted with the apparently more scientific attempt to judge according to objective facts assumed characteristic of the inquest. This shift in attitude has often been associated with the growth of the Carolingian state and with what have been seen as the latter's attempts to

---

[42] For the Lucca case, see Wickham above, pp. 106–7.
[43] See Davies above, pp. 80–1.
[44] See Wormald above, p. 160.

rationalize existing judicial institutions and practices. For this view there are basically two sources of inspiration: one an optimistic view of the Carolingian state as progressively distinct from its predecessors and neighbours, the other a teleological view of the evolution of law which homes in on those elements of practice which have import for the future – here, for instance, the development of the inquest is perceived as having exciting implications for the later evolution of the jury system. But in contemporary practice, distinctions between the different kinds of testimony were blurred. Our cases have revealed such easy permutations of the types just outlined that the traditional contrasts between them seem disquietingly anachronistic. We must observe, instead, that the combination between a *de facto* need for some knowledge of a given case, and the general fear of perjury the courts drew upon to solemnicize their proceedings, put oath-helping, witnessing and the inquest all in the same spectrum. As we have seen, courts were essentially pragmatic in their use of procedures: they drew on the type of testimony appropriate to the situation, and judgement drew its strength in part from the involvement of people of high local standing. As Susan Reynolds has recently remarked, it is to this general process of collective judgement that we should look for the origins of juries, not to one specific element in a whole range of testimentary procedures[45]. We must also observe that collective judgement and a pragmatic approach to testimony are found in all our societies except Ireland. It is wrong, therefore, to single out the Carolingian state as making a breakthrough into a more scientific approach, and, anyway, it is not at all clear that it was the Carolingians who 'invented' the inquest, or even that they used it to any great extent.

Testing by oath was only one way of submitting a case before God. God's judgement – usually referred to as precisely that – was also sought through the casting of lots and through the ordeal. In these practices divine judgement was revealed through a physical manifestation which was made certain by the use of a binary decision-making process. It is the reliance on chance and strength rather than on reason here which, from the twelfth century onwards, as we saw at the outset, has led to the classification of these procedures in particular, and early medieval judicial procedure in general, as fundamentally irrational. We must now examine this issue in greater depth. So far we have seen that the procedures adopted in the great variety of cases we have discussed have been more or less comprehensible. That is to say that we can understand why the participants reached the conclusions they did, or if we cannot, we can point to obvious gaps in the recording of the disputes as they have come down to us. So when we do see people using irrational procedures we cannot conclude that they were doing so because they did not know how to argue in a reasoned manner. Nor should we simply associate a more cerebral approach to law and legal practice with the

---

[45] S. Reynolds, *Kingdoms and Communities in Western Europe 900–1300*, pp. 33–4.

growing sophistication of states, an assumption which underpins the view of the Carolingians as great innovators in the practice of justice. Legal anthropologists present to us a wide range of ethnographic examples that show us societies with weak states, or no states at all, where people in dispute come to terms, or even coerce losers, through procedures that can be rough and ready and that can mix abstract legal norms and everyday morality; we do not think we use such procedures in western courts (though we do in our ordinary lives, all the time), but they make sense to us[46]. We would see them, in other words, as basically rational.

Students of medieval ordeal and oath-helping, the so-called irrational proofs, have shown us that God's judgement was, although not based on evidence, far from random; it was often only a ritualized version of community decisions, and, further, was normally a judgement of last resort, in genuinely difficult cases, or cases associated with so much social tension that only the most dramatic religious rituals could end them – it hardly mattered which way. By the same token, oath-helping was, at the very least, less violent than feud, an alternative means of mobilizing support for a cause. Often it simply expressed group solidarities that were necessary for any successful action in any court; indeed, the presupposition behind oath-helping, that a juror ran the risk of eternal damnation, sometimes visibly prevented people from taking the oath. Essentially, in all small-scale societies, people know what is going on; they know who is untrustworthy, who may be a thief, who has farmed this land, just as they know who is sleeping with whom. And that basic knowledge (generally accurate, although it may for the outcast, the weak or the unlucky, only be prejudice) underlies all the procedures, rational or irrational, of local dispute settlement, just as it is the basis too of collective judgement: the ordeal and the jury alike draw on it.

Actually, in the cases we have seen, ordeal, lots and oath-helping have not been all that visible. One could not argue from this that appeals to divine judgement were rare; our cases are, above all, disputes about land and status, in which documents (outside Ireland at least), sworn witness and inquest have an obvious rôle. For accusations of theft, or disputes involving violence and 'honour' in its various forms, that is, where there is suspicion rather than something which can be proved, most of our societies often employed various types of ordeal. Although few such cases were recorded by ecclesiastical archivists, their potential existence is clear in laws and is dramatized in formal narratives. But the cases we have, with their stable procedures and intelligible results, go a long way to reinforce the argument that people knew what they were doing when they went to law, even at the times when it was only to watch someone being thrown bound into a river to see if they floated. As Susan Reynolds has observed, we nowadays believe in the justice of the jury system, even though we may disagree with the verdicts of

---

[46] See, for examples, M. Gluckman, *The Judicial Process among the Barotse of Northern Rhodesia*, W. MacGaffey, *Custom and Government in the Lower Congo*, and S. Roberts, *Order and Dispute*.

individual juries; so one could with ordeal, if one accepted its basic premiss, that God was capable of direct intervention in human affairs[47]. Rational and irrational elements in early medieval judicial procedure do not, therefore, stand in opposition to each other, nor can they be separated and ascribed higher and lower places respectively in some continuum of human cognitive development[48]. Both must be seen as integral to a whole battery of procedures that drew its power in part from its very comprehensiveness.

The provision of procedural remedies for any eventuality, the presidency of powerful men, the involvement of men of high local standing in judgement and in impartial witness, the entrapment of parties – once they had begun a formal case – to finish or bust for sure, the lacquering of the whole process with a sense of religious accountability, all these were means to making binding the settlement of disputes in the courts. We must now look at what other means there were to give durability to settlements. Most obviously, in the light of these particular sources, court decisions were trumpeted in formal records. The use of notaries in court has already been discussed in the previous section of the conclusion. Suffice it to say here that a statement of public recording was an important part of procedure at the end of cases: in our cases the most detailed example of this is the ending of the Sandlaw dispute. Most often, notaries were named so that, as in the Tours case of 857, they could, if necessary, testify at a later date to the authenticity of the record. In Byzantium it was the actual writing down of the court's decision which activated it legally. At the heart of the record's usefulness lay its corroboration, simultaneously a device for expressing authenticity and a device, at least in the short-to-medium term, for invoking the support of those on record as witnesses to the proceedings.

In England, where the recording traditions are least formal, it is significant that the records speak of very large numbers of supporters for, and witnesses to, cases. Supporters appear here as oath-helpers, but mass oath-swearing is also mentioned in a corroborative context, and a further means to corroboration in England was the publication of legal business in gatherings of the shire court. Here an airing before the public was also associated with the backing of the ruler, and in addition, in legislation from the mid-tenth century onwards, kings called lords to guarantee the judicial process where their men were concerned. Everywhere, when very powerful people were in dispute, equally powerful people were involved in making binding the settlement of those disputes. In such cases norms of procedure may have mattered less than the exercise of power. But in cases of a more humdrum nature, procedures for upholding court decisions yet again involved that ubiquitous class of 'law-worthy' men which, generically, we

---

[47] Reynolds, *Kingdoms and Communities*, pp. 36–7.
[48] Cf. C. Radding, 'Nature, fortune and the passing of the medieval ordeal', *American Historical Review*, 84 (1979).

can term *boni homines*. These we have already seen associated with judgement, with impartial witness and, probably, with the monitoring of procedure in courts in general. In the same way, they bore public witness to the judgement and its execution. Normative Frankish legislation, the Edict of Chilperic, provides perhaps the clearest indication of this process, with the *rachymburgi* deciding in court to seize an individual's property in lieu of a fine, and then accompanying the count charged with that seizure to make sure that their own instructions were carried out properly.

Another method of guarantee was the use of named sureties, and naming extended the collective and public responsibility of the guarantors into the realm of personal obligation. With the possible exception of Byzantium, all societies, in their various ways, reveal the use of men who stood in surety for fines imposed by courts. The most common term for them in Latin is *fideiussores**: if a person who was fined defaulted, then his *fideiussor* was liable to pay instead or distrain to enforce payment. Their use is clearly associated with punishment procedures, and Wendy Davies cites an extreme example of this in the case of one Anau, whose sureties were required to kill him should he continue to flout the court's decision[49]. But in Brittany, Ireland and Italy those standing in surety are also visible implementing court decisions over a much wider range of business. The material from the Redon cartulary, the only collection considered here to deal with peasant communities in any detail, suggests that at village level the use of named sureties was the usual means to guarantee publicly acknowledged obligations. As has been suggested, there is no reason why at this level eastern Brittany should be markedly different from those other societies which shared an evolution from late Roman forms of local government[50].

At whatever level, the machinery of the courts described above seems to have been fairly accessible and in regular use. It is unlikely that in the great majority of cases presented in this volume a court was convened specially to settle the dispute in question. Frankish formal terminology makes this plain: the account of each case follows a statement that the court is sitting 'to hear the cases of many persons', and both Frankish and English legislation called for regular meetings of the courts. It is also clear that often a case was heard before several court sessions: in the Lucca case of 847, for example, the parties were in and out of court on four separate days, and in the case between the villagers of Zacors and the monastery of Celanova, the parties in dispute made at least three court appearances over a nine-week period[51]. In the unfolding of procedure courts were quite likely to postpone judgement until a later session, and from Byzantium, England and

---

[49] See Davies above, p. 77.
[50] The theme of parallel functions across a wide range of continental societies once subject to Roman rule is also basic to Nehlsen-von Stryk's observations on the *boni homines*.
[51] For the dispute between Zacors and Celanova, see Collins above, pp. 89–90.

Francia our case records show litigants seeking fresh hearings before a higher judicial authority. Where multiple hearings, before different courts, were allowed, cases could drag on for a very long time. When this was the case, usually people or institutions of importance were involved, but peasants too were prepared to have a crack at taking disputes before the higher courts. People of every status, it seems, were aware of what could be done in pursuit of their cause, and it is important to note that they thought it worthwhile doing a lot: in Francia the peasants in the Mitry case of 861 made a round trip of 120 km to seek a hearing in the royal court; in Byzantium the parties in the Athos case were prepared to make the 7–10 days' journey from Chalcidike to Thessalonika to bring their dispute before a court[52]. It was this desire to use the courts and the latters' provision of accessible facilities based on potentially comprehensive settlement procedures that gave the early medieval court its institutional value, a theme which is taken further in the next section of the conclusion.

So far we have seen that procedures have been directly comparable over the whole range of societies under discussion. The Sandlaw case shows us that centuries later, in the sixteenth century, similar procedures were used to settle disputes in Scotland. In this case a long-running dispute was finally brought to an end by entry into a formal process that drew its strength from public witness by men of high local standing. Settlement through these channels proved more effective than the invocation of distant authority, however great the latter's potential in this early modern state. Here similarity in function is the basis of comparability. Elsewhere it is both similarity in function and a common institutional inheritance that makes procedures look alike. But the point should not be stretched too far. Although one can draw attention to the ways in which, say, Byzantine and Irish practices worked to the same ends, there is a world of difference between the precise forms of procedure employed in the two societies – between the personal application of the law by the *brithem* in Ireland, and the emphatically bureaucratic framework of settlement in Byzantium.

We must also observe that the nature of the record makes different procedures appear comparable. Records of court decisions, naturally, advertise dispute settlement through the formal process, and tend to portray normative procedures operating smoothly. This is clearly illustrated by the progressive formalization of the court record in Italy from the mid-ninth century onwards. Yet when other kinds of sources talk of dispute settlement, we see that there is a range of procedures in addition to those on formal record. Some of the letters of Sidonius Apollinaris, for instance, show settlement through the informal lobbying of the influential, and everywhere when narrative sources mention dispute, they give far more emphasis to open conflict than to the formal process[53].

---

[52] For the Mitry case, see Nelson above, pp. 51–3.
[53] For Sidonius Apollinaris, see Wood above, p. 8, and for further contrasts in the evidence of narrative and diplomatic sources, see Fouracre above, pp. 38–9.

This is not to suggest that the evidence of case records is substantially misleading, simply a reminder that the courts did not have a monopoly over the settlement process.

Differences in the form of legal procedure employed by these societies are best explained in terms of historical development, the relationship of past to present practices, and important here is an ideological mediation between past and present. Law in action tends to make a virtue out of past practice. Just how much of a virtue was made out of it, with what self-awareness, precision, force and coherence, affects the development of the forms of legal procedure. We have seen clearly how in Gaul in the early sixth century past practice was subjected to a whole range of pressures and influences. Indeed, this society may have been more of a melting-pot for disparate influences than any other we have looked at. The result was the breeding of the hybrid procedures so evident in the seventh-century Frankish *placita**. As soon as we see these procedures – and the assumption that we see them not long after they had crystallized is, on circumstantial grounds, a sound one – they appear as strongly established custom. Yet their marked formalism, and the high profile of their ritual, precisely those elements which give them a customary look, may betray the process of bringing a new, and plainly visible, order to the confusion of disparate traditions. The precise formation of the new order fixed on significant aspects of the old – especially the rituals binding people to accept the rules – and thereby presented itself as customary. Thereafter as adherence to custom gained ideological momentum in Francia, and as the kings set themselves up as the guardians of legitimate custom, these hybrid procedures were maintained relatively un-changed throughout the Carolingian period.

Whereas in Francia fixed procedure grew out of preceding change, in England change grew out of the steady pressure put on traditional procedures by king and church. The details of the beginning of this process are lacking, but it is clear that by the late Saxon period the king had come to regulate the judicial process, at least in the area south of the river Trent. The principle of legality in England thus came to be derived not simply from custom, but from custom defined and approved by the king. Legal ideology encompassed both past practice and present (or even future) claims to power.

Byzantium had a markedly different approach to past practice. There, legal machinery was directly descended from Roman prototypes. The Byzantines knew this, and they enjoyed knowing it. They were perfectly able to articulate legal principles deriving from past practice, and guided by the general principle of bringing order to the world, their legal officials seem to have approached disputes methodically, but without a great deal of conscious formalism. Although we can generally say that the Byzantines worked under an umbrella of written law, reference to it tended to be through the intermediary of handbooks such as the *Peira*. The kingdoms of northern Spain, like the Byzantines, laid great ideological emphasis on written law, but with the important difference that they used it directly, sometimes quoting chapter and verse from Visigothic law. Procedural development was thus circumscribed by a very clearly conserved memory of past practice and the development of local customs moved procedures away from this fixed point only very slowly. No contradiction seems to have been perceived when newer practices were used in conjunction with the *Forum Iudicum*, and this may go some way to explaining the tenacity of the latter.

Use of the *Forum Iudicum* conserved the heritage of the late Roman practices in Spain into the thirteenth century. In Italy too the heritage of these practices was strong, but not represented to us through continual reference in our cases to a single text of written law. We see them maintained here through a continuity of legal and procedural institutions controlled by a high proportion of literate men who were themselves fully trained in law and written tradition. In such conditions procedure could be fairly flexible in Italy, at least until the late ninth century, when, as we have seen, it became rigidly formulaic. This was the result of the activity of the same legal experts who quarried the written record of past practice to produce *formulae* for the courts to use.

In Brittany, at village level, the evidence presents no hint of any principle expressed in relation to past practice, not in terms of written law, nor in terms of custom. Perhaps this was because there was no consciousness of change in this milieu and, simply, no need to define practice in ideological terms. Procedure in Brittany was thus marked by informality and flexibility. Ireland presents a very different picture. Here the form of procedure resulted from a fusion of Christian teachings with native law. Expressed principles referred to both, and were both numerous and complex. The result was procedure unique in form and variety. Even so, functions and conditions were not so different in Ireland that procedure there cannot be discussed in the same terms used to discuss procedures elsewhere in Europe.

In many of these societies it was a common complaint that people were too keen on the process of litigation, too ready to use the courts. One can see why this might have been so: the procedure of the courts was pragmatic and comprehensive enough to accommodate most kinds of problems, it allowed people to be proclaimed right and it was important members of the public who were present in court. The formal process also produced written affirmation of property, and this was so valued that in some societies people developed the habit of clothing their transactions as disputes in order to get it. A survey of early medieval court procedure should leave us not with the old image of barbaric ritual and arbitrary decision, but with the impression of a system of procedures which reflects the conditions of early medieval society perfectly. People with calloused hands may well have had an unfair advantage in the ordeal by hot water, but in the kind of cases we have looked at, only very rarely would they have had an opportunity to play to that sort of advantage. In practice it was usually smooth-handed operators brandishing charters and marshalling witnesses who won cases, and won, too, according to the rules.

DISPUTE PROCESSES AND SOCIAL STRUCTURES

A major aim of this book has been to show that the traditional picture of early medieval law, as presented in the early twentieth-century legal histories, and indeed still accepted by many modern experts on the legal changes of the twelfth and thirteenth centuries, cannot be maintained. That picture derived largely from an over-simple reading of Germanic law codes, which were too often accepted simply as a straightforward description of what happened in courts; as a result, early medieval dispute settlement has been seen as ritualistic and irrational, a semi-conscious and organic outgrowth of community identity, rather than a set of procedures that, however rough, were workable, and made some sense to the people that used them. By contrast, it is fundamental to the understanding of medieval dispute settlement that we have developed as a group that a credible picture of how it worked cannot be constructed without consideration of disputes themselves. Our records are not perfect for this purpose, of course; they are not disinterested sociological descriptions, and we should not treat them as if they were. But they are where we must start; actual cases, despite all their problems, are as close as we can get to how things happened – certainly far closer than the idealizations of written law. The results we have obtained show that the process of dispute was very unlike that of the traditional picture. We can see that, although the law codes do have some practical reality, they are overschematic; legal practice was more matter-of-fact than has been recognized by many legal historians. Even ritual, cornerstone of the conventional view of early medieval irrationality, fitted clearly into a social context that gave it meaning, as we have already seen. Let us look, then, at the place of disputing in early medieval society as a whole.

Generalization about early medieval dispute is problematic. The commonest characterization we find, that of the early middle ages as marking a gap between the legal coherence and coercive power of the late Roman state and the revival of law in the twelfth century, is certainly misleading. Indeed, the rôle of the state itself in our period has often been underestimated. We must, therefore, begin our generalizations by discussing the issue of the nature of the state in these societies. We can best see it through analysis of three broad questions: the problem of what the state actually was in the early middle ages; some of the major differences in the patterns of state intervention in dispute across space and time; and some of the restrictions on intervention from above, as contrasted with the informal rôle of local communities and lords in dispute settlement. This will give us a framework for discussion of further problems.

Every one of the societies discussed in this book had some sense of collective identity, that could be described as public. And, as a consequence, each recognized the existence of public powers that could be coercive, based on what could broadly be called public institutions – a recognized hierarchy, and a set of recognized responsibilities for the men in that hierarchy that could be separated, at least in theory, from the private relationships and interested activities of the individuals concerned. There was no part of Europe without some central public authority, however weak, which could be called on for judgement when necessary and which, with few exceptions, had the theoretical right to enforce judgements if it needed to. It is this public authority that can be loosely characterized as the state. Its roots were largely Roman: even procedures that have always been thought of as typically 'Germanic' could have Roman origins, or at least analogues; it is the classical Latin word *publicus* that is used to describe this authority in most of our societies. But it would be wrong to see such ideas as purely Roman; traditional Germanic and Celtic societies, too, had a sense of the public. The institutions of the early medieval world were not merely classical survivals, slowly decaying in a more barbarous reality; they could be created as well, or recreated, and not only in the political reorganization and developed public ideology of the Carolingian state, even if the latter is the most obvious example. Legal processes were a major part of a pattern of public power; indeed, the law-suits that we have for England, Francia, Italy and Spain, show how far the institutions and personnel of the state actually defined themselves as having power through the direction of dispute settlement. Central powers thus had some control over the rules of social life. All our kings could legislate, and such legislation could have an effect on the way people behaved. This was so most obviously and explicitly in southern Europe, with its widespread literacy and deep-rooted institutional complexity, but was no less so, in different ways, in late Saxon England, where kings kept as tight a control as they could of legal procedure, even if no-one in court ever invoked their norms. Even in Ireland, people behaved to each other in courts with the knowledge that they were operating inside a highly complex framework of rules laid down by someone other than themselves. Only in Brittany at the village level can we not see any external power in control of such rules at all, and even this may be a distortion of our evidence[54].

There were differences, of course, in the way these institutions interrelated with local society and local dispute processes. Some states were obviously very much stronger than others. A standard opinion on the subject is that early medieval state power was determined more or less by the political and cultural inheritance of the Roman empire: the more remote the inheritance, the weaker the successor state. But a picture of this kind is misleading. For a start, the variability of political/juridical power across Europe was not represented by

[54] See Davies above, pp. 76, 78, 82–3.

neatly bounded political or geographical units like 'Francia' or 'Spain', or even 'Anjou' and 'Catalonia'; it was far more geographically diverse. The impact of royal control, for instance, was in most of our examples closely related to social and geographical distance from the king; in England, say in 1000, a line taken from Penzance to London probably would have traversed examples of most of the types of judicial practice that we have seen in this book, outside the Byzantine empire. Every political unit, no matter how small, was built up of extremely diverse local societies, with their own rules of activity and their own relationship to the centre. States could be strong, too, in different ways, and the precise nature of their strength affected the relationship between state and dispute settlement. Otto I's Saxony or Æthelstan's England were far more effective political units than Hugh of Arles's Italian kingdom of the early tenth century, but the coherence and stability of judicial procedure was far greater in the latter than in either of the former. And when the state broke down in much of post-Carolingian continental Europe, to be replaced by the principalities and *seigneuries** of the 'feudal' world in what is now France, it is far from clear that justice always changed in type, even if external influences on judicial practice were very much weaker. The spatial and temporal heterogeneity of early medieval Europe does not prevent us from generalizing, but it does require that anyone who tries to generalize about any aspect of it must recognize such a lack of homogeneity and be prepared to discuss the reasons for it.

What this means, for our purposes, is that if we want to understand the rôle of the state in justice, we must look at it from beneath, from the standpoint of the social groups involved in disputing. The first point to recognize here is the limits of external intervention. Courts could have smoothly running formal procedures, with a rationality that we can recognize, as we saw in the previous section. Early medieval institutions were, however, difficult to use against the strong; people were not always prepared to accept the judgements of an external body, be it the count's court, or any other part of the state's institutional apparatus. In some cases, indeed, the courts accepted this as their right. The most obvious instance of this is the accepted right of people to feud, best described in Frankish and Icelandic narratives; among our contributions here, the recognition by people that the rôle of the courts was limited is most explicit in Jenny Wormald's paper on Scotland[55]. But even when courts did make judgements that they intended to have carried out, they did not always succeed; the strongest local powers tended to prevail whether they were the winners or the losers in court. And, for that matter, the judgements themselves, however rational, were not invariably in accordance with either our notions of justice or those of contemporaries; judges, even if legal experts, were often aristocrats, and the early middle ages is full of hostile rhetoric about their actions: legislation, hagiography,

---

[55] For feud in Francia, Iceland and Scotland see J. Wallace-Hadrill, *Long-haired Kings*, pp. 121–47; J. Byock, *Feud in the Icelandic Saga*; Wormald above, pp. 202–4.

even poetry, stress their oppression, partiality, or corruption (for followers, or kinsmen, or friends, or money, as the Lombard king Ratchis put it in 746)[56].

Statements of this kind, taken on their own, are banal; very few institutions have worked properly in history, and only the naive would believe in the flawless functioning of our own. But their context is more interesting. It is legitimate to say that the power of justice could be weak, for otherwise contemporaries would not have complained about its absence. But it is perhaps more helpful to put it differently: abstract justice (if and when it existed) coexisted with the different expectations of the participants themselves about how disputes ought to turn out, expectations that often had more to do with local, private, patterns of power than with our crude conceptions of right and wrong. And states, kings and princes above all, even if they could have an important rôle in early medieval dispute, had a highly mediated one. Kings, that is to say, intervened in local societies from the outside; even when they made law, they could not get it put into practice unless the men who controlled their courts accepted it. Kings, law-makers or no, were by no means necessarily more 'just' than private powers, of course; they simply had different objectives. But if we wish to understand either, we must give as much attention as we can to what went on at the local level.

Court procedures in early medieval Europe, as we have seen, tended to be collective: in most cases, this meant that they were the responsibility of the free men of the area concerned. As in the Roman world, the Celtic and Germanic concept of the public hung directly on the participation of 'good men', *boni homines** and their innumerable variants; the coherence of justice itself depended on the fact. But this meant that the bulk of judicial decision, and the effectiveness of any such decision, hung, not on any abstract institutional structure, but on the local community, its social attitudes and its private personal relationships. The relative remoteness of the state from this world is best expressed by the absence of any real distinction between civil and criminal cases. There were no broad categories of crime that were outside the purview of community procedures; even homicide could be cancelled out by the payment of compensation. There were, certainly, offences against the king that were his responsibility to act on (forgery, rebellion, the breaking of the king's peace in his court), but even they were in effect offences against his own person, that he was bound to seek remedy for as anyone would for theft or assault; when he was satisfied, the course of justice need go no further[57]. The existence of collective criteria for determining the outcome of disputes must not be read, however, as a claim that there was anything egalitarian about any of our societies. The local community was controlled in

---

[56] Ratchis ch. 10 in *Leges Langobardorum 643–866*, ed. F. Beyerle, p. 190.

[57] Kings did tend to legislate on homicide and other major offences, and increasingly regarded it as their concern (see, most forcefully, Wormald above, pp. 162–6). It is true that our notions of crime and felony derive historically from these developments, but we should not read the latter back straightforwardly to them.

practice by the local élite; anywhere outside the purview of the ninth-century Redon charters, and those other – ill-documented – areas of Europe with a relatively independent peasantry, this meant the aristocracy. The relationship between the state and the community was thus often simply represented by the relationship between aristocrats acting in their various capacities, both as public officials and as local landowners. This two-fold rôle became more formalized in the ninth century and onwards, with the growth of clearly bounded private (seigneurial) jurisdictions, above all but not only in France. Such jurisdictions certainly excluded the formal intervention of the state; but they did not necessarily change the way the process of disputing was organized. Seigneurial justice was often in practice based on very similar procedures to the informal dispute settlement of the *rachymburgi** of the seventh century, or even the *placita** of the Carolingian world. In each case, the process and the result would have been determined very largely by the will of the most powerful local personages, whose institutional position changed as their political environment changed, but whose practical control remained much the same. Conversely, however, this did not mean that non-aristocrats had no rôle at all in courts; local aristocrats, with or without seigneurial rights, needed the rest of the community by them to make their legal decisions effective. The *boni homines* of the seventh or even the tenth century had a real not just symbolic legal function; the agreement of people such as them was in practice necessary for any settlement to be effective[58]. At all levels of society, then, we can see a dialectic working, between state and locality, between lord and community, between external power and local values and processes. They were not necessarily in opposition, and above all they were not mutually exclusive; each had an effect on the other. And both state and local society must be seen as having an effect on the way that dispute settlement worked, in every one of our societies, however diverse.

Generalizations such as these are not an end-point; they are only the bases for a new set of questions. Under what *circumstances* would men, at different places and times kill their enemies, or take them to court, or make peace with them? What was the purpose of going to court at all? Could courts ever judge against the powerful, and could they ever do so effectively? It must be recognized that these questions will be answered differently in each region of Europe, perhaps differently among different social groups inside the same region, and certainly differently at different times. We are not going to be able to rewrite the legal history of early medieval Europe from our case-law standpoint until we have answered each of these questions for each region, and explained the differences in the answers. We cannot do this yet. But we can already see, across the studies contained in this book, that regional divergencies in legal proceedings were

---

[58] Cf. S. Reynolds, *Kingdoms and Communities in Western Europe 900–1300*, pp. 12–66, for all this and other valuable discussions of issues highly pertinent to this section of the conclusion.

enormous. The extreme localization of power in ninth-century east Brittany, with its striking lack of legal ritual and formality, makes one think of the very matter-of-fact legal procedures of various parts of Africa; but contrast that with the obsession with looking up the exact law in the law book in ninth- and tenth-century Spain, or the extreme standardization of procedures in land disputes in tenth-century Italy[59]. The generalizations that have been outlined only serve to point up such contrasts; it will take a lot more work to explain them. Here, we can only look at a few aspects of these questions that lie at the core of any sociological understanding of dispute settlement: the different circumstances in which people came to the courts and the different ways people could use them.

Early medieval court cases were political. This is one of the motifs that runs most constantly through the chapters of the book. That is to say, they fitted into the network of local social relationships that preceded each case, and indeed succeeded it, slightly modified by the case itself. 'It is not so much that quarrels are never wholly resolved, but rather that cases have their sources in the ceaseless flow of social life, and, in turn, contribute to that flow.'[60] Only if we recognize this can we regard court cases as history; otherwise, they are merely law. And the first consequence to be recognized is that the purpose of much dispute settlement was not in any strict sense justice, but the restoration of peace. 'Peaceful coexistence' was an ideal in most medieval societies, as elsewhere, indeed a critical necessity. No dispute was too serious for resolution between the parties, at least in principle, even, as we have seen, those hanging on what we would now call 'criminal' offences. But we must not idealize the notion of peace. Disputes were in themselves sufficiently common to constitute in themselves part of normal social interaction; 'peace', that is to say, was already pretty contentious. Some disputes may well have been undertaken for reasons other than those which were the immediate object of the dispute; their seriousness was a function of the social relationships between the parties, quite as much as of the importance of the object of dispute itself. Going to court, that is, often fitted into a set of wider social strategies for each party; at the least, the court case was only one part of the dispute and its settlement, which could have a far longer time-scale. Such a strategic framework is, unfortunately, the hardest aspect of early medieval dispute to document, so rarely do we have any other information on the parties in question. But some of our more detailed case records show how complex such processes often were, and we can get an idea from them of how such processes worked.

[59] For Brittany, Spain and Italy, see Davies, Collins and Wickham above, pp. 76–8, 88, 117–18. The vast range of attitudes to law in Europe alone is well exemplified in J. Bossy (ed.), *Disputes and Settlements*. For anthropological guides, see S. Roberts, *Order and Dispute* and S. Moore, *Law as Process*; the great classic is M. Gluckman, *The Judicial Process among the Barotse of Northern Rhodesia*.
[60] A. Epstein, 'The case method in the field of law', in *idem* (ed.), *The Craft of Social Anthropology*, p. 230.

Early medieval people were often enough prone to anger and violence: unthought-out action as an instant response to offence. Violent action did not exclude its perpetrator from social support; indeed, feud, present in all the societies we have studied, presupposed it. So why bother to go to court at all? It might be thought that it would be enough for a party to convince enough people of his right for him to take reprisals against an opponent – for example, in a land dispute, which most of our cases are, to occupy the land in question. We certainly should not assume that people were more prone to think coolly about land disputes than about other offences; it is quite clear in our cases, as in those of later centuries, that disseisin, the seizure of land, was a common recourse as an initial claim to it. But such an act, as far as we can see, was normally intended, in most of our societies, not to be the conclusion of an action, but to force one's opponent to court. We must conclude that courts were everywhere seen, with a few exceptions we will look at at the end, as the major *locus* for the climax of dispute. And, if that is so, then courts must have been of some use for disputants; we should not assume that people went to court out of a disinterested love for the law.

The key advantage of going to court was the width of support potentially available to a party there. The detail of how one of the disputing parties could construct support in the court – and the other see it dissolve – is most visible, out of our own examples, in the Tours case of 857. Here, the church of St Hispanus persuaded each of its three opponents in turn to concede the case, against the opposition of those remaining in dispute; the church had already persuaded the witnesses of the charter its opponents possessed to state that they had not witnessed it fully, thus invalidating it – these witnesses were clearly changing sides, for when they had participated in the redaction of the charter they must have known quite well that the transaction ran against the interests of the church. The church, that is to say, was able to break up an alliance of opponents and emerge victorious; both as a result of threats and (it would appear) as a result of its opponents' sense that they were genuinely in the wrong, but above all because its 'persuasion' took place in the law court, the most public form for the airing of such grievances, and one in which most pressure could be brought to bear. Such pressure was probably negotiated for. We cannot see the negotiations in this case, but there are others where we can: in Alfred's England, for example, the friendless Helmstan could only build up support for his defence of his land in a legal dispute by ceding the land itself to his noble protector – again, both the threat to his land and his eventual defence were posed in terms of public judicial proceedings. All across Europe, people recognized that the public, formal, airing of disputes was serious. In Brittany, indeed, it could be sufficient that a party should begin to collect evidence for production at court for his opponent to come to terms. We do not, in our court cases, have the drama of the slow build-up of support that was pursued by medieval Icelanders, from booth to booth at the Althing; but it is clear that the courts in our cases were a focus for political negotiation and confrontation, and that support could be constructed, in order to gain a court victory, that was not necessarily present at all before a party to a dispute threatened to bring the case to the court[61].

Going to court was, then, making a dispute public. Private disputes – feuds – could certainly exist, but feuding parties could only get their closest kin to participate, particularly if the dispute became violent, or went on for a long time. And no-one in Europe lived only among kin; one needed support from neighbours, dependants, lords, and this was available above all in the public arena. Such men could testify and swear for their associates; they would not necessarily fight for them. Going to court was the only way that much of one's reserve of support could be brought into play at all. The importance of the court was sufficiently great that a party could seldom refuse to take his case there in the end if his opponent demanded it, or, if he did, might well lose even the support of his kin. Courts were only a part of disputing, but they were that part that was most likely to bring a party the backing he needed to construct victory, or at least advantageous compromise.

It follows that the other major function of the court was, simply, to conclude dispute. Parties could leave court as losers, and still refuse to come to terms; but by and large the support one received at court was available on the assumption that a lasting end to the dispute could be obtained thereby, by agreement or else coercion. And in all the societies we have looked at here, no matter how violent, it was recognized that it was better for disputes to end. It is true that enmity was never easy to extinguish, and disputes could easily flare up again. Recent work on feud has emphasized its persistence across long periods; longstanding social relationships themselves can be expressed in terms of acts of hostility, as a negative of the links represented by the exchange of gifts[62]. But individual disputes had a shorter life-span; they could be and were resolved. And courts were the most public, that is definitive, arena available to people in most of our societies; decisions and agreements made there were more binding than any *fait accompli* established outside them.

At this point, however, we come back to the purview of the state. When people went to court, they abandoned, at least in part, their desire to prevail over their opponents by strength alone. We have been looking at this in terms of the informal negotiation possible in any court; but public courts were also the principal *locus* of state intervention in local society, and parties recognized that once they went to law, the rules of law themselves began to matter. Such rules expressed above all the values of the state, even if they were often transformed by

---

[61] For Tours, see Nelson above, pp. 56–7; Helmstan, *Cartularium Saxonicum*, ed. W. de Gray Birch, no. 591 (*English Historical Documents*, vol. 1, ed. D. Whitelock, no. 102); Brittany, Davies above, p. 76; Iceland, *Brennu Njáls Saga*, ed. E. Sveinsson, cc. 115–45. Cf. S. Humphreys, 'Social relations on stage', *History and Anthropology*, 1, pt 2 (1985).

[62] See J. Black-Michaud, *Cohesive Force*, pp. 63–89 and references there cited.

local interpretation. It is far from clear, however, that the involvement of the state necessarily affected the social patterns that have just been outlined in any simple way. This double rôle of the court, the point where state and community met, has sometimes been seen as a contrast between adjudication and mediation (judgement and compromise, justice and peace), the strength of the state being measured by the frequency of uncompromising judgements in courts, potentially cutting across all local social relationships. Even now, for example, some historians still see the fall of the Roman and the Carolingian empires as logically to be associated with a decline in judgements and a rise in compromise procedures. But this contrast is misleading; the state could mediate, just as the local community could judge. Some of our most unambiguous instances of courts acting as mediators come from places where Roman law was most influential and the state was strongest. In reality, neither Roman nor German law was in itself hostile to mediation. In practice, whether mediation or adjudication was employed, or in what measure, must have depended almost totally on the local political circumstances, the pattern of relationships in specific instances; but both, whether formally or informally, were always available. Indeed, so far from judges encouraging compromise only because they had not the strength to coerce people, we can sometimes find compromise seen as a positive good, a real basis for future social interaction[63].

This balance between judgement and compromise was very various. In some cases, courts produced outright judgements which were then followed up by compromise; the final judgement could sometimes deliberately hide the fact that settlement had in reality been worked out in the court itself. Sometimes courts were expected to make outright decisions, but were themselves used politically: cases were raised at court, but then withdrawn, as a compromise was reached; such a settlement could then be ratified by the court separately, as in our Athos case. Sometimes people stepped back from the final oath at the end of the case, which could be seen as a hostile or humiliating increase in the stakes, itself capable of making subsequent peaceful coexistence impossible; we have clear English instances of this. But courts could often regard it as their direct responsibility to ensure 'friendly agreement' (*amica pactuatio**, and its analogues) between the two sides. Some judges in Italy were prepared to stop adversarial proceedings and press a settlement on parties; in Aragón such *convenienciae/ cominenzas* were regarded as a normal, and, sometimes, compulsory part of formal law. Compromise was often a real negotiation, with sweeteners to the weaker and losing party, to save face, as in our Scottish example[64]. Conversely,

---

[63] On arbitration in a strong state run by Roman law, see P. Toubert, *Les Structures du Latium médiéval*, pp. 1244–57. For arbitration and mediation, see S. Roberts, *Order and Dispute*; for the positive side of compromise, see S. White, 'Settlement of Disputes', *American Journal of Legal History*, 22 (1978), 301–7.

[64] For Athos, see Morris above, pp. 131–5; stepping back from the final oath, see *Anglo-Saxon Charters*, ed. A. Robertson, nos. 66, 83, and in Italy, *Regesto di Farfa*, ed. I. Giorgi and U. Balzani,

the rhetoric of peacemaking could often cover the total defeat of one of the parties, and his acceptance of that defeat. And we must not forget that courts could also give outright and binding judgements, backed up by the might and influence of its representatives, in every one of our societies from Byzantium to Ireland.

This array of examples can allow us to draw an anthropological conclusion. Adjudication and mediation are in principle opposites, and can be separated analytically. But they do not represent *historical* oppositions. In practice, they were, and are, present in most European courts, sometimes in the same decisions. There are societies in the world (even if none can be seen to have existed in Europe in historical times) without formal procedures for judgement, but there are none without legitimate procedures for mediation. One could see peace and justice as two ends of a spectrum, each legitimating the other. If one believes that the purpose of legal decisions is only to produce objectively just results, according to the letter of the law (as in modern western legal ideology – less so legal practice), then one does not disbelieve in peacemaking; one simply believes that peace follows from justice. If, however, one believes that the purpose of law is to negotiate an end to dispute to the (greater or lesser) satisfaction of (stronger or weaker) parties, then one believes that such endings are just in themselves. And these beliefs are not necessarily in contradiction. Different situations produce different results; western family law tends classically towards compromise, whereas few early medieval kings would have accepted such a thing in cases of treason. The ways our court cases turn out show that early medieval concepts of justice were not unrecognizable to us; at most, early medieval societies were often further across the spectrum towards compromise than we tend to be. We inhabit the same world as they did, even if its contours are utterly changed.

The impact of the state on early medieval courts did not, then, have any straightforward effect on the ways that disputes were settled. It has been argued, however – indeed, it is generally accepted – that this would change in the twelfth and thirteenth centuries, the 'age of law', the world of Henry II of England and the Roman lawyers of Bologna, when, at last, law suits came to be dominated by the rules laid down by kings. And it is certainly the case that we ourselves have seen early medieval dispute settlement in apposition to that of the twelfth century. Not, however, because twelfth-century law was different in *content*; the real difference between the two periods is a dramatic shift in the documentation at the historian's disposal, which requires different methods of analysis and poses different problems. We would argue, indeed, that the changes of the twelfth

no. 34. *Amica pactuacio*: see Wickham above, p. 122; *cominenza*: see Collins above, pp. 99–101; incentives to the losing party in the Sandlaw case: see Wormald above, pp. 199–200.

century and onwards have been exaggerated. Let us, to finish, look briefly at the issue.

The twelfth century certainly did see a conscious effort on the part of kings and princes, even lawyers themselves, to take over and systematize the practice of law. What we contest in this book is not only that this was particularly new, but even that it was as yet all that much more effective than previous attempts. The new world of the twelfth century was more legally articulate, but court procedures did not change all that much, and it is far from clear that they were supposed to. We must not get misled by the rhetoric of system and authority emanating from Henry II or the lawyers, any more than we are misled by the rhetoric of king as judge and teacher emanating from the court circles of the Carolingians. In practice, the ways Henry intervened in the disputing process were very much like the ways of Liutprand or Charlemagne or Æthelred II; local relationships carried the weight of dispute settlement, the king at best managing to change some of the rules, perhaps regularize some of them, certainly direct as many judicial profits as possible towards himself. Above all, the impact of the state was not yet destined, or even designed, to undermine traditional methods of settling disputes. Law was not yet the abstract and disinterested process of the Common Law* handbooks; at best, the carapace of legal institutions began to take shape in this period, to proceed throughout the rest of history largely according to its own rules[65].

That is not to say that the twelfth century had no importance in the history of law; only that its historical position has been misunderstood. We have just looked at how court proceedings could be used strategically, and at the circumstances in which people felt it advantageous to pursue a dispute through legal institutions rather than fight it out. It is arguable that the true variability of dispute settlement in Europe lies here: not in the varying impact of state intervention, or even in the varying acceptance of judgement rather than compromise, but in the extent to which people, high and low in the social hierarchy, were prepared to use public institutions when disputing rather than fight or negotiate privately. Legal institutions, that is to say, varied most of all in their *internal* strength: not their coercive power, but their acceptability as a means for the settlement of disputes, and their capacity for holding people to their procedures until resolution was achieved. This is what Henry II, or Frederick II, or Louis IX, or any Italian city, were aiming at in their judicial innovations, rather than the securing of abstract justice[66]. But, even then, the novelty of these innovators was above all their conscious awareness that they could use such changes to enhance their own political power. The public legal procedures of the early middle ages, too, could serve to funnel dispute towards peace, and were certainly intended to by their originators.

[65] Cf. E. Thompson, *Whigs and Hunters*, pp. 258–69.
[66] See, for instance, M. Clanchy, 'Law and love' in Bossy (ed.), *Disputes*, pp. 51–7; R. Bartlett, 'Royal government in the French Ardennes', *Journal of Medieval History*, 7 (1981), 91–2.

The strong will, of course, always use the institutions that are available to them, to assert and enhance their own power, and so did they in our period. But the interesting thing about our period is that the weak often did so too. Even tenants, who certainly knew that they could seldom win against their lords, and who sometimes explicitly said so in public, came back again and again to courts in the Carolingian world, and indeed were even very occasionally victorious. One must recognize that this constant use of courts was what the Carolingians intended, and that it therefore represented a real success for them – even if one could not exactly agree with those, like Bonnassie and Toubert, who argue that justice was therefore somehow classless[67]. A similar success can be recognized in the tenth-century English kingdom, where, even if cases were constantly reopened as the kings changed, they were constantly reopened *in court*; public legal procedures were genuinely already beginning to encompass the private tensions of late Anglo-Saxon society, two centuries before the Writ of Novel Disseisin[68]. We see the same in Byzantium, where state legal procedures could be readily available to, and were sought by, even the most distant and insignificant of the emperor's subjects. There was a risk here, which was not always overcome: that court procedures became so different from private settlement that the two were clearly seen as alternatives; this probably underlies, for example, the avoidance of courts that we can see in fifth- and sixth-century southern Gaul, or the conscious use of private settlement in both tenth-century Byzantium and sixteenth-century Scotland[69]. Once state procedures were crystallized, private agreements could be seen as more flexible – one must not forget that courts, as they became institutionalized, became increasingly expensive and corrupt; and, indeed, violent, as in the notorious case of the courts of late Rome, which no-one could have been blamed for wishing to avoid. The more institutionally ambitious a state, by and large, the more systematically violent its methods. This was the other side of the coin to the ready availability of relatively standard legal procedures; there were many who found private violence not only more rewarding, but actually less bloodthirsty. But public procedures did have the advantage that they could end dispute more comprehensively, and they were used in each of our societies, as they were later, in the twelfth century and beyond. We must stress, however, that they were not simply an emanation of state power; even in Iceland, despite the near absence of any coercive rôle for legal institutions at all, and despite a society probably more oriented towards interpersonal violence than any of the ones we have studied here, people tended to make peace through

---

[67] P. Bonnassie, *Catalogne du milieu du Xe à la fin du XIe siècle*, p. 198; Toubert, *Structures*, pp. 1254f.
[68] Wormald above, pp. 162–3. The Ottonian kings signally failed to achieve this in contemporary Saxony; see K. Leyser, *Rule and Conflict in an Early Medieval Society*.
[69] Gaul: see Wood above, pp. 8–9; Byzantium: see Morris above, p. 147; Scotland: see Wormald above, pp. 202–5. For Italian parallels, see Wickham above, pp. 121, 123–4, with J. Delumeau, 'L'exercice de la justice dans le comté d'Arezzo (IXe-début XIII siècle), *Mélanges de l'École française de Rome*, 90 (1978), 598–603.

the courts in the end; the homogeneity of the legal system and the subtlety of the complex legal procedures that the Icelanders had worked out were themselves largely responsible for this[70].

By the standards of most of the world, all European societies are violent. It is likely that the ritual embodied in most of the court processes we have looked at derives precisely from a consciousness that this was the only way for legal institutions to make an impact on societies perpetually riven by antagonism and oppression. Ritual was the most effective way to channel off resentments in the direction of the ideal of renewed peace, through a close association with religious practice (as with the endless oaths in all courts, or, at the most extreme, ordeal), and through elaborate and lengthy procedures that could, in all senses of the word, be called dramatic. Many of these procedures must have existed for a long time before our period; the need to mediate in societies as tense as these can hardly have been new in the early middle ages. (The point has been argued particularly forcefully in Ireland[71].) But, as time went on, the institutionalization of conflict through court procedures became more acceptable, and more accepted: not completely in the early middle ages, or in the twelfth century either – nor yet in a linear process, for the influence of legal institutions would continue to fluctuate in most of Europe – but, over time, increasingly. Kings and lawyers may not have felt the need to legislate against feud and private settlement (indeed, when they did so it was fruitless); what they could do instead was absorb the feuding process and its analogues into their *own* institutional structures, by making these available for the conduct of conflict at all levels. As Palmer has recently noted, the very fact that thirteenth-century English court cases could always be reopened encouraged people to use the courts instead of fighting, and then, eventually, to come to terms; these were just the procedures that were beginning to develop in tenth-century England. And the whole process is summed up for us by our example of the resolution of a feud right at the end of the middle ages, in sixteenth-century Scotland: here, the practice of feud itself was coming inside the purview of professional lawyers[72]. Above all in this example, we can see how the victory of the state was not the victory of its legislation, or even of its interest in and capacity for direct intervention, but of the success of its institutions and their representatives in capturing the disputing processes of local élites. And our Scottish example illustrates more clearly than anything else how the case-law approach illuminates, not just the disputes themselves, but the social structure that expressed itself through them[73].

[70] Byock, *Feud*; for legal homogeneity and complexity in Iceland, see *Laws of Early Iceland*, vol. 1, ed. A. Dennis, P. Foote, R. Perkins.

[71] On drama see also V. Turner, *Dramas, Fields and Metaphors*, pp. 35–44. For Ireland see, for example, D. Binchy, 'Linguistic and legal archaisms', *Trans. Philological Soc.*, 1959.

[72] R. Palmer, *The Whilton Dispute*, pp. 212–15, though in other ways the argument of the book is profoundly alien to that proposed here. For Scotland see Wormald above, pp. 201–5.

[73] Thanks are due to Nicholas Brooks and Gervase Rosser for reading this section and for their helpful comments.

Appendix

I

Formulae Arvernenses, no. 1.

SOURCE: MS Paris BN lat. 4697 (s. ix), fols. 47r–48v, edited by K. Zeumer, *Formulae Merowingici et Karolini Aevi, MGH LL in quarto, sectio* 5, p. 28.

nascuntur[1], per hanc occassionem non perdant. Ob oc igitur ego ille et coiuues mea illa conmanens orbe Aruernis, in pago illo, in uilla illa, dum non est incognitum, qualiter cartolas nostras per hostilitatem Francorum in ipsa uilla illa, manso nostro, ubi uisi sumus manere, ibidem perdimus; et petimus uel cognitum faciemus, ut, quit per ipsas stromentas eo tempore habere noscuntur[2], possessio nostra per hanc occasionem nr̄um pater[3], inter epistolas illas de mansos in ipsa uilla illa, de qua ipso atraximus in integrum, item et uindedit, ista omnia superius consscripta, uel quod memorare minime possimus, iudicibus, breuis, nostris[4], spondiis, incolcacionibus uel alias stromentas, tam nostras, quam et qui nobis commendatas fuerunt, hoc inter ipsas uillas suprascriptas uel de ipsas turbas ibidem perdimus; et petimus, ut hanc contestaciuncula seu plancturia per hanc cartolas in nostro nomine collegere uel adfirmare deberemus; quo ita et fecimus; [5]ista principium Honorio et Theodisio consilibus eorum[5] ad hostio sancto illo, castro Claremunte per triduum habendi[6] uel custodiuimus, seu in mercato puplico, in quo ordo curie duxerunt aut regalis uel manuensis uestri aut personarum ipsius carta[7], ut, cum hanc contestatiuncula seu plancturia iuxta legum consuetudinem in presentia uestra relata fuerit, nostris[8] subscriptionibus signaculis subroborare faciatis, ut quocumque perdictionis nostras de supascripta per uestra adfirmatione iusta auctoritas remedia consequatur, ut nostra firmitas legum auctoritas reuocent in propinquietas.

Gesta

'Unde ergo te uir laudabilis illum defensore necnon et uos honerati, que curas puplicas agitis adsidue, oportet me curiae in hoc contestatiuncula seu plancturia per triduum partibus foris puplicis apensa uestris subscriptionibus uel signaculis subter faciatis adfirmare, ut, quomodo mihi necessarium fuerit, causella meas aut in presentia dominorum uel iudicibus aduersariorum meorum reuocent in proquietas[9]. Pro hoc que contra hanc contestaciuncula seu plancturia deponere percurauimus, ut, quando uolueritis et malueritis, uel mihi necessarium fuerit, ut mos est, gestis municipalibus eam faciatis ablegare cum petitiones nostras. Maximas uobis ex hoc gratias agere ualeamus'.

---

[1] *? read* noscuntur *Zeumer*   [2] *? read* noscimur *Zeumer*   [3] nr̄um pater *i.e.* nostrorum pater *MS*] *read* n̄ rumpatur *i.e.* non rumpatur *Zeumer*   [4] *? read* notitiis *Rozière*   [5] iste . . . eorum *MS*] *read* iuxta principum Honorii et Theodosii consulum decretum *Rozière*   [6] *read* appendimus *Zeumer*   [7] *editors print* castri   [8] *read* uestris *Zeumer*   [9] *read* propinquietas *Zeumer*

II

Liber Constitutionum, viii.

SOURCE: Edited by L. R. de Salis, *MGH LL in quarto, sectio* I, vol. 2, pt 1, pp. 49–50, from numerous eighth- and ninth-century manuscripts.

De obiectione criminum, quae ingenuis intenduntur.

[1.] Si ingenuus per suspicionem uocatur in culpa, tam barbarus quam Romanus, sacramenta praebeat, cum uxore et filiis et propinquis sibi duodecimus iuret. Si uero uxorem et filios non habuerit, et patrem aut matrem habuerit, cum patre et matre numerum impleat designatum. Quod si patrem aut matrem non habuerit, cum duodecim proximis impleat sacramentum.

[2.] Quod si ei sacramentum de manu is, cui iurandum est, tollere uoluerit, antequam ecclesiam ingrediantur illi, qui sacramentum audire iussi sunt, quos a iudicibus ternos semper ad sacramentum audiendum praecipimus delegari, contestantur se nolle sacramenta percipere, et non permittitur qui iuraturus erat post hanc uocem sacramenta praestare; sed ad nos illico diriguntur Dei iudicio committendi.

[3.] Si autem permissus iurauerit et post sacramentum potuerit forte conuinci, in nouigildo se nouerit redditurum eis, quibus praesentibus iudex iusserit dare sacramenta.

[4.] Si ad locum statuto die uenire dissimulauerint et non ab aliqua fuerint infirmitate aut publica occupatione detenti, senos solidos multae nomine inferant. Quod si infirmitate aut occupatione detenti fuerint, faciant hoc ipsum iudicem scire aut loco suo tales personas dirigant, quorum fide possint in loco sacramenta praestare.

[5.] Si autem is, qui sacramenta daturus erat, ad locum non uenerit, usque horam sextam diei ipsum expectet pars altera; quod si usque ad sextam non uenerit, causam absque dilatione dissoluat.

[6.] Quod si ille alius non uenerit, ille, qui sacramenta praebiturus erat, discedat indempnis.

III

Liber Constitutionum, xlv.

SOURCE: as for II.

De his, qui obiecta sibi negauerint et praebendum obtulerint iusiurandum.

Multos in populo nostro et per uacationem causantium et cupiditatis instinctum ita cognoscimus deprauari, ut de rebus incertis sacramenta plerumque offerre non dubitent et de cognitis iugiter periurare. Cuius sceleris consuetudinem submouentes praesenti lege decernimus, ut, quotiens inter homines nostros causa surrexerit, et is, qui pulsatus fuerit, non deberi a se quod requiritur, aut non factum quod obicitur, sacramentorum oblatione negauerit, hac ratione litigio eorum finem oportebit inponi: ut, si pars eius, cui oblatum fuerit iusiurandum, noluerit sacramenta suscipere, sed aduersarium suum ueritatis fiducia armis dixerit posse conuinci, et pars diuersa non cesserit, pugnandi licentia non negetur; ita ut unus de eisdem testibus, qui ad danda conuenerint sacramenta, Deo iudicante confligat; quoniam iustum est, ut si quis ueritatem rei incunctanter scire se dixerit et obtulerit sacramentum, pugnare non dubitet. Quod si testis partis eius, qui obtulerit sacramentum, in eo certamine fuerit superatus, omnes testes, qui se promiserant iuraturos, trecenos solidos multae nomine absque ulla induciarum praestatione cogantur exsoluere. Uerum si ille, qui renuerit sacramentum, fuerit interemptus, quidquid debebat, de facultatibus eius nouigildi solutione pars uictoris reddatur indempnis, ut ueritate potius quam periuriis delectentur.

Data sub die V kalendas Iunias Lugduno, Abieno uiro clarissimo consule.

IV
Pactus Legis Salicae, xxxix. 2.

SOURCE: Edited by K. A. Eckhardt, *MGH LL in quarto, sectio* 1, vol. 4, pt 1, pp. 142–3, from numerous manuscripts, of which the earliest are from the eighth century.

Si quis seruus alienus fuerit plagiatus et ipse trans mare ductus fuerit et ibidem a domino suo fuerit inuentus et, a quo ipse in patria sua plagiatus est, in mallo publico nominauerit, tres ibidem testes debet colligere. Iterum cum seruus ipse detrans mare fuerit reuocatus, in alterum uero mallum debet iterum nominare, ibidem simul tres testes debent collegi idoneos; ad tertium uero mallum similiter fieri debet, ut nouem testes iurent, quod seruum ipsum equaliter per tres mallos super plagiatorem audierint dicentem, et sic postea qui eum plagiauit, mallobergo mallo uuiridarium hoc est, praeter capitale et dilaturam MCCCC denarios qui faciunt solidos XXXV culpabilis iudicetur. Qui confessio serui usque ad tres plagiatores admittitur, sed ea tamen ratione, ut nomina hominum et uillarum semper equaliter debeat nominare.

V
Royal judgement in dispute between Chaino, abbot of St Denis, and Abbot Ermenoald, over wine and oil pledged by Ermenoald to Chaino, given in the king's court at the royal palace of Nogent-sur-Marne, 5 May 691 or 692.

SOURCE: Based on editions by G. Pertz, *MGH Diplomata*, vol. 1, pp. 53–4 (no. 60), and P. Lauer, C. Samaran, *Les diplômes originaux des Mérovingiens*, no. 21, from MS Paris, Archives nationales, K3, no. 4; facsimile also in *ChLA*, vol. 14, no. 573.

✝ Chlodouius rex Francorum, u. inl.

Uenientis agentis basilice domni Dionisii, ubi ipsi preciosus domnus in corpure requiiscit et uenerabilis uir Chaino abba praeesse uiditur, Nouiento in palacio nostro, nobis suggesserunt eo quod itemque uenerabili uiro Ermenoaldo abbati ante hus annus uuaddio pro olio milli quignentas liberas, et uino bono modios cento, pro Anseberctho episcopo ipsi Chaino abba ei conmendassit; et taliter ipsi Ermenoaldus spondedisset ut hoc ei dare et adinplire debirit, et hoc menime ficisset. Unde et ante dies per eorum noticias paricolas ante domno Sygofrido pontefeci placita inter se habuerunt, ut medio minse Aprile iam preterito ipsi Ermenoaldus abba apud tris homenis, sua mano quarta, ante ipso pontefeci aut hoc coniurare debirit, quod ipso uuaddio de mano memorato Chainone abbati numquam adchramissit, nec hoc ei dare et adinplire spondedisset; quod se menime faciebat, argento liberas dece ad ipso diae ei dare debirit. Quod se hoc non faciebat, postia, istas Kalendas Madias iam preteritas, ante nus debirint coniungire et, inspectas eorum noticias, eorum inter se de ac causa debirint deducire racionis; unde et per ipsas eorum noticias paricolas taliter inter se placitum habuerunt initum. Sed uenientis ad eo placitum ipsi agentis iam dicto abbati Nouiento, in ipso palacio nostro, per triduo seo per pluris dies, ut lex habuit, placitum eorum uise sunt custudissent, et ipso

Ermenoaldo abbati abiectissent uel solsadissent; ipsi nec uinissit ad placitum, nec misso in uice sua derixsissit, nec nulla sonia nunciassit adfirmat. Proinde nus taliter una cum nostris procerebus constetit decriuisse, ut se euidenter per eorum noticias paricolas taliter inter se pro ac causa placitum habuerunt initum, et inluster uir Uuarno, comis palacii noster, testimuniauit quod memorati agentis iam dicto Chainone abbati placitum eorum ligebus custudierunt, et suprascriptus Ermenoaldus abba placitum suum custudire neclixsit: iobemmus, ut quicquid lex loci uestri de tale causa edocit, memoratus Ermenoaldus abba partibus ipsius agentibus ad parte suprascripti Chainone abbati uel basilice sui domni Dionisii, omnemodis uobis distringentebus, conponire et satisfacire non recusit.

✠ Aghilus recognouit.   Bene ualete.

Datum quod ficit minsis Madius, dies quinque. Anno secundo rigni nostri. Nouiento. In Dei nomene feliciter.

VI

Royal judgement in dispute between Chrotcharius, representing the orphan Ingramnus, and Amalbert, over the property of Bayencourt on the River Matz, given in the king's court at the royal palace of Valenciennes, 28 February 692 or 693.

SOURCE: Based on editions by G. Pertz, *MGH Diplomata*, vol. 1, pp. 58–9 (no. 66), and P. Lauer, C. Samaran, *Les diplômes originaux des Mérovingiens*, no. 23, from MS Paris, Archives nationales, K3, no. 7; facsimile also in *ChLA*, vol. 14, no. 576.

✠ Chlodouius rex Francorum, u. inl.

Cum nos in Dei nomene Ualencianis in palacio nostro una cum apostolicis uiris in Christo patribus nostris Ansoaldo, Godino, Ansoberctho, Protadio, Sauarico, Uulfochramno, Chaduino, Turnoaldo, Constantino, Abbone, Stefano, Gribone episcopis; seu et inlustribus uiris Godino, Nordoberctho, Sarroardo, Ragnoaldo, Gunduino, Blidegario, Magnechario, Uualdramno, Ermechario, Chagnerico, Bucceleno, Sigoleno optematis; Angliberctho, Ogmire, Ettherio, Chillone, Adreberctho, Adalrico, Ghislemaro, Ionathan, Modeghiselo comitebus; Chrodmundo, Godino, Sigofrido, Ghiboino, Ermenteo, Madlulfo, Arigio, Auriliano grafionibus; Raganfredo, Maurilione, Ermenrico, Leudoberctho domesticis; Uulfolaico, Aiglo, Chrodberctho, Waldramno refrendariis; Chugoberctho, Landrico seniscalcis; necnon et inlustri uiro Audramno, comite palati nostro, uel reliquis quampluris nostris fedilebus, ad uniuersorum causas audiendas uel recta iudicia termenanda resediremus; ibique ueniens uenerabilis uir Chrotcharius diaconus in causa Ingramno orfanolo, filio Chaldedramno quondam, ordenante inlustri uiro Nordeberctho, qui causas ipsius orfanolo per nostro uerbo et praecepto uidetur habire receptas, aduersus homene nomene Amalberctho repetibat, dum dicerit, eo quod locello noncupanti Baddanecurte super fluuium Masso, qui fuit ipsius Chaldedramno genitore praedicto Ingramno, malo ordine post se retenuit. Unde et per nostras equalis praecepcionis pluris placeta inter se pro ac causa habuerunt initas, aeciam et ad praesens, ad dies quinque ante istas Kalendas Marcias, per alias nostras equalis praecepcionis memmoratus Chrotcharius apud ipso Amalberctho de ac causa placitum habuit initum. Sed ueniens ad eo placeto praedictus Chrotcharius Ualencianis in ipso palacio nostro, et dum placetum suum ligebus custodibat uel ipso Amalberctho sulsadibat, sic ueniens ex parte filius ipsius Amalberctho, nomene Amalricus, sulsadina sua contradixissit; et dum exinde in nostri uel suprascriptis uiris praesencia in racionis adstabant, interrogatum fuit ipsius Amalrico: dum ipsi genitur suos per nostra requalis praecepcionis placitum apud ipso Chrotchario habibat initum, quo ordine in ac causa introire uolibat. Sed ipsi Amalricus nulla euidentem potuit tradire racionem qualiter in ac causa structus aduenissit, nisi inuentum fuit quod contra racionis ordinem ipsa sulsadina contradixissit uel in ac causa introissit. Sic ei fuit iudecatum, ut in exfaido et fredo solidos quindece pro ac causa fidem facere debirit; quod ita et in praesenti per fistuga uisus est ficisse. Et postia memmoratus Chrotcharius per triduum aut fer amplius placitum suum, ut lex habuit, custodissit, et ipso Amalberctho abiectissit uel sulsadissit, ipsi Amalbercthus nec uenissit ad placitum, nec ipso mundeborone suo, inlustri uiro Ermechario, quem per ipsas praecepcionis habuit achramitum, nullatinus praesentassit, nec nulla sunnia nonciasse adfirmat. Proinde nos taliter una cum nostris proceribus constetit decreuisse: ut dum suprascripti uiri renonciauerunt, aeciam et praedictus uir Audramnus suum praebuit testimonium quod ac causa taliter acta uel iudicata seu definita fuissit denuscitur, iubimus ut antedictus Amalbercthus ipso locello Baddanecurte, quicquid ibidem ipsi Chalded-ramnus uisus fuit tenuisse uel moriens dereliquisse, cum omni integritate sua uel aieciencias, sicut ab ipso Chaldedramno fuit possessum cum ligis beneficium, memmorato Chrotchario ad partem suprascripti Ingoramno omnimodis reddire et satisfacere non recusit, ita ut praesentaliter ipso locello praedictus Chrotcharius ad partem ipsius Ingramno omni tempore habiat euindecatum adque elidiatum. Et quicquid de fructa aut paecunia uel reliqua rem, quod dici aut nomenare potest, de ipso locello ipsi Amalbercthus aut mithius suos exinde abstraxit uel minuauit, de quod Chaldedramnus moriens dereliquid, hoc cum ligis beneficium semiliter reddere studiat, et sit inter ipsis ex ac re in postmodo subita causacio; et ipsos solidos dece, quod antedictus Amalricus ad partem ipsius Chrotchario fidem ficit, hoc ei omnimodis conponire et satisfacere non recusit.

✠ Uualderamnus recognouit.   Bene ualete.

Datum pridiae Kalendas Marcias. Annum tercio rigni nostri. Ualencianis. In Dei nomine feliciter.

VII

Edict of Chilperic, 8.

SOURCE: MS Leiden, University Library, Voss. Lat. Q 119 (s. x[1]), fols. 83v–84r; edited by A. Boretius, *MGH LL in quarto, sectio* 2, vol. 1, p. 9, and with emendations by K. A. Eckhardt, *MGH LL in quarto, sectio* 1, vol. 4, pt 1, pp. 262–3.

Quale conuenit modo, ut si seruum sors nunciata fuerit de furtum, tunc dominus serui inter x noctes mittat seruum ad sortem. Si ibi illum in illas x noctes non miserit in praesente, tunc in XL et duas noctis eum mittat, et tunc[1] ibi seruus ad sortem uenire debet, et illi qui[2] furtum pertulit ius sit cum VI uidere. Et si ad XL et duas noctis non uenerit nec sunnia adnuntiauerit, tunc seruus culpabilis iudicetur; et causa super domino magis non ascendat nisi quantum de seruo lex est, aut ipsi[3] seruus decidat[4] aut dominus pro seruo conponat, hoc est solidos XII et capitale et delatura. Et si in XL et duas noctis legibus sunnia nuntiauerit, in octuaginta et quatuor noctis postea placitum intendatur; et si ibi se non eduxerit, sicut supra scriptum[5] est, culpabilis iudicetur; nam ⟨si⟩[6] ad XL et II noctes sunnia ⟨non⟩ nuntiauerit[7], iectus[8] XV[9] solidos componat. Et si inter ipsas XL et II noctes nec fidem

---

[1] tunc *Boretius*] eum *MS*   [2] *i.e.* cui   [3] *i.e.* ipse   [4] cedatur *Boretius*] decidat *MS*   [5] scriptum *Eckhardt*] scriptu *MS*   [6] *added by Boretius*   [7] sunnia non nuntiauerit *Boretius*] sunni adnuntiauerit *MS*   [8] iectus *Boretius*] lectus *MS*   [9] XL *Eckhardt*

facere nec conponere uoluerit, tunc rogat ille qui consecutus est, ut de lege[10] inter XIIII ⟨noctes⟩[11] soluat quod antea dictum est; et si adhuc inter ipsas XIIII noctes noluerit soluere, rogit inter VII noctis. ⟨Et si inter ipsas VII noctis⟩[12] nec fidem facere nec componere uoluerit, tunc in proximo mallo ante rachymburgiis sedentes et dicentes, quod ipsi illum ante audierint[13] sic inuitetur graphio, cum fistuco mittat super se, ad res suas ambulet et prendat quantum rachymburgii antea audierint[14]; et graphio cum VII rachymburgiis antrutionis bonis credentibus aut quis sciant accionis ad casam[15] illius ambulent et pretium faciant et quod graphio tollere debet. Et si graphio ante rachymburgiis sedentes non fuerit inuitatus, non ibi presummat ambulare. Et si inuitatus fuerit et ibidem noluerit ambulare, de uita sit culpabilis. Et si graphio super pretium aut extra legem aliquid tollere presumpserit, nouerit se uitae suae perire[16] dispendium . Et si dixerit illi[17] cui res tolluntur, quod male eum destruat et contra legem et iustitiam[18], tunc maniat[19] graphio eum inter noctis quadraginta et duo et ille et suo contractorem qui eum inuitauit similiter maneat. Et si non negauerit ille qui inuitauit, adducat VII rachymburgiis ferrebannitus qui antea audissent causam illam: nobis praesentibus erit. Et si VII uenire non potuerint et eos certa sonia detrigauerit et toti uenire non possint, tunc ueniant III de ipsis qui pro fide[20] sua dicant et pro paris suos sunia nuntiant. Et si rachymburgiis nec VII nec III dare potuerit nec dat, graphio et ille qui accepit, res illius, quem contra legem et iustitiam extruderit, ⟨reddat⟩[21] et ille qui male inuitauit soluat cui res fuerunt.

Et quicumque ingenuus de actione et ui reiecte mallauerit de qualibet causa, simili modo ubi habet lege directa sic facere debet. Et si homo malus fuerat qui male facit et si res non habet unde sua mala facta conponat, legibus consecutus super illum nihilhominus graphio ad legem que antea auditus est e lege inuitetur[22], et auferat per tres mallus ante rachymburgiis, ut eum, si[23] uoluerint, parentes aut de suis rebus redimant, aut se sciant, si noluerint in quarto mallo, nobis presentibus ueniant: nos ordinamus, cui malum fecit tradatur in manu et faciant exinde quod uoluerint. Nam agens et qui mallat ipsum ad nos adducant, et adtrutionis secundum legem consecutus habuerit inter octuaginta et quatuor noctes ipsa inuitatio et lex faciat sicut superius scriptum est.

[10] lege *Eckhardt*] legem *MS*   [11] *added by Eckhardt*   [12] *added by Merkel*   [13] audierint *Eckhardt*] audierit *MS*   [14] audierint *Eckhardt*] odierit *MS*   [15] ad casam *Eckhardt*] a casa *MS*   [16] perire *Boretius*] periret *MS*   [17] *i.e.* ille   [18] iustitiam *Eckhardt*] iustitia *MS*   [19] maniat *i.e.* manniat *Eckhardt*] muniat *Boretius*   [20] pro fide *Eckhardt*] preside *MS*   [21] *added by Boretius*   [22] a lege inuitetur *Eckhardt*] inuita elegitur *Boretius*   [23] eum si *Boretius*] ea nisi *MS*

VIII

Royal judgement in dispute between several *coloni* of the monastery of Cormery and the monastery itself, about rents and renders, given in the king's court at the royal palace of Chasseneuil, 9 June 828.

SOURCE: Edited by L. Levillain, *Recueil des actes de Pépin I et Pépin II, rois d'Aquitaine (814–848)*, pp. 46–7 (no. 12), from parchment original now bound up as MS Paris, BN lat. 8837, fol. 17.

Pipinus, gratia Dei rex Aquitanorum. Cum nos, in Dei nomine, die martis, Casanogilo uilla palatio nostro in pago Pictauo secus alueum Clinno, ad multorum causas audiendum rectaque iudicia terminandas resideremus, ibique uenientes aliqui homines nomen Aganbertus, Aganfredus, Frotfarius et Martinus, tam ipse quam eorum pares coloni sancti Pauli de uilla Antoniaco ex monasterio Cormaricum siue Iacob abbate, ibique se proclamabant incontra ipso abbate uel suum aduocatum nomine Ageno, eo quod iam dictus abba uel sui missi eis super querissent uel exactassent amplius de censum uel de pro soluta quam ipse per drictum facere nec soluere non debebant nec eorum antecessores antea ad longum tempus non fecerant nec solserant nec talem legem eis non conseruabant quomodo eorum antecessores habuerant. Sed ipse Agenus aduocatus et Magenarius prepositus ex ipso monasterio de presente adstabant et taliter incontra ipsos intendebant quod iam dictus abba nec ipsi nullas functiones nec redibutiones eis non exactauerant nec exactare iusserant, nisi quale ipsi per drictum uel per triginta annos partibus ipsius monasterii tam ipsi quam et eorum antecessores desolserant; et discriptionem ibidem optulerunt ad relegendum, in quo continebatur quomodo sub tempus Alcuino abbate ipsi coloni ex ipsa uilla, qui ad presente adstabant unacum eorum pares, cum iuramento dictauerunt quid per singula mansa ex ipsa curte desoluere debebant et habebant daturum: ipsa discriptio, anno trigesimo quarto regnante Carolo rege. Interrogatum fuit ad iam dictis colonis qui ibidem de presente adherant si ipsa discriptione dictauerant uel ipsa redibutione per annorum spacia dissolserant, sicut in ipsa continebatur, aut si ipsa discriptio uera aut bona adherat, aut si contra ipsa aliquid dicere aut opponere uellebant, an non. Ipsi ipsam discriptionem ueram et bonam dixerunt uel recognouerunt, et hoc minime denegare non potebant quod ipsa redibutione per annorum spacia non desolsissent uel ipsam discriptionem ipsi non dictassent uel antecessores eorum. Proinde nos taliter unacum fidelibus nostris, id sunt Himmoni comiti, Dadeno, Bobilone, Launaldo, Dodone, Sigoino, Gyrlebaldo, Hisario, Dauid, Helinberto, Adalberto, Acsindo, Amalfredo, Ioseph, Arcambaldo, Erinfredo, Geraldo, Ruben, Rotgaudo, Leotgario, Ingilberto, Deotimio, Salacone seu et Iohanni comiti palacii nostri uel reliquis quampluris, uisi fuimus iudicasse ut, dum ipsi coloni taliter se recognoscebant, sicut superius est insertum, ut ipsa discriptione, sicut ipse dictauerant uel conscripta adherat, uel ipse ipsa redibutione per spacia annorum fecerant, ita et per singulos annos partibus ipsa casa Dei facere uel dissoluere debeant. Propterea iubemus ut, dum ac causa sic acta uel perpetrata esse cognouimus, ut memoratus Agenus aduocatus siue Maginarius prepositus tale scriptum partibus ipsa casa Dei exinde recipere deberet, quod ita et de presente manifestum est fecisse.

✝   Deotimius ad uicem Iohanni comiti palacii recognoui et subscripsi.

✝   Datum quinto idus Iunio in anno xv imperium domni Hludowici serenissimi imperatoris. ✝   Nectarius scripsit et subs.

IX

Notitia recording hearing in county court by two royal *missi* of dispute between Wulfad, archbishop of Bourges, and Count Eccard, about the estate of Perrecy, at Mont, *c.* 875.

SOURCE: Edited by M. Prou and A. Vidier, *Recueil des chartes de Saint-Benoît-sur-Loire*, pp. 57–9 (no. 24), from several seventeenth- and eighteenth-century transcripts of the cartulary of Perrecy; the text given follows MS Paris, BN lat. 17721 (s. xviii), p. 4.

INQUISTUM CUM EXEMPLARIBUS DE CARTIS QUEM FECERUNT LEUDO ET ADELARDUS COMES INTER UULFALDUM ET HECCARDUM DE UILLA PARICIACO.

Uenerunt Leudo episcopus et Adelardus comes, missi dominici, in comitatu Augustidunense, in uilla quæ dicitur in Monte, et fecerunt ibi uenire ipsos pagenses nobiliores et cæteris quampluris de iam dicto comitatu per bannum domni Regis, et fecerunt requistum inter Uulfaldum episcopum et Heccardum comitem, per illos quem

Uulfaldus ibi denominauit uel per cæteros, per illum sacramentum quem domno Karolo rege habebant iurata et per illam professionem quam in baptismo promiserunt ut ueritatem dixissent de uilla quæ dicitur Patriciacus, quem Uulfaldus dicebat quod de sua ecclesia essere debebat. Unde ibi kartas ostendidit ad relegendum de temporibus Hildeberti et Chilperici regum, et una de temporibus domni Pipini regis, siue de nomen Niuelongi, in loco præstaria, ut interueniente per bonorum hominum consensum et per uoluntatem ipsius episcopi Bituricensis in precaria iam dictus Niuelongus habuisset, et III libras in festiuitate sanctæ Mariæ transsoluisset. Et Heccardus ibi præceptum domni imperatoris Ludouici præsentauit ad relegendum, et sua notitia, per quem super Iohanne reconquisiuit res, quæ de ipso præcepto ei abstractas fuerunt, in placito generale domno nostro Karolo. Tunc interrogatum per istos fuit Leutbaldo, Ildrico, Suauono, Girbaldo, Iohanne, Ildebodo, Eruilfo, Uulfardo, item Leutbaldo, Honesteo, uel per cæteros, per illum sacramentum, quid de ueritatem de isto inquisto superius denominatum sciebant, ueritatem exinde dixissent. Deinde isti unanimiter dixerunt: neque antecessores nostros audiuimus dicere, neque nos ipsi nec audiuimus, nec uidimus dicere ueritatem quod ipsa uilla aliter fuisset nisi ad fiscum domni Pipini et domno Karoli et domno Ludouici imperatoris, sine ullo censu, uel ullo uestidura, aut ulla causa dominii, usque domnus imperator per suum præceptum Heccardo dedit. Deinde interrogatum fuit Leutboldo et Iacob, per cuius exortationem Uulfaldus ad ipsum placitum uenutus erat, quid inde sciebant? Et dixerunt quod Heccardo ipsam uillam habere uidimus, et audiuimus dicere quod de ipsa ecclesia Uulfaldo essere debuisset, quod adhuc multi auditum habent postquam ista ratio exorta fuit, sed non de ueritate quod umquam exinde fuisset. Deinde interrogatum fuit Guntfrido, et dixit quod Hildebrando illam habere uidi, ad fiscum regis, et deinde Heccardo, ad alodum, et audiuit dicere quod de ecclesia Uulfaldo fuisset. Deinde interrogatum fuit Maurono et dixit quod uenit ad illum Suauus ut fuisset locutus cum Odelrico seniori suo quod ipsa uilla acaptasset et ei dedisset, sed Odelricus uidit quod ratio non erat, hoc demisit. Deinde fuit loqutus cum Uinfredo alii seniori sui, et uidit quod ratio non fuisset, dimisit similiter, deinde audiuit quod uenit ad Odono comiti pro ipsa ratione, sed nesciebat quod inde fecit, amplius illi cognitum non erat.

X

Notitia recording hearing before Saraman, provost of St Martin, Tours, of dispute between the priest Notbert, and Agintrude and others, about land at *villa Malebuxis*, heard on the property, June 857.

SOURCE: Edited by M. Thévenin, *Textes relatifs aux institutions privées et publiques aux époques mérovingienne et carolingienne*, pp. 120–3 (no. 89), from a transcript of the lost 'Pancarte noire' of St Martin, Tours.

Notitia hic habetur iure assignata, qualiter et quorum presentia anno DCCCLVII dominice incarnationis, XVII regni piissimi regis Karoli III nec non et Hilduini saluberrimi abbatis, parte et maxima, deo propitiante, iam sopita seuissima tempestate quam hostis antiquus inter Christicolas crudelissime excitauerat: iamque iura legum rediuiuum quasi exordium dum capere per loca aliqua nitens, et Deo cooperante in hac sedatione clarissimo uiro Hilduino egregio abbate prepollente; dumque in sua pene omni dictione precipiente atque compellente eius missi iustitias facere studerent, presbiter quidam Ecclesie sancti Hispani ipsa ex dictione nomine Notbertus presentiam Saramiani prepositi gregis beati Martini, aliorumque nobilium uirorum eiusdem potestatis IV idus

Iunii adiens proclamabat qualiter res Ecclesie sancti Hispani que in precepto eiusdem ecclesie cum aliis rebus prefixe erant, quas et in sua potestate post mortem auunculi sui Esaïe qui ipsas res emerat diu legitime partibus ipsius ecclesie in uilla Malebuxis possiderat, faciente Autberto et Agintrude sorore eius et eius uiro Amalgario, iniuste ex potestate sancti Hispani ablate forent. Tunc Saramannus prepositus precepit ut hi homines qui ipsas res tenebant eius in praesentia ad constitutum placitum suas auctoritates ostenderent, quas auctoritates Turonis eius in conspectu aliorumque nobilium uirorum deferentes, nullatenus ipsam rationem propter absentiam uicinorum quibus haec ratio nota erat, diffinire ualebant. Tunc deliberatum est ibi ut in ipsa uilla de qua eaedem res erant, unde ratio haec agebatur, iudicio uicinorum aliorumque bonorum uirorum diffiniretur. Aliquamdiu post dum Saramanus praefatus praepositus cum aliis clericis gregis beati Martini aliisque bonis uiris uillam Briusgalum de qua memoratae erant res, pridie kalendarum Augustarum adisset, ut ibi ex precepto senioris sui diuersas sciscitaretur ac deliberaret causas, et residerent infra atrium sancti Spani propter congruentiam maiorum conuentus, uentum est ut et haec altercatio deliberaretur. Tunc iudicatum est ibi a multis nobilibus uiris et colonis, qui subter tenentur inserti, ut Norbertus presbiter suum ibi statueret aduocatum, et predicti homines suas deferrent auctoritates. Mox unus ex ipsis, uidelicet Autbertus, nutu, ut uisum est, Dei professus est palam quia ⟨il⟩lorum auctoritates false erant: et ne ob hoc gehennam uenturam liceret, nolens in hac obstinatione durare, proiecerat ipsas auctoritates super altare sancti Spani. Tunc prescriptus Amalgarius in aduocationem Agintrudis sue scilicet uxoris accusauit Autbertum dicens quod iniuste contenderet auctoritates sue mulieris. Super haec diu, omnes residentes et astantes attoniti, deliberatum est, ut idem Autbertus ipsas cartas in palam differret, quod et actum est. Sed ipse primus testificatus est, uidelicet illam quae ex nomine Esaïe detulit, et illam quae Turonis ingeniose facta fuerat quas recitatas inuente sunt falsae publiciter, scilicet, quia ipsi quorum nomina prefixa ibi habebantur, id est Notfredus et Geroinus testificati sunt iureiurando quod nequaquam illam ullo tempore firmassent, nec etiam unquam corroborata fuisset. Etiam et affuit scriptor eiusdem cartae qui ibidem professus est palam, quod ipsam cartam scripsisset, sed non eam corroborrasset. Sic pene et omni coloni testificati sunt, quod non eam uidissent corroborare, nec tamen nomina colonorum ipsius uillae ibi adnotata erant, unde ipse res habebantur, sed alterius preter eorum tamen qui memorati sunt. Hinc iudicio omnium qui ibidem aderant, tenuit prenotatus Amalgarius cartas in manibus et sciscitatus a residentibus utrum testes ipsius potestatis habere potuisset, qui illas cartas ueras iurati dixissent, mox palam professus est quod non potuisset. Tunc memorata femina Agintrudis proclamauit quod causa timoris predicti presbiteri testes huius rei habere nequaquam potuissent; et denominauit quosdam colonos quos dixit peritos esse huius rationis. Tunc prepositus iussit offerre ibi reliquias; et denominauit colonos, id est [9 names], et alios plurimos adiuratus est per Deum et eorum christianitatem atque fidelitatem et presentes Sanctorum reliquias, si ipsa carta scilicet titulus uenditionis qui ex nomine Esaïe eorum partibus erat, legitime et iure corroboratus esset, et si haberet legitimam uestituram et si ipse res iure potius Notberto presbitero partibus sancti Hispani debite essent, quam Agintrudis. Ad haec mox singuli sub ipsa testificatione eodem modo iureiurando testificati sunt: quod ipse titulus uenditionis nec iure corroborratus foret, sed furtim, nec legitimam habuisset uestituram: similiter et ille scriptus quem ingeniose Turonis impetrauerant, inutilis et inofficiosus esset; et ipse res magis debite essent partibus sancti Spani quam partibus Agintrudis. Tunc Amalgarius palam professus est, quod testes nec ibi presentialiter nec deinceps habere potuissent, et inofficiose forent ipse carte quas ibi tenebat. Mox iudicio omnium, qui ibidem aderant, interrogauit Saramanus prepositus Otbertum aduocatum prelibati Notberti presbiteri, si ipsas cartas quas adhuc

Amalgarius in manibus tenebat, facere falsas potuisset. Statim ille respondit: quod omnimodis potuisset illas facere falsas. Tunc iure prefixo cum testibus prenotatis fecit eas omnimodis falsas, et in manibus ipsius Amalgarii eas punxit, et hinc penitus scidit, sicut ei ab omnibus iudicatus est et deliberatum. Sunt enim ipse res in uilla que uocatur Malebuxis, quas quondam Esaias presbiter de Amalberto datis suis preciis emerat que in titulo uenditionis cum suis terminationibus adnotate habentur. Sicque res istas iure partibus sancti Spani iudicio omnium ibidem residentium atque astantium redditas ac euindicatas eorum consilio, Notberto presbitero uisum fuit ut hanc exinde acciperet notitiam, scilicet ut, si futuris temporibus insidiante inimico humani generis inde aliqua motio ei suisque successoribus aduenerit, manifestum sit quomodo iure rationabiliterque deliberatum a plurimis nobilibus uiris ac deffinitum sit qui hic ex parte habentur adnotati. Saramannus prepositus subscripsi. Autbertus presbyter subsc. Azaneus diaconus subsc. Gislemarus accolitus subsc. Gislarius subdiaconus subsc. Signum ✦ Nautfredi Iudicis. Signum ✦ Geruini. S. [*3 names*]. S. ✦ Restoduni. S. [*2 names*].

XI

Out of court agreement between Abbot Conuuoion of Redon and the peasant Fomus, made at Augan, 29 January 852.

SOURCE: MS Rennes, Archiepiscopal Palace, s.n. ('Cartulary of Redon'), fol. 81r; also printed by A. de Courson, *Cartulaire de Redon*, pp. 96–7 (no. 127).

Noticia in quorum presentia qui subtertenentur qualiter uenit Fomus ad interpellandos monachos Sancti Saluatoris in Rotono monasterio habitantes, de hereditate Arbiuan, et dicebat quod suam hereditatem erat; et habuit Conuuoionus abbas consilium cum fratribus suis super hac re, et dediderunt et illi consilium ut trammitteret tres doctissimos ex suis fratribus usque ad supradictam illam terram, in conspectu uirorum nobilium qui manebant illa plebis, et interrogarent eos utrum uerum quereret an non. Et abierunt Leumelus, presbyter et monachus, et Uuinkalunus, presbyter et monachus e Rituere, monachus, usque ad supradictam illam terram, in IIII feria, in decollatione sancti Iohannis; et dederunt illi illam terram terciam partem hereditatis Degnum; et donauit ille Fomus fideiiussores et securitates, Iarnhobrit et Dumuuoret, ut non quereret ille amplius super illos de hereditate Dignum et de hereditate Arbeuuan, nec ipse, nec filius eius, nec filii filiorum eius usque in aeternum, quandiu mundus staret; et in annis singulis promisit ille dare ex illam tertiam partem unum semodium ex frumento, denarios XVIII. Factum est hoc in plebe quae uocatur Alcam, in Coluuoretan, coram multis nobilibusque uiris quorum haec sunt nomina: Reinbert, presbyter, testis; Haelhoiarn, presbyter, testis; Catuueten, testis; Cenetlor, presbyter, testis; Arthanael, testis; Uuoletec, testis; Rethuualt, testis; Alunoc, clericus, testis; Iarnican, testis; Uuorbili, testis; Maenuuallon, testis; Pascuuoret, testis; Seferia, testis. Factum est hoc IIII kal. Februarii, anno XII regnante Karolo rege, dominante Erispoe Britaniam.

XII

Appearance of the machtiern Ratfred before the *princeps* Salomon at *Aula Colroit*, 857.

SOURCE: Cartulary of Redon (as for XI, fols. 74v–75r; also printed by de Courson, *Cartulaire de Redon*, pp. 79–80 (no. 105).

Noticia in quorum presentia requisiuit Salomon, princeps Brittaniae, Ratfrid quare fregisset securitatem suam super Conuuoiono abbatem et monachos Sancti Saluatoris in illa perturbatione post mortem Erispoe, quia supradictus Ratfred et fratres eius in supradicta perturbatione uenerunt ad monasterium Roton, dicentes se esse heredes in Bain, et nisi Conuuoion abbas et sui monachi redderent eis suam hereditatem in Bain, totam abbatiam Sancti Saluatoris incenderent et predarent. Tunc supradictus abbas et eius monachi inuiti et necessitate conpulsi, dederunt eis quod querebant, id est, octo partes in Bain et IIII partes et dimidium in Siz. Nec in hoc eis satisfuit, nisi supradicti monachi IIII homines in securitate istius redditionis eis darent; nec non et illud constricti et coangustati fecerunt ne tota illa plebs arderetur. Sed postquam Salomon totum dominum Brittanniae obtinuit et hoc audiuit, ualde ei displicuit. Deinde iussit Ratfrid uenire ad se, et interrogauit cur monachia sempiternam Sancti Saluatoris per uim et tirannidem teneret. Tunc ipse respondit per uim se nihil tenere, sed quod tenebat, id est, VIII partem in Bain et IIII et dimidium in Siz, Conuuoion abbas et sui monachi ei, sponte et uoluntariae ac pacifice, dedisse. Postea Salomon iratus[1] interrogauit Conuuoion abbatem et suos monachos cur abbatiam Sancti Saluatoris sponte tirannis dedissent. Tunc Conuuoion abbas et sui monachi responderunt se nihil uoluntariae dedisse, sed inuiti et coacti et necessitate conpulsi dederunt quod dederunt. Tunc Salomon dixit ad Ratfred ut redderet in manu sua quicquid tenebat de abbatia Sancti Saluatoris. Quod et fecit, et reddidit in manu Salomonis. Tunc Salomon dixit ad Ratfred: Ecce dedisti in manu mea quod tenebas ex abbatia Sancti Saluatoris; nunc quere tuum sumptum, et fac quod tua hereditas sit secundum legem et ueritatem ac rationem, et ego mutabo illam monachis et ibi illam reddam. Tunc respondit Ratfred se ibi non habere sumptum quod non erant ibi sui pagenses. Deinde Salomon dixit: Do tibi spatium X dierum ut congregas tuum sumptum et tuos testes in aulam Penard. Tunc confessus est Ratfred se non habere testes uel sumptum unde posset facere quod haberet hereditatem in Bain. Tunc Salomon dixit: Si non potes facere quod tua hereditas sit, promitte et da securitatem, et pro te et pro omnibus tuis parentibus, ut nunquam dicas neque tu neque tui parentes uos esse heredes in Bain, et quod non queratis illam hereditatem super Conuuoion abbate et super suos monachos. Et tunc promisit Ratfred et dedit securitatem et pro se et pro suis fratribus et omnibus suis parentibus, quod non quererent hereditatem in Bain, et quod non inquietaret Conuuoion abbas et suos monachos, ex hoc quod iniuste ac per uim ab illis monachis acceperat, et iterum iuste ac legaliter in manu Salomonis reddiderat. Et tunc reddidit Salomon Sancto Saluatori et Conuuoion abbati, pro anima sua et pro anima Nominoe sui nutritoris, in elemosina sempiterna, hoc quod Ratfred iniuste ac per uim a supradictis monachis acceperat. Factum est hoc in aula Colroit, coram multis nobilibus uiris quorum ista sunt nomina: Salomon, testis; Bran, testis; Boduuan, testis; Pascuueten, testis; Urscant, testis; Festien, presbyter, testis; Felix, diaconus, testis; Roenuualart, presbyter, testis; Communoc, presbyter, testis; Finois, presbyter, testis; Moetien, diaconus, testis; Uuocondelu, testis; Hincant, testis; Sabioc, testis; Hoiluualart, testis; Drelouuen, testis.

---

[1] Salomoni ratus *MS*

XIII

Lawsuit between the peasants Uuobrian and Uuetenoc at Ruffiac, 17 June 860.

SOURCE: Cartulary of Redon (as for XI), fol. 84v; also printed by de Courson, *Cartulaire de Redon*, p. 106 (no. 139).

Noticia in quorum presentia qualiter interpellauit quidam homo nomine Uuobrian alterum hominnem nomine Uuetenoc, propter alodum quem supradictus Uuobrian illi, multo ante tempore, uendiderat; dicebat enim Uuobrian non se uendidisse ei tantum de terra quantum ille tenebat. Tunc supradictus Uuetenoc placitum inde leuauit, adunatis suis quorum ista sunt nomina: Fomus, Iacu, Rethuualart, Drehuuobri; et lecta sua carta, et adtestantibus suis testibus et dilisidis, reuelauit quod totum quod tenebat, comparauerat a supradicto Uuobrian. Tunc Uuobrian, uictus tam ad carta quam a testibus et dilisidis, confessus est. Factum est hoc in aecclesia Rufiac, xv kalendas Iulii, feria II, coram Iarnhitin machti n et Hinuualart et Litoc, hoc misso Salomonis principis, et coram multis nobilibusque uiris quorum haec sunt nomina: Uuorcomet, testis; Nominoe, testis; Miot, testis; Omnis, testis; Tuduual, testis; Hoiarn, testis; Sulmin, abbas, testis; Iuna, abbas; Comaltcar, presbyter, testis; Adaluuin, testis; Eusorchit, clericus, testis, qui tunc cartam publice legit quod totum ei uendiderat sicut sua carta dicebat supradictus Uuetenoc.

XIV

Account of dispute between the monastery of Celanova and the villagers of Zacors in Galicia, together with a record of the oath taken by the villagers, 11 May 987.

SOURCE: MS Madrid, Archivo histórico nacional, sección de códices, 986 B (s. xii/xiii) ('Cartulary of Celanova'), fols. 38v–39r; also printed in C. Sánchez-Albornoz, 'Documentos para el studio del procedimiento judicial en el reino Asturleones' in *Homenaje a D. Agustín Millares Carlo*, pp. 1750 (no. 9).

Nos homines qui sumus habitantes in uilla Zacors, id sumus prenominati Hordonio, Ueremudo, Habze, Abdella et Timimi uobis domni Manillani abbati et domni Didaci et fratrum uestrorum monasterio Cellenoue. Plerisque manet cognitum quod obtinuimus quandam partem uillule Sancti Felicis iuri nostro de dato pontificis domni Rudesindi episcopi, beate memorie, quod nobis dederat ad stipendium usufructuario. Et peccato nobis inpediente misimus illam in contemptione ad fratrem uestrum frater Oduario qui ipsam deganeam Sancti Felicis obtinebat pro quo peruenimus in ipsam uillam in presentia iudicum Froyla Monniiz, Abraham abba, Pelagius Aspasandiz, Oluario Tezoniz, Gemondo Froilaiz, Alfidio Gulderes, Pelagius Tructesendiz, Fagildus confessor, Hoduario confessor, Vimara Froylaz et aliorum multorum filii bene natorum turba non modica qui in ipsos terminos preuiderunt secundum in uestra diuisione resonat. Et cuncti dixerunt quia uestra est ueritas. Proinde causatus fuit nobis mandator uester nomine Saluator et roborauimus manifestum et placcitum ut fuissemus ad legem et quod nobis ordinasset adimplessemus. Obinde agnouimus nos in ueritate et adsignauimus uobis in uestra uilla per textum scripture placiti et per saionem nomine Gudesteo et fecimus uobis ligali placiti ut si in quacumque tempus, an nos an filii neptis uel bisneptis nostris, uobis aut fratribus uestris, qui ipsam deganeam contenuerint, aliquam calumpniam in ipsam uillam uobis in ferre uoluerint pro ipsis terminis sicut in istam diuisionem resonat, quomodo pariemus uobis tam nos quam qui hoc ausus fuerit infringere, ipsam uillam duplatam et in super per singula capita xx.xx boues. Notum die v, ydus Magii era xxv^a post millessima Hordonius in hoc placitum manu mea ✛ Ueremudo manu mea ✛ Habze manu mea ✛ Abdella manu mea ✛ Timimi manu mea ✛ Qui presentes fuerunt: Didacus presbiter, Crizila presbiter, Timimi presbiter, Melhe presbiter, Gudesteo presbiter, Nouidius presbiter, Teodemirus diaconus, Geodesindus Pepizi, Froyani Gaudio, Berosindus Iohanniz, Ero Audinizi, Azo Uimarizi, Fonso Sunilla et alii plures. In iuditio Froyla Nunniz, Pelagio Spasandizi et aliorum iudicum ape⟨ti⟩tione Saluator qui asseret in uoce Domini Saluatori et de Manillani abbatis et fratribus Cellenoue contra istum Ordonium qui uoce intendit sua et de suos heredes nominibus Ueremudo, Abze, Abdella, Temimi, manifestus sum ego Ordonio uerum est, quod negare non ualeo, quia abeo quintam de ipsa uilla Sancto Felice per ubi eam designauimus ad predictos iudices et que abeo manifestum et ad manifestum nichil abeo que apponere. Hordonio in hoc meum manifestum manu mea ✛ Saluator et Hordonio tibi saioni nostro Gudesteo per hunc nostrum placitum tibi compromittimus ut presentemus nostras personas ista IIII^a feria in presentia iudicis, Abrahame abba, pro ad lege, pro quinta de ipsa uilla et quod nobis lex iusserit adimpleamus, et qui unus ex nobis hunc placitum excesserit pariet de quo agitur in duplum. Saluator et Ordonio in hoc placitum manus nostras ✛ Saluator qui uoce intendit de fratribus Cellenoue et Ordonio qui uoce intendit sua et de suos heredes tibi saioni nostro Gudesteo per hunc nostrum placitum tibi compromittimus ut presentemus nostras personas et testimonias in presentia iudicis Froyla Nunnizi die ista v^a feria hic in ad Sanctum Christophalum ad Malage et firme ego Saluator qui ipsas quattuor rationes de ipsa uilla Sancto Felice per ubi eam designauimus iste Ordonio et suos heredes tollerunt ad ipsos fratres de eas iure et abent illas contra se. Et ego Ordonio mea persona et meas testimonias quia ipsas quattuor rationes nec eas presumsi neque ego neque meos heredes uel uoce intendo neque illas abemus contra nos et qui hunc plactum exierit pariet ipsa uilla in duplum et insuper c solidos. Saluator et Ordonio in hoc placitum manus nostras ✛. Exceptis illa quinta unde manifestum roboraui. Hordonio ad persona mea et heredum meorum, nominibus Ueremudo, Abze, Abdella et Timimi tibi saioni nostro Gudesteo per hunc placitum nostrum ad implendo tibi compromittimus quomodo adsignemus tibi ipsam uillam cum omnia sua per terminos suos et locis antiquis ab integro sicut in illa diuisione resonat quam frater Fagildo et frater Oduario in concilio presentant die ista IIII^a feria quod est v^o ydus Magii, era Millessima xxv^a. Et tu in manu Saluatoris qui uocem fratrum obtinet sicut veritas et lex gotica docet, et si minime fecerimus et de nostro placito excesserimus quomodo duplemus tibi ipsam uillam et insuper pariemus per singula capita xx.xx boues. Nos superius nominati in hoc placitum manus nostras ✛.

XV

A variant copy of the record of the oath of the villagers of Zacors (XIV).

SOURCE: 'Cartulary of Celanova' (as for XIV), fol. 54r.

Nos homines qui sunt habitantes in uilla Zacoris adsumus praenominati Hordonio Uermudo Habze Abdella et Timimi uobis domini Manillani abbati et domini Didaci et fratrum uestrorum monasterii Cellenoue. Plerisque manet cognitum quod obtinuimus quandam partem Sancti Felicis uillule iuri nostro de dato pontificis domini Rudesindi episcopi beate memorie quod nobis dederat adstipendium usufructuario. Et peccato nobis impediente misimus illam in contemptione ad frater uestrum nomine Oduario qui ipsam deganeam Sancti Felicis obtineat pro quo peruenimus in ipsa uilla in presentia iudicum Froila Nuniz Abraham abba Pelagius Spasindiz Oduario Tetoniz Gemondo Froylaz Alfidio Gulderes Plagi Tructerendiz Fagildus confessor Oduario confessor Uimara Froilaz et aliorum multorum filii bene natorum turba non modica qui ipsos terminos peruiderunt secundum in uestra diuisione resonat et cuncta dixerunt quia est uestra ueritas. Proinde causatus fuit nobis cum mandator uester nomine Saluator Grouprauiz. Manifestum et placitum ut fuissemus ad legem et quod nobis ordinassent adimplessemus. Obinde agnouimus nos in ueritate uobis uestram uillam per textum scripture placiti et per saione nomine Godesteo et facimus uobis legale placitum ut si inquacumque tempus an nos an filii nepti uel binepti uobis uel fratribus uestris qui ipsam deganeam continuerint aliam calumniam in ipsam uillam uobis inferre uoluerint pro ipsis terminis sicut in istam diuisionem resonat quomodo pariemus uobis tam nos quam qui hoc ausus fuerit infringere ipsam uillam duplatam et insuper per singula capita xx.xx boues.

Notum die v ydus Magii era xxᵃ vᵃ post millenia. Hordonio in hoc placitum manum meam. Uermudo manum meam. Habze manum meam. Abdella manum meam. Timimi manum meam. In presentes fuerunt Boresindus Iohanniz testis. Ero Audiniz testis. Azo Uimariz testis. Fonso Sunilla et alii plures.

XVI

Recognitio made by García Refugano repudiating his claim to the church of Tobiella and recognizing the rights to it of the monastery of Cardeña, 14 January 957.

SOURCE: Edited by L. Serrano, *Becerro Gótico de Cardeña*, pp. 224–5 (no. 210), from the thirteenth-century Cartulary of Cardeña (then in private hands: untraced), fol. 57v.

In presentia domno et cum summa ueneratione nominando comitis nostri Fredinando Gundissalbiz uel aliorum multorum manifestus sum ego Garsea Refugano, ad petitione de domno Auriolfo qui est in uoce de Recesuindus abba; uerum est quod negare non ualeo quia ypsa casa Sanctorum Petri et Pauli, qui est sita in locum quem uocitant Tobiella, quia cognosco me in ueritate quem ego germano Obeco presbiter tradidit illa et suum corpus et anima ad Sanctorum Apostolorum Petri et Pauli simulque Domino, et ad Stefano abbati uel ad collatione de Caradigna, et post inde sic iactabi uestros fratres, id est, Fortuni confessor et Garsea presbiter siue et Gemellus presbiter cum suos sotius manibus de ipsa casa; et postea sic uenit Dominico presbiter seu Rapinatus presbiter cum saione de comite, pernominato Sarracino Obecoz, et miserunt ipsos fratres in sua casa per mandato de comite, et fecimus exinde placitum quarto die post Natale Domini si non uenissem ante comite cum meas cartas que ipso meo germano iam supradicto presbiter mici tradiderat ypsa casa coram multis testibus et ante Adefonso Sendiniz, que pariassem CCC solidos a parte comite per manuberrende fide iussore; et non potui firmare; et cum mea superuia feci uobis contemptio et iudicio ante comite et ante domno Sebuldo abba; et pro meo peccato negaui ipsa carta de tradictione ecclesie et ipsa pagina, quia non fecit meo germano carta nisi pro gubernio et continentia de undecim fratres, et non potui firmare. Deinde cognosco me in ueritate que hoc manifestum uerum esse fateor et in hoc manifestum nicil abo quod apponam.

Factum manifestum XVIIII kalendas Februarias, era DCCCCLXXXXVᵃ regnante rex Sancio in Legione, et comite Fredinando Gundissalbiz in Castella.

Ego Garsea, qui hoc manifestum fieri uolui et relegendo audiui, manu mea sygnum feci. Munnio Didaz hic.—Beila Didas hic.—Sarracino hic.—Garsea testis.—Belasco testis.—Sancio testis.—

XVII

Oath taken by the inhabitants of Kastro Aquilanido in settlement of their dispute with the inhabitants of Jonsedh, 1 April 987.

SOURCE: Edited by R. d'Abadal i de Vinyals, *Catalunya Carolingia*, vol. 3, p. 427 (no. 270), from two printed texts of a lost original.

In nomine Domini Dei eterni. Congregati sunt homines de kastro Aquilanido et homines de Jonsedh pro altercatione que cecidit inter illos pro illorum hereditatem quod uendiderunt unus ab aliis, et postea fecerunt inde sacramenta homines de Aquilanido ad homines de Jonsed. Hec sunt nomina illorum: Fertunio filius Aberla, et Ferruzo filius Hecca, et Guisandi filius Christoforo, et Nunnus filius Hondemar, et Endura filius Ramio, et Exipio filius Ramio, et Altemir filius Axenci, et Rechesendi filius Oriolfi, et Albin filius Hichila, et Uddi filius Sabila, et Rechesindi filius Altemir. Et fecerunt sacramenta isti homines supra nominati, in domum Sancti Sebastiani martyris Christi, quod habebant terciam partem in ipso puteo salinarum pro hereditate, et quia non comparauerunt nulla hereditatione de homines de Jonsed, nec agrum nec uineam, post Azeka cecidit super illos, et fecerunt ista sacramenta per iussionem de Fertunio presbitero, iudicem cunctis christianis Leridense, sub imperio Zamega aluazir. Et fuerunt auditores de sacramenta eorum, Comparati filius Aquila, et Exebi presbitero filius Bia, et Bonofilio filius Homar. Et hoc ipsas kalendas Aprelis, sub era MXXV.

XVIII

Account of successive hearings relating to the dispute concerning the ownership of the allod of Gausa in the county of Aragón, 958.

SOURCE: Parchment original in the Cathedral Archive of Jaca; printed by R. del Arco, 'El archivo de la catedral de Jaca', *Boletín de la Real Academía de la historia*, 65 (1914), 49–51, and by M. Serrano y Sanz, 'Un documento del obispo aragonés D. Atón' in *Homenaje a D. Carmelo de Echegaray*, pp. 41–8.

In Dei nomine et eius gratia. Hec est chartula corraborationis de alode de Gausa et suo termino quod tenuit domnus Furtunio episcopus cum suos germanos, alode parentum suorum, nullo herede nisi Deum, terminum dilectum plus de centum annos, nullo querellante. Post hec dederunt terras ad laborare ad homines de illas billas qui sunt a giro. Quando transiuit ille episcopus negaberunt illas terras qui illas tenebant. Sic se adunaberunt barones et comis et iudiciales et abbates super illo terminum, et iudicarunt ut firmassent suas terras et suo termino, et perdissent ipsas terras et suo termino, et pariassent lege quomodo iudicius mandat, et illas terras bestitas. Sic ducibi ego episcopus Atto et mei germani testes bonos barones senes de illo bicinato, et testificarunt et bolebant iurare et firmare. Sic conplacuit ad Furtunio Scemenonis comite, et abbas Bancio, et ad alios barones ut non iurassent, et debiserunt illo termino et fecerunt cominenza sicut est lege de terra, et lascabimus deciso quod uiderunt boni barones quod nec illi abuissent nulla querella, nec ego contra illos. Et post histum factum exibit Furtunio Scemenonis de Aragone; disficerunt illi homines illa cominenza et miserunt Sancio Scemenonis Galiffa, et introierunt in placitum ante rege domno Sancio cum suos barones, et non potuerunt illi homines pro nullo parente abere ibi partem. Post hec fuerunt ad rege Garcia Sancionis quando beniebat de illa partitione de Enneco Sancionis, et iudicabit illis in illa histrata ad Santi Stefani de Binaqua, quid firmassent illa alode, et non potuerunt abere testes. Post histum factum mandabit rex Garcia Sancionis et suus filius quod pedificasset ille pater de illo episcopo domno Attoni, Oriolus Galindonis, illo termino, et iurasset super illa regula sancta, et sic fecit in Sancti Bincenti in Larbesa, quod nullus alius debuit ibi abere parte nisi filii de domna Inchalzata quando tradidit domna Inchalzata suo filio domno Furtunio episcopo in Sesabe, sic dedit illo monte Besauni ad sancti adtrium, et bir suus sic donabit Charastos exitu de filios et filias et de omni parentela sua nisi quid serbiunt in sancti adtrium. Propter hoc firmauit Oriolus Galindonis, et fuerunt ibi testes abbas Bancio et Datu Forti, Asner Hundisculi, Enneco Donati presbiter, Bradila Belascus, Garcianis Tollus, Ato Banzonis, Garcia Bradilanis, Lope Enneconis, Galindu Banzonis, Psalla Asnari cun suos germanos, Belascu Sancionis cum suos germanos, Garcia Scemenonis cum suos germanos et alii multi quod longum est scribere. Et qui histum factum boluerit disrumpere, in primis ira Dei descendat super eum, et cum Iuda traditore abeat portione infernum inferiori, amen. Facta chartula sub era DCCCCLXLVI. Pax sit audientibus uel legentibus dicta. Garsea Sancionis confirmans. ✠ Sancio Garseanis prolis predicti Regis confirmans. ✠ Saluus Albaildensis licet indignus abba hoc testamentum Regum manu mea roboraui. ✠

XIX

Record of the procedures used to establish the boundaries between the villages of Banassa and Katamesas in the county of Aragón, 928.

SOURCE: Edited by A. Ubieto Arteta, *Cartulario de San Juan de la Peña*, pp. 47–50 (no. 14), from the eleventh-century cartulary in the University of Zaragoza, Faculty of Law, fols. 71v–72r.

✠ Sub Christi nomine et eius gratia.
Noticia uel explanatio de termino Sancti Iohannis.

In temporibus illis, regnante Fortunio Garcianes in Pampilona, fuit contentio facta pro ipso termino de uillis que prope erant, una que uocatur Benassa et alia que uocatur Katamesas. Et uenit rex Fortunio Garcianes cum suos filios et uiros nobiles de sua patria et abbates et presbiteri, et fecit placitum pro ipso termino, et uenit ipse rex cum multitudine uirorum et posuerunt terminum. Ipse rex in equo suo pedificando antecedebat, et alii uiri post eum. Agmina multitudo confirmauerunt, ipse uero precedebat omnes.

Hoc explicito, post multum temporis cursu, illo adhuc uiuente, erexit Deus regem Sancio Garcianes domnum et gubernatorem de patria et defensorem populi, et regnauit in Pampilonia et in Deio. Regnauit autem annis XX, et mortuus est.

Et post obitum eius uenit domnus Galindo episcopus et pro confirmatione iterum congregauit alios uiros, qui sciebant ipsum terminum. Et abbates et presbiteri circuierunt eum, sicut uiderant regem transientem, transierunt et ipsi per illam lineam de rigo qui descendit de Sancto Uincentio in directum ad illa uinea de Enneco Asnari, et peruenit usque ad male traie in partibus orientis; et de parte occidente de illo nauigio de Banassa, sicut aqua uertit. Et scripserunt cartam istam, ut nulla contemptio sit apud nos et illos.

Et super hec iurauerunt testes pronominati fratres Isinarius, qui fuit magister de equis de Fortunio Garsianis, et Sancio Centulli presbiter, et Enneco Sancionis presbiter: et isti tres iurauerunt in Sancto Iohanne, sicut audierant olim auribus suis et uiderant oculis suis, ante rege Scemeno Garcianes et suo creato domno Garsea, filio de rege Sancio Garsianes. Et ipse domnus Galindo episcopus posuit testes pronominatos abbates et presbiteros domnum abbatem Uerilam et domnum Galindonem de Lisabe et Galindo Galindones de

Sancto Petro, abbas Eximinus de Sancto Martino et de Elessu, presbiter Trasiricus, presbiter Gustrimarius, frater Sancio Mauri, presbiter Belasco de Benasso, presbiter Sazzenus de Baguasse, presbiter Garsias de Iscodie, presbiter Bradila de Kasela, presbiter Sancio de Lizarraga, presbiter Belasco de Uncquosse, presbiter Fortunio de Isorre, presbiter Salitu de Turrillas, presbiter Belasco de Ausuni, presbiter Ferruzu de Selbanianu, presbiter Fortunio de Onse, presbiter Kardellu de Bassobauzo, presbiter de Sabalza, presbiter Abeiza de Catamesas, presbiter Fortunio de Aspera, presbiter Arrebellus de Undosse. Seniores uiros pronominatos Sancio Scemenones et suo filio Enneco Sanciones et suus frater Asnari Scemenones et suo creato Incalzato, Enneco Iupi de Eisi, Fortunio Garsianes de Benassa, Galindo Ennecones et Bellaco frater eius, Zaccarias de Benassa, Galindo Fortuniones, Galindo Garcianes, Garcia Fortuniones, Eximino Dacones et alii multi quorum nomina longum est scribere.

Facta carta sub era DCCCCLXVI, regnante Scemeno Garsianes cum suo creato domno Garsea in Pampilona et in Deiu, et domnus Galindo episcopus similiter in Pampilona et in Deiu et in Castro Sancti Stefani regebat.

XX

Notitia recording hearings in dispute between the church of S. Giulia, Controne, and Draco, Walperto and Fraimanno, over land at Granaiola, heard in the ducal court at Lucca, dated 25 June 847.

SOURCE: Edited by C. Manaresi, *I Placiti del 'Regnum Italiae'*, vol. 1, pp. 169–73 (no. 51), from the parchment original, MS archivio Arcivescovile di Lucca, *G 22.

✠ In nomine Domini. Dum Adelbertus inlustrissimo dux una cum Ambrosio uenerabili episcopo istius ciuitatis Lucense, residentibus hic ciuitate Luca, curte uidelicet docalis, in iudicio, cum ipsis et nos Aron gastaldius, Ardo, Petro, Andreas et Gherimundo schabinis, ad singulorum hominum causas deliberandas, erantque nobiscum Cuniperto uassus domni imperatoris, Uuichelmo, Hildiperto, Teudimundo, Rodilando, Hildiprando, Sichiprando germanis, Aroghisi, Angalperto germanis, Fridiano clerico, Toto, Cunerado, Gastaldulo, Albolfo, Gausprando, Adelperto, Adelghisi et reliquos plures. Ueneruntque ibi ante nos Andreas aduocatus ecclesie sancte Iulie, que est plebis babtismalis, sita loco Controne, nec non Draco et Ualperto germanis altercationem inter se abendum, dicendum nobis Andreas aduocatus: 'Istis Draco et Ualperto germanis abere uidetur iniuste rebus ecclesie sancte Iulie, cuius sum aduocatus, que esse uidetur in loco Filectulo prope loco Granariolo, unde quero, ut detis inter nos iudicio'. Respondebat ipsis Draco et Ualperto germanis: 'Nescimus res de quo dicis'. Dictum hoc sic, ipse Andreas per nostrum iudicium dedit uuadia sepius dictis germanis de rebus ipsis illis monstrandum, et ipsis germanis fecimus ei dare uuadia essent parati aput locum ostensio ipsa recipere ab eo et rem ad iudicium ponendi. Exinde rationem posuerunt inter se fideiussores et statuimus inter eis constituto. Constituta uero die utrumque ante nos in iudicio reuersi, dixit nobis ipse Andreas: 'Ostensi huic Drachi et Ualperti germanis antedict[as res][1] in loro Filectulo; uolo ut ponant mihi ante uos rationem, cur eas abere uidentur iniuste'. Respondebant ipsis Draco et Ualperto: 'Abemus res ipsa, sed non iniuste, eo quod comparauimus eas da Flaiperto filio quondam Pini, et ecce c[artula pre] manibus abemus, et secundum textum cartule istius autores et defensatores exinde dare uolumus Fraimanno filio et heredes eidem Flaiperti'. Nos ita audientibus, fecimus nobis cartula ipsa relegi, ubi inter reliqua

---

[1] *Square brackets indicate reconstructed text where manuscript is illegible.*

continebatur ut ipsis germanis adserebant. Et secundum textum cartule dederunt uuadia eidem Andree de autorem ipsum ei dandum, et Andreas fecimus eis dare uuadia paratus essed ab eis autorem ipsum recipere. Posuerunt inter se fideiussores et constituto. In quo constituto ambas partes, ipsis Andreas, Draco et Uualperto, in iudicio reuersi ante nos qui supra Petrus et Andreas schabinis, ubi nobiscum aderant Teudimundo, Ardimanno, Albolfo, Adalprando, Rodilando et Teusprando germanis, Flaiperto clerico, Petro et Altiperto de Suburbano, Hodolpaldo, Heripaldo clerico, Teutpaldo notario, Adelghisi et reliquis. Tunc ipsis Uualperto et Draco germanis iuxta suprascriptam suam uuadiam detulerunt coram nobis suprascripto Fraimanno suum [autorem et dixerunt] eidem Andree: 'Ecce autorem nostrum, age cum eo'. Quibus ipse Fraimanno narrabat contra ipso Andreas: 'Ego ex res ipsa istorum Drachi et Uualperti autorem existo, pro eo quod antedicto Flaiperto genitor meus, qui eas istorum germanorum uende[rat nunc sunt] plus annorum triginta, abuit ad suum proprietario'. Hoc dicto, interrogauimus ipsum Fraimanno, si ita hec per testes adprobare poteret sicut dicebat. Qui dixit: 'Non possum'. Tunc ipse Andreas proclamandum dicebat: 'E[go adpro]bare possum per testes, qualiter res ipsa infra istos triginta annos pars suprascripte ecclesie sancte Iulie abuit ad proprietatem'. Dicebat ipse Fraimanno: 'Non est ueritas hoc quod dicis'. Et dum inter eis talis uerteretur causatio iudicauimus et uuadiam dare fecimus ipsum Andreas eidem Fraimanni, ut sicut adserebat ita adprobaret. Et Fraimanno fecimus ei dare uuadia paratus essed adprobatio ipsa ab eo recipere. Posuerunt inter se fideiussores et constituto. Constituta uero die, dum nobis qui supra Aron gastaldius, Petrus, Andreas et Gherimundo schabinis, resedentes nos in eadem curte docalem, ubi simul nobiscum resedebat Iohannes et Adelperto schabinis, Ambrosius et Iohannes episcopis, Heriprando et Cuniperto uassis regalis, etiam simul nobiscum aderant Ildiperto, Teudimundo, Teufridi notarius, Ghisolfo, Samuel, Leo, Odolpaldo, Auriperto, Liuderamo notarius, Ildo, Aggo, Gastaldulo, Gundelprando notarius, Petro, Alo, Ardimanno, Gumperto [et rel]iqui plures. Tunc ipse Andreas detulit ante nos testimonia sua, idest Cunimundo et Iohannes germani et Uuito, qui, dum nobis presentati fuissent, interrogauimus ipsum Fraimanno si aliquid aduersos ipsos testes aberet quod dicere. [Iam dictus Fraimanno] dixit: 'De is duobus germanis nihil abeo quod contradicere, ut receptibilis non sint; de isto alio autem nomine Uuito ueritatem dico, quia de suo proprio non abet ualentes centum quinquaginta solidos; propterea uolo ut testimo[nia audiatis super] hoc'. Tunc suprascripto Gherimundo schabino seu Adelperto et Appo germani unusquisque singulatim testificauerunt dicentes: 'Uere nes scimus, quia iste Uuito inter proprium et mouilem amplius abet quam centum quinquaginta solidos ualentes et suum bene potest dicere testimonium'. Et dum taliter ipse Uuito a predictis hominibus testificatus fuisset, sic nos quorum supra Aron gastaldius, Petrus, Andreas et Gherimundo schabinis predicta testimonia separauimus et diligenter illos unum ad unum inquirere cepimus. In primis [dictus] Cunimundo dixit: 'Scio res illa in Filectulo, unde intentio est inter isto Fraimanno et isto Andreas da parte sancte Iulie, scio infra istos triginta annis eas abentem parte eadem ecclesie sancti Iulie ad proprietatem'. Iohannes similiter dixit et Uuito equaliter dixit. Redduto testimonio, tunc presenti sancti Dei euangelie aduci fecimus; sic ipse testi[monia] unusquisque, qualiter suum reddiderunt testimonium, ad Dei euuangelie adfir[mati] sunt. Insuper ipse Andreas aduocatus iuratus dixit per as Dei euangelie quia: 'Qualiter testimonia iste de hac causam testimonium reddiderunt, ueritatem dixerunt'. Et dum hec omnia ante nos taliter facta fuissent, paruit nobis recte una cum reliqui nobiliores et ceteros nobiscum adessentibus ita iudicauimus, ut liceat pars suprascripte ecclesie sancte Iulie supradicta res aberet, secundum qualiter adprobatio ipsa ante nos facta fuerat, sine contraditionem ipsius Fraimanni; nam et [ipse Frai]manno permaneat exinde in hoc contemptus et remotus. Et statim ipse Fraimanno predicta res eidem Andree a parte eidem ecclesie reddere fecimus. Et post hec per nostrum iudicium dedit uuadia ipse Fraimanno eidem Andree de fruges, quitquit ex ipsis rebus post illius compellatio tullerat, omnino reddendi sub sagramentum retro tempus secundum legem. Unde qualiter ante nos acta et deliuerata est causam, presentem notitia iudicati nostri pro securitatem a parte suprascripte ecclesie sancte Iulie emitti preui[dimus], ut in eadem permaneat deliberationem et Petrum clericum notarium scribere admonuimus, anno imperii domni nostri Hlotharii magni imperatoris, postquam in Italia ingressus est, uigisimoquinto, septimo kalendas Iulias, indictione decima.

Signum ✠ manus Petri schabino, qui in is actis interfuit.
✠ Ego Iohannis clericus scauinu in quantu de me supra legitur interfui.
✠ Ego Andreas notarius et schabinus interfui.   ✠ Ego Gerimundu scauinu interfui.
Signum ✠ manus Adelghisi que Appo uocatur, qui ibi fuit.
Signum ✠ manus Aroghisi filio quondam Ghisi, qui ibi fuit.
Signum ✠ manus Adelberti germani ipsius Adelghisi, qui ibi fuit. ✠ Ego Teufridi notarius ibi fui.
✠ Ego   Angilperto ibi fui.

XXI

Form of agreement between the inhabitants of Ierissos and monks of Athos about their common boundary, May 942.

SOURCE: Based on diplomatic text edited by D. Papachryssanthou, *Actes du Prôtaton*, vol. 1, *Archives de l'Athos*, vol. 7, pp. 191–2 (no. 4), from the contemporary copy in the Archives of the Prôtaton of Mount Athos, Karyes.

[12 signatures]

Εν ονοματι του πατρος και του υιου και του αγιου πνευματος. Ημις οι προγεγραμενοι, οι και τους τημιους και ζωοποιους σταυρους ηδιοχειρως πηξαντες, την παρουσαν εγγραφον ασφαλειαν και τελhαν διαλοισην ποιουμεν ης οιμας Θωμαν βασιλικον πρωτοσπαθαριον και ασηκριτην και επωπτην Θεσσαλονικης, ημhς αν οι ηγουμενοι μετα τον χωρηατον υπερ πασης της κοινοτητος της χωρας, ημης δε οι μοναχοι Αθωνιτε οιπερ παντον τον μωναχων του Αθωνος του ορους. Επηδι πρω χρωνου τηνος επωλησας τους χωρηατας την παρ' αυτον κατεχωμενιν κλασματηκην γην, ου διεχωρισας δε το εος που οφειλουσην δεσπωζιν οι αγωρασαντες και εκηθεν οι Αθωνιτε, και δια τουτω εισηλθομεν εν Θεσσαλονικη και ενοπιον του πανευφημου στρατηλατου Κατακαλων, και Γρηγοριου του αγιοτατου ημον αρχιεπισκοπου, Θωμα βασιλικου πρωτοσπαθαριου του Τζουλα, και Ζωητου βασιλικου πρωτοσπαθαριου και κριτου, και σου του πρωηρημενου εποπτου, εγκλησιν εποιεισαμεθα επιζητουντες χωρισθηνε τα του Αθωνος απω της διαπραθεισης γης. Και ημεις μεν οι της χωρας ελεγαμεν εινε την ημετεραν δεσπωτειαν εος τον Ζυγον εκηθεν δε των Αθωνιτον, ημεις δε οι Αθωνιτε αντελεγαμεν παλιν οτι κατα πολυν μερος ανηκει προς ημας εκ της παρ' οιμον εξωνειθεισης γης περι τουτων πολλα φηλονικησαντες, συνιδομεν αμφοτεροι και σοινεβιβασθημεν γενεσθαι ουτως ινα απο το πληρωμα των χωραφιων του κυρ Μεθοδιου ως προς τον Ζοιγον κοπουν τα συνορα απο θαλασσαν εις θαλασσα και τα μεν προς τον Ζοιγον παντα χωραφια τε και χερσα ηνα εισην της δεσποτιας των Αθωνιτων, απο δε τα τοιαυτα συνορα και προς τον Ερισον ινα εισιν παντα της δεσποτειας των αγορασαντων και του Κολοβου, και μητε ημεις οι Αθωνιτε απω τα τοιαυτα συνορα και προς τον Ερισον ινα εχομεν εξουσιαν το συνολον επιζητει⟨ν τι⟩, μητε ημεις[1] οι της χωρας απο τα τοιαυτα συνορα και προς τον Αθωνα εχει⟨τε⟩ τηνα εξουσιαν. Και εις ταυτα συνφωνησαντες και αρεσθεντες εξησφαλισαμεθα προς ⟨σ⟩ε τον εποπτην ηνα κατανευγης[2] και εξελθης και διαχωρισης ημας, καθως και εσοινεβειβασθημεν · οιον δε μερος ανηλογησει και ουκ ασμενησει εις ταυτα τα προηρημενα, εν πρωτοις αρνητης εστην της αγιας και ομοουσιου Τριαδος και ξενος της των Χριστιαν[ων][3] πιστεος και της μοναχικης καταστασεος, επειτα και καταδικαζεται, δικεουμευου του εμμενους και στεργοντος μερους εις τα ειρημενα συμφωνα. Εξωθεν δε τουτον εχην ημας και την καθεδρα τον γεροντων την εν τω χρυσοβουλιω μνημονευομενη. Εις ταυτα παντα αρεσθεντες προεταξαμεν τους τιμιους και ζωοποιους ημων σταυρους, γραφεν το υφος δια χειρος Δημητριου κληρικου κουβουκλησιου και ορφανοτροφου, μηνι Μαιω ινδικτιωνος ιε′ ✠

✠ Γρηγοριος ελαχιστος αρχιεπισκοπος Θεσσαλονηκης μαρτυρων τοις προγεγραμενοις οιπεγραψα ιδιοχειρως ✠

✠ Εν ονοματι του πατρος και του υιου και του αγιου πνευματος Θωμας βασιλικος πρωτοσπαθαριος και νοταριος του κομερκιου παρημη επι πασιν τοις προγεγραμενοις μαρτυρων υπεγραψα ιδιοχειρως ✠

✠ Βασηλειος βασιλικος κανδιδατος ο Σκρινιαρης παρημη επι πασιν τοις προγεγραμμενοις μαρτυρων υπεγραψα ιδιοχειρως ✠

[✠ Εν ονοματι του πατρος] και του υιου και του αγιου πνευματος Γρηγωριος βασιλικος σπαθαριος ο Φουσκουλος παρημη επι πασιν τοις [προγεγραμμενοις μαρτυρων υπεγραψα ιδιοχειρως ✠

✠ Εν ονοματι του πατρος και] του υιου [και] του αγιου πνευματος Μιχαηλ κληρικος της Μεγαλης Εκκλησιας παρημη επι [πασιν τοις προγεγραμμενοις μαρτυρων υπεγραψα] ιδιοχειρως ✠

[1] υμεις.
[2] κατανευγης] *read* κατανευης
[3] *Square brackets indicate reconstructed text where manuscript is illegible.*

XXII

Molybdobull recording settlement of dispute between the inhabitants of two neighbouring districts in southern Italy, Tricarico and Acerenza, about common rights, heard in the court of the katepan, Bari, 1001–2.

SOURCE: Based on normalized text edited by A. Guillou and W. Holzmann, 'Zwei Katepansurkunden aus Tricarico', *Quellen und Forschungen aus italienischen Archiven und Bibliotheken*, 41 (1961), 18–19, from 'une copie moderne' (p. 17).

✠ Επειδηπερ εν τω καιρω Λουκα του καφιρου του και αποστατου γεγονοτος, ωστις και την κατακτισιν ειχεν εν τω καστελλιω Πετραπερτουσαν, ουκ ολιγας τυραννιας και σκομιδας υπηρχε πεποιηκως εν ωλη τη Ιταλια, και ου μονον τα τοιαυτα ατοπιματα εχομενος διεπραττετο, αλλα και τοπους αλλοτριους και ωρια ληστρικως κατεκρατη, εν ω και απαν τον τοπον τε και διακρατησιν κατεσχεν των οικειτορων καστρου Τρικαρικου, ατινα και υπειρχον δεσποζωντες απο παλαιων των χρονων οι αυτοι οι οικητωρες του ειριμενου καστρου Τρικαρικου, και μηκετι παραχωρειν τουτους το συνολον εισερχεσθαι ειτε νεμεσθαι τους ιδιους αυτων τοπους. Δι' ου τοινυν απελαυθεντος παρ' ημων του αυτου Λουκα απο τε του ειρημενου καστελλιου Πετραπερτουσας αμα των συνοικειτορων και ομοφρονων αυτου καφυρων, εγκλησιν εποιησαντω οι αυτοι οικειτωρες καστρου Τρικαρικου περι τε των συνορων και της διακρατησεως του τοπου αυτων. Και το μεν προτερον απεσταλη παρ᾽ ημων Κωνσταντινος ταξιαρχης ο και καλουμενος του Κοντου, ωστις αγαγων και τους οικειτωρας καστελλιου Τουλβας ομοθυμαδων παρεγενοντω, και εξ αρεσκειας των εκατερων μερων διεχωρησεν τα τοιαυτα συνορα τε και τοπια τα αναμεταξυ υπαρχοντα των τε οικειτορων καστρου Ἀκερεντζας και των οικειτορων καστρου Τρικαρικου, καθο και παλαιων των χρονων υπειρχων αμφωτεροι δεσποζοντες. Μεθ᾽ ου πολυ δε ημεις, βουλομενοι ετι την τοιαυτην υποθεσιν επι πλειον γυμνασαι, απεσταλη παρ᾽ ημων κατα τον Δεκεμβριον μηνα την ιε΄ ινδικτιονος Ρωμανος ο και προξημος ημων αμα Αργυρου του μαγιστρου και Βαρινου, ομοιως και Μυρωνος του και γεγονοτος χαρτουλλαριου των Σχολων, οιτινες παραγενομενοι ηγαγον παλιν τους αυτους οικειτωρας καστρου Τρικαρικου αμα των οικειτορων καστελλιου Τουλβας, και ερανησαντες περι των τοιουτων συνορων απελογησαντω και εξειπων ουτως οι οιριμενοι οικειτωρες καστελλιου Τουλβας, ωσει μεχρι τον αριθμον πεντε, λεγω δη Χαρζανετην και Σικηνουλφον, Ιωαννην της Καρας, Γοηνανδον και Ιωαννην Βαρσιανον, ως οτι ημεις εκατεροι απο παλαιων των χρονων ανακοινομενοι υπειρχωμεν και εν τω μεσω ημων ουτε νομιστρον ουτε χυλωτικον αλλ᾽ ουτε κρατησιμον ανελαβετω τις εξ ημων πωποτε, αλλα καθως και διεχωρησεν τα τοιαυτα συνορα ο ριθεις Κωνσταντινος, ουτως και υπειρχον αναμεταξυ ημων των τε οικειτορων καστρου Ακερεντζας και των οικητορων καστρου Τρικαρικου, ατινα και ταυτα εισιν · απο μεν το Βουγητον και ως αναβενη το ξηροποταμην το καλουμενον Καναπινον μεχρι του ποδηματος του ωρους του Μαρκου και ως απερχεται η λαγκαδα προς δυσμας μεχρι της τρυπιμενης πετρας και εως την ετεραν πετραν ην εστησεν ο στρατηγος Σελαντζηανος και αποδιδει εως του εριμωκαστελλιου του καλουμενου Κερβανου μεχρι της στρατας της δημοσιας, οπου και τα λιθαρια υπαρχωσιν τα μεγαλα καθο στικουσι τα δενδρα σιμηομενα απο χειρων του αυτου στρατηγου και ως κατερχεται το ροιακην και το μεγαν λιθον τον ισταμενον μεσων των δυο ροιακηων και αποδηδον εις τον ποταμον τον καλουμενον Τρατον και αποδιδει ο αυτος Τρατος εις το ετερον ποταμην το Βασενδον και κατερχεται προς τον ναον της Θεοτοκου του καλουμενου Ρεσβουγηου. Και απο την σημερον εχειν εξουσιαν τους αυτους οικειτωρας καστρου Τρικαρικου τους ιδιους αυτων τοπους εις τελειαν αυθεντιαν και αναφερετον δεσποτιαν, ετι δε και εις τους εξης απαντας και διειναικης χρονους · δηλονοτι μη εχοντες εξουσιαν απο του παροντος μητε οικειτωρες καστρου Ακερεντζας μητε οι αυτοι οικειτορες του καστελλιου Τουλβας μητε ετεροι οικητορες απο των καστελλιων των και πλησιαζοντων του ειριμενου καστρου Τρικαρικου υπερβενειν εις τα συνορα του ειριμενου καστρου Τρικαρικου και καταρπαζειν τους ιδιους αυτων τοπους. Δι᾽ αυτο, ως ειριται, εξ αρεσκειας των εκατερων μερων διαχωρισθηναι τα τοιαυτα συνορα καθος και υπειρχων απο παλαιων των χρονων. Επι τουτω γαρ και το παρων υπομνημα εγενετω παρα Γρηγοριου του πρωτοσπαθαριου κατεπανω Ιταλιας του Τρακανιωτου και επεδωθη εις δικαιωσιν των οικειτορων καστρου Τρικαρικου και αποπαυσιν των οικειτορων καστρου Ακερεντζας και του καστελλιου Τουλβας, υπογραφεν τη οικεια μου χειρι βουλλωθεν και τη συνηθη ημων βουλλη τη δια μολυβδου ετει ͵ϛϙι΄.

✛ Γρηγοριως πρωτοσπαθαριος και καταπανω Ιταλιας ο Ταρχανηωτης.

XXIII

Charter recording judgement by King Beornwulf of Mercia, Archbishop Wulfred of Canterbury, and the royal court, in dispute between Bishop Heaberht of Worcester and the community at Berkeley over the minster at Westbury and its endowments, 30 October 824.

SOURCE: Edited by W. de G. Birch, *Cartularium Saxonicum*, vol. I, pp. 519–22 (no. 379), from two eleventh-century cartulary copies.

✠ Regnante inperpetuum domino nostro Ihesu Christo qui mundi monarchium sua semper uirtute gubernat in æternum . Anno uero ab incarnatione domini nostri Ihesu Christi . DCCC° . XXIIII° . Indictione autem . II . regnante BEORNUULFO rege Merciorum factum est pontificale et sinodale conciliabulum in loco qui dicitur CLOFESHOAS . Præsidente ibi rege præfato . ac uenerando uiro ÞULFREDO archiepiscopo . illo conuentu regente ac moderante illic omnes episcopi nostri et abbates et uniuersi Mercentium principes et multi sapientissimi uiri congregati adessent . ibi in alia plura colloquia aliqua contentio allata est . INter Heaberhtum episcopum et illam familiam æt BERCLEA de hereditate Æðelrici filii Æðelmundi hoc est monasterium quod nominatur ÞESTBURHG . Habuit autem episcopus ante nominatus terram illam cum libris . sicut Æðelricus ante præcepit ut ad ÞEOGERNENSEM aecclesiam redderetur . Statuta est autem atque decreta ab archiepiscopo et ab omni sancta sinodo illa consententia . ut episcopus qui monasterium et agellum cum libris haberet . cum iuramento Dei seruorum presbiterorum diaconorum et plurimorum monachorum sibi in propriam possessionem terram illam cum adiuratione adiurasset . Et ita finita et proscripta illa contentione coram episcopo post . XXX . noctes illud iuramentum to ÞEstmynstre deducatum est . Qua propter siquis hunc agrum ab illa aecclesia in ceastre nititur euellere contra decreta sacrorum canonum sciat se facere quia sancti canones decernunt quicquid sancta synodus uniuersalis cum catholico archiepiscopo suo adiudicauerit nullo modo fractum uel irritum esse faciendum . Haec autem gesta sunt. Hii sunt testes et confirmatores huius rei quorum nomina hic infra notantur a die . III^a . k'l Nouembris .

✠ Ego Beoruulf rex Merciorum hanc cartulam synodali decreti signo sanctæ crucis Christi confirmaui . ✠ Ego Þulfred archiepiscopus hanc synodalem sententiam cum signo gloriose crucis corroboraui .

✠ Ego Oeðeluuald episcopus consensi . ✠ Hræðhun episcopus consensi . ✠ Eadpulf episcopus consensi . ✠ Heaberht episcopus consensi . ✠ Beonna episcopus consensi . ✠ Ego Þigðegn episcopus consensi . ✠ Ego Cioberht episcopus consensi . ✠ Ego Þermund episcopus consensi . ✠ Ego Cynred episcopus consensi . ✠ Ego Hunberht episcopus consensi . ✠ Ego Eanmund abba consensi . ✠ Ego Cuðpulf abba consensi . ✠ Ego Þihtred abba consensi . ✠ Ego Þilferð abba consensi .

✠ Æt ðam aðe pæs æt Þest mynstre efen fiftig mæsse preosta 7 x . diaconas 7 ealra oðra preosta sixtig 7 hund teontig .

✠ Ego Beornoð dux . ✠ Eadberht dux . ✠ Sigered dux . ✠ Ecgberht dux . ✠ Eadpulf dux . ✠ Alhheard dux . ✠ Mucel dux . ✠ Uhtred dux . ✠ Ludeca dux . ✠ Bynna frater regis . ✠ Piot presbiter . ✠ Cyneberht . ✠ Noðhelm præco a domno Eugenio papa . ✠ Bola . ✠ Aldred thelonius consensi . ✠ Þighelm . ✠ Beadheard . ✠ Eadbald consensi .

✠ Her sindon þara maesse preosta naman þe on þam aðe stodon 7 on þaeron . (There follows a list of 56 names.)

XXIV

Charter recording judgement of King Cenwulf of Mercia, Archbishop Æthelheard of Canterbury and 'the whole synod' that Æthelric, son of Æthelmund, had freedom to dispose of his lands, including Westbury; followed by Æthelric's declaration before a similar synod of his disposition of Westbury and other estates, 804.

SOURCE: Edited by W. de G. Birch, *Cartularium Saxonicum*, vol. 1, pp. 438–40 (no. 313), from two eleventh-century cartulary copies.

✠ In nomine domini Dei summi rex regum . qui in altis habitat et prospicit omnia cælestia et terrestria .

Anno . ab incarnatione Christi . DCCC° . IIII° . Indictione . XIIᵃ . Ego ÆÐELRIC filius Æðelmundi . Cum conscientia synodali inuitatus ad synodum et in iudicio stare in loco qui dicitur Clofeshoh . Cum libris et ruris . id est æt Ðæst mynster quod prius propinqui mei tradiderunt mihi et donauerunt . ibi Æðelheardus archiepiscopus . mihi regebat atque iudicauerat cum testimonio Coenpulfi regis et optimatibus eius coram omni synodo quando scripturas meas perscrutarent ut liber essem terram meam atque libellas dare . quocunque uolui .

Postea commendaui amicis meis ad seruandum . quando quæsiui sanctum Petrum et sanctum Paulum pro remedio animae meae . Et iterum me reuertente ad patriam . accepi terram meam et prætium reddidi quasi ante pacti sumus et pacifici fuerimus ad inuicem . Facta est autem post paucos annos alia synodus æt ACLEA . Tunc in illo synodo coram episcopis rege et principibus eius ememoraui pristinæ libertatis mei . quæ mihi ante iudicatum est . et cum licentia eorum testificaui in præsenti testimonio quem ad admodum meam hæreditatem dare uoluissem . Et sic dixi .

'Haec sunt Nomina illarum terrarum . quae dabo ad locum qui dicitur Deorhyrst pro me et Æðelmund patrem meum . Si mihi continguat ut illic corpus meum requiescat . Todanhom . 7 æt Sture . Screfleh . 7 Cohhanleh . ea condicione ut illa congregatio uota eorum faciat firma sicut mihi promiserunt . Iterum dabo Ðærferðe . XI . manentium Bremes grefan 7 Feccanhom ut habeat suum diem et postea reddat ad Ðigorna cestre . Uerum etiam do . XXX . manentium under Ofre ad Gleape cestre . Et quando mihi contingat exitus mei diei . tunc dabo Ciolburge matri meae si diutius uiuit quam ego . terram illam æt Ðest mynster 7 æt Stoce ut habeat suam diem et postea reddat ad Ðeogornensem aecclesiam . Pro qua re ea uiuente ut ibi habeat protectionem et defensionem contra Berclinga contentione . Et si aliquis homo in aliqua contentione iuramentum ei decreuerit contra Berclingas . liberrima erit ad reddendum cum recto consilio propinquorum meorum . qui mihi donabant hereditatem et meo quo ei dabo . et si non habeat patrocinium in ciuitate Ðeogornensi . Post ea primum quærat ad archiepiscopum in Cantia et si ibi non habeat sit libera cum libris et ruris ad elegandam patrocinium ubi placitum sibi fuerit . Si aliter fiat ut non opto aliquis homo contendat contra libros meos uel hereditatem indigne tunc habet Aldpulfus episcopus in Licetfelda istius cartulæ comparem et amici necessarii mei et fidelissimi alias . id est . Eadbyrht Eadgaring . 7 Æðelheh Esning . ad confirmationem huius rei.'

Rogo etiam Æðelric pro amore omnipotentis Dei . et præcipio et obsecro per omnes uirtutes cœlorum . Ut nullus homo hanc positionem crucis Christi . quæ tantorum uirorum testimonio confirmata est . non præsumat minuere . Si ausus est aliquis confirmationem istam infringere . deletur de laude Dei . si non satisfactione emendauerit .

✠ Ego Coenpulf rex Merciorum hanc munificentiam signo sanctæ crucis subscripsi .
✠ Ego Æðelheardus . archiepiscopus Dorouernensis ciuitatis signum sanctæ crucis

subscripti . ✠ Ego Aldpulfus Licetfendensis episcopus consensi . ✠ Ego Þærnberht episcopus consensi . ✠ Ego Denebyrht episcopus consensi . ✠ Ego Þulfheard episcopus consensi . ✠ Ego Eadpulfus episcopus consensi . ✠ Ego Heaberht dux subscripti . ✠ Ego Beornoð dux subscripti . ✠ Ego Ciolpard dux subscripti . ✠ Ego Cynehelm dux subscripti . ✠ Ego Þicga dux subscripti . ✠ Ego Þigheard dux subscripti . ✠ Ego Byrnpald dux subscripti . ✠ Ego Aldred dux consensi et subscripti .

XXV

Record of dispute between the bishop of Rochester, and Brihtric and Brihtwaru, over estates at Bromley, Fawkham and Snodland, between 975 and 982.

SOURCE: Edited by A. Campbell, *The Charters of Rochester, Anglo-Saxon Charters*, vol. 1, pp. 53–4 (no. 36), from the cartulary copy, MS Rochester Cathedral Library, *Textus Roffensis* (s. xii[1]), fols. 162v–163v.

Þus pæron ða land . æt Bromleage . 7 æt Fealcnaham . þam cinge Eadgare gereht . on Lundenbyrig . ðurh Snodinglandes landbec . ða þa preostas forstælon þam biscope on Hrofesceastre . 7 gesealdan heo Ælfrice Æscpynne sunu . pið feo dearnunga . 7 heo Æscpyn Ælfrices modor sealde heo ær ðiderin . ða geacsode se biscop þæt ða becc forstolene pæron . bæd þara boca ða geornlice . under ðam þa gepatt Ælfric . 7 he bæd ða lafe syððan . oð man gerehte on cinges ðeningmanna gemote ðære stope 7 ðam biscope ða forstolenan becc Snodiglandes . 7 bote æt ðære ðyfðe . þæt pæs on Lundene . þær pæs se cing Eadgar . 7 se arcebiscop Dunstan . 7 Aðelpold biscop . 7 Ælfstan biscop . 7 oðer Ælfstan . 7 Ælfere ealdorman . 7 fela cynges pitena . 7 man agæf ða into ðære stope ðam biscope ða becc . ða stod ðara pydepan are . on ðæs cinges handa . Ða polde Þulfstan se gerefa niman þa are to ðæs cinges handa . Bromleah . 7 Fealcnaham . ða gesohte seo pydepe ða halgan stope . 7 ðane biscop . 7 agæf ðam cinge Bromleages boc . 7 Fealcnahames . 7 se byscop gebohte ða becc 7 ða land æt ðam cinge on Godeshylle . mid fiftigan mancesan goldes . 7 hundteontigan . 7 ðrittigum pundum . þurh forespræce . 7 costnunge . into Sanctę Andrea . siððan ða lefde se biscop ðare pydepan . ðara lande bryces . under ðam ða gepatt se cing . Ongan ða syððan Byrhtric ðare pydepan mæg . 7 heo to ðam genedde þæt hy brucan ðara landa on reaflace . gesohtan ða ðane ealdorman Eadpine . 7 þæt folc ðe pæs Godes anspreca . 7 geneddan ðane biscop be ealre his are agiftes ðara boca . ne moste he beon þara ðreora nanes pyrðe ðe eallum leodscipe geseald pæs on pedde . Tale . ne teames . ne ahnunga .

Þis is seo gepitnesse ðæs ceapes . Eadgar cing . 7 Dunstan arcebiscop . 7 Ospald arcebiscop . 7 Aðelpold . biscop . Æðelgar . biscop . 7 Æscpi . biscop . 7 Ælfstan . biscop . 7 oðer Ælfstan . biscop . 7 Sideman . biscop . 7 ðæs cinges modor Ælfðryð . 7 Osgar . abbod . 7 Ælfere ealdorman . 7 Þulfstan on Dælham . 7 Ælfric . on Ebbesham . 7 seo duguð folces on Þestan Cænt . þær þæt land . 7 þæt læð toli̇ð .

XXVI

Record of judgement of the Kentish shire court in the dispute between Bishop Godwine of Rochester and Leofwine, son of Aelfheah, over the estate at Snodland, between 995 and 1006.

SOURCE: Edited by A. Campbell, *The Charters of Rochester*, pp. 54–5 (no. 37), from *Textus Roffensis*, fols. 155r–156v.

⁜ Her cyð on ðysum geƿrite . hu Godƿine biscop on Hrofeceastre . 7 Leofƿine Ælfeages sunu ƿurðon gesybsumode ymbe þæt land æt Snoddinglande . on Cantƿarabyrig .
Þa ða se biscop Godƿine com to ðam biscopstole þurh hæse his cynehlafordes Æðelredes cynges æfter Ælfstanes forðsiþe biscopes þa gemetæ he on ðam mynstre þa ylcan sƿutelunga þe his foregenga hæfde . 7 þærmid on þæt land spæc . ongan ða to specenne on ðæt land . 7 elles for Godes ege ne dorste . oððæt seo spræc pearð þam cynge cuð . Þa ða him seo talu cuð pæs . þa sende he geƿrit 7 his insegl to þam arcebisceope Ælfrice . 7 bead him þæt he 7 hys þegenas on East Cent . 7 on Ðest Cent . hy onriht gesemdon . be ontale . 7 be oftale . Þa þæt pæs þæt bisceop Godƿine com to Cantƿarabyrig to ðam arcebiscope . þa com ðider se scyresman Leofric . 7 mid him Ælfun abbod . 7 þegenas ægþer ge of East Cent ge of Ðest Cent . eal seo duguð . 7 hy ðær þa spæce sƿa lange handledon . syððon se bisceop his sƿutelunge geeoƿod hæfde . oþ hy ealle bædon þone biscop eaðmodlice . þæt he geunnan scolde þæt he moste mid bletsunga þæs landes brucan æt Snoddinglande his dæg . 7 se biscop þa þæs getiðode on ealra þæra ƿitena þanc þe þær gesomnode ƿæran . 7 he behet þæs truƿan þæt land æfter his dæge unbesacen eode eft into þære stoƿe þe hit ut alæned pæs . 7 ageaf þa sƿutelunga þe he to þam lande hæfde þe ær of þære stoƿe geutod pæs . 7 þa hagan ealle þe he bepestan þære cyrcan hæfde into þære halgan stoƿe . 7 þises loces ærendracan ƿæran . Ælfun abbod 7 Ðulfric abbod . 7 Leofric sciresman . 7 Siƿeard . 7 Ðulfstan æt Sealtpuda . 7 Ælfelm Ordelmes sunu . Ðonne is her seo geƿitnes þe æt þisum loce pæs . þæt is ærest se arcebiscop Ælfric . 7 se biscop Goduuine . 7 Ðulfric abbod . 7 Ælfun abbod . 7 Ælfnoð æt Orpedingtune . 7 se hired æt Cristes cyrcan . 7 se hired æt Sancte Augustine . 7 so burhƿaru on Cantƿarebyrig . 7 Leofric sciresman . 7 Lifing æt Meallingan . 7 Siƿeard . 7 Sired his broðor . 7 Leostan æt Mærseham . 7 Godƿine Ðulfeages sunu . 7 Ðulstan æt Sealtpuda . 7 Ðulfstan iunga . 7 Leosƿine æt Dictune . 7 Leofric Ealdredes sunu . 7 Goda Ðulfsiges sunu . 7 Ælfelm Ordelmes sunu . 7 Sideƿine æt Peallespyrðe . 7 Ðærelm . 7 Æþelred portgerefa on byrig . 7 Guðƿold . Gif hƿa þis ðence to aƿendenne . 7 þas foreƿord to abrecenne . aƿende him God fram his ansyne on þam miclan dome . sƿa þæt he si ascyred fram heofena rices myrhðe . 7 sy eallum deoflum betæht into helle . Amen .

XXVII

Record of grant of land at Int Ednan by the church of Killeshin to the church of Durrow, in resolution of a dispute over a previous grant, between 1103 and 1116.

SOURCE: Edited by R. I. Best, 'An early monastic grant in the Book of Durrow', *Ériu*, 10 (1926–8), 137–8, from the contemporary entry written into the seventh-century Gospel Book of Durrow, MS Dublin, Trinity College Library 57 (formerly A.4.5), fol. 13v.

Ostende nobis domine et salutare tuum da nobis. Óentu mór eter Comgan 7 Colum Cille. Recles dano dorat Comgan do Cholum Chille [   ] léged fáill fair co fotta cen íarraid ó muintir Choluim Chille .i. o muintir Darmaige. Táncatar dano muinter Darmaige imma n-appaid 7 imma saccart d'iarraid in reclése et haec sunt nomina eorum .i. Gilla na Nóem hÚa hÉnluáin isé ropp app 7 Gilla Adamnáin hÚa Corten isé ropo haccartt tunc. 7 alii plurimi cum illis uenerunt. Ní fúaratar dano a rrecles fein. ideo scilicet ar dorattad side do Dal Chais. Conid ed doronsat muinter Glinne hUssen deside cutrumma a n-erlese eter fot 7 lethet do muinter Darmaige ár forémdes a n-erlese fein do thabairt dóib for culu. Erlese ind ednain dano isí tuccad dóib dar ése a n-erlese féin 7 mathe muintere Glinne hUsen i ccommairge dóib fria ond airchenniuch .i. Ó Chathasach Ú Chorcráin. IS siat so dano anmand na slanta féin .i. Dublittir hÚa hUádgaile in fer legind 7 Dúnchad hÚa hUádgaile 7 Saírgal Ua Subne 7 a mac .i. Saírbrethach. 7 Artgal mac Culinnáin 7 fratres eius. 7 Mael Choluim mac Cortáin 7 fratres eius 7 Amalgaid hÚa hAiru(d)áin 7 fratres eius i n-amsir dano Muridaich meic Meic Cormáin dorattad 7 Muircertaich Ú Briaín ríg Érend. Bennacht dano don lucht dosrat 7 dia tuccad. Flannchad filius Filii scientis scripsit.

XXVIII

Contract between Sir Walter Ogilvy of Dunlugus and Thomas Baird of Burnside, in settlement of a dispute over the lands of Sandlaw, 14 March 1546.

SOURCE: MS Edinburgh, Scottish Record Office, Abercromby of Forglen Papers, GD 185, box 2, bundle 11/1.

At Huntlie the fourtene day of the monethe of merche the zeir of god ane thousand five hundretht & fourtie five zeiris It is appoyntit concordit & finalie contractit betuix schir walter ogilvy of dunlugus knycht one that ane part & thomas baird off burnesid one that uther part At the counsaill and command of ane nobill & mychty lord George Erle of huntlie lord gordoun & badzenocht Alexander ogilvy of that ilk and off fynletter And George gordoun of schewes In maneir as followis That is to say The said schir walter Quhowsoun he thinkis expedient sall warne lauchfullie and require Alexander baird the sone and air of umquhill [*the late*] william baird of Sandlauche and the said thomas baird his tutour to compeir in the perroche kirk of banff to resawe [*receive*] the sowme off sax hundretht markis Togidder witht ane sufficient letter of tak and bailzere [*lease and bailliery*] off the saidis landis off Sandlaw for the spaice of nyntene zeiris fra the said schir walter ogilvy ass assigna lauchfullie constitut be the said alexander ogilvy off that ilk to the letter of reversioun maid be the said umquhill walter baird to the said alexander ogilvy and his assignais for redemptioun and outquitting off the saidis landis off Sandlauche: And at the day to be assignit therto the said schir walter sall Realie and with effect deliver the said sowme of sax hundretht markis letter of tak and bailzere to the said thomas baird as tutour forsaid eftir the tenour of the said reversioun Quhilk sowme and letter of tak and bailzere the said thomas as tutour forsaid sall resawe but ony dilay in the said kirk he beand lauchfullie warnit therto as saidis aftir the tenour of the said reversioun and compeir personalie him self in the said kirk to the resaitt [*receipt*] theroff and grant the samin landis of sandlauche lauchfullie redemit and deliver to the said schir walter ogilvy all charteris instrumentis off sasing documentis and evidentis maid to the said umquhill William baird george baird his fadeir or to the said alexander baird of the saidis landis of Sandlauche: And as tutour forsaid Remitt the samin for ewir wytht all rycht & titill of rycht propirte & possessioun that he hes to the saidis landis of sandlauche: And thereftir incontinent the said schir walter sall discharge the said alexander baird pupill and the said thomas his tutour and all utheris quhome [*whom*] it efferis [*concerns*] off all mailis fermis profittis and dewteis of the sandlauche aucht to him as superiour therof of all zeiris and termis precedand the dait heirof be ressoun of nonentreis or utherwais and in speciall sene the deceiss of the said umquhill william baird extending to the sowme of ane thousand markis And therefor the said thomas baird as tutour to the said alexander and in his name sall remitt and ourgiff [*give up*] the rycht and titill of rycht at the said alexander and thomas baird his tutour hes or may hawe in & to the saidis takis and bailzere off the saidis landis off sandlauche for ewir sua that it salbe lesum [*lawful*] to the said schir walter ogilvy and his airis to labour the saidis landis of sandlauche witht thair awin propir gudis in all tymes tocum eftir the redemptioun to be maid therof as saidis or to sett the samen to tennentis as thai sall think expedient nochtwithstanding the saidis letteris of tak and bailzere for nyntene zeris Quhilkis letteris of tak & bailzere in takin of the said renunciatioun the said thomas sall Randoure restoir and deliver agane to the said schir walter incontinent eftir the said redemptioun And for the awfald [*honest*] fulfilling of thir premissis & ewir ilk part theroff safer [*and each part thereof so far*] as concernis the said alexander baird pupill & thomas baird his tutour The said thomas baird as tutour forsaid sall contract and be the tenour heirof contractis witht the said schir walter ogilvy in the maist large & ampill forme the said schir walter or his freyndis can dewiss and at the redemptioun of the saidis landis sall seile & subcrive letteris of contract in the best forme the said schir walter will dewyiss to the effect abone wretin and salbe oblist & askit in the officialis bukis of aberdene to fulfull the samin under the panis of cursing in the name of the said alexander baird pupill & mak fayth befoir the said officiall at the same contract is maid in ewident utilite and profitte of the said alexander pupill & thairfor desyire the authorite of the said officiall as Juge ordiner to be interponit therunto in the largest maneir the said schir walter will dewyiss And the said schir walter sall thoill the said thomas baird joiss and brwik the takkis sett till him be the freris of banff [*shall allow the said thomas baird to enjoy and keep the leases set to him by the friars of Banff*] of dalhauche for the spaice & termes to Ryn [*run*] contenit in ane assidatioun maid till hym therof be the priour of the freris forsaidis for nyntene zeiris or ellis the said schir walter now fewar of the saidis landis of dalhauche sall of new mak ane sufficient assidatioun & letter of tak of the saidis landis of dalhauche to the said thomas baird forsamonye termes as is to Rin of the assidatioun of xix zeiris forsaidis maid be the priour of the saidis freris for zeirlie pament of sic fermis & deweteis as is contenit in the said priouris assidatioun and at sic termes of pament And attoure the said schir walter sall Remitt the said thomas baird and james baird of forfaldis all Rancoure that he hes or ony wyiss haid aganis thame or ony of thame for the slauchter off umquhill alexander ogilvy his brothersone and schir johnne cristesoun cheplane And sall deliver ane letter of slanis in deu forme to thame therfor for himself & all that he ma latt betuix this and the feist of witsounday nixtocum: And sall fra thinfurtht stand in amite and kyndness witht the said thomas and james bard and sall manteyne and defend thame as his speciall servandis & men in tymetocum in all thir actionis querellis & contraverseis lefull & honest aganis all deidlie [i.e. *living*] during thir lifetymis As it accordis ane gentilman of the maneir of Scotland to manteyne & defend his man and servand and therfor the saidis thomas & james baird salbecum & be thir presentis becumis thrall men & serwandis to the said schir walter during thir lifetymis and sall mak sufficient lettres & bandis of manrent therupoun in the best forme as the said schir walter will dewyss the qwenis graice the authorite & thir forinfeftouris allanerlie except [*those who have already infeft them only excepted*]: And als the said thomas sall pay to the freris of banff & priour therof all the (?)restis of victualis aucht to thame for the fermis of the dalhauche sene the dait of his last assidatioun conforme to the samin befoir this last crop off the quhilk [*which*] crop he sall pay the fermis to the said schir walter And frathinfurtht sall ansueir in the said schir walteris court as he salbe chargitt:

And grynd his cornis at his myln as the Remanent of his tennentis dois for free multouris Attoure the said thomas sall pay the saidis fermis betuix this and witsounday: And als all teyndschevis & utheris dettis aucht be him to the said schir walter safer as he can sufficientlie preif awand [*proof owing*]: And for the obserwing of the premissis athir off the saidis parteis ar bundin oblist & suorne to utheris be thir gryte aythis the haly ewangelis tuichit & in takin therof [*each of the said parties is bound, obliged and sworn to the other by their great oath, the gospels touched, and in token thereof*] hes subscrivit this present contract with thir handis zeir day & plaice forsaidis And sall off new subscrive & seil ilkane to uther the doubill & copyis of the principall als oft as thai salbe Requirit therto baytht in paper & parchment this wreit subscrivit befoir thir witnes Robert carnegy of kynard maister john gordoun burgess of aberdene james currour of inchdrwie & maister william gordoun parsoun of duchell witht utheris diverss

I Walter Ogilvy
Thomas bard witht my hand

Glossary

JANE CARPENTER (ED.)

N.B. Where no time or place is specified, the period and geographical area are those covered by the book.

Adchramire To promise, hence to undertake an obligation in court; often to make a binding agreement to appear in court at a later date, or to undertake to make a third party appear in court. Common in Francia.

Adstans, pl. adstantes Free man present at a public tribunal, to give it public status (see *boni homines*). The legal requirement for all free men to be present at court, as in Carolingian capitularies, in theory would have produced very large numbers of *adstantes* indeed, but in practice their presence would have varied according to the importance of the court.

Advocatus The legal representative in court of parties without capacity to act on their own behalf at law: children, women (in most European societies) and (again, in most places) churches. The latter often had professional advocates in Italy, but the term does not have to apply to a professional lawyer; in Germany, for instance, advocateship (*Vogtei*) tended to be in the hands of the aristocratic family who patronized (and, until the Gregorian Reform, owned) the church.

Agentes pl. Representatives, especially of an ecclesiastical institution. *Agentes* are most clearly associated with monasteries and appear as the means by which a community of monks fixed to a locality conducted their legal and commercial affairs over a wider area.

Althing The principal, and final, court of tenth- to thirteenth-century Iceland. It met annually at Thingvellir, in the south west of the island.

Amica pactuacio 'Friendly agreement'; the standard phrase used mainly in eighth- to twelfth-century Italy for peaceful settlement, above all settlements and compromises obtained in court.

Apokentarchôn, pl. apokentarchontes Retired commander of a group of one hundred men, possibly the personal guard of a *stratêgos** of a *theme* (province) in the Byzantine Empire.

Asekrêtês Byzantine official of an imperial bureau.

Author The principal party to a document; in a land transaction, the alienator of the land. By extension, the person who can defend (guarantee and justify) the right of tenure of the person to whom the land is alienated, if that right is challenged in court by a third party. The concept of *auctoritas* is Roman in origin. Cf. warranty*.

Basilikos Byzantine term implying employment in Byzantine imperial service.

Boni homines, boni viri, pl., 'good men' A term applied to *adstantes** or 'law-worthy' males of legal competence, and often reserved for those whose local knowledge was especially valued. Hence they might act as or sit with the judges (see *scabini*), be called on to give evidence as impartial witnesses, act as signatories or intervene as official mediators. According to formularies*, their functions in Francia appear to be very close to those of the *rachymburgi**. In Brittany they were free and propertied but nothing suggests that they were wealthy men – rather, respectable peasant proprietors, 'worthies'; cf. *gwyr da* ('good men') in Welsh law codes. In Spain and in Francia they appear to have had to have been of sufficient (if unstipulated) social and economic standing. In Italy, generally speaking, they tended to be the local élite: in local courts, they could be peasants, whereas in cities they were the urban aristocracy.

Centena; centenarius, pl. *centenarii* 'Hundred' and 'hundred man'. An administrative unit and its leader, first encountered in Frankish and Visigothic legislation, possibly derived from the organization of the Roman fisc. The significance of the number 100 is obscure. Cf. hundred*.

Charter In modern English usage, the generic historical term for nearly all the documents considered in this book. Charters record the transfer or confirmation of property rights or privileges or other transactions.

Chartoularios tôn scholôn Byzantine officer; third-in-command to Domestic of the Schools (commander-in-chief of army in the absence of the emperor).

Chirograph *Cyrographum* (literally 'written by hand') was used to refer to a legal deed, especially by Anglo-Saxons. In modern usage, the chirograph was a record reproduced in two (or more) copies on the same sheet, with a word such as *cyrographum* inscribed between them and then cut through the middle, so that parties to a transaction each had identical versions whose authenticity could be proved by matching the truncated letters. This technique originated in England, perhaps by the 850s, and was often used in the late Saxon period for dealings involving laity.

Chôrion*, pl. *chôria Byzantine rural commune usually centred on a village or larger settlement. It constituted a single fiscal unit whose landholders contributed to a common tax payment and enjoyed communal rights to land and priority to purchase plots within the *chôrion*.

Chrysoboullon Gold seal used only by the Byzantine emperor. Gives its name to type of imperial document.

Colonus In late Roman law, and in some areas later on, term denoting peasant of free status. In Frankish contexts, hereditary peasant tenant owing fixed customary renders, and (rarely) labour service, to lord. Distinguished from serf (*servus*) by limited nature of his renders and services, and access to public courts.

Common Law The principle that all free subjects of the English king shared the same ('Common') law, enforced in the king's courts by his judges.

Defensor Late and post-Roman official theoretically responsible for protecting those without legal standing. The duties and the title were established under the Roman empire, but during the fifth century their character may have altered. Some bishops took the title of *defensor* and may have exercised its functions.

***Denarii*, pl.** See *solidus*.

Despoteia Byzantine term for full ownership of property, implying free right of disposal, gift and sale.

Dilisidus*, pl. *dilisidi Breton term. See sureties.

Diploma*, pl. *diplomata A term for the most formal type of charter*, usually one issued by emperor, pope or king.

Distraint The taking of property in lieu of unpaid penalty formally imposed by a court; sometimes used in a more general sense of punishment. In Ireland, used as a means of coercing a defendant to come to a settlement.

Doux = Latin *dux*. Used in the Byzantine empire before the mid-tenth century to designate high-ranking military officers. After this date, the governor of a frontier region.

Ealdorman The standard Anglo-Saxon term for a senior provincial officer, converted to 'earl' in the eleventh century. He had judicial responsibilities in the seventh century and the military leadership of a shire* by the ninth. In the later Saxon period, he was joint president with the bishop of the shire-court, and was entitled to one third of its proceeds, but his jurisdiction often came to extend over several shires.

Engraphon asphaleia Byzantine term for final confirmatory document.

Enklêsis Byzantine term for formal request for legal action.

Enoria Byzantine fiscal and administrative district comprising a number of *chôria**.

Epoptês Byzantine tax official responsible for revising cadasters (land surveys).

Era, the Spanish A calculation of dating peculiar to the Iberian peninsula, widely used from the sixth to the thirteenth century, it begins thirty-eight years earlier than the Christian era (i.e. AD). It derived from the notional date of the completion of the Roman conquest of Spain.

Exfaida In Merovingian Francia, a fine paid to an injured party to avoid a feud (Latin *faida*). In practice, however, *exfaida* could be demanded by a court merely on technical grounds.

Exousia Byzantine term for the right to cultivate, improve or build upon land as opposed to *despoteia**.

Festuca Rod used in Frankish and Italian courts in the context of formal legal procedure. The *festuca* was grasped to show that the decision of the judges had been accepted. Grasping the *festuca* thus bound the party to carry out the court's decision, and agreements made between parties in court were likewise made binding *per festucam*.

Fideiussor, pl. fideiussores See sureties; not oath-helper nor *iurator*.

Fidiator A synonym for *fideiussor**; see sureties.

Formula, pl. formulae A standard phrase in a document; or a model document. See formulary.

Formulary Collection of a whole range of legal documents, or parts of documents, relating to land, dowry, jurisdiction, rights of attorney etc. for use as models. For the most part, surviving collections come from central and northern France, southern Germany and northern Italy.

Fredus In Francia, the proportion of a fine which was paid to the king or his representatives. Fines demanded by courts were levied as compensation to an injured party, but some of the fine, usually one third, was the king's due. By the later seventh century, the *fredus* was an important source of royal revenue.

Fuero, pl. fueros In Spain, a local law or privilege granted by king or lord to a town or rural community. In its earliest form the *fuero* was a simple charter of immunity*, modifying the applicability of royal law (the *Forum Iudicum*), restricting powers of officers such as the *saio** in matters of search and arrest, and in many cases establishing tariffs of compensation to be paid for injuries and homicides. The earliest examples date from the tenth century; and in later medieval centuries *fueros* grew substantially in the compass of their provisions.

Gastald A royal official, either holding public authority in an Italian city, instead of a duke or count, or the administrator of royal property in a given city territory. By extension from the latter, from the tenth century, an estate manager.

Graphio Germanic title for an officer resembling the fifth- and sixth-century *comes* (count) set in charge of a *civitas* (city-based administrative district).

Hêgoumenos, pl. hegoumenoi Head of a Byzantine monastic house or community, like a western abbot.

Hundred   The standard sub-division of English local government below the shire*. In the mid-tenth century it appears, probably under Frankish influence, as the name for a court of first instance and a unit of policing. See *centena*. In records of dispute, it is normally encounted as a body of 'several' or 'many' hundreds lending support to a party, or giving evidence.

Immunity   An area exempted from interference by secular and ecclesiastical authorities, and especially from state fiscal demands, and which sometimes stood outside the local public court system. See further *seigneurie*. The monks of Redon, in eastern Brittany, in the ninth century, viewed their lands as 'islands in the sea without tax and without tribute' (*CR* 136).

Inquest   A form of inquiry originally used by the Roman imperial fisc to pursue misappropriations. Used similarly in the Carolingian period, and also against male-factors and in property disputes. Public officials took sworn evidence from a number of theoretically impartial witnesses.

Iudex, pl. *iudices*   Person or persons involved in advising on, giving or enforcing judgement. The word thus applies both to those exercising real power and those whose rôle was merely participatory. In Irish contexts it translates the word *brithem*, a legally qualified and professional judge whose judgement all parties bound themselves to accept.

Iurator, pl. *iuratores*   Oath-taker. The word *iurator* is to be found primarily in Frankish or Frankish-derived law, but it is also used in the Burgundian Code. Oath-takers could be summoned to testify to the extent of a man's property and over issues of theft, dowry, loss to an enemy and slavery. They could also be called upon to support a defendant's assertion of innocence in litigation where there was no evidence: this overlapped with the rôle of oath-helping*.

Kastellion   Byzantine term for small fortified settlement; see *kastron*.

Kastron   Byzantine term for fortified settlement; see *kastellion*.

Katepan, Gk *katepanô*   Overall commander of Byzantine southern Italy.

Klasma   Land abandoned for more than 30 years (cf. Thirty-year rule*), taken over by the Byzantine state, detached from the *chôrion** and leased, regranted or sold. Became property independent from the *chôrion** and was entered separately in the tax registers.

Koinotês tês chôras, koinotês tou chôrion   Byzantine term for the collectivity of the *chôrion**, made up of the owners and cultivators of the land within it.

Koubouklêsios   Byzantine term for official of the private office of a high-ranking churchman.

Kritês   Byzantine term for judge; cf. *iudex**.

Locopositus   In eighth- and ninth-century Italy, the official subordinate of a count, or, more rarely, of a bishop.

Machtiern   A hereditary minor aristocrat who presided at meetings and sometimes initiated investigations and proceedings in the village communities of eastern Brittany, well-evidenced only in ninth-century texts. Usually each parish (*plebs*) had its own, although one man might in practice serve several communities.

Magistros   Rank in a Byzantine court.

Maior   In Carolingian rural contexts, official appointed by a lord to supervise affairs on one estate.

Mallus   The official meeting-place of a local community in the Frankish world, and thus also the place at which legal issues were settled.

Missus, pl. *missi*   Agent appointed by ruler to inspect count's administration in a group of counties (*missaticum*) and to remedy abuses, in Francia, Burgundy and Italy.

Ninth-century *missi* were often local magnates: sometimes a bishop and a count together.

Molybdoboullon   Lead seal used by Byzantine officials.

Mundeboro   Pledge-guarantor. In seventh-century Francia, one who is named as representative in legal affairs for another unable to plead in court by reason of age or infirmity.

Mundeburdium   Germanic term for formally recognized legal guardianship over those unable to protect themselves.

Muwallad   A Muslim of non-Arab descent, either a convert to Islam or the descendant of earlier converts.

Notitia   Record, often of legal proceedings.

Notarios tou kommerkiou   Byzantine official concerned with the levying of the *kommerkion*, a 10 per cent tax on the circulation and sale of commodities.

Oath-helping   Oaths in early medieval judicial procedure might be taken by a contestant and/or supporters, as evidence of his good faith, and hence used as proof of the justice of his case. They may often have been little different in practice from oaths sworn by ostensibly impartial witnesses as evidence of fact; cf. inquest*. Even when cases were decided on other grounds, oath-helping, often involving very numerous supporters, could appear – usually at the conclusion of proceedings.

Orphanotrophos   Head of a Byzantine state orphanage.

Ostensio cartae   In tenth- and eleventh-century Italy, the practice of showing one's charter in public in the court; by extension, the formalized procedure by which such a demonstration won a court-case for the charter owner without contest. Cf. *swutelung**.

Pagenses   People of the *pagus*, the word used for 'county' in much of Francia. In ninth-century Breton texts it is used to refer to men of legal competence, suitable to give evidence in court, with detailed local knowledge of properties and persons in an area much smaller than the county, i.e. 'locals'.

Periorismos   Byzantine term for demarcation of land, usually consisting of a detailed description of property boundaries with reference to natural or man-made landmarks.

Placitum, pl. placita   A word generally used by historians to refer to a specific type of document recording the final composition at the end of a law suit; for example, a mutual agreement or a formal royal permission. This usage is attested in early medieval sources, but the word has a very much wider range of meanings in classical and late Latin. The document now called a *placitum* appears to have developed only in the sixth century. By the eighth century in Francia and Italy, the meaning was extended to that of a public court hearing ('an agreement to appear in court' or a 'royal licence for a public hearing') and later to the whole of a public court-case, across many hearings; and to the document recording the case.

Pledge-guarantor   See *mundeboro*.

Precaria   In Francia and Italy, the granting of land on revocable tenure, usually but not always in return for rent or service (often military); and also, by extension, a charter* making such a grant. How far such grants were in practice revocable certainly varied from case to case. *Precaria* became assimilated to fief; both were in practice very similar.

Prôtospatharios   Rank in a Byzantine court.

Rachymburgus, pl. rachymburgi   A word doubtless of Germanic origin, of uncertain derivation, possibly meaning 'law-worthy men', worthy by virtue of property ownership, good character and knowledge of legal custom. In Frankish law *rachymburgi* appear at the *mallus** as lawmen, usually in groups of seven; they were expected to know *Lex Salica* and were subject to heavy penalties if they failed to state the law when requested. When problems were not immediately solved within the locality they acted in concert with the *graphio**, witnessing the correctness of his action. Their functions seem to be remarkably similar to those of the *boni homines** and, from the late eighth century, the *scabini**.

Rechtsschule The school of legal historians dominant in Germany and elsewhere from the early nineteenth century; characterized by a tendency to develop the rules of the Germanic law codes into a large-scale legal system, with as great a consistency as possible.

Roman vulgar law Legal custom current in the later Roman empire, not necessarily coinciding with the law of imperial edicts, other official enactments or the writings of classical jurists; not properly codified, it has to be reconstructed from a variety of Roman and post-Roman legal sources. The major work of elucidating Roman vulgar law is that of E. Levy.

Saio A Gothic judicial officer, generally of royal appointment, or, under the terms of some *fueros**, locally elected. In medieval Spain the *saio* was involved in various stages of dispute settlement, receiving the pledges of both parties to appear before the judges, conducting the ordeal when applied, and overseeing the handing over of the loser's renunciation of his claim and the restitution of the disputed property to the victor. The *saio* also had powers of search and arrest.

Scabinus, pl. scabini The word is found in the late eighth century in Francia and after 774 in Italy. Originally, and often still in the ninth century in Francia, the term was equivalent to *rachymburgus**. In Carolingian law it denotes a land-holder of some local standing appointed by the count or the *missus** for life to serve as a judgement-finder in the courts of the *missus*, count or *vicarius**. In Italy, *scabini* often ran the courts, except for the most important hearings when counts or bishops or royal *missi* presided. In eastern Brittany, it was the task of the *scabini* to conduct investigations and make judgements, usually under the presidency of one or more machtierns* or *missi*.

Seigneurie A territory in which powers normally exercised by public authority were exercised by a private landlord. This meant that the landlord (*seigneur*) might hold his own court there, and impose penalties, and that he might receive dues from the residents, direct and indirect. His own lands were usually exempt from public dues, thereby creating an immunity*.

Sheriff In England, the reeve (or steward) of the shire* was the official primarily responsible for English administration and justice at local level. Originally subordinate in theory to the ealdorman*, but there is evidence from *c.* 1000 that he had his own direct links with the king, in judicial and other matters, and the writ* was often addressed to him.

Shire County in England, although it is not certain that it originally corresponded to the modern English administrative county. The shires of Wessex, however, were serving under their modern names as military units in the ninth century, and the shire system, as it existed until 1974, was established in all but the far North by the eleventh. In the tenth century, if not before, the shire court was the normal forum of judgement in property dispute, and of local administration.

Solidus, pl. solidi In origin in the late Roman empire, a gold coin weighing $\frac{1}{72}$ of a pound and equivalent to twelve silver *denarii*. In the early middle ages, its equivalence to other coins was variable. In *Lex Salica*, a *solidus* was equivalent to forty *denarii*. In the Carolingian empire twelve *denarii* to one *solidus* became the standard pattern, although there were variations. *Solidi* were very rarely minted in the early medieval period; by the early ninth century the silver *denarius* was the normal coin. However, references in our texts to both units may often represent weights of metal rather than specifically coins.

Stratêgos, stratelatês Military governor of a Byzantine province. Both terms mean a general.

Sulsadire In Francia, to establish the fault of an opposing party in a dispute by proving that he has not turned up to a hearing, without a *sunia**, inside three days of an agreed date.

Sunia A legally valid reason for not turning up to a dispute hearing within three days of an agreed date. This term is more familiar to legal historians in its later form, *essoin*.

Sureties People who guaranteed the fulfilment of obligations by other parties, frequently appointed when an agreement was made or a dispute was settled. The many words for surety include *fideiussor**, *fidiator**, festerman, *dilisidus**; see also *wadia**. Generally their responsibilities could involve payment from their own resources or distraint* on a defaulter's property, either the goods at issue or the fine owed in punishment; very occasionally they had to punish a persistent defaulter, and might even execute a death penalty. In Spain, the concept also included those guarantors who acted for persons themselves disqualified from giving testimony and pledges in court on their own behalf. In Brittany, the use of sureties was very common and the machinery was entirely private. In late Saxon England, the adult male population was divided into groups which had the obligation of standing surety for each other's good behaviour. In Ireland, a distinction was made between the surety who enforced fulfilment of the obligation on the defaulter (*naidm*) and the surety who fulfilled it himself (*ráth*); almost all transactions were secured by sureties.

Swutelung Old English word meaning 'demonstration' or 'manifestation'. Frequently used for presentation of written evidence in dispute settlement; see charter and cf. *ostensio carta**.

Taxiarchês Byzantine commander of 1,000 infantrymen subordinate to *stratêgos**.

Teleia dialysis Final settlement in Byzantine law.

Thirty-year rule The period of time after which uncontested long possession of land became *prima facie* proof of ownership. Some special categories of land, above all royal and ecclesiastical, could require a longer time period, up to sixty years. The rule seems to originate in Roman vulgar law*.

Vicarius, pl. vicarii Subordinate or deputy of count, probably appointed by him. In Francia, the area of a *vicarius*'s jurisdiction could sometimes be a sub-division of a county; for example, eleven vicariates are known for the ninth-century county of Angoulême. *Vicarii* held courts and were empowered to demand attendance of defendants, *scabini** and witnesses.

Villa Primary meaning is estate. Hence also, a village inhabited by the tenants of an estate; sometimes specifically a royal estate, hence royal residence.

Wadia, wadium; Old English wedd A judicial pledge, represented by the offer of an object. More specifically, a pledge by either party to continue with a court-case, to offer or accept specific types of evidence, to make a successful oath, to return after adjournment, to pay a fine, to return property, to cede any sort of goods or service, or to come to a future agreement. More generally, any formal promise signified by the offer of an object, whether substantive or symbolic: for instance, the offer of a ring representing a promise to transfer land.

Warranty The legal principle whereby the validity of a property claim could be defended by tracing back its ownership through successive donors or vendors. Cf. author*. It was a normal aspect of procedure in Anglo-Saxon property disputes, as in the phrase *tale ne teames ne ahnunga*; the word *tale* is best translated as 'my story' or 'my case', but in extant judicial records it involved no obvious specific procedure; OE *team* meant either human genealogy or harnessed animals, its legal significance being the connection between one legal right and the preceding one on which it was based.

Werewolf; Latin *uuiridarium* To denounce a man as a werewolf is probably no more than to say that he is depriving another man of life, or in the case of *Pactus Legis Salicae*, xxxix. 2, of livelihood, by taking away his slave. This is the most picturesque of several Frankish words used in the *Pactus* to categorize different crimes.

Wergeld In Germanic Europe, 'man-money' or 'blood-money', reflecting the principle that a human life has a compensatory value, payable in full if a person is killed, or proportionately for injury or insult. Reckoned according to a person's standing, it provided a means of measuring his legal status and liability.

Writ In Anglo-Saxon usage, a sealed letter, usually in the vernacular, from the king or otherwise established authority to an individual subject or collective institution, generally on issues of property, including disputes.

Works cited

1 MANUSCRIPTS

Archivo Histórico Nacional, Madrid, sección de clero, Carpeta 701, Carpeta 709 and Carpeta 1405 (Navarra).
Archivo Histórico Nacional, Madrid, sección de códices, 986B, 'Cartulario de Celanova'.
Biblioteca Nacional, Madrid, MS 18387, 'The Cartulary of Samos'.
Bibliothèque Nationale, Paris, MS lat. 5411, 'Instrumentarium Casauriense'.
British Library, London, Additional MS 358444.
Scottish Record Office, Edinburgh, Abercromby of Forglen Muniments, GD 185.
Scottish Record Office, Edinburgh, Gordon Castle Muniments, GD 44.

2 PRINTED PRIMARY SOURCES

Actes de Lavra, vol. 1, ed. A. Guillou, P. Lemerle, N. Svoronos, D. Papachryssanthou, *Archives de l'Athos*, vol. 5, Paris, 1970.
Actes du Prôtaton, vol. 1, ed. D. Papachryssanthou, *Archives de l'Athos*, vol. 7, Paris, 1974.
Actus Pontificum Cennomanis in urbe degentium, ed. G. Busson and A. Ledru, Le Mans, 1901.
Adrevald of Fleury, *Ex Miraculis Sancti Benedicti*, ed. O. Holder-Egger, *MGH SS*, vol. 15, pt 1, Hannover, 1887, pp. 474–500.
Agobard, *Liber adversus legem Gundobadi*, ed. J.-P. Migne, *Patrologia Latina*, 217 vols., Paris 1841–64, vol. 104, cols. 113–26.
Anglo-Saxon Charters, ed. A. J. Robertson, 2nd edn, Cambridge, 1956.
Annales de St Bertin, ed. F. Grat, J. Vielliard and S. Clémencet, Paris, 1964.
Archives de l'Empire – Inventaires et Documents. Monuments historiques, ed. J. Tardif, Paris, 1866.
Asser's Life of King Alfred, ed. W. H. Stevenson, repr. with new introduction by D. Whitelock, Oxford, 1959.
Avitus, *Opera*, ed. R. Peiper, *MGH Auctores Antiquissimi*, vol. 6, pt 2, Berlin, 1883.
Balsamon, Theodore 'Responsa ad interrogationes Marci patriarchae', *Patrologia Graeca*, vol. 138, Paris, 1865, cols. 951–1012.
Basilicorum libri lx, ed. C. E. Heimbach, 6 vols., Leipzig, 1833–70.
Basilicorum libri lx, series A, Textus, ed. H. J. Scheltema and N. van der Wal, Groningen, 1955—; *series B, Scholia*, ed. H. J. Scheltema, Groningen, 1953.
Berrad Airechta: sect. 1–43, ed. K. Meyer, 'Bretha Airechta', *Zeitschrift für celtische Philologie*, 13 (1921), 19–24; sect. 44–84, ed. (and the whole work trans.) R. Thurneysen, *Die Bürgschaft im irischen Recht*, *Abhandlungen der Preussischen Akademie der Wissenschaften, phil.-hist. Kl.*, Berlin, 1928, pt 2.

Bethu Phátraic, ed. K. Mulchrone, Dublin, 1939.
Brennu–Njáls Saga, ed. E. O. Sveinsson, *Íslensk fornrit*, vol. 12, Reykjavik 1954.
Cáin Adamnáin, ed. and trans. K. Meyer, Oxford, 1905.
'Canones Wallici' in *The Irish Penitentials*, ed. L. Bieler, pp. 136–59.
Capitularia Regum Francorum, ed. A. Boretius, 2 vols., *MGH LL in quarto*, sectio 2, Hannover, 1883.
Cartulaire de Beaulieu, ed. M. Deloche, Paris, 1859.
Cartulaire de Cormery, ed. J.-J. Bourassé, *Mémoires de la Société archéologique de Touraine*, vol. 12, Tours, 1861.
Cartulaire de l'abbaye de Saint-Victor de Marseille, ed. B. Guérard, 2 vols., Paris, 1857.
Cartulaire de Redon, ed. A. de Courson, Paris, 1863.
Cartulario de San Juan de la Peña, ed. A. Ubieto Arteta, Valencia, 1961.
Cartulario de San Millán de la Cogolla, ed. A. Ubieto Arteta, Valencia, 1976.
Cartulario de Santo Toribio de Liébana, ed. L. Sánchez Belda, Madrid, 1948.
Cartularium Langobardicum = Additio Tertia. Cartularium, ed. A. Boretius, *MGH LL*, vol. 4, Hannover, 1868, pp. 595–601.
Cartularium Saxonicum, ed. W. de Gray Birch, 4 vols., London, 1885–99.
Catalunya Carolíngia III: Els Comtats de Pallars i Ribagorca, ed. R. d'Abadal, 2 vols., Barcelona, 1955.
Cecaumeni Strategicon, ed. B. Wassiliewsky and V. Jernstedt, St Petersburg, 1896; rep. Amsterdam, 1965.
Chartae Latinae Antiquiores, ed. A. Bruckner, R. Marichal; vol. 4, ed. A. Bruckner, R. Marichal, Olten and Lausanne, 1967; vol. 13, ed. H. Atsma, J. Vezin, Zurich, 1981; vol. 14, ed. H. Atsma, J. Vezin, Zurich, 1982; vol. 17, ed. H. Atsma, R. Marichal, J.-O. Tjäder, J. Vezin, Zurich, 1984; vol. 20, ed. A. Petrucci, J.-O. Tjäder, Zurich, 1982; vol. 21, ed. A. Petrucci, J.-O. Tjäder, Zurich, 1983.
Charters of Rochester, ed. A. Campbell, *Anglo-Saxon Charters*, vol. 1, Oxford, 1973.
'Chartes de l'Église de Valpuesta', ed. L. Barrau-Dihigo, *Revue Hispanique*, 7 (1900), 273–389.
Childeberti Decretio in *Legum*, ed. G. H. Pertz, *MGH LL*, vol. 1, Hannover, 1835, pp. 9–10.
Chlotharii Praeceptio in *Capitularia Regum Francorum*, vol. 1, ed. A. Boretius, pp. 18–19.
Chronicon Abbatiae Rameseiensis, ed. W. D. Macray, *Rolls Series*, vol. 83, London, 1886.
Codex diplomaticus Amiatinus, ed. W. Kurze, 3 vols., Tübingen, 1974–81.
Codex diplomaticus langobardiae, ed. G. Porro-Lambertenghi, Turin, 1873.
Codex Theodosianus, ed. T. Mommsen and P. M. Meyer, Berlin, 1904–5.
Codice diplomatico longobardo, 5 vols., Rome, 1929—; vols. 1, 2, ed. L. Schiaparelli, 1929–33; vol. 3, pt 1, ed. C. R. Brühl, 1973.
Codice diplomatico veronese, ed. V. Fainelli, 2 vols., Venice, 1940–63.
Coibnes Uisci Thairidne: ed. D. A. Binchy in 'Irish law-tracts re-edited: I. *Coibnes Uisci Thairidne*', *Ériu*, 17 (1955), 52–85.
Coic Conara Fugill, ed. R. Thurneysen, *Abhandlungen der Preussischen Akademie der Wissenschaften, phil.-hist. Kl.*, Berlin, 1925, pt 7.
Colección diplomática de la Catedral de Huesca, ed. A. Duran Gudiol, 2 vols., Zaragoza, 1965–9.
Colección diplomática de Obarra, ed. A. J. Martin Duque, Zaragoza, 1965.
Colección diplomática de Pedro I de Aragón y Navarra, ed. A. Ubieto Arteta, Zaragoza, 1951.
Colección diplomática de San Salvador de Oña, ed. J. del Alamo, 2 vols., Madrid, 1950.
'Concilium Burdegalense' in *Concilia Galliae 511–695*, ed. C. de Clercq, *Corpus Christianorum, Series Latina*, vol. 148A, Turnhout, 1963, pp. 311–13.

Constantine Porphyrogenitus, *De Administrando Imperio*, ed. G. Moravcsik, Eng. trans. R. J. H. Jenkins, *Dumbarton Oaks Texts*, vol. 1, Washington, D.C., 1967.
　Commentary, ed. F. Dvornik, R. J. H. Jenkins, B. Lewis, G. Moravcsik, D. Obolensky, S. Runciman, London, 1962.
Corpus Iuris Hibernici, ed. D. A. Binchy, 6 vols., Dublin, 1978.
Costantino Porfirogenito, *De Thematibus*, ed. A. Pertusi, *Studi e testi*, vol. 160, Vatican, 1952.
Críth Gablach, ed. D. A. Binchy, *Mediaeval and Modern Irish Series*, vol. 11, Dublin, 1941.
Die Gesetze der Angelsachsen, ed. F. Liebermann, 3 vols., Halle, 1903–16; rep. 1961.
Die irische Kanonensammlung, ed. F. W. H. Wasserschleben, 2nd edn, Leipzig, 1885.
Die nichtliterarischen Papyri Italiens aus der Zeit 445–700, ed. J.-O. Tjäder, 3 vols., Lund and Stockholm, 1955–82.
Diplomata, chartae, epistolae, leges aliaque instrumenta ad res Gallo-Francicas spectantia, ed. J. Pardessus, 2 vols., Paris, 1843–9.
Diplomata regum Francorum e stirpe Merowingica in *MGH Diplomata Imperii*, vol. 1, ed. K. Pertz, Hannover, 1872.
'Do Macuib Úa Suanaig' in *Bethada Náem nÉrenn*, ed. and trans. C. Plummer, 2 vols., Oxford, 1922, vol. 1, pp. 312–16, vol. 2, pp. 303–7.
Ecloga, Das Gesetzbuch Leons III und Konstantinos' V, ed. L. Burgmann, *Forschungen zur Byzantinischen Rechtsgeschichte*, vol. 10, Frankfurt, 1983.
Edictus Chlotharii in *Capitularia Regum Francorum*, vol. 1, ed. A. Boretius, pp. 20–3.
Edictus Rothari in *Leges Langobardorum*, ed. F. Beyerle, pp. 16–94.
Ekloga in *Jus graecoromanum*, ed. J. and P. Zepos, vol. 2, pp. 5–62.
El Becerro gótico de San Pedro de Cardeña, ed. L. Serrano, Valladolid, 1910.
El Cartulario de San Pedro de Arlanza, ed. L. Serrano, Madrid, 1925.
'Els documents, dels segles IX i X, conservats a l'Arxiu Capitular de la Seu d'Urgell', ed. C. Baraut, *Urgellia*, 2 (1979), 7–145.
Eparchikon biblion in *Jus graecoromanum*, ed. J. and P. Zepos, vol. 2, pp. 371–92 (English translation by E. H. Freshfield, *Roman Law in the Later Roman Empire*).
Formulae Andecavenses in *Formulae Merowingici et Karolini Aevi*, ed. K. Zeumer, pp. 1–25.
Formulae Arvernenses in *Formulae Merowingici et Karolini Aevi*, ed. K. Zeumer, pp. 26–31.
Formulae Merowingici et Karolini Aevi, ed. K. Zeumer, *MGH LL in quarto*, sectio 5, Hannover, 1886.
Formulae Turonenses in *Formulae Merowingici et Karolini Aevi*, ed. K. Zeumer, pp. 128–59.
'Gesta Sanctorum Rotonensium' in L. d'Achéry, *Acta Sanctorum ordinis sancti Benedicti*, ed. J. Mabillon, 9 vols., Paris, 1668–1701, vol. 4, pt 2, pp. 193–222.
Gregory of Tours, *Decem Libri Historiarum*, ed. B. Krusch and W. Levison, *MGH SRM*, vol. 1, pt 1, Hannover, 1951.
　Miracula, ed. W. Arndt and B. Krusch, *MGH SRM*, vol. 1, pt 2, Hannover, 1885.
Gúbretha Caratniad: ed. R. Thurneysen, 'Die falschen Urteilssprüche Caratnia's', *Zeitschrift für celtische Philologie*, 15 (1924–5).
Hincmar of Rheims, *Ad Episcopos Regni*, ed. J.-P. Migne, *Patrologia Latina*, 221 vols., Paris, 1841–64, vol. 125, cols. 1007–18.
Illustrations of the Topography and Antiquities of the Shires of Aberdeen and Banff, ed. J. Robertson and G. Grub, 5 vols., Aberdeen, 1843–69.
Instrumenta Ecclesiae Ausciensis in *Instrumenta* section, *Gallia Christiana*, vol. 1, ed. D. Sammarthani, Paris, 1715, pp. 159–72.
I placiti del 'Regnum Italiae', ed. C. Manaresi, 3 vols., Rome, 1955–60.
'Itinerarium Bernardi Monachi' in *Descriptiones Terrae Sanctae ex saeculo VIII. IX. XII. et XV*, ed. T. Tobler, Leipzig, 1874, pp. 85–99.

Jus graecoromanum, ed. J. and P. Zepos, 8 vols., Athens, 1931–6; rep. Aalen, 1962.

Justinian, *Codex Iustinianus*, ed. P. Krueger in Justinian, *Corpus Iuris Civilis*, vol. 2, Berlin, 1900.

Digest, ed. T. Mommsen in Justinian, *Corpus Iuris Civilis*, vol. 1, Berlin, 1902.

Laws of Early Iceland: Grágás 1, ed. A. Dennis, P. Foote, R. Perkins, Winnipeg, 1980.

Leges Grimvaldi in *Leges Langobardorum*, ed. F. Beyerle, pp. 95–8.

Leges Langobardorum 643–866, ed. F. Beyerle, 2nd edn, Witzenhausen, 1962.

Leges Liutprandi in *Leges Langobardorum*, ed. F. Beyerle, pp. 99–176.

Leges Ratchisi in *Leges Langobardorum*, ed. F. Beyerle, pp. 183–93.

Leges Visigothorum, ed. K. Zeumer, *MGH LL in quarto*, sectio 1, vol. 1, Hannover and Leipzig, 1902.

Les diplômes originaux de Mérovingiens, ed. P. Lauer, C. Samaran, Paris, 1908.

Les Novelles de Léon VI le sage, ed. P. Noailles and A. Dain, Paris, 1944.

Lex Romana Burgundionum in *Leges Burgundionum*, ed. L. R. de Salis, *MGH LL in quarto*, sectio 1, vol. 2, pt 1, Hannover, 1892, pp. 123–63.

Lex Romana Visigothorum, ed. G. F. Haenel, Leipzig, 1847–9.

Liber Angeli in *The Patrician Texts in the Book of Armagh*, ed. L. Bieler, pp. 184–91.

Liber Constitutionum in *Leges Burgundionum*, ed. L. R. de Salis, *MGH LL in quarto*, sectio 1, vol. 2, pt 1, Hannover, 1892, pp. 29–122.

Liber Eliensis, ed. E. O. Blake, *Camden 3rd series*, vol. 92, London, 1962.

Liber Historiae Francorum, ed. B. Krusch, *MGH SRM*, Hannover, 1888, vol. 2, pp. 238–328.

Liber legis langobardorum Papiensis dictus, ed. A. Boretius, *MGH LL*, vol. 4, Hannover, 1868, pp. 289–585.

Marca, P. de *Marca Hispanica sive Limes Hispanicus*, ed. S. Baluze, Paris, 1688.

Marculfi Formularum Libri Duo, ed. and French trans. A. Uddholm, Uppsala, 1962.

Memorie e documenti per servire all' istoria del ducato di Lucca, vol. 5, ed. D. Barsocchini, 3 vols., Lucca, 1837–44.

Nomos georgikos in *Jus graecoromanum*, ed. J. and P. Zepos, vol. 2, pp. 65–71 (trans. W. Ashburner, 'The Farmer's Law', *J. Hell. Stud.*, 32 (1912)).

Oxyrhynchus Papyri, vol. 1, ed. B. P. Grenfell and A. S. Hunt, London, 1898.

Pactus Legis Salicae, ed. K. A. Eckhardt, *MGH LL in quarto*, sectio 1, vol. 4, pt 1, Hannover, 1962.

Pactus pro tenore pacis domnorum Childeberti et Chlotharii regum in *Capitularia Regum Francorum*, vol. 1, ed. A. Boretius, pp. 3–7.

Passio Praejecti, ed. B. Krusch, *MGH SRM*, vol. 5, Hannover and Leipzig, 1910, pp. 225–48.

Patrick, Saint, *Confessio* in *Libri Epistolarum Sancti Patricii*, ed. L. Bieler, 2 vols., Dublin, 1952, vol. 1; also ed. R. P. C. Hanson and C. Blanc, *Saint Patrick. Confession et Lettre à Coroticus, Sources chrétiennes*, vol. 249, Paris, 1978, pp. 70–133.

Paul, *Historia Langobardorum*, ed. L. Bethmann and G. Waitz, *MGH Scriptores Rerum Langobardicarum*, Hannover, 1878, pp. 12–187.

Practica ex actis Eustathii Romani in *Jus graecoromanum*, ed. J. and P. Zepos, vol. 4, pp. 11–260.

Procheiros Nomos in *Jus graecoromanum*, ed. J. and P. Zepos, vol. 2, pp. 109–228 (English translation in E. Freshfield, *A manual of Eastern Roman law*).

Recueil des Actes de Charles II le Chauve, ed. G. Tessier, 3 vols. Paris, 1943–55.

Recueil des Actes de Pépin I et de Pépin II, rois d'Aquitaine (814–848), ed. L. Levillain, Paris, 1926.

Recueil des chartes de l'Abbaye de Cluny, ed. A. Bruel, 6 vols., Paris, 1872–1903.

Recueil des Chartes de l'abbaye de St Benoît-sur-Loire, ed. M. Prou and A. Vidier, *Documents publiés par la Société historique et archéologique du Gâtinais*, vol. 5, Paris–Orleans, 1900.
Regesto di Farfa, ed. I. Giorgi and U. Balzani, 5 vols., Rome, 1879–1914.
Regiam Maiestatem et Quoniam Attachiamenta, ed. T. M. Cooper, Stair Society, vol. 11, Edinburgh, 1947.
Registrum Magni Sigilli Regum Scotorum, ed J. M. Thomson and others, 11 vols., Edinburgh, 1882–1914.
Registrum Secreti Sigilli Regum Scotorum, ed. M. Livingstone and others, 8 vols., Edinburgh, 1908—.
Sacrorum conciliorum nova et amplissima collectio, ed. J. D. Mansi, 31 vols., Florence–Venice, 1757–98.
Sidonius Apollinaris, *Poèmes et Lettres*, ed. A. Loyen, 3 vols., Paris, 1960–70.
Syllabus Graecarum membranarum, ed. F. Trinchera, Naples, 1865.
Synodus Patricii in *The Irish Penitentials*, ed. L. Bieler, pp. 184–97.
Syntagma tôn theion kai hierôn kanonôn, ed. G. A. Rhalles and M. Potles, 6 vols., Athens, 1852–9.
Tacitus, *Germania*, ed. J. G. C. Anderson, Oxford, 1938.
The Acts of the Lords Auditors of Causes and Complaints, ed. T. Thomson, Edinburgh, 1839.
The Acts of the Parliaments of Scotland, ed. T. Thomson and C. Innes, 12 vols., Edinburgh, 1814–75.
The Annals of Banff, compiled by W. Cramond, 2 vols., Aberdeen, 1891–3.
The Cartulary of the Benedictine Abbey of St Peter of Gumay (Croatia), ed. E. Pivčevič, Bristol, 1984.
The Charters of the Abbey of Crosraguel, ed. F. C. Hunter Blair, 2 vols., Edinburgh, 1886.
'The Farmer's Law', ed. and trans. W. Ashburner, *Journal of Hellenic Studies*, 30 (1910), 85–108 (Text); 32 (1912), 68–95 (Commentary and Translation).
The Fourth Book of the Chronicle of Fredegar, ed. and trans. J. Wallace-Hadrill, London, 1960.
The Irish Penitentials, ed. L. Bieler, *Scriptores Latini Hiberniae*, vol. 5, Dublin, 1963.
Theodulf, 'Versus contra Iudices' in *Poetae Latinae Aevi Carolini*, vol. 1, ed. E. Dümmler, *MGH Poetarum Latinarum Medii Aevi*, vol. 1, Berlin, 1881, pp. 493–517.
The Patrician Texts in the Book of Armagh, ed. L. Bieler, *Scriptores Latini Hiberniae*, vol. 10, Dublin, 1979.
Theophanes continuatus, *Chronographia*, ed. I. Bekker, Bonn, 1838.
The Practicks of Sir James Balfour of Pittendreich, ed. P. G. B. McNeill, 2 vols., Stair Society, vols. 21 and 22, Edinburgh, 1962–3.
The Theodosian Code, trans. C. Pharr, Princeton, 1952.
The Will of Æthelgifu, ed. D. Whitelock, with N. R. Ker and Lord Rennell, London, 1968.
Tírechán (writings of) in *The Patrician Texts in the Book of Armagh*, ed. L. Bieler, pp. 124–63.
Urkundenbuch der Abtei Sanct Gallen, ed. H. Wartmann, 2 vols., Zürich, 1863–6.
Venantius Fortunatus, *Opera Poetica*, ed. F. Leo, *MGH Auctores Antiquissimi*, vol. 4, pt 1, Berlin, 1881.
Vita Amandi, ed. B. Krusch, *MGH SRM*, vol. 5, Hannover and Leipzig, 1910, pp. 428–49.
Vita Ansberti, ed. W. Levison, *MGH SRM*, vol. 5, Hannover and Leipzig, 1910, pp. 619–41.
Vita Eligii, ed. B. Krusch, *MGH SRM*, vol. 4, Hannover, 1902, pp. 663–741.
Vita Germani Grandivallensis, ed. B. Krusch, *MGH SRM*, vol. 5, Hannover and Leipzig, 1910, pp. 33–40.

Vita Landiberti Vetustissima, ed. B. Krusch, *MGH SRM*, vol. 6, Hannover and Leipzig, 1913, pp. 353–85.

Vita Nivardi, ed. W. Levison, *MGH SRM*, vol. 5, Hannover and Leipzig, 1910, pp. 160–71.

Volpini, R. 'Placiti del "Regnum Italiae" (secc. IX–XI). Primi contributi per un nuovo censimento' in P. Zerbi (ed.), *Contributi dell'Istituto di storia medioevale*, vol. 3, Milan, 1975, pp. 245–520.

3 SECONDARY WORKS

Ahrweiler, H. *L'idéologie politique de l'Empire byzantin*, Paris, 1975.

'Recherches sur l'administration de l'empire byzantin aux IXe–XIe siècles', *Bulletin de correspondance héllenique*, 84 (1960), 1–111; rep. in H. Ahrweiler, *Études sur les structures administratives et sociales de Byzance*, London, 1971.

Angold, M. *The Byzantine Empire 1025–1204*, London, 1984.

Arbois de Jubainville, H. d' 'Des attributions judiciaires de l'autorité publique chez les celtes', *Revue celtique*, 7 (1886), 2–37.

Études sur le droit celtique, 2 vols., Paris, 1895.

'La procédure du jeûne en Irlande', *Revue celtique*, 7 (1886), 245–9.

Arce, R. del 'El Archivo de la Catedral de Jaca', *Boletín de la Real Academia de la Historia*, 65 (1914), 49–51.

Azkue, R. M. de *Diccionario Vasco–Español–Frances*, 2 vols., Bilbao, 1969.

Baldwin, J. 'The intellectual preparation for the canon of 1215 against ordeals', *Speculum*, 36 (1961), 613–36.

Balfour Paul, J. (ed.), *The Scots Peerage*, 9 vols., Edinburgh, 1904–14.

Bankton, Andrew McDouall lord, *An Institute of the Laws of Scotland*, Edinburgh, 1751.

Baraut, C. 'Els documents, dels anys 981–1010, de l'Arxiu Capitular de la Seu d'Urgell', *Urgellia*, 3 (1980), 7–166.

Bartlett, R. 'The impact of royal government in the French Ardennes: the evidence of the 1247 enquête', *Journal of Medieval History*, 7 (1981), 83–96.

Beaucamp, J. 'La situation juridique de la femme à Byzance', *Cahiers de civilisation médiévale*, 20 (1977), pts 2 and 3, 145–76.

Bergmann, W. 'Untersuchungen zu den Gerichtsurkunden der Merowingerzeit', *Archiv für Diplomatik*, 22 (1976), 1–186.

Best, R. I. 'An early monastic grant from the Book of Durrow', *Ériu*, 10 (1926–8), 135–42.

Besta, E. *Fonti: legislazione e scienza giuridica*, Milan, 1923 (= P. Del Giudice (ed.), *Storia del diritto italiano*, vol. 1, pt 1).

Bigelow, M. M. (ed.), *Placita Anglo-Normannica*, London, 1879.

Binchy, D. A. 'An archaic legal poem', *Celtica*, 9 (1971), 152–68.

'Ancient Irish law', *The Irish Jurist*, n.s., 1 (1966), 84–92.

'A pre-Christian survival in mediaeval Irish hagiography' in D. Whitelock, R. McKitterick and D. Dumville (eds.), *Ireland in Early Mediaeval Europe*, Cambridge, 1982, pp. 165–78.

'Bretha Nemed', *Ériu*, 17 (1955), 4–6.

Celtic and Anglo-Saxon Kingship. The O'Donnell Lectures for 1967–8, Oxford, 1970.

'Distraint in Irish law', *Celtica*, 10 (1973), 22–71.

'Féichem, fethem, aigne', *Celtica*, 11 (1976), 18–33.

'Irish history and Irish law', *Studia Hibernica*, 15 (1975) 7–36, and 16 (1976), 7–45.

'Linguistic and legal archaisms in the Celtic law-books', *Transactions of the Philological Society*, 1959, 14–24.

'Patrick and his biographers, ancient and modern', *Studia Hibernica*, 2 (1962), 7–173.

'Secular institutions' in M. Dillon (ed.), *Early Irish Society*, Dublin, 1954, pp. 52–65.

'The date and provenance of *Uraicecht Becc*', *Ériu*, 18 (1958), 44–54.

'The linguistic and historical value of the Irish law-tracts', *Proceedings of the British Academy*, 29 (1943), 195–227.

'The passing of the old order' in B. Ó. Cuív (ed.), *The Impact of the Scandinavian Invasions on the Celtic-speaking Peoples, c. 800–1100 A.D. Papers read at the International Congress of Celtic Studies, Dublin, 1959*, Dublin, 1975, pp. 119–32.

Black-Michaud, J. *Cohesive Force*, Oxford, 1975.

Bognetti, G. P. *L'età longobarda*, 4 vols., Milan, 1966–8.

Bonnassie, P. *La Catalogne du milieu du Xe à la fin du XIe siècle*, 2 vols., Toulouse, 1975–6.

Bossy, J. (ed.), *Disputes and Settlements: Law and Human Relations in the West*, Cambridge, 1983.

Boulet-Sautel, M. 'Aperçues sur le système des preuves dans la France coutumière au moyen âge' in *La Preuve*, vol. 2, *Recueil de la Société Jean Bodin*, vol. 17, pp. 275–325.

Bouras, C. 'City and village: urban design and architecture', *Akten, XVI Internationaler Byzantinistenkongress*, Vienna, 1981, vol. 1, pt 2, pp. 611–53.

Breatnach, L. 'Canon law and secular law in early Ireland: the significance of *Bretha Nemed*', *Peritia*, 3 (1984), 439–59.

Bresslau, H. *Handbuch der Urkundenlehre*, 2 vols., Leipzig, 1912–17.

Brooks, N. *The Early History of the Church of Canterbury*, Leicester, 1984.

'The pre-conquest charters of Christ Church Canterbury', Univ. Oxford D.Phil. thesis, 1969.

Brown, K. M. *Bloodfeud in Scotland, 1573–1625: Violence, Justice and Politics in an Early Modern Society*, Edinburgh, 1986.

Brown, P. 'Society and the supernatural: a medieval change', *Daedalus*, 104 (1975), 133–51.

Browning, R. *Byzantium and Bulgaria*, London, 1975.

Brunner, H. *Deutsche Rechtsgeschichte*, 2 vols., Leipzig, 1887–92; 2nd edn, Leipzig–Munich, 1906–28; 3rd edn, with C. F. von Schwerin, Berlin, 1961.

Die Entstehung der Schwurgerichte, Berlin, 1871.

Buchner, R. *Die Rechtsquellen*; Beiheft to W. Wattenbach and W. Levison, *Deutschlands Geschichtsquellen im Mittelalter*, Weimar, 1953.

Bullough, D. A. '*Europae Pater*: Charlemagne and his achievement in the light of recent scholarship', *English Historical Review*, 85 (1970), 59–105.

'Leo, *qui apud Hlotharium magni loci habebatur*, et le gouvernement du *Regnum Italiae* à l'époque carolingienne', *Le moyen âge*, 67 (1961), 221–45.

Byock, J. L. *Feud in the Icelandic Saga*, Berkeley, 1982.

Caenegem, R. C. van 'La preuve dans le Droit du moyen âge occidental' in *La Preuve*, vol. 2, *Recueil de la Société Jean Bodin*, vol. 17, pp. 691–753.

Royal Writs in England: from the Conquest to Glanville, Selden Society, vol. 77, London, 1958–9.

Cam, H. M. 'The Evolution of the mediaeval English franchise', *Speculum*, 32 (1957), 427–42.

Campbell, J. 'Observations on English Government from the tenth to the twelfth century', *Transactions of the Royal Historical Society*, 5th s., 25 (1975), 39–54.

(ed.), *The Anglo-Saxons*, Oxford, 1982.

Canellas Lopez, A. *Diplomática Hispano-Visigoda*, Zaragoza, 1979.

Castan, N. 'The arbitration of disputes under the *ancien régime*' in J. Bossy (ed.), *Disputes and Settlements*, pp. 219–60.

Chanock, M. 'Making Customary Law – men, women and courts in Northern Rhodesia' in M. Hay, M. Wright (eds.), *African Women and the Law: Historical Perspectives*, Boston University Papers on Africa, vol. 7, Boston, 1982, pp. 53–68.

Chaplais, P. 'The Anglo-Saxon chancery: from the diploma to the writ', *Journal of the Society of Archivists*, 3 (1965–9), 160–76.

Charles-Edwards, T. M. 'Boundaries in Irish law' in P. H. Sawyer (ed.), *Medieval Settlement: Continuity and Change*, London, 1976, pp. 83–7.

'The *Corpus Iuris Hibernici*', *Studia Hibernica*, 20 (1980), 141–62.

Chédeville, A. and Guillotel, H. *La Bretagne des saints et des rois, V^e–Xe siècle*, Rennes, 1984.

Clanchy, M. T. 'A medieval realist: interpreting the rules at Barnwell Priory, Cambridge' in E. Attwool (ed.), *Perspectives in Jurisprudence*, Glasgow, 1977, pp. 176–94.

From Memory to Written Record, London, 1979.

'Law and love in the middle ages' in J. Bossy (ed.), *Disputes and Settlements*, pp. 47–67.

Classen, P. 'Fortleben und Wandel spätrömischen Urkundenwesens im frühen Mittelalter' in P. Classen (ed.), *Recht und Schrift im Mittelalter*, pp. 13–54.

'Kaiserreskript und Königsurkunde. Diplomatische Studien zum römisch-germanisch Kontinuätsproblem', *Archiv für Diplomatik*, 2 (1956), 1–115.

(ed.), *Recht und Schrift im Mittelalter, Vorträge und Forschungen des Konstanzer Arbeitskreis für mittelalterliche Geschichte*, vol. 23, Sigmaringen, 1977.

Claude, D. 'Untersuchungen zum frühfränkischen Comitat', *ZRG, Germ. Abt.*, 42 (1964), 1–79.

Collins, R. J. H. 'Charles the Bald and Wifred the Hairy' in *Charles the Bald: Court and Kingdom*, ed. M. Gibson and J. Nelson with D. Ganz, pp. 169–89.

Early Medieval Spain: Unity in Diversity, 400–1000, London and Basingstoke, 1983.

'*Sicut Lex Gothorum continet*: law and charters in ninth- and tenth-century León and Catalonia', *English Historical Review*, 100 (1985), 489–512.

'The Basques in Aquitaine and Navarre' in *War and Government in the Middle Ages*, ed. J. Gillingham and J. C. Holt, Cambridge, 1984, pp. 3–17.

Colman, R. V. 'Reason and Unreason in Early Medieval Law', *Journal of Interdisciplinary History*, 4 (1974), 571–91.

Conrad, H. *Deutsche Rechtsgeschichte*, Karlsruhe, 1962.

Cooper, T. M. *Select Scottish Cases of the Thirteenth Century*, Edinburgh, 1944.

Crook, J. A. *Law and Life of Rome*, London, 1967.

Davies, W. 'Disputes, their conduct and their settlement in the village communities of eastern Brittany in the ninth century', *History and Anthropology*, 1, pt 2 (1985), 289–312.

'Land and power in early medieval Wales', *Past and Present*, 81 (1978), 3–23.

'On the distribution of political power in Brittany in the mid-ninth century' in M. Gibson and J. Nelson with D. Ganz (eds.), *Charles the Bald: Court and Kingdom*, pp. 87–107.

'Priests and rural communities in east Brittany in the ninth century', *Études Celtiques*, 20 (1983), 177–97.

'Suretyship in the *Cartulaire de Redon*' in T. M. Charles-Edwards, M. E. Owen and D. Walters (eds.), *Lawyers and Laymen*, Cardiff, 1986, pp. 72–91.

'The Latin charter-tradition in western Britain, Brittany and Ireland in the early mediaeval period' in D. Whitelock, R. McKitterick and D. Dumville (eds.), *Ireland in Early Mediaeval Europe*, Cambridge, 1982, pp. 258–80.

Villages, Villagers and the Structure of Rural Society in Early Medieval Brittany, London, 1986 (forthcoming).

Delumeau, J.-P. 'L'exercice de la justice dans le comté d'Arezzo (IXe–debut XIIIe siècle)', *Mélanges de l'École française de Rome. Moyen âge, Temps modernes*, 90 (1978), 563–605.

Díaz y Díaz, M. C. *Libros y librerías en la Rioja altomedieval*, Logroño, 1979.
'Los documentos hispano–visigóticos sobre pizarra', *Studi Medievali*, 7 (1966), 75–107.
Dictionary of the Irish Language (incorporating *Contributions to a Dictionary* . . .), ed. E. G. Quin and others, Dublin, 1913–76.
Dilke, O. A. W. *Roman Land Surveyors*, Newton Abbot, 1971.
Dillon, M. *Celts and Aryans*, Simla, 1975.
Doherty, C. 'Some aspects of hagiography as a source for Irish economic history', *Peritia*, 1 (1982), 300–28.
'The monastic town in early medieval Ireland' in H. B. Clarke and A. Simms (eds.), *The Comparative History of Urban Origins in Non-Roman Europe: Ireland, Wales, Denmark, Germany, Poland and Russia from the ninth to the thirteenth century*, British Archaeological Reports, International Series, vol. 255, Oxford, 1985, pp. 45–75.
Dölger, F. *Ein Fall slavischer Einsiedlung im Hinterland von Thessalonika im 10. Jahrhundert, Sitzungsberichte der Bayerische Akademie der Wissenschaft, phil.-hist. Klasse*, Munich, 1952, pt 1.
Dölger, F. and Karayannopoulos, J. *Byzantinische Urkundenlehre, Handbuch der Altertumswissenschaft*, vol. 12, pt 3, 1/1, Munich, 1968.
Donaldson, G. 'The legal profession in Scottish society in the sixteenth and seventeenth centuries', *Juridical Review*, n.s., 21 (1976), 1–21.
Drogin, M. *Medieval Calligraphy*, London, 1980.
Du Cange, C. Dufresne, *Glossarium ad Scriptores Mediae et Infirmae Latinitatis*, 3 vols., Frankfürt-am-Main, 1681.
Duchesne, L. *Fastes épiscopaux de l'ancienne Gaule*, 3 vols., Paris, 1907–15.
Dumville, D. N. 'On the dating of the early Breton lawcodes', *Études Celtiques*, 21 (1984), 207–21.
Duncan, A. A. M. 'The Central Courts before 1532' in *Introduction to Scottish Legal History*, Stair Society, vol. 20, Edinburgh, 1958, pp. 321–40.
Ebling, H. *Prosopographie der Amtsträger des Merowingerreiches*, Beiheft der *Francia*, vol. 2, Munich, 1974.
Emilia, A. d' 'Il diritto bizantino nell' Italia meridionale', *Atti del convegno internazionale sul tema: l'Oriente christiano nella storia della civiltà, Florence, 1963, Quaderno dell' Accademia nazionale dei Lincei*, 62 (1964), 343–74.
Epstein, A. L. 'The case method in the field of law' in *idem* (ed.), *The Craft of Social Anthropology*, London, 1967.
Estey, F. N. 'The *scabini* and the local courts', *Speculum*, 26 (1951), 119–29.
Falkenhausen, V. von 'I bizantini in Italia' in G. Cavallo *et al.*, *I bizantini in Italia*, Milan, 1982, pp. 1–136.
La Dominazione bizantina nell' Italia meridionale, Bari, 1978.
Ferrari, G. *I documenti greci medioevali di diritto privato dell' Italia meridionale, Byzantinisches Archiv*, 4 (1910).
Finberg, H. P. R. *The Early Charters of Wessex*, Leicester, 1964.
Fleckenstein, J. *Grundlegung. Die karolingische Hofkapelle, Die Hofkapelle der deutschen Könige*, vol. 1, *Schriften der MGH*, vol. 16, Stuttgart, 1959.
Fleuriot, L. 'Un fragment en Latin de très anciennes lois bretonnes armoricaines du VIᵉ siècle', *Annales de Bretagne*, 78 (1971), 601–60.
Foss, C. 'Archaeology and the twenty cities of Byzantine Asia', *American Journal of Archaeology*, 81 (1977), 469–86.
Ephesus after Antiquity, Cambridge, 1979.
Freshfield, E. H. *A Manual of Eastern Roman Law: the Procheiros Nomos*, Cambridge, 1928.
Roman Law in the Later Roman Empire, Cambridge, 1938.

Galbraith, V. H. 'The death of a champion (1287)' in R. W. Hunt, W. A. Pantin and R. W. Southern (eds.), *Studies in Medieval History presented to F. M. Powicke*, Oxford, 1948, pp. 283–95.

Ganshof, F. L. *Feudalism*, 3rd English edn, London, 1964.

Frankish Institutions under Charlemagne, Providence, Rhode Island, 1968.

'La preuve dans le droit franc' in *La Preuve*, vol. 2, *Recueil de la Société Jean Bodin*, vol. 17, pp. 71–98.

Ganz, D. 'Bureaucratic shorthand and Merovingian learning' in P. Wormald, D. Bullough and R. Collins (eds.), *Ideal and Reality in Frankish and Anglo-Saxon Society: Studies presented to J. M. Wallace-Hadrill*, Oxford, 1983, pp. 58–75.

Gasnault, P. 'Les actes privés de l'abbaye de St Martin de Tours du VIIIe au XIIe siècle', *Bibliothèque de l'École de Chartes*, 112 (1954), 24–66.

Gaudemet, J. *L'Église dans l'empire romain*, Paris, 1958.

'Les ordalies au moyen âge' in *La Preuve*, vol. 2, *Recueil de la Société Jean Bodin*, vol. 17, pp. 99–135.

Gay, J. *L'Italie méridionale et l'empire byzantin*, Paris, 1904.

Gibert, R. *Historia general del derecho español*, 2 vols., Granada, 1968.

Gibson, M. and Nelson, J. with Ganz, D. (eds.), *Charles the Bald: Court and Kingdom*, British Archaeological Reports, International Series, vol. 101, Oxford, 1981.

Gluckman, M. *Custom and Conflict in Africa*, Oxford, 1956.

The Judicial Process among the Barotse of Northern Rhodesia (Zambia), 2nd edn, Manchester, 1973.

Goebel, J. *Felony and Misdemeanour*, New York, 1937.

Goñi Gaztambide, J. *Catálogo del Archivo Catedral de Pamplona*, Pamplona, 1965.

Catálogo del Becerro antiguo y del Becerro menor de Leyre, Pamplona, 1963.

Historia de los obispos de Pamplona, 2 vols., Pamplona, 1979.

Goody, J. *The Development of family and marriage in Europe*, Cambridge, 1983.

Graus, F. *Volk, Herrscher und Heiliger im Reich der Merowinger*, Prague, 1965.

Grimm, J. *Deutsche Rechtsaltertümer*, Göttingen, 1828.

Guillou, A. *Culture et société en Italie byzantine*, London, 1978.

La civilisation byzantine, Paris, 1974.

Studies on Byzantine Italy, London, 1970.

Guillou, A. and Holtzmann, W. 'Zwei katepansurkunden aus Tricarico', *Quellen und Forschungen*, 41 (1961), 1–28; rep. in A. Guillou, *Studies on Byzantine Italy*.

Halphen, L. 'La justice en France au XIe siècle' in *idem*, *À travers l'histoire du Moyen Age*, Paris, 1950, pp. 175–202.

Heinzelmann, M. 'Une source de base de la littérature hagiographique latine: le recueil de miracles' in *Hagiographie, cultures et sociétés, IVe–XIIe siècles*, ed. E. Patlagean and P. Riché, Études Augustiniennes, Paris, 1981, pp. 235–57.

Hennebicque, R. 'Structures familiales et structures politiques au IXe siècle: Un groupe familial de l'aristocratie franque', *Revue Historique*, 265 (1981), 289–333.

Hirschfeld, B. *Die Gesta Municipalia in römischer und frühgermanischer Zeit*, Marburg, 1904.

Hübner, R. 'Gerichtsurkunden der fränkischen Zeit', *Zeitschrift der Savigny-Stiftung für Rechtsgeschichte; germanistische Abteilung*, 12 (1891) and 14 (1893), appendixes, pp. 1–118, 1–258; also published separately.

Hughes, K. W. *Early Christian Ireland: Introduction to the Sources*, London, 1972.

Humphreys, S., 'Social relations on stage: witnesses in classical Athens', *History and Anthropology*, 1, pt 2 (1985), 313–69.

Hurnard, N. D. 'The Anglo-Norman Franchises', *English Historical Review*, 64 (1949), 289–327, 433–60.

'The Jury of Presentment and the Assize of Clarendon', *English Historical Review*, 56 (1941), 374–410.

Iglesia Ferreirós, A. 'La creación del derecho en Cataluña', *Anuario de Historia del Derecho Español*, 47 (1977), 99–423.

Jackson, K. H. *The Gaelic Notes in the Book of Deer*, Cambridge, 1972.

Jaeger, H. 'La preuve judiciaire d'après la tradition rabbinique et patristique' in *La Preuve*, vol. 1, *Recueil de la Société Jean Bodin*, vol. 16, pp. 415–594.

James, E. '*Beati pacifici*: bishops and the law in sixth-century Gaul' in J. Bossy (ed.), *Disputes and Settlements*, pp. 25–46.

The Origins of France, London, 1982.

Jolowicz, H. F. *Historical Introduction to the Study of Roman Law*, 2nd edn, Cambridge, 1952; 3rd edn, Jolowicz, H. F. and Nicholas, B., Cambridge, 1972.

Jones, A. H. M. *The Later Roman Empire*, 3 vols., Oxford, 1964.

Keller, H. 'I placiti nella storiografia degli ultimi cento anni' in Istituto storico italiano per il medioevo, *Fonti medioevali e problematica storiografica*, vol. 1, Rome, 1976, pp. 41–68.

Kennedy, A. 'Disputes about *bocland*: the forum for their adjudication', *Anglo-Saxon England*, 14 (1985), 175–96.

Keynes, S. D. *The Diplomas of King Æthelred 'the Unready', 978–1016*, Cambridge, 1980.

Kienast, W. 'La pervivencia del derecho godo en el sur de Francia y Cataluña', *Boletín de la Real Academia de Buenas Letras de Barcelona*, 35 (1973/4), 265–95.

La Borderie, A. Le Moyne de *Histoire de Bretagne*, 6 vols., Rennes, 1898–1914.

Lacarra, J. M. *Aragón en el pasado*, Madrid, 1972.

Lapidge, M. and Sharpe, R. *A Bibliography of Celtic–Latin Literature 400–1200*, Dublin, 1985.

La Preuve, 2 vols., *Recueil de la société Jean Bodin*, vols. 16, 17, Brussels, 1964–5.

Laughlin, J. Laurence, 'The Anglo-Saxon Legal Procedure' in H. Adams *et al.*, *Essays in Anglo-Saxon Law*, Boston, 1876, pp. 183–305.

Lawson, M. K. 'The collection of danegeld and heregeld in the reigns of Æthelred II and Cnut', *English Historical Review*, 99 (1984), 721–38.

Lemarignier, J.-F. 'La dislocation du *pagus* et le problème des *consuetudines* (Xᵉ–XIᵉ siècles)' in *Mélanges d'histoire du moyen âge dédiés à la mémoire de L. Halphen*, Paris, 1951, pp. 401–10.

Lemerle, P. *Agrarian History of Byzantium*, Galway, 1979.

Levillain, L. 'Les Nibelungen historiques et leurs alliances de famille', *Annales du Midi*, 49 (1937), 337–407.

Levison, W. *England and the Continent in the Eighth Century*, Oxford, 1946.

Levy, E. *West Roman Vulgar Law. The Law of Property*, Philadelphia, 1951.

Lewis, A. *The Development of Southern French and Catalan Society, 718–1050*, Austin, Texas, 1965.

Leyser, K. *Rule and Conflict in an Early Medieval Society. Ottonian Saxony*, London, 1979.

Lyall, R. J. 'Two of Dunbar's Makars: James Affleck and Sir John the Ross', *Innes Review*, 27 (1976), 99–109.

Lysaght, G. A. 'Fleury and S. Benedict: monastery and patron saint (640–877)', Univ. Oxford D.Phil. thesis, 1985.

MacCana, P. 'The three languages and the three laws', *Studia Celtica*, 5 (1970), 62–78.

MacGaffey, W. *Custom and Government in the Lower Congo*, Berkeley, 1970.

MacNeill, E. 'Ancient Irish law. The law of status or franchise', *Proceedings of the Royal Irish Academy*, 36 (1923), C, 265–316.

'Dates of texts in the Book of Armagh relating to St Patrick', *Journal of the Royal Society of Antiquaries of Ireland*, 58 (1928), 85–101.
'Ireland and Wales in the history of jurisprudence', *Studies*, 16 (1927), 262–77, 605–15.
'Prolegomena to a study of the *Ancient Laws of Ireland*', *The Irish Jurist*, n.s., 2 (1967), 106–15.
MacNiocaill, G. 'Admissible and inadmissible evidence in Irish law', *The Irish Jurist*, n.s., 4 (1969), 332–7.
'Aspects of Irish law in the thirteenth century', *Historical Studies*, vol. 10, ed. G. A. Hayes-McCoy, Galway, 1976, pp. 25–42.
'Meabhrán dlí ó mhuintir Eolais, 1497–1513', *Galvia*, 4 (1957), 25–6.
'Notes on litigation in late Irish law', *Irish Jurist*, n.s., 2 (1967), 299–307.
Notitiae as Leabhar Cheanannais 1033–1166, Dublin, 1961.
'The interaction of laws' in J. F. Lydon (ed.), *The English in Medieval Ireland*, Dublin, 1984, pp. 105–17.
MacQueen, H. L. 'Jurisdiction in Heritage and the Lords of Council and Session after 1532' in *Miscellany of the Stair Society*, vol. 2, ed. D. Sellar, Stair Society, vol. 35, Edinburgh, 1984, pp. 61–85.
Maddicott, J. R. 'Magna Carta and the local community', *Past and Present*, 102 (1984), 25–65.
Manaresi, C. 'Della non esistenza di processi apparenti nel territorio del regno', *Rivista di storia del diritto*, 23 (1950), 179–217; 24 (1951), 7–45.
Márquez-Sterling, M. *Fernán González, First Count of Castille*, Mississippi, 1980.
Martindale, J. 'Charles the Bald and the government of Aquitaine' in M. Gibson, J. Nelson, D. Ganz (eds.), *Charles the Bald: Court and Kingdom*, pp. 109–35.
'The Kingdom of Aquitaine and the "Dissolution of the Carolingian fisc"', *Francia*, 11 (1985), 131–91.
Martínez Díez, G. *Fueros locales en el territorio de la Provincia de Burgos*, Burgos, 1982.
Maxwell, D. 'Civil procedure' in *Introduction to Scottish Legal History*, Stair Society, vol. 20, Edinburgh, 1958, pp. 413–25.
McDonald, C. 'The perversion of law in Robert Henryson's fable of *The Fox, the Wolf and the Husbandman*', *Medium Aevum*, 49 (1980), 244–53.
McKitterick, R. 'Some Carolingian law-books and their function' in B. Tierney and P. Linehan (eds.), *Authority and Power. Studies on Medieval Law and Government presented to Walter Ullmann on his seventieth birthday*, Cambridge, 1980, pp. 13–28.
The Carolingians and the Written Word, Cambridge, 1987 (forthcoming).
The Frankish Kingdoms under the Carolingians, 751–987, London, 1983.
McLeod, N. 'Parallel and paradox. Compensation in the legal systems of Celtic Ireland and Anglo-Saxon England', *Studia Celtica*, 16/17 (1981–2), 25–72.
Ménager, L.-R. 'Notes sur les codifications byzantines et l'occident', *Varia*, 3 (1958), 240–303.
Menéndez Pidal, R. *Los orígenes del Español*, 3rd edn, Madrid, 1950.
Meyer, K. 'Bretha airechta', *Zeitschrift für celtische Philologie*, 13 (1921), 19–24.
'Cenēla airechta', *Zeitschrift für celtische Philologie*, 12 (1918), 359–60.
The Instructions of King Cormac Mac Airt, Todd Lecture Series, vol. 15, Dublin, 1909.
Moore, S. F. *Law as Process: an Anthropological Approach*, London, 1978.
Mor, C. G. 'Considerazioni minimi sulle istituzioni giuridiche dell' Italia meridionale bizantina e longobarda' in *L'Italia meridionale nell'alto medioevo e i rapporti con il mondo bizantino, Atti del 3° congresso internazionale di Studi sull'alto medioevo*, Spoleto, 1959, pp. 139–52.

Morice, H. *Mémoires pour servir de preuves à l'histoire ecclésiastique et civile de Bretagne*, 3 vols., Paris, 1742–6.
Morris, R. 'The Powerful and the poor in tenth-century Byzantium', *Past and Present*, 73 (1976), 3–27.
Mortreuil, J. *Histoire du droit byzantin*, 3 vols., Paris, 1843–7.
Mundó, A. 'Para una historia de la escritura visigótica' in *Bivium: Homenaje a Manuel Cecilio Díaz y Díaz*, Madrid, 1983, pp. 175–96.
Murray, A. L. 'Sinclair's *Practicks*' in *Law-Making and Law-Makers in British History*, ed. A. Harding, London, 1980, pp. 90–104.
Nehlsen-von Stryk, K. *Die boni homines des frühen Mittelalters, Freiburger Rechtsgeschichtliche Abhandlungen*, n.s., vol. 2, Berlin, 1981.
Nelson, J. L. 'Kingship, law and liturgy in the political thought of Hincmar of Rheims', *English Historical Review*, 92 (1977), 241–79.
'Kingship and Empire' in J. H. Burns (ed.), *The Cambridge History of Medieval Political Thought*, Cambridge, 1986, forthcoming.
'Public *Histories* and Private History in the work of Nithard', *Speculum*, 60 (1985), 251–93.
'Queens as Jezabels: the careers of Brunhild and Balthild in Merovingian history' in D. Baker (ed.), *Studies in Church History, Subsidia*, vol. 1, 1978, pp. 67–72.
Niermeyer, J. F. *Mediae Latinitatis Lexicon Minus*, Leiden, 1976.
O'Brien, M. A. 'Some questionable emendations', *Ériu*, 11 (1930–2), 154–9.
Ó Corráin, D. 'Nationality and kingship in pre-Norman Ireland' in T. W. Moody (ed.), *Nationality and National Independence, Historical Studies*, vol. 11, Belfast, 1978, pp. 1–35.
Ó Corráin, D., Breatnach, L., Breen, A. 'The laws of the Irish', *Peritia*, 3 (1984), 382–438.
Ó Cróinín, D. *The Irish Sex Aetates Mundi*, Dublin, 1983.
O'Curry, E. *On the Manners and Customs of the Ancient Irish*, ed. W. K. Sullivan, 3 vols., Dublin, 1873.
O'Hanlon, J. and O'Leary, E. *History of the Queen's County*, Dublin, 1907.
Oikonomidès, N. *Les listes de préséance byzantines des IXᵉ et Xᵉ siècles*, Paris, 1972.
Palmer, R. C. *The Whilton Dispute, 1264–1380*, Princeton, 1984.
Palol, P. de and Hirmer, M. *Early Medieval Art in Spain*, London, 1967.
Parsons, M. P. 'Beiträge zum angelsächsischen Urkundenwesen bis zum Ausgang des neunten Jahrhunderts', Universität Wien, Unpublished Dissertation, 1937 (Vienna University Library, D5083).
Pérez de Urbel, J. *Historia del Condado de Castilla*, 3 vols., Madrid, 1970.
Pieler, P. 'Byzantinischer Rechtsliteratur' in H. Hunger (ed.), *Die hochsprachliche profane Literatur der Byzantiner*, 2 vols., *Handbuch der Altertumswissenschaft*, vol. 12, pt 5, 1/2, Munich, 1978, vol. 2, pp. 343–80.
Pita Merce, R. *Lérida Arabe*, Lérida, 1974.
Planiol, M. *Histoire des Institutions de la Bretagne*, 5 vols., Mayenne, 1981–4 (rep., with additional material, of 3 vol. edn of 1953).
Plucknett, T. *Concise History of the Common Law*, 5th edn, London, 1956.
Plummer, C. 'Notes on some passages in the Brehon laws, I–V', *Ériu*, 8 (1915–16), 127–32; *ibid.*, 9 (1921–3), 31–42, 109–17; *ibid.*, 10 (1926–8), 113–29.
Pollock, F. and Maitland, F. W. *History of English Law*, 2nd edn, ed. S. F. C. Milsom, Cambridge, 1968.
Poly, J.-P. and Bournazel, E. *La Mutation féodale*, Paris, 1980.

Poole, A. L. *Obligations of Society in the Twelfth and Thirteenth Centuries*, Oxford, 1946.
Poole, R. L. *The Papal Chancery*, Cambridge, 1915.
Radding, C. 'Nature, fortune and the passing of the medieval ordeal', *American Historical Review*, 84 (1979), 945–69.
Reynolds, S. *Kingdoms and Communities in Western Europe, 900–1300*, Oxford, 1984.
Rintelen, M. 'Die Urteilfindung im angelsächsischen Recht' in M. Krammer (ed.), *Historische Aufsätze Karl Zeumer zum sechsigsten Geburtstag als Festgabe dargebracht*, Weimar, 1910, pp. 557–77.
Roberts, S. *Order and Dispute. An Introduction to Legal Anthropology*, London, 1979.
'The study of disputes: anthropological perspectives' in J. Bossy (ed.), *Disputes and Settlements*, pp. 1–24.
Robertson, J. J. 'The development of the law' in *Scottish Society in the Fifteenth Century*, ed. J. M. Brown, London, 1977, pp. 136–52.
Robertson, W. *The History of Scotland during the Reigns of Queen Mary and King James VI*, 2 vols., London, 1759.
Robinson, F. N. 'Notes on the Irish practice of fasting as a means of distraint' in *Putnam Anniversary Volume: Anthropological Essays presented to F. W. Putnam*, New York, 1909, pp. 567–83.
Rodríguez, J. *Ordoño III*, León, 1982.
Ramiro II Rey de León, Madrid, 1972.
Ronayne, L. 'Seandlithe na nGael: an annotated bibliography of the ancient laws of Ireland', *The Irish Jurist*, n.s. 17 (1982), 131–44.
Rossetti, G. *Società e istituzioni nel contado lombardo durante il medioevo. Cologno Monzese*, vol. 1, Milan, 1968.
Rowlands, M. E. 'Robert Henryson and the Scottish Courts of Law', *Aberdeen University Review*, 39 (1962), 219–26.
Salvioli, G. *Storia della procedura civile e criminale*, 2 vols., Milan, 1925–7 (= P. Del Giudice (ed.), *Storia del diritto italiano*, vol. 3).
Sánchez-Albornoz, C. 'Documentos para el estudio del procedimiento judicial en el reino asturleonés' in *Homenaje a don Agustin Millares Carlo*, 3 vols., Las Palmas de Gran Canaria, 1975, vol. 2, pp. 143–56.
Sawyer, P. H. *Anglo-Saxon Charters: an annotated List and Bibliography*, Royal Historical Society Guides and Handbooks, London, 1968.
Kings and Vikings, London, 1982.
'The Vikings and Ireland' in D. Whitelock, R. McKitterick and D. Dumville (eds.), *Ireland in early mediaeval Europe: Studies in memory of Kathleen Hughes*, Cambridge, 1982, pp. 345–61.
Scheltema, H. J. 'Byzantine law' in *Cambridge Medieval History*, vol. 4, pt 2, 2nd edn, Cambridge, 1966, pp. 55–77.
L'Enseignement de droit des antécesseurs, Leiden, 1970.
Schilbach, E. *Byzantinische Metrologie*, Handbuch der Altertumswissenschaft, vol. 12, pt 4, Munich, 1970.
Schmitt-Weigand, A. *Rechtspflegedelikte in der Fränkischen Zeit*, Berlin, 1962.
Serrano y Sanz, M. 'Un documento del obispo aragonés D. Aton' in *Homenaje a D. Carmelo de Echegaray*, San Sebastian, 1928, 41–8.
Sharpe, R. 'Armagh and Rome in the seventh century' in P. Ní Chatháin and M. Richter (eds.), *Irland und Europa. Die Kirche im Frühmittelalter*, Stuttgart, 1984, pp. 58–72.
Review of L. Bieler (ed.), *Patrician Texts in the Book of Armagh*, *Éigse*, 18 (1980–1), 329–32.
Simon, D. *Rechtsfindung am byzantinischen Reichsgericht*, Frankfurt-am-Main, 1973.

Simonet, F. *Historia de los Mozárabes de España*, Madrid, 1897.

Simpson, G. G. *Scottish Handwriting, 1150–1650*, Edinburgh, 1973.

Sinatti D'Amico, F. *Le prove giudiziarie nel diritto longobardo*, Milan, 1968.

Smith, R. M. 'A tract on pleading' in J. Fraser, P. Grosjean and J. G. O'Keeffe (eds.), *Irish Texts*, 5 vols., London, 1930–3, vol. 4, pp. 20–2; and *idem*, '*Urchoillte Brithemoin*', *ibid.*, vol. 4, pp. 24–7.

Snyder, F. 'Colonialism and legal form: the creation of customary law in Senegal' in C. Sumner (ed.), *Crime, Justice and Underdevelopment*, London, 1982, pp. 90–121.

Stafford, P. 'The reign of Æthelred II, a study in the limitations on royal policy and action' in D. Hill (ed.), *Ethelred the Unready: Papers from the Millenary Conference*, British Archaeological Reports, vol. 59, Oxford, 1978, pp. 15–46.

Stanihurst, R. *De rebus gestis in Hibernia*, Antwerp, 1584.

Stein, P. 'The Source of the Romano-Canonical Part of *Regiam Maiestatem*', *Scottish Historical Review*, 48 (1969), 107–23.

Stenton, F. M. *Anglo-Saxon England*, 3rd edn, Oxford, 1971.

Stern, S. M. *Fātimid Decrees*, London, 1964.

Stokes, W. 'Sitting dharna', *The Academy*, 28 (1885), 169.

Stokes, W. and Strachan, J. *Thesaurus Palaeohibernicus*, 2 vols. and supplement, Cambridge, 1901–10.

Stuart, J. (ed.), *The Miscellany of the Spalding Club*, 5 vols., Aberdeen, 1841–52.

Stubbs, W. (ed.), *Select Documents illustrative of English Constitutional History*, 9th edn, revised by H. W. C. Davis, Oxford, 1913.

Sutherland, J. N. 'Aspects of continuity and change in the Italian *placitum*, 962–72', *Journal of Medieval History*, 2 (1976), 89–118.

Svoronos, N. G. *Recherches sur la tradition juridique à Byzance: la Synopsis Major des Basiliques et ses appendices*, Paris, 1964.

Ter-Ghewondyan, A. *The Arab Emirates in Bagratid Armenia*, trans. N. Garsoïan, Lisbon, 1976.

Tessier, G. *Diplomatique royale française*, Paris, 1962.

Thomas, J. A. C. *Textbook of Roman Law*, Amsterdam, 1976.

Thompson, E. P. *Whigs and Hunters. The Origin of the Black Act*, London, 1975.

Thurneysen, R. '*Ancient Laws of Ireland* und Senchas Már (Aus dem Irischen Recht 6 (i))', *Zeitschrift für celtische Philologie*, 16 (1927), 167–95.

'Das Fasten beim Pfändungsverfahren', *Zeitschrift für celtische Philologie*, 15 (1924–5), 260–75.

'Das Keltische Recht', *ZRG, Germ. Abt.*, 55 (1935), 81–104; English trans. in D. Jenkins (ed.), *Celtic Law Papers*, Brussels, 1973, pp. 51–70.

Die Bürgschaft im irischen Recht, Abhandlungen der Preussischen Akademie der Wissenschaften, phil.-hist. Klasse, Berlin, 1928, pt 2.

'Die falschen Urteilssprüche Caratnia's (Aus dem Irischen Recht 4)', *Zeitschrift für celtische Philologie*, 15 (1924–5), 302–70.

'Zum ursprünglichen Umfang des Senchas Már (Aus dem Irischen Recht 8)', *Zeitschrift für celtische Philologie*, 18 (1929), 356–64.

Torkar, R. (ed.), *Eine altenglische Übersetzung von Alcuins De Virtute et Vitiis, Texte und Untersuchungen zur englischen Philologie*, vol. 7, Munich, 1981.

Toubert, P. *Les Structures du Latium médiéval*, 2 vols., Rome, 1973.

Turner, V. *Dramas, Fields and Metaphors*, Ithaca, 1974.

Ubieto Arteta, A. 'La diocesis Navarro-Aragonesas durante los siglos IX y X', *Pirineos*, 10 (1959), 179–99.

Udina Martorell, F. *El Archivo Condal de Barcelona en los siglos IX–X*, Barcelona, 1951.

Vannier, J.-F. *Familles byzantines: les Argyroi, Byzantina Sorbonensia*, vol. 1, Paris, 1975.

Verhulst, A. 'La genèse du régime domanial classique en France au haut moyen âge' in *Agricoltura e mondo rurale in Occidente nell' alto medioevo, Settimane di Studio del Centro Italiano di Studi sull'Alto Medioevo*, vol. 13, Spoleto, 1966, pp. 135–60.

Villanueva, J. de *Viage literário a las iglesias de España*, 22 vols., Madrid, 1803–51.

Vismara, A. 'La legislazione di Ottone I', *Archivo storico lombardo*, 53 (1925), 40–73, 221–51.

Vollrath, H. 'Herrschaft und Genossenschaft im Kontext frühmittelalterlicher Rechtsbeziehungen', *Historisches Jahrbuch*, 102 (1982), 33–71.

Vryonis, S., Jnr. 'The *Peira* as a source for the history of Byzantine aristocratic society in the first half of the eleventh century' in *Near Eastern Numismatics, Iconography, Epigraphy and History: Studies in Honor of George C. Miles*, ed. D. Koumjian, Beirut, 1974, pp. 279–84.

Wallace-Hadrill, J. M. *Early Germanic Kingship in England and on the Continent*, Oxford, 1971.

'The bloodfeud of the Franks' in *idem, The Long-Haired Kings*, pp. 121–47.

The Frankish Church, Oxford, 1983.

The Long-Haired Kings, London, 1962.

Warren, W. *Henry II*, London, 1973.

Watson, A. *The Law of Property in the Later Roman Republic*, Oxford, 1968.

Weinberger, S. 'Cours judiciaires, justice et résponsabilité sociale dans la Provence médiévale: IXᵉ–XIᵉ siècles', *Revue Historique*, 267 (1982), 273–88.

Wenskus, R. *Stammesbildung und Verfassung*, Cologne, 1961.

Werner, K.-F. 'Die Nachkommen Karls des Grossen bis um das Jahr 1000' in W. Braunfels and H. Beumann (eds.), *Karl der Grosse, Lebenswerk und Nachleben*, 5 vols., Düsseldorf, 1965–8, vol. 4, pp. 403–79.

'*Missus–marchio–comes*. Entre l'administration centrale et l'administration locale de l'empire carolingien' in W. Paravicini and K.-F. Werner (eds.), *Histoire comparée de l'administration*, Beiheft der *Francia*, vol. 9, Munich, 1980, pp. 191–239.

White, S. D. 'Feuding and peace-making in the Touraine around the year 1000', *Traditio* 42 (1986), pp. 195–263.

'*Pactum ... legem vincit et amor judicium*: the settlement of disputes by compromise in eleventh-century western France', *American Journal of Legal History*, 22 (1978), 281–308.

Whitelock, D. (ed.), *English Historical Documents*, vol. 1, 2nd edn, London, 1979.

The Audience of Beowulf, Oxford, 1951.

Wickham, C. J. *Early Medieval Italy*, London, 1981.

Studi sulla società degli Appennini nell'alto medioevo, Bologna, 1982.

Wood, I. N. 'Avitus of Vienne: religion and culture in the Auvergne and the Rhône valley 470–530', Univ. Oxford D.Phil. thesis, 1979.

'Pagans and holy men, 600–800' in P. Ní Chatháin and M. Richter (eds.), *Early Irish Christianity and Western Christendom: the Bible and the Missions*, Stuttgart, forthcoming.

The Merovingian North Sea, Alingsås, 1983.

Wormald, J. 'Bloodfeud, kindred and government in early modern Scotland', *Past and Present*, 87 (1980), 54–97.

Court, Kirk and Community: Scotland, 1470–1625, London, 1981.

Lords and Men in Scotland: Bonds of Manrent, 1442–1603, Edinburgh, 1985.

Wormald, P. 'Æthelred the Lawmaker' in D. Hill (ed.), *Ethelred the Unready: papers from the Millenary Conference, British Archaeological Reports*, vol. 59, Oxford, 1978, pp. 47–80.

Bede and the Conversion of England: the Charter Evidence, Jarrow Lecture, 1984.

'Bede, the *Bretwaldas* and the Origins of the *Gens Anglorum*' in P. Wormald, D. Bullough and R. Collins (eds.), *Ideal and Reality in Frankish and Anglo-Saxon Society: studies presented to J. M. Wallace-Hadrill*, Oxford, 1983, pp. 99–129.

'*Lex Scripta* and *Verbum Regis*: legislation and Germanic kingship from Euric to Cnut' in P. H. Sawyer and I. N. Wood (eds.), *Early Medieval Kingship*, Leeds, 1977, pp. 105–38.

'The uses of literacy in Anglo-Saxon England and its neighbours', *Transactions of the Royal Historical Society*, 5th s., 27 (1977), 95–114.

Wright, R. P. *Late Latin and Early Romance in Spain and Carolingian France*, Liverpool, 1982.

Zachariae von Lingenthal, K. E. *Geschichte des griechisch-römischen Rechts*, 2nd edn, 3 vols., Berlin, 1892.

Zimmermann, M. 'L'usage du droit wisigothique en Catalogne du IXe au XIIe siècle: approches d'une signification culturelle', *Mélanges de la Casa de Velasquez*, 9 (1973), 233–81.

Index

abbots, *see* Alcuin, Bancio, Chaino, Conuuoion, Ermenoald, Germanus, *hêgoumenos*, Hilduin, Lupus
Aberdeen, 196, 198, 201
Acerenza, *see* Akerentza
Adriatic Sea, 121
adstantes, 56, 109, 269
advocates, 45, 56, 61, 74, 269; *assertores*, 86, 93, 94, 103; *feithem*, 184, 185, 187, 188; *mandatarii, mandatores*, 89, 90, 93, 103; *see also* Andreas, Salvator
Æthelberht, king of Kent, 19
Æthelmund, owner of Stoke and Westbury, 152, 154–6, 263
Æthelred II, king of England, 152, 158, 161, 163, 166, 238
Æthelric, son of Æthelmund, 152, 154–7, 161, 263
Æthelsige, *minister* of Æthelred II, 158–9, 161, 164, 166
Æthelwine, ealdorman, 167
Aganbert, *colonus*, 49, 50, 51, 246
agentes, 27, 269; *cf. missi*
Agintrude, 56–9, 61, 64, 212, 248–50
Agobard, archbishop of Lyons, 21
airecht, see court
Akerentza (Acerenza), Byzantine Italy, 136, 137, 146, 260
Al-Andalus, 96–7
Alcuin, abbot of St Martin, Tours, 49, 51
Alfred, king of Wessex, 152, 164, 166, 234
allod/*alodium*, 98, 100
Alpert, cleric in Lucca, 116
Amalbert, claimant to Bayencourt, 28–9, 31–2, 244–5
Amalric, son of Amalbert, 29, 31, 34, 35, 41, 244–5
amica pactuacio, 122–3, 236, 269; *cf. cotach*, 175 n.19; *see also* compromise, settlements
Anau, 73, 77, 224

Andreas, advocate of S. Giulia in Controne, 106–11, 257–8
Angers, 9
Angilbert II, archbishop of Milan, 120
Anjou, county of, 212, 230
Ansbert, bishop, 27, 30–1
Anspert, archbishop of Milan, 119
Antoigné, dép. Maine-et-Loire, 49, 50, 51, 63
antrustions, 11, 17, 19
Aquitaine, 46, 48, 49, 57
Aragón, county of, 90, 97, 100–4, 213, 236, 255, 256
arbitration, 173, 181, 188, 197, 199–200, 202–4; *see also* compromise, mediation, settlements
archbishops, *see* Agobard, Angilbert II, Anspert, Dunstan, Gregory, Hincmar, Wulfad, Wulfred; *see also* bishops
archives, 1, 49, 52, 54, 125, 159, 161, 208, 209; in Constantinople, 125; of Prôtaton on Mt. Athos, 147; *see also* charters, *gesta municipalia*, records
aristocracy, 230, 232, 234–5, 238; Anglo-Saxon, 152, 166–7; Breton, 72–3 and n.20, 74, 82; Frankish, 48; Scottish, 205; *see also* antrustions, counts, ealdormen, gastald
Arlanza, San Pedro de, monastery of, 92 and n.26, 94
Armagh, 172, 174, 176, 177
Armenia, Bagratid kingdom of, 207
Arezzo, diocese of, 114
Asclepiodatus, referendary, 19
assault, 70, 231
assemblies, local, 71, 76, 162, 186; *cf. chôrion*, *forrach*
assertores, see advocates
assessors, in Byzantine courts, 138–40
Atto, bishop, 98, 99
Auchlady, George Mortimer of, 199
Audiprando, owner in Pieve Fosciana, 115–16